The Political Economy of Argentina in the Twentieth Century

In this work, Roberto Cortés Conde describes and explains the decline of the Argentine economy in the twentieth century, its evolution, and its consequences. At the beginning of the century, the economy grew at a sustained rate, a modern transport system united the country, a massive influx of immigrants populated the land, and education expanded, leading to a dramatic fall in illiteracy. However, by the second half of the century, not only had growth stalled, but a dramatic reversal occurred, and the perspectives in the median and long term turned negative, and growth eventually collapsed. This work of historical analysis defines the most important problems faced by the Argentine economy. Some of these problems were fundamental, whereas others occurred without being properly considered, but in their entirety, Cortés Conde demonstrates how they had a deleterious effect on the country.

Roberto Cortés Conde is Professor Emeritus of Economy at the Universidad de San Andrés in Argentina. He is Honorary President of the International Economic History Association. He is coeditor, with Victor Bulmer-Thomas and John Coatsworth, of *The Cambridge Economic History of Latin America* (2006) and coeditor, with Michael D. Bordo, of *Transferring Wealth and Power from the Old to the New World: Monetary and Fiscal Institutions in the 17th through the 19th Centuries* (2001). He was a Robert Kennedy Professor of Latin American Studies at Harvard University in 1998. He was a visiting professor at the University of Chicago in 1990 and 1991. Also, he is a member of the National Academies of Economic Science and History of Argentina.

CAMBRIDGE LATIN AMERICAN STUDIES

General Editor
Herbert S. Klein
Gouverneur Morris Emeritus Professor of History, Columbia University
Director of the Center of Latin American Studies, Professor of History,
and Hoover Senior Fellow, Stanford University

92
The Political Economy of Argentina in the Twentieth Century

Other Books in the Series

(Continued after index)

The Political Economy of Argentina in the Twentieth Century

ROBERTO CORTÉS CONDE

Universidad de San Andrés

CAMBRIDGE UNIVERSITY PRESS
Cambridge, New York, Melbourne, Madrid, Cape Town, Singapore, São Paulo, Delhi

Cambridge University Press
32 Avenue of the Americas, New York, NY 10013-2473, USA

www.cambridge.org
Information on this title: www.cambridge.org/9780521882323

© Roberto Cortés Conde 2009

First published 2009

Printed in the United States of America

A catalog record for this publication is available from the British Library.

Library of Congress Cataloging in Publication Data
Cortés Conde, Roberto
[Economía política de la Argentina en el siglo XX. English]
The political economy of Argentina in the twentieth century / Roberto Cortés Conde.
p.   cm. – (Cambridge Latin American studies ; 92)
ISBN 978-0-521-88232-3 (hardback)
1. Argentina – Economic conditions – 20th century.   I. Title.   II. Series.
HC175.C669813   2009
330.982'06 – dc22   2008019060

ISBN   978-0-521-88232-3 hardback

Contents

Acronyms

AGA	Anuario Geográfico Argentino
BCRA	Banco Central de la República Argentina
BID	Banco Interamericano de Desarrollo
BNA	Banco de la Nación Argentina
CAP	Compañía Argentina de Productores de Carne
CEPAL	Comisión Económica para América Latina y el Caribe
CGE	Confederación General Económica
CGT	Confederación General del Trabajo
CINA	Confederación Industrial Argentina
CONADE	Consejo Nacional de Desarrollo
DNEC	Dirección Nacional de Estadística y Censos
DNGPS	Dirección Nacional de Programación del Gasto Social
ECLAC	Economic Commission for Latin America and the Caribbean
FIEL	Fundación de Investigaciones Económicas Latinoamericanas
FMI	Fondo Monetario Internacional
GOU	Grupo de Oficiales Unidos
IAPI	Instituto Argentino del Promoción del Intercambio
IMF	International Monetary Fund
IMIB	Instituto Movilizador de Inversiones Bancarias
IMIM	Instituto Mixto de Inversiones Mobiliarias
INDEC	Instituto Nacional de Estadísticas y Censos
INTA	Instituto Nacional de Tecnología Agropecuaria
NYSE	New York Stock Exchange
OAS	Organization of American States
OEA	Organización de Estados Americanos
SRA	Sociedad Rural Argentina
UIA	Unión Industrial Argentina
YPF	Yacimientos Petrolíferos Fiscales

Acknowledgments

I express my thanks to Mercedes María Campi, Ariel M. M. Meije, and Mariano Scapin for their invaluable contribution in searching and collecting statistical and bibliographical references contained herein; to the translator of the Spanish version of this book, Hope Doyle D'Ambrosio, Ph.D., for her professionalism and arduous work; and most especially to the series editor, Professor Herbert Klein, for his extremely helpful observations and comments. I am also grateful to Frank Smith of Cambridge University Press for the interest showed in this work. And finally, I thank my wife, without whose patient company my years of obsessive work in investigating and writing this book would never have been possible. Any errors or omissions are the sole responsibility of the author.

San Isidro, Buenos Aires, December 2007

Introduction

I

This book discusses the evolution of the Argentine economy in the twentieth century. It covers a century that actually begins a few years earlier, in the decade of the 1880s, with the foundation and expansion of modern Argentina, and ends in 1989. This analysis does not include the last decade of the twentieth century because the 1989–1990 hyperinflationary period marks the end of an era and the beginning of a new one that is beyond the scope of this book. The convertibility system of the 1990s ushered in new problems, the recession starting in 1998 and the crisis of 2001–2002 afterward, following which was the recent and significant recovery (2003–2006). These more recent developments are part of an ongoing process that will only be understood as patterns emerge.

In the span of that century Argentina went through numerous and contradictory experiences. At its beginning it saw a rapid expansion followed by a deceleration after World War I. In the second half of the century there was only one decade of growth, the 1960s, and ever since then, it has suffered a clear decline. Until Word War I it grew at a rate that was greater than that of some more industrialized countries, converging to those levels of per capita income. During the second half of the century, however, Argentina fell behind, and the difference between it and more developed countries became evident.

The purpose of this book is to describe the economic events of the century within the framework of the changing institutions in which they occurred, providing some – albeit tentative – answers to these worrisome trends. The operative question regarding the Argentine economy is not whether it was successful but whether it had the political and legal institutions, and appropriate standards, necessary to make it so.

The book's focus is historical, not only because it tells what happened but also because it attempts to understand, at least partially, current behavior by observing past behavior and shows the contingent nature of economic behavior. Although the past does not determine the present, it limits future options and choices. No one, neither governments nor individuals, made decisions in isolation; each choice was contingent on a range of possibilities that resulted in current conditions but that were also restricted by past conditions. Decisions depended on the circumstances of a given moment and individual preferences, but also on previous choices, which were often manifest in institutions. The past limited the range of possible actions. So choices were conditioned in this sense not only by existing technologies and the nature of available resources but also by past decisions. The choice of an institutional system in a given historical framework produces constraints. Thus, no society begins with blank slate, a complete *tabula rasa*, even when a new political system causes a break from the previous one. It can never break entirely.

The first chapter describes the problems that emerged during the first half of the nineteenth century, with its long regional conflicts following independence, which were an obstacle to the effective exercise of government and which, by increasing the cost of violence[1] and maintaining segmented markets, retarded development. During the second half of the nineteenth century this trend discontinued because technologies of more developed countries were incorporated and because the expectations of benefits from technology allowed important consensus building, an end to civil wars, and the consolidation of the national state, which fomented movement of capital and labor, which in turn promoted growth. The consolidation of that national state was a condition that was possible because of the incorporation of technologies and great economic expansion.

II. A New Country Conflict between Heterogeneous Regions

With the breakup of the colonial regime, the new governments of the old viceroyalty – claiming authority inherited from the crown in their previous jurisdictions – had to exercise that authority over vast and often unpopulated territories.[2] The Spanish monarchy had determined the scale of these large administrative units to maintain control over silver mining. However, once separated from the Upper Peru and this income lost, the country, now oriented to the coast, had to rely on another source of income, namely, the customs at the Port of Buenos Aires.[3] The new postcolonial governments tried, unsuccessfully, to impose their authority over distant

---

1 By monopolizing the supply of protection, the state diminishes the cost of violence. Frederik C. Lane, "Economic Consequences of Organised Violence," *Journal of Economic History*, vol. XVIII, no. 4, December 1958, pp. 401–451.

2 In this regard, see also Alberto Alesina and Enrico Spolara, *The Size of Nations*, Cambridge, MA, The MIT Press, 2003.

3 Roberto Cortés Conde, *Progreso y Declinación de la Economía Argentina*, Buenos Aires, Fondo de Cultura Económica, 1998, p. 13.

and heterogeneous regions and were constantly involved in conflicts with the interior provinces (see Map I.1).[4]

The Latin American ex-colonies experienced not only the traumatic transition to independent regimes but also a transition from an absolutist rule to a constitutional one, much like Spain itself in the nineteenth century. Revolution as part of liberal movements in Europe was embedded in the difficult change from the *ancien régime* to a modern one. During colonial times all decisions were concentrated in a central authority within the viceroyalty. Dissension was hidden in the severe absolutist regime, but in the transition toward a more open society, a high price was paid for the disagreement over who was the central authority, a conflict that finally ended with the fragmentation of that authority. However, although the colonial regime had been formally centralist, many cities had treasury offices (main or subordinate ones, *Cajas principales y secundarias*), which gave them free use of the taxes (*alcabalas*) they collected, supposedly for the crown, and with which they paid for the local bureaucracy. With the end of the colonial regime, every city that had a revenue-collecting treasury fought to retain control of interior customs, which became a right granted along with provincial autonomy. This was the origin of Argentinean federalism. "During a large part of the 19th century a central state with a monopoly of legitimate coercive power never managed to consolidate itself, and regional and provincial access to fiscal resources was a source of unending conflicts."[5]

The unitarian formula of the 1826 Constitution, reapplied in the 1853 federal constitution, transferred external customs to the nation. This was against the interests of Buenos Aires. Likewise, the formula eliminated internal customs, hurting the province's public finances. But this was the only viable formula for the formation of a national state. The geography of Argentina, which at that time was landlocked, made the whole country subordinate to the only seaport on the Rio de la Plata. Yet, at the same time, the vast distances, transportation costs, and the plethora of vested interests led to fiscal and political fragmentation. Multiple domestic customs, in addition to the already high built-in transportation cost, made merchandise

---

4 Herbert Klein mentions this with respect to the fact that the heterogeneity of interests compared with those of the River Plate had led to the separation from Alto Peru. Alberto Alesina and Enrico Spolara have addressed the problem of the size of nations and the trade-off between economies of scale and the cost of heterogeneity. Long before, this had been implicitly suggested by Augustin Edwars Vives in *La Fronda Aristocratica* when he compared the different institutional evolutions in the decades following the independence of Chile and Argentina. See Herbert S. Klein, "Las Finanzas del Virreinato del Río de la Plata," *Desarrollo Económico*, vol. 13, no. 50, 1973; Alberto Alesina and Enrico Spolara, *Size of Nations*, 2003; Alberto Edwards Vives, *La Fronda Aristocrática en Chile*, Santiago de Chile, Editorial Universitaria, 1997.

5 Roberto Cortés Conde, *Progreso y Declinación*, 1998, p. 14.

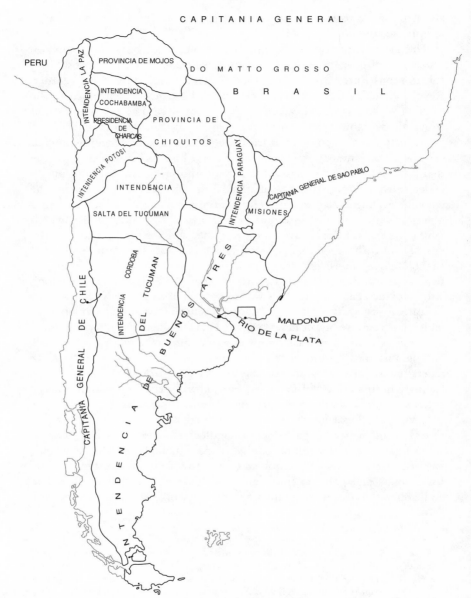

Map I.1. Viceroyalty of the Rio de la Plata, 1776–1810. *Source:* Archivo General de la Nación, "Documentos referentes a la guerra de la independencia y emancipación política de la República Argentina: y de otras secciones de América a que cooperó desde 1810 a 1828," 1914.

more expensive and hindered the growth of markets, keeping them small and segmented.

The state is an enterprise that ensures protection. But because the geography and technology of the period did not help to consolidate the state, various centers that disputed with the central government the monopoly on the legitimate use of force emerged, thereby increasing the cost of violence.[6] Poverty was not a propitious environment for producing anyone able to consolidate power over the entire territory and put an end to the interminable conflict. (Rosas, who was closest to achieving this, was ultimately unable.)[7] The threat to life and property limb and to the safe transportation of goods – because of constant confiscations – was an obstacle to savings and investment and contributed to the retardation of economic development during the first half of the nineteenth century.

III. New Technologies in the Formation of a Market and a National State: Economic Growth

During the second half of the twentieth century new technologies in transportation marked a clear break from the past and gave a glimpse of progress to come. The railroad integrated the country, and the reduction in shipping freights allowed the agricultural production of the Pampas to reach European markets. Thus, the most enlightened thinkers of the period, such as Sarmiento and Alberdi, maintained that the desert areas could become populated, following the model of the United States.

Prospects for progress were a strong incentive to end civil wars. So a political solution was found to the conflict that had afflicted the River Plate ever since independence. In 1862, at the end of the war of attrition between the different regions, the Buenos Aires Customs Authority was ultimately placed under national control, just as the 1853 National Constitution had stipulated. This was coupled with the elimination of internal customs.

The exploitation of natural resources, the increase in the wage-earning population, and the construction of transportation networks created a market that broadened the tax base and constituted the sustenance of the modern state. This fiscal agreement that included the provinces, the national government, and wide social sectors lasted, with some exceptions, until

6 Frederick Lane, "Economic Consequences," 1958.

7 In this regard see also Alberto Alesina and Allan Drazen, "Why Are Stabilizations Delayed?" *American Economic Review*, no. 5, 1991; Barry Eichengreen, *Golden Fetters: The Gold Standard and the Great Depression, 1919–1939*, New York, Oxford University Press, 1995. Alesina and Drazen argue that when there are divergent interests of groups that do not manage to get their way, there is a "war of attrition" with negative effects because no measures are taken to improve the economy. This thesis was applied especially in the case of Eichengreen to the analysis of European problems in the interwar period.

1930. This was largely the result of circumstances that broadened markets and favored progress and was also a condition of the state's sustainability.

IV. Growth Trends: International Comparisons

The twentieth century may be characterized by several different trends. The first period, 1870–1914, was one of rapid expansion of such dimensions that it reached income levels of many more industrialized countries. The second trend encompasses the interwar period, 1914–1945, in which the world economy decelerated, like that of Argentina. During this period, open economies were exposed to external shocks, especially Great Britain and countries with ties to Great Britain, and the European economy, whereas the United States and Canada recovered more quickly. During the 1930s, when economies became insular and protectionist measures abounded ("beggar your neighbor policies"), Argentina, which had suffered a gradual drop in GDP until 1932, recovered beginning in 1934.[8] During World War II, thanks to its relative isolation, Argentina did not suffer the negative effects that it had endured during World War I. Comparing these trends with those of Western countries in the twentieth century, just as Maddison describes them,[9] we see that until World War II those of Argentina coincide with world trends (see Figures I.1 and I.2).[10]

However, circumstances following World War II were different. Whereas the Western countries and Australia experienced significant growth, Argentina stagnated and later declined, so that by the end of the twentieth century it lagged not only behind other industrialized countries but also behind other Latin American ones, such as Mexico and Brazil (see Figure I.3).

The strong growth spurt that had begun around 1934 and that had intensified during the 1940s began to be much more limited after World War II. Unlike Brazil and Mexico – not to mention Australia – where the postwar growth was very significant, Argentina had economic crises

---

8 Argentina's annual growth rate in the 1930s was 5.61%, whereas Great Britain grew by 2.45%, France by 0.90%, Italy by 2.19%, and the United States by 1.98%.

9 Angus Maddison, *Dynamic Forces in Capitalist Development*, Oxford, Oxford University Press, 1991, chap. 4.

10 According to the neoclassical model of growth, the presence of decreasing capital production determines that there is an inverse ratio between the initial level of GDP of an economy and the ultimate growth rate that it can achieve. This is the hypothesis of convergence or catching up. See Robert Solow, "Technical Change and the Aggregate Production Function," *Review of Economics and Statistics*, August 1957. See also Robert Solow, "A Contribution to the Theory of Economic Growth," *Quarterly Journal of Economics*, no. 70, February 1956, pp. 65–94, and Robert Barro and Xavier Sala i Martin, "Convergence across States and Regions," *BPEA*, no. 1, 1991, pp. 107–158.

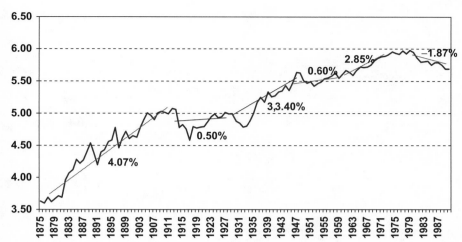

Figure I.1. Evolution of per Capita GDP, Argentina 1875–1989: Growth Trends (Index numbers: 1900 = 100, in natural logarithm). *Source:* Up to 1935: Roberto Cortés Conde, with María Marcela Harriague, *Estimaciones del Producto Bruto Interno de Argentina 1875–1935*, Documento de Trabajo, Departamento de Economía, Universidad de San Andrés, Buenos Aires, 1994 (updated series). Since 1935: GDP published by the Central Bank (updated series).

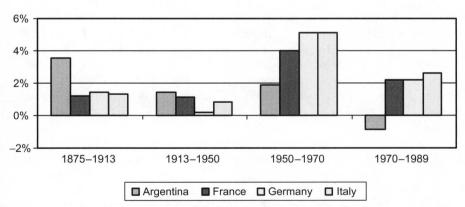

Figure I.2. Comparative Growth Trends: Argentina, France, Germany, and Italy, 1875–1989 (Average growth rate of per capita GDP). *Source:* Roberto Cortés Conde, with María Marcela Harriague, *Estimaciones del Producto Bruto Interno de Argentina 1875–1935*, Documento de Trabajo, Departamento de Economía, Universidad de San Andrés, Buenos Aires, 1994 (updated series), for Argentina; and Angus Maddison, *Monitoring the World Economy: 1820–1992*, OECD Development Centre Studies, Paris, 1995.

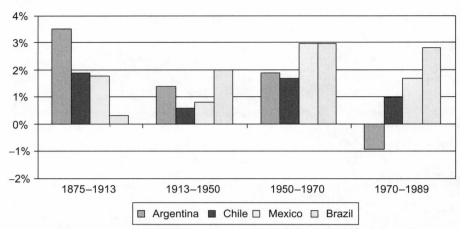

Figure I.3. Comparative Growth Trends: Argentina, Chile, México, and Brazil,
1875–1989 (average growth rate of per capita GDP). *Source*: Roberto Cortés Conde,
with María Marcela Harriague, *Estimaciones del Producto Bruto Interno de Argentina
1875–1935*, Documento de Trabajo, Departamento de Economía, Universidad de
San Andrés, Buenos Aires, 1994 (updated series), for Argentina; and Angus
Maddison, *Monitoring the World Economy: 1820–1992*, OECD Development Centre
Studies, Paris, 1995.

in 1949 and 1951–1952; these were the *stop-and-go* years. After the end
of the brief postwar boost, characterized by an exceptional increase in
international demand and an increase in prices on foodstuffs, it was clear
that in Argentina there were obstacles to continued growth. The country
suffered difficulties in the export and domestic sectors and had come to the
realization that painful adjustments were necessary. After World War II,
not until the mid-1960s, in 1963, did another growth spurt begin and
would last until 1974, when the new experience of nearly two years of
decline began.

In Argentina, the different growth phases – except for the first and
longest one – never seemed to be sustainable over time. Throughout most
of the twentieth century, initial growth impetuses, in some cases longer
ones, were always interrupted by a crisis that provoked a drop in GDP
followed by a slow recovery, only to return years later to previous levels.[11]

11 A discussion about the stages of growth in Argentina and a comparison with the economic devel-
opment of other countries is found in Roberto Cortés Conde, *La Economía Argentina en el Largo
Plazo*, Buenos Aires, Sudamericana, 1998, chap. 1. There are other studies on this subject, starting
with that of Carlos Díaz Alejandro, *Essays on the Economic History of the Argentine Republic*, New
Haven and London, Yale University Press, 1970, and also that of Juan José Llach, *Reconstrucción o
Estancamiento*, Buenos Aires, Thesis, 1987; that of Vicente Vázquez Presedo, *Auge y Decadencia de la
Economía Argentina desde 1776*, Buenos Aires, Academia Nacional de Ciencias Económicas, Buenos

In other countries the breaks from the past that we have highlighted as a characteristic of Argentinean growth were exceptional and due to international wars (Germany) or civil wars (Spain). What the book explores, then, is why until 1914 the Argentine economy grew at a rate that was greater than that of the world and why it declined and diverged from all of the world economic trends since World War II.

V. Problems of Growth in the Twentieth Century

In this analysis, it is assumed that there were multiple factors that caused the 1870–1914 economic expansion (Chapter 1) and its subsequent deceleration (Chapter 2) and decline in the years that followed World War II (Chapter 3 onward). Between the end of the nineteenth century and the 1930 world crisis the influence of external factors was extraordinary. Growth was positive until 1914 and then negative during World War I and in the 1930 crisis. But after 1930, and especially following World War II, the economy was affected more by internal factors (primarily policies decisions). Nevertheless, these are general statements that should not be taken in absolute terms. It is generally agreed that after 1930 the economy was geared more toward the domestic market with exchange measures that bolstered industrial import substitution and monetary measures that reduced the impact of the external shock. But the external factors of the 1930 recovery were also significant; international agricultural prices improved starting in 1934, especially during the war years, when the United States and the Allied countries were a source of continual demand for foodstuffs, raw wool, and hides. Moreover, export prices, as well as the terms of exchange, became more favorable in 1963 and 1973.

However, after World War II domestic policy decisions noticeably affected the profitability of economic factors, savings, investment, and consequently growth. Regarding the causes of the initial period of economic expansion, which was discussed in Chapter 1, two are most significant: technology and institutions. European markets were accessible to the American countries' supply of raw materials and foodstuffs thanks to the low cost of transportation. The railroad network connected the agricultural production of the interior to the ports, and the low cost of shipping allowed American

Aires, 1992; that of Pablo Gerchunoff and Lucas Llach, *El Ciclo de la Ilusión y el Desencanto*, Buenos Aires, Ariel Sociedad Económica, 1998; and more recently Gerardo della Paolera and Allan M. Taylor, *Tensando el Ancla: La Caja de Conversión Argentina y la Búsqueda de Estabilidad Macroeconómica 1880–1935*, FCE, Buenos Aires, 2003. Others have discussed growth by referring to some periods or specific aspects that will be cited in each case. Juan Carlos de Pablo's recently published book *La Economía Argentina en la Segunda Mitad del Siglo XX*, Buenos Aires, La Ley, 2005, is also an invaluable resource, as is the statistical series by Orland Ferreres, *Dos Siglos de Economía Argentina (1810–2004): Historia Argentina en Cifras*, Buenos Aires, El Ateneo and Fundación Norte y Sur, 2005.

products to reach Europe. The flow of capital and people to Argentina was a result of these changes. This allowed growth on a great scale, based on the incorporation of the factors of production (labor, capital), increased productivity due to changes in land use, and also incorporation of technology from countries with advanced agricultural and industrial methods.[12]

Prospects for progress were an incentive to achieve a political solution to old regional conflicts. The increase in the cost of protection (military expenditures) had consumed resources that would otherwise have been applied to productive activities. The monopoly on the supply of protection on the part of the central government was consolidated by newly available technologies that reduced its costs and provided an institutional framework that allowed the flow of the factors of production. These went from where they were abundant and less remunerated to where they were scarce and better compensated. The framework gave them the legal assurance that the effective remuneration they would receive would relate to their marginal productivity. Refraining from using force gave the impression that neither earnings nor savings would be confiscated. Such were the conditions of growth until World War I, when the Argentine economy became an integral part of the international community.[13]

A Changing World

But this world in which Argentina had become incorporated so successfully changed drastically with World War I (Chapter 2). While previous economic and political conditions internationally were beneficial for Argentina,[14] after the changes and following the 1930 crisis and World War II, they were no longer so. Although it was believed that after the war normalcy would return, and there was a significant recovery in the 1920s, soon problems emerged that unleashed enormous imbalances in international markets of capital and goods. The world agricultural oversupply

---

12 On technological "catching up," see M. Abramovitz, "Catching Up, Forging Ahead and Falling Behind," in *Thinking about Growth, and Other Essays on Economic Growth and Welfare*, Cambridge, Cambridge University Press, 1989, pp. 220–244. The idea is that countries that arrive later to the industrialization process can grow more quickly by learning from and imitating countries that achieved industrialization earlier. See also A. Gersenkron, *Economic Backwardness in Historical Perspective*, Cambridge, MA, Harvard University Press, 1962.

13 Argentina became more involved in international trade, according to Williamson and O'Rourke, more because of the low cost of transportation than because of the low tariffs. See Jeffrey Williamson and Kevin O'Rourke, *Globalization and History: The Evolution of a Nineteenth-Century Economy*, Cambridge, The MIT Press, 1999. Regarding propitious conditions for work, the same applies, in addition to the lack of restrictions on immigration to American countries, until 1914. Conditions for capital were also positive, under the stability that the gold standard provided.

14 Víctor Bulmer-Thomas, *The Economic History of Latin America since Independene*, Cambridge, Cambridge University Press, 2005.

beginning midway through the decade affected the continuous drop in international prices and affected import capacity that was sustained thanks to loans from the United States, which intensified the imbalances in the long run. With the 1930 financial crisis, the belief that normalcy would ever be possible again dissipated, and Argentina reacted to the isolationism with defensive and interventionist measures.

With markets in decline and increasingly numerous difficulties, every country tried to protect itself by transferring its losses to others (Chapter 2). Coalitions of corporate interests were formed and income distribution conflicts emerged and would continue throughout the century, much like those that afflicted the European countries in the 1920s and 1930s.[15] Protection of trade implied relying on political power, which in the long run was traduced in the attempts to capture the state to defend private corporate interests.

Institutional innovations were born of the need to confront economic emergencies. (Some had been tried during the war.) These would endure and influence the economy and society, causing changes in relative prices and in income distribution. Although they were seen as emergency measures and applied prudently, they were instruments that developed further in the years after World War II (Chapter 3) and were proof that Argentina had changed profoundly and permanently. From this point on, the country set its gaze inward and closed out the international community, of which it had been such an integral part. Thus, although putting an end to regional conflicts in the mid-nineteenth century marked a break from the previous period, which was initiated in the 1930s, and particularly accentuated after World War II, this time was characterized by sector conflicts and growing isolationism.

The Political Economy of Populism

Whereas the 1930 coup d'état had curbed the increase in real wages, which had decreased somewhat, at the beginning, the Perón administration showed a tendency to raise workers' real wages. Maintaining full employment and improvements in workers' incomes were central features in the social changes occurring and would have long-term consequences. Policies that favored workers until 1950 and subsidy policies that were a response to corporate pressure were the source of conflicts over income distribution and the ever-more rampant inflation. Investment was sacrificed for the sake of consumption, which the government itself tried to change toward the end of its administration, but rather unsuccessfully.

---

15 On wars of attrition between World War I and World War II in Europe see Eichengreen, *Golden Fetters.*

Perón left behind an economy that was not very productive, extravagantly regulated, and highly inflationary. The problem was that he had faced competing objectives, wanting on the one hand to keep real wages high, but on the other to apply a protectionist approach that generated levels of low productivity. Because overall wealth did not increase, the official measures to keep real wages high consisted of curbing the price of foodstuffs and public service prices and to privilege consumption over investment. But this approach was not sustainable in the long term (Chapter 3).

In the decades following the postwar period Argentina continued to be isolated so as to prevent the negative external shocks that so afflicted the country from 1914 to 1917, and again from 1929 to 1932, but at the same time it could not take advantage of the favorable economic shocks that spurred the "golden decades" of Western economies.[16]

A Divided Society

The limited and feeble efforts made after 1955 to open up and deregulate the economy caused new and greater conflicts during the eighteen years in which Perón was out of power (Chapter 4). Ever since the balance-of-payments crisis, which had occurred chronically since 1949, there was a chokehold on imports and that hindered industrial development. Between Perón administrations there were attempts to obtain foreign capital (Frondizi) in order to break the chokehold. Although these attempts were unsuccessful in changing institutions that had been inherited (particularly protectionist and corporate ones), thanks to greater stability during the years immediately subsequent to 1959, they allowed industry to become modernized and permitted a more appropriate set of relative prices that spurred the only decade of growth in the second half of the century (1963–1974).

The Hong Decline

In a framework in which there were no winners, the answer was to seek arbiters that would help all parties to disentangle themselves. The military officers, who believed that their profession made them more effective and less susceptible to pressures from vested interests, took on this role and effectuated coups d'état to manage the government in the 1960s and 1970s, failing significantly. Perón himself assumed this role on returning to power in 1973, in the middle of those military periods. At first, unions and management appeared to have reached an agreement, but in 1974 it began to crumble and ended up failing, paving the way for a rampant three-digit

16 Maddison, *Dynamic Forces*.

inflation that would last fifteen years and coincide with the longest period of decline that the country had known.

Attempts to achieve macroeconomic balance (both fiscal and monetary), essential conditions for investment and capital inflows, led to repeated devaluations, increases in public service prices, elimination of subsidies, and contraction of credit. These provoked angry reactions from popular sectors and corporations, causing dire social and political upheaval. With protectionist policies, the cost of capital was elevated. In a society involved in interminable zero-sum sector conflicts, savings and investment were extremely reduced and economic decline ever-more accentuated.

Such is the story told in the following pages, from its very beginning in the nineteenth century to the dramatic hyperinflation of 1989 that marks the end of an epoch.

I

Period of Rapid Economic
Expansion: 1880–1914

The 1880s were characterized by intense economic activity. The bustling Port of Buenos Aires epitomizes this decade, with the arrival of ships packed with goods and immigrants from a panoply of nations. These ships left Buenos Aires filled with raw wool, hides, and later, grains. Argentine goods poured into European ports, but European goods returning to Argentina occupied less space. So the unused cargo space on these ships was filled with human cargo. This became an inexpensive way for European immigrants to reach Argentina, where the rapidly growing economy held the promise of work, either in agriculture or in urban centers.

Europeans became a significant part of Argentina's population. Although a majority of the new immigrants identified themselves as farmers, during the 1880s the railroad had not yet reached the interior, so the European immigrants remained in Buenos Aires and in other costal cities where the dizzying pace of investment created an insatiable need for labor. In the Argentine Pampas, without navigable rivers – except the Paraná – the development of agriculture would have to wait for the construction of the railroad, the cost of which was well beyond Argentina's saving capacity. Thus, when it took on the project, the government financed railroad construction by accruing external debt. When private investment was allowed to enter the picture, it was through concessions to foreign companies that were guaranteed profits. The government and foreign investors assumed, correctly, that the railroads would generate enough wealth to provide for repayment of the debt incurred by their construction, with ample profits to boot. However, the railroad enterprise did not enjoy a long-lasting monopoly, for despite the profitability of investment in rail transportation, beginning in the 1920s, but especially in the 1930s and 1940s, railroads faced stiff competition from the automobile industry. Given the size of the initial investment, the railroad's natural monopoly was short lived.

Safe from the perils of abuse and corruption, thanks to the consolidation of the National Government, foreign capital flowed in, because the yield on investment was higher than in Europe. Duties on foreign goods provided a firm financial basis of power for the National Government. And the new railroad and telegraph networks, which allowed the deployment of the army to maintain effective control over Argentina's vast national territory, provided an infrastructure for this power.

Fiscal centralization, which provided the basis of power for the National Government, created a systemic imbalance whereby the provinces became chronically dependent on the National Government. This dependence became particularly evident as the government's power grew. In addition to customs duties, tariffs were charged on exports beginning in 1866 and taxes on internal revenue in 1890.

Not only was there an agreement between the national and provincial governments regarding the appropriation of fiscal resources, but there was also consensus regarding the fairness and legitimacy of the burden of the tax levied. Indirect taxes (on imports, which represented the majority of those levied) were established without political opposition despite the fact that they tax consumption without regard to income. The lack of opposition can be attributed to two factors: the amount imposed was considered by consumers to be a small sum, and with wages higher than their European counterparts, consumers could purchase food grown in their own country and were able to afford inexpensive imported manufactured goods (thanks to the strong peso and low transportation cost). A small duty on imported goods did not seem like much of a sacrifice to make for the benefit of receiving public goods (including education) that the government provided with proceeds from the expanding economy. This understanding was the foundation of the social pact between the government and taxpayers, and the bedrock of the consensus regarding the tax burden that persisted until 1930. These circumstances have not since been repeated.

Not everyone shared in the national prosperity to the same degree. Per capita GDP increased 3.6% yearly between 1875 and 1913, yet real wages increased by only 1% per year during the same period.[1] We compare wages of a homogeneous category representing unskilled labor. It is likely that for any individual, over the span of several decades, education as well as other investments in human capital would have resulted in greater wage increases. Thus, even if income distribution favored some more than others, since everyone benefited, there was wide consensus in this social pact, and this was evidenced in the continual influx of immigrants that lasted for more than three decades.

The 1880s, however, proved to be a tumultuous decade. Imbued with a thirst for progress, administrations did not always govern judiciously and committed a number of serious errors. Occasionally, they were tainted by

---

[1] The growth rate is calculated using three-year averages in order to soften for anomalies in any one particular year, as in the case of the decrease in GDP per capita in 1914 because of the outbreak of World War I.

Table 1.1. *Indicators of Argentine Growth, 1869–1914*

	1869	1914
Population (millions)	1.8	7.9
Railroad (thousands of kilometers)	0.6	34.5
Exports (millions of *pesos oro*)	32.4	349.3
Imports (millions of *pesos oro*)	41.2	271.8

Source: Dirección General de Estadística de la Nación, *Extracto Estadístico de la República Argentina correspondiente al año 1915*, Compañía Sudamericana de Billetes de Banco, Buenos Aires, 1916.

conflicts of interest, simply betraying the public trust in pursuit of personal benefit. There was a brief attempt at making the currency convertible, lasting only from 1881 until 1885. The failure of this policy created a climate of distrust, which, combined with considerable deficits and the excessive issuance of paper money by the Guarantee Banks (*Bancos Garantidos*), caused an inordinate flight of capital, culminating in inflation and the financial crisis of 1890, which would be the country's worst, until 1930.

The agricultural sector was essentially spared in the crisis. The downturn primarily affected the financial and government sectors, causing a reduction in GDP in 1891. The deceleration of the strong growth experienced during the second half of the previous decade was due to a broad reduction in imports and a contraction in transportation, commerce, and industry. On the other hand, wheat exports, which in 1888 had reached 100 thousand tons, had increased tenfold by 1893. This agricultural expansion is even more remarkable considering that as late as 1876 Argentina was still importing wheat. As a further demonstration of Argentina's growing agricultural prowess, the country began exporting live sheep to Europe during the 1890s.

Although the agricultural sector was left unscathed, urban economies felt the brunt of the financial crisis. Monetary issuances were kept at 1890 levels, requiring an increase in cash reserves as well as in interest rates, which was more damaging to cities than to rural areas. The peso devalued significantly and continued that way until 1893, causing a substantial reduction in real wages. During the second half of the decade, as a result of the application of austerity measures, prices fell, real wages increased, and the peso recovered its value. By the end of the 1890s, Argentina greeted the new century with an economy on the gold standard, a convertible currency, and a Currency Board offering a fixed exchange rate of 2.2727 pesos per dollar, or one *peso oro* (a convertible paper currency with an official par value of 1.45 grams of fine gold) (see Table 1.1).

At the start of the twentieth century there was cause for great optimism, which was only reconfirmed by the emerging economic reality. The country had suffered a difficult period of contractionary measures and stabilization that had followed the crisis of 1890, and now its finances were in order, payments on the national debt were being made, and the currency had been stabilized. After the debt agreements of 1893 and 1896, debt payments were made, and by the end of the nineteenth century, these had little effect on public spending and exports. Argentina again began to attract substantial amounts of foreign capital. There was another surge in railroad construction and investments reached their apex in 1913.

Investments were redirected as a result of changes in the Argentine economy. From this point on, government bonds became less attractive and direct investments the more desirable option because, since the turn of the century, profits earned in Argentine pesos could be converted at a fixed exchange rate. Transportation, real estate, insurance, and banking were the sectors that attracted the most foreign capital. At the same time immigration rates increased anew.

But the most important factor in the economic expansion in the first decade of the twentieth century was the technology that permitted an enormous transformation in the cattle industry. At the end of the previous century, Argentina was exporting hides. But now, at the beginning of the new one, a more profitable commodity could be exported – meat. The emergence of a brand-new technology, the refrigerated ship, made this new export possible. (Located in the South Atlantic, Argentina had a geographical disadvantage with regard to the United States where the shipment of live cattle to Great Britain was concerned.) The export of Argentine beef also became possible because of modifications in cattle stocks, for which British cattle had to be imported for reproductive purposes. Beef exportation also required a change in land use, including sowing pastures to feed cattle. These changes required a reorientation of investments and of technology, and cattle producers responded appropriately.

Restructuring the national debt by means of successive consolidations and conversions (1893–1896 and 1906) helped the national economy to recuperate and allowed a substantial reduction in interest on the debt. A fixed exchange rate based on the gold standard enforced a stable monetary policy, one that impeded the government from simply printing money in order to finance its deficit. At the same time, it allowed the considerable inflow of capital in those years.

Factors Endowment

The availability of land, capital, and labor produced a remarkable economic expansion in Argentina. Growth was also due, to some extent, to an increase in productivity. As is well known, the economic calculation underlying the flows of capital or labor from one place to the other is based on the assumption that such movements would be profitable (given the relative scarcity of the resource). However, transportation and other costs have to be deducted from this calculation. Among the most significant of these other costs would be those levied by the state; the owner of capital should pay for the services actually rendered, as well as for those that were simply promised but not delivered.

With the establishment of a stable National Government, Argentina could guarantee the returns on foreign capital, which had never happened before. Thus the enormous flows of capital and labor from European countries, where there was a surplus, to Argentina, where there was a scarcity. Of course the reduction in transportation costs was an extremely relevant factor in the economic and demographic influx, but we cannot underestimate the effect of the reduction in institutional costs, which had been the hallmark of Argentina, which had long discouraged foreign investment. During much of the nineteenth century it was not unusual for the state to impose compulsory and highly inflationary financing, and when the debt was disavowed, resort to confiscation. This was reflected in the difference in income yields generated by Argentine versus English government bonds, which implied not greater returns on the capital invested, but rather the inclusion of a risk premium.

Economic Expansion

Argentina experienced the highest and most sustained rate of economic growth in the country's history. Excepting cyclical fluctuations and the drop in GDP during the crises of 1890 and of 1900,[2] the country enjoyed uninterrupted economic expansion for thirty-four years (see Figure 1.1). This growth marked a clear break from the economic trends of the first half of the nineteenth century. Although there are no data regarding GDP during that period, all of the circumstantial evidence and some variables related to economic activity support the thesis that the second half of the century marked a clear change from the trends of the previous decades.

The work of Carlos Newland appears at first glance to contradict this conclusion, demonstrating a high growth rate during the first half of the nineteenth century. He finds that the growth rate was 6.1% annually, higher than the estimated growth for later decades.[3] However, his work refers specifically to the Province of Buenos Aires and has a bias because exports are used as a proxy for total output, a category that should also include other less modern activities. Newland's estimates use as a point of departure a low level of economic activity (see Appendix). Lastly, the discrepancy may be accounted for by the fact that he is comparing the

---

2 Roberto Cortés Conde with the collaboration of Marcela Harriague, *Estimaciones del Producto Bruto Interno de Argentina 1875–1935*, Buenos Aires, Universidad de San Andrés, 1994.

3 Carlos Newland and Barry Poulson, "Puramente Animal: Pastoral Production and Early Economic Growth, 1825–1865," Seminarios Universidad de San Andrés, 1994.

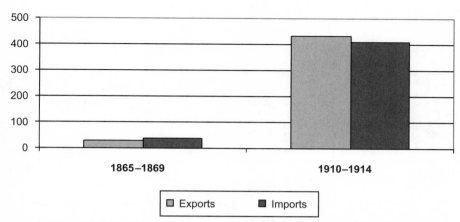

Figure 1.1. Foreign Trade, 1865–1914 (in millions of *pesos oro*). *Source:* Dirección General de Estadística de la Nación, *Extracto Estadístico de la República Argentina correspondiente al año 1915*, Compañía Sudamericana de Billetes de Banco, Buenos Aires, 1916.

averages for two specific decades: the 1820s and the 1860s. The variation in averages for the decades may be skewed by the sharp upturn experienced in the 1860s.[4]

But, as we have observed, there are other indicators that support the notion that the first half of the nineteenth century was characterized by sluggish economic growth, if any could be detected at all. This expansion began only in the 1850s, thus not entirely contradicting Newland's estimates. Figure 1.2 shows data regarding tax revenue, which, though not an estimate of the growth in GDP, should be related to its evolution, especially because this revenue is derived from tax on consumption. Because during this period no changes were made to the system of tax contribution, it was difficult to fathom that economic expansion could square with declining tax revenue between 1819 and 1850.

Economic growth in Argentina was greater than that of Australia, the United States, Canada, and the majority of European countries. Davies and Gallman assert that although growth in Argentine per capita GDP until World War I hovered around 6.5% to 6.6% per year, Australia, Canada, and the United States saw growth rates around 3.5% to 4% annually. "Argentina, thus, was the fastest growing economy by a considerable margin."[5] Thus argument is made by Carlos Díaz Alejandro, who claimed that:

4 Carlos Newland and Barry Poulson, "Puramente Animal."

5 Lance E. Davies and Robert E. Gallman, "Argentine Savings, Investment, and Economic Growth before World War I," in *Evolving Financial Markets and International Capital Flows: Britain, the Americas, and Australia, 1865–1914*, Cambridge, Cambridge University Press, 2001, cap. 6, p. 647: "Virtually all of the relevant evidence indicates that Argentine economic growth in the several decades before

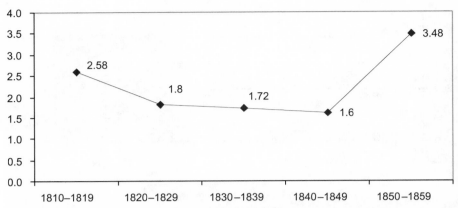

Figure 1.2. Revenue from the National Treasury (1810–1820) and Buenos Aires
(1820–1860) (in millions of *pesos fuertes*). *Source:* Roberto Cortés Conde, "Fiscal
Crisis and Inflation in XIX Century Argentina," Harvard University y
Universidad de San Andrés, November 1998.

not all regions beyond the capital enjoyed spectacular growth during the period
between 1880 and 1913. One could speculate that the difference in circumstances
between Argentina and Australia during these years can be attributed to a greater
capacity for adaptation where Argentine exports were concerned. Between 1875
and 1879, Argentine exports were still comprised of raw wool, hides, and cured
meats. During the period between 1890 and 1904 corn and linen had each come
to represent the same proportion of exports as hides. Lastly, during the period
between 1910 and 1914, frozen meat exports were almost as great a proportion of
exports as raw wool.

Argentina's increasing integration into the Atlantic markets was due to the
reduction in transportation costs, both domestically and internationally, as well as
to the relative scarcity of governmental restrictions on commerce and the portability
of the factors of production. Inclusion in Atlantic markets implied a supply of labor
and capital sufficiently elastic to produce Argentina's expansion, to the extent that
they could pay the going prices on the Atlantic market. Among the classical factors
of production, the least elastic was land.[6]

How did each of the factors of production contribute to this expansion?
Beginning with land, it is clear that during the last three decades of

World War I was extraordinarily rapid for that period; it was probably the most dramatic growth
experienced in the entire world. The most recent estimates indicate that real per capita GDP was
growing at an average rate of 6.5–6.6% per year. Over the same period the closest competitors,
Australia, Canada and the United States, recorded rates of from 3.5 to 4.0% per year."

6 Carlos Díaz Alejandro, "Economía Argentina, 1880–1913," in *La Argentina del Ochenta al Centenario*,
ed. Gustavo Ferrari and Ezequiel Gallo, Buenos Aires, Editorial Sudamericana, 1980.

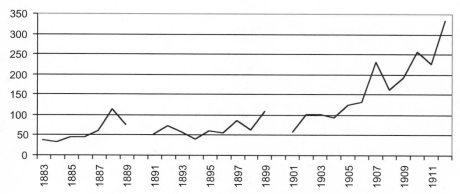

Figure 1.3. Price of Land in 1903 Pesos. *Note:* Price of land divided by the food price index. Base index numbers: 1903 = 100. *Source:* Roberto Cortés Conde, *El Progreso Argentino 1880–1914*, Buenos Aires, Sudamericana, 1979, p. 281.

the nineteenth century an increasing number of land tracts became part of Argentina's agricultural explotation. The Alsina and Roca expeditions of desert exploration in the period between 1876 and 1890[7] resulted in virgin land that was immediately exploited for cattle raising.[8] Later, as land became accessible by rail,[9] the tracts could be farmed, if climatic and soil conditions permitted.

Even before the construction of the railroad, the first expansion of Argentine *frontier* provided new land for already established cattle ranchers and made this land more valuable, inasmuch as the ranchers were allowed to freely exploit it because the security deployment had forced the withdrawal of a nomadic indigenous population that had been stealing cattle. However, as has been demonstrated elsewhere, land was relatively inexpensive for quite a number of years, because of the limited size of the population and the vast amount of land.[10] Lack of monopolistic control so that land could not be taken off the market to extract higher prices[11] allowed for an active land market. The price of land increased during the second half

7 Roberto Cortés Conde, *El Progreso Argentino, 1880–1914*, Buenos Aires, Sudamericana, 1979, p. 55.
8 The expansion of the frontier was not simply a military operation nor simply the assignment of previously unexploited land. It was effectively an occupation that led to the exploitation of new territories. "Border frontier expansion in the Province of Buenos Aires was essentially an expansion of its cattle frontier." Roberto Cortés Conde, *El Progreso Argentino*, p. 58. See also Roberto Cortés Conde, *La Economía Argentina en el Largo Plazo (Siglos XIX y XX)*, Buenos Aires, Sudamericana, 1997.
9 Roberto Cortés Conde, *El Progreso Argentino*, p. 177.
10 See Chapter III, "El mercado de tierras," in Roberto Cortés Conde, *El Progreso Argentino*, pp. 149–190.
11 Roberto Cortés Conde, *El Progreso Argentino*. For an alternate point of view see Jorge Federico Sábato, *La Clase Dominante en la Argentina Moderna: Formación y Características*, Buenos Aires, Imago Mundi, 1991.

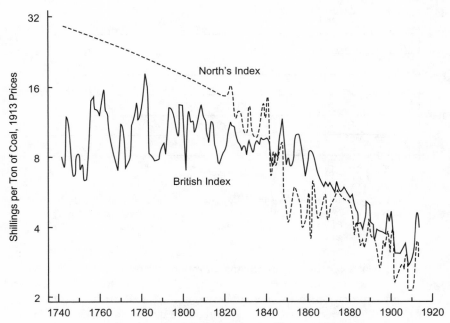

Figure 1.4. Cost of Transatlantic Transport of Coal. *Source:* Jeffrey Williamson and
Kevin O'Rourke, *Globalization and History: The Evolution of a Nineteenth-Century
Atlantic Economy*, The MIT Press, Cambridge, 1999, p. 36, and Douglass C. North,
"Ocean Freight Rates and Economic Development: 1750–1913", *Journal of
Economic History*, vol. XVIII, 1958.

of the 1880s because of inflationary pressures declined in the 1890s (see
Figure 1.3). The first decade of the twentieth century brought the most
significant increase in the value of land, and this was a result of changes in
cattle ranch exploitation, because these tracts became increasingly used for
meat production. As income from meat production increased, so did the
value of the land.

Whereas the first frontier movement allowed for the exploitation of
newly occupied lands, the second expansion brought with it a fundamental
change in the cattle industry, and this was a consequence of the reduction
in the cost of both maritime[12] and land transportation (see Figure 1.4 and
Maps 1.1–1.4).

---

12 See also Jeffrey Williamson and Kevin O'Rourke, *Globalization and History: The Evolution of a
Nineteenth-Century Atlantic Economy*, Cambridge, The MIT Press, 1999, p. 36, and Douglass C.
North, "Ocean Freight Rates and Economic Development, 1750–1913," *Journal of Economic History*,
vol. XVIII, 1958.

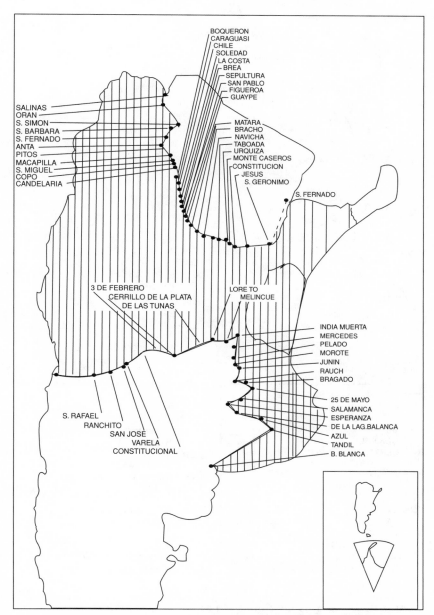

Map 1.1. Argentine *Frontier*, 1864. *Source:* Roberto Cortés Conde, *El Progreso Argentino 1880–1914*, Buenos Aires, Sudamericana, 1979.

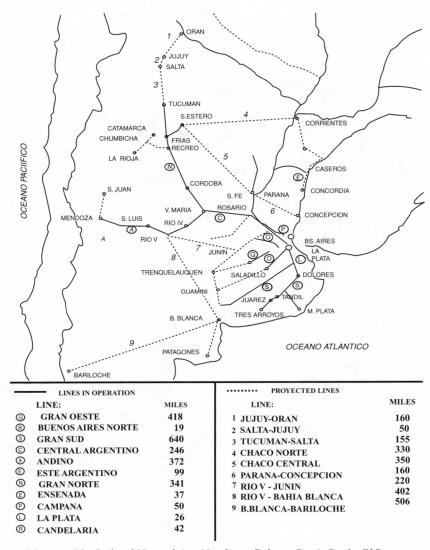

LINES IN OPERATION			PROYECTED LINES	
LINE:	MILES		LINE:	MILES
ⓖ GRAN OESTE	418		1 JUJUY-ORAN	160
ⓑ BUENOS AIRES NORTE	19		2 SALTA-JUJUY	50
ⓢ GRAN SUD	640		3 TUCUMAN-SALTA	155
ⓒ CENTRAL ARGENTINO	246		4 CHACO NORTE	330
ⓐ ANDINO	372		5 CHACO CENTRAL	350
ⓔ ESTE ARGENTINO	99		6 PARANA-CONCEPCION	160
ⓝ GRAN NORTE	341		7 RIO V - JUNIN	220
ⓔ ENSENADA	37		8 RIO V - BAHIA BLANCA	402
ⓟ CAMPANA	50		9 B.BLANCA-BARILOCHE	506
ⓛ LA PLATA	26			
ⓡ CANDELARIA	42			

Map 1.2. The Railroad Network in 1884. *Source:* Roberto Cortés Conde, *El Progreso Argentino 1880–1914*, Buenos Aires, Sudamericana, 1979.

As we have seen, Argentine land products became accessible (in terms of costs) in European markets because of a reduction in freight costs and the advent of the railroad, which carried agricultural output from the interior to the ports. The Argentine interior, now reachable, replaced European peripheral regions such as Italy, Spain, and Russia, which to that

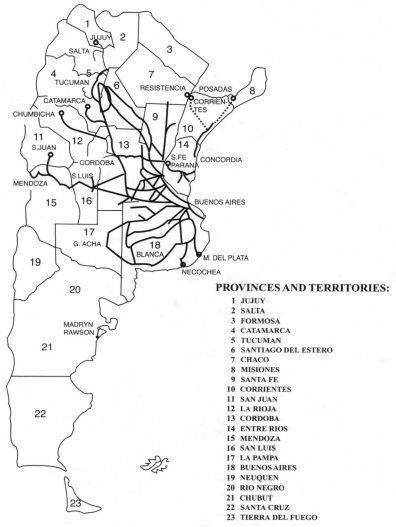

PROVINCES AND TERRITORIES:

1 JUJUY
2 SALTA
3 FORMOSA
4 CATAMARCA
5 TUCUMAN
6 SANTIAGO DEL ESTERO
7 CHACO
8 MISIONES
9 SANTA FE
10 CORRIENTES
11 SAN JUAN
12 LA RIOJA
13 CORDOBA
14 ENTRE RIOS
15 MENDOZA
16 SAN LUIS
17 LA PAMPA
18 BUENOS AIRES
19 NEUQUEN
20 RIO NEGRO
21 CHUBUT
22 SANTA CRUZ
23 TIERRA DEL FUEGO

Map 1.3. The Railroad Network in 1896. *Source:* Roberto Cortes Conde, *El Progreso Argentino 1880–1914*, Buenos Aires, Sudamericana, 1979.

point had provided food for the more industrialized countries in northern Europe.

In terms of capital, it was the infrastructure that received the largest share of capital flows, as significant investments were made in railroads and ports. Referring to the stages of railroad construction, Eduardo Zalduendo points out that the system grew fivefold between 1880 and 1915 and

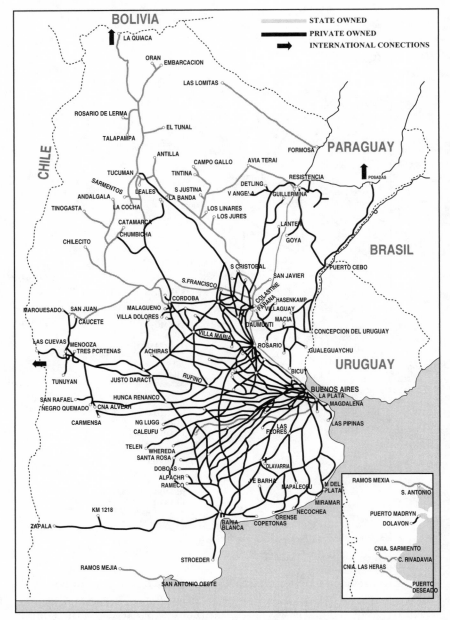

Map 1.4. The Railroad Network in 1916. *Note:* We are grateful to the Publisher
and the authors for their permission to include the map in this book. *Source:* Mario
Justo López, Jorge Waddell (comp.), *Nueva Historia del Ferrocarril en la Argentina:
150 Años de Política Ferroviaria*, Buenos Aires, Lumiere, 2007.

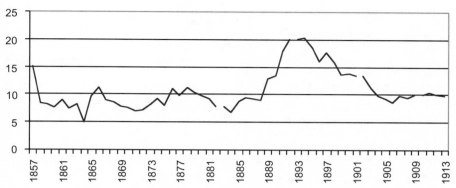

Figure 1.5. Ratio between Total Capital and Total Product of Argentine Railroad.
Source: Dirección General de Estadística de la Nación, *Extracto Estadístico de la
República Argentina Correspondiente al año 1915*, Compañía Sudamericana
de Billetes de Banco, Buenos Aires, 1916.

reached a peak of construction in the 1905–1910 period. By the turn of the
century, he notes, the network was the tenth largest in the world.[13]

Investment in railroads is necessarily large scale, with the added difficulty
of indivisibility. In the case of Argentina, rail construction required not only
the mobilization of enormous amounts of capital but also an investment
that would not be highly productive in the short term (high capital/product
ratio). This is because the endeavor required enormous construction projects
that would not yield profits immediately. It would take years to finish the
stretches of rail network required to join regions with vast distances between
them, install functioning rolling stock cars, and fully utilize the rail system,
thereby rendering profits.

The Baring Crisis, as Colin Lewis noted, led to the collapse of the guarantee system. Argentines felt that the companies had abused their privileged
positions, whereas British opinion faulted the Argentine authorities (see
Figure 1.5). He noted that

circumstances surrounding the revocation of the guarantees during the early 1890s
tended to foster many misconceptions, not least that the system was peculiar to
Argentina. It was overlooked that the guarantees had been applied in virtually
every country at some stage of the nineteenth-century railway development, with
the possible exception of Great Britain. The vast sums needed for modernization of
infrastructure invariable demanded some form of official participation, irrespective
of whether the capital was to be raised home or abroad, though the nature of state
intervention might differ from country to country. . . . Railway guarantees were not

13 Eduardo A. Zalduendo, "Sistema de Transportes de la Argentina", in *La Argentina del Ochenta al
Centenario*, ed. Gustavo Ferrari y Ezequiel Gallo, Buenos Aires, Editorial Sudamericana, 1980.

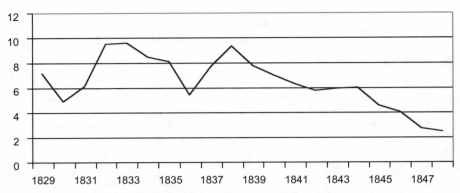

Figure 1.6. Price of Debt Securities, 1829–1848. Difference between Argentine
and British interest rates on public debt (in percentage points). *Source:* Price of
Argentine National Treasury Bonds: 1829–1848: Burgin; Price of Bonds on the
British Market: Pedro Agote: "Informe del Presidente del Crédito Público
Nacional", Libro II, 1884, Buenos Aires, Imprenta La Universidad, 1884,
pp. 109–116; T. S. Ashton, "Some Statistics of the Industrial Revolution", in *Gold
and Prices*, ed. G. F. Warren and A. Pearson, New York, John Willey, 1935, p. 403,
or in B. R. Mitchell and P. Deane, *Abstract of British Historical Statistics*, Cambridge
University Press, 1962, p. 455, table 8.

peculiar to the Argentine Republic, nor a mechanism that was especially designed
for foreign interest to serve their ends in the River Plate, as some Argentine authors
appear to believe. The fact was that in Argentina during the 1880s a well-tried
policy was ruined through over-use.[14]

What Were the Returns on Capital?

As we have seen, capital investment flows from where it is abundant but
yields low returns to where it is scarce and renders a higher rate of return.
The differences in profitability between Argentina and more developed
countries were due to the fact that in Argentina capital was scarce. Transactions on the Stock Exchange were limited primarily to gold and foreign
money, government debt or bills of exchange, and, to a much lesser degree,
stock transactions. The interest rate, measured as return on Argentine
government securities, was higher than that of Great Britain, which is
measured as return on British bank annuities or gilded bonds (see Figure 1.6). Part of this difference is due to a risk premium and the cost of
insurance, determined according to investors' analysis of the institutional
factors that might not be favorable to investment, those that might hinder

14 Colin Lewis, *British Railways in Argentina, 1857–1914: A Case of Study of Foreign Investment*, Institute
of Latin American Studies, University of London, 1983, pp. 97–98.

the maximization of profits that would be yielded in a market in which earnings are strictly dependent on profitability. When risk premium is too costly, capital investment is discouraged; greater returns on capital will be required to attract more capital, but the opposite is actually true. High risk, which is reflected in costly hazard premium, discourages investment, because only those who are willing to assume that risk, at a premium, enter the capital market.

Experience with debtors' behavior creates the perception of risk, as do systemic mechanisms that hinder governments' ability to appropriate savings or influence returns on investments. It is usual to estimate country risk in this case by calculating the ratio between the yield on Argentine government debt securities and the British consolidated treasury bonds. In the early years of Argentine independence the difference between Argentine public debt and British consols was great, as investment in Argentine debt was considered highly risky because in 1827 the government defaulted on payment on external debt (the Baring loan) and only renewed payments in 1857. Government debt bonds were highly discounted on the market, and this was reflected in the price of these bonds and the difference in their yields from stable countries such as Great Britain.

But the perception of risk with regard to foreign investment in Argentina began to change. There were several factors that shifted international expectations regarding the capacity of the Argentine government to fulfill its obligations without having to recur to confiscations. Among the first were the establishment of the Constitution and the 1857 Buenos Aires Baring agreement concerning the payment of foreign debt. Another factor was the founding of the Bank of the Province of Buenos Aires (*Banco de la Provincia de Buenos Aires*) with a bimonetary system, along with the final 1862 agreement between the central and the provincial governments, with the central government taking over the Buenos Aires Custom House. Added to these factors were the Buenos Aires Currency Conversion Act of 1863, the agreement regarding floating debt,[15] and the establishment of a sinking fund. These changes in Argentina were reflected in the price of bonds (a decline both in returns on bonds and in the interest rate). On the other

---

15 "Law 30 (November 1, 1862) consolidated the Confederation's floating debt from April 1, 1861 to December 12, 1861: 'may it be recognized as legitimate' and provided for the formation of a commission chosen by the Executive branch to verify this credit. Later, Law 66 (October 20, 1863) required the government to sell off the Confederation's debt in bonds, bills of customs exchange and treasury bills. This debt would then be consolidated at 6% interest in Public Funds. The same law established verification procedures and the National Public Credit [Agency] and ordered the issue of 7 million *pesos fuertes* (convertible currency) from Public Funds." Roberto Cortés Conde, *Dinero Deuda y Crisis: Evolución Fiscal y Monetaria en la Argentina, 1862–1890*, Buenos Aires, Sudamericana, 1989, p. 23.

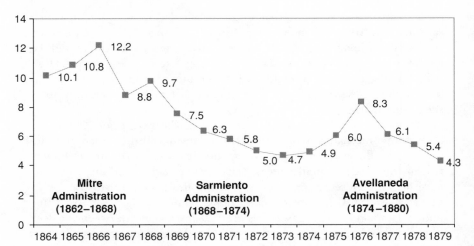

Figure 1.7. Difference in yields on Argentine Public Debt and British Bonds,
1864–1879 (in percentage points). *Source:* Roberto Cortés Conde, "Fiscal Crisis
and Inflation in XIX Century Argentina," Universidad de San Andrés,
November 1998.

hand, that same year Argentina experienced something nearly unheard of
before: a fiscal surplus (see Figure 1.7).

As the international perception of Argentine finances shifted, the country
could rely on international capital markets to raise funds. First, the Province
of Buenos Aires was able to accomplish this in 1857 – when it managed to
recuperate from the Baring debt – and later the National Government was
able to do so in 1865,[16] in that it "could resort to the international market,
negotiating a loan in the amount of 2.5 million pounds with Barings of
London in order to finance the Paraguay War."[17] Furthermore, despite the
fact that the country had to resort to financing by successive currency issues
(with *metallic* notes issued from the Bank of the Province of Buenos Aires),
the war did not cause a spike in inflation.

The adoption of the gold standard, which gave the exchange rate some
stability, was another factor that affected capital returns on foreign investment in Argentina. A depreciated local currency allows the purchase of
assets at a lower price, but when profits must be sent abroad, back to the

---

16 "In 1865 the Executive requested Congress' authorization to negotiate a foreign loan in the amount of
   12 million *pesos fuertes*. After arduous negotiations, in 1866, a loan from London was finally arranged
   in the amount of 2.5 million pounds (at 75 and 77$\frac{1}{2}$, with 6% interest and 2$\frac{1}{2}$ amortization). Of
   this amount, only 1.7 million was paid out: 379,000 pounds in 1866; 31,000 in 1867; 918,000 in
   1868; and 367 thousand in 1869." Roberto Cortés Conde, *Dinero, Deuda y Crisis*, p. 40.
17 Roberto Cortés Conde, "Finanzas Públicas, Moneda y Bancos (1810–1899)", in *Nueva Historia de la
   Nación Argentina*, Buenos Aires, Planeta, 1999, vol. V, p. 482.

foreign investors, they are reduced when there is an unfavorable exchange rate resulting from the depreciated currency. However, government debt securities were safe from depreciation because they were issued in gold or in foreign currency; where direct investment was concerned, profits from private companies that sold goods and services locally were earned in the local currency.

The desire to attract foreign capital was an important aspect of the pressure to adopt the gold standard not only in Argentina but also in other countries (Mexico since 1905 and Brazil). Demonstrating conflicting goals, several administrations, in pursuit of foreign capital, tried to implement policies that led to stability in the exchange rate,[18] while on the other hand inflationary fiscal and monetary policies of the government caused depreciation of the currency. These conflicting goals were the result of failed fiscal management and also pressure from export interests or from producers on the domestic market in pursuit of protection and in favor of depreciation of the local currency.

In terms of labor, higher immigration rates added labor, another important factor of production, to the equation for economic expansion. Argentina was sparsely populated, roughly a million inhabitants mostly concentrated in urban centers (Buenos Aires, Rosario, Cordoba) and in the Pampas and the central and northwestern regions of the country. Massive immigration brought an enormous increase not only in the population but also in the population growth rate and broadened the regional distribution of this growing population, shifting it from the center and northwest to the coast. In 1869, 42% of the population lived in the center and northwest, and a similar proportion, 41%, on the coast, but by 1914 only 22% lived in the center and northwest and 64% on the coast.

But the greatest impact of immigration was felt on the labor market, because the majority of new immigrants were adult males. In the period between 1880 and 1891, 70% of immigrants were men, but between 1900 and 1910 the number rose to 73%. This situation, in turn, affected the dependency rate, which is the ratio of the dependent population to the active-age one. This rate dropped from 0.839 in 1869 to 0.734 in 1895 and to 0.688 in 1914,[19] as the ratio of the dependent to the active population diminished. Taylor maintains that the dependency rate was greater in Argentina than in Australia and Canada, which would explain the lower domestic savings rate (see Figure 1.8 and Chapter 2).

---

18 This also happened in Brazil with the Rothschild loan.
19 "The dependency rate is the ratio of dependent population (0–15) + (over 64) to active population (15–64)." Blanca Sánchez-Alonso, "Labour and Immigration in Latin America," in *Cambridge Economic History of Latin America*, vol. II, ed. Victor Bulmer-Thomas, John Coatsworth, and Roberto Cortés Conde, Cambridge and New York, Cambridge University Press, 2005.

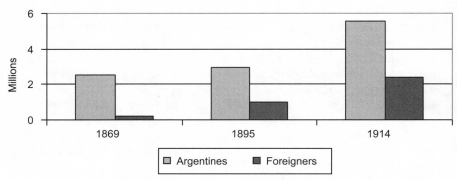

Figure 1.8. Population. *Source:* República Argentina, *Tercer Censo Nacional, levantado el 1° de junio de 1914*, Buenos Aires, 1916 (Third National Census).

European workers emigrated to Argentina for a number of reasons, among them the entitlement to the same civil rights as the native population and access to universal education. However, what was most attractive to immigrants was the difference in wages between European countries and Argentina. A 1979 study demonstrated the existence of this important difference and its fluctuations (see Figure 1.9).

Argentina had many more fertile lands than Europe, and these were exploited for grain cultivation, allowing more efficient use of labor and increasing the marginal productivity. At the same time, the GDP per

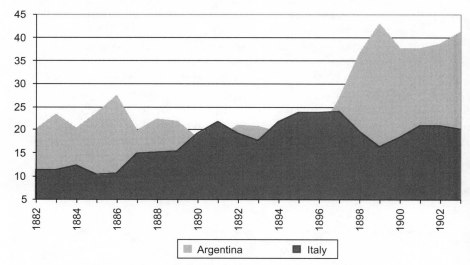

Figure 1.9. Real Wages in Argentina and Italy (Wages in 1882 Pesos). *Source:* Roberto Cortés Conde, *El Progreso Argentino 1880–1914*, Buenos Aires, Sudamericana, 1979.

capita increased, and this translated into higher wages for the workers than in their country of origin and greater remittances for the family members they had left behind.[20]

One important feature of this economic expansion is that it occurred during a time of relative macroeconomic stability after the 1890 crisis. Thus, an analysis of the fiscal and monetary development of the period is essential. The long expansion of these years took place in the context of macroeconomic stability sustained by a tax system whose revenues were based on an ever-growing level of importations and by a monetary regime suffering sharp oscillations in the 1880s and the crisis of 1890 but that entered a period of stability under the gold standard regime.

The greatest source of income for the National Government came from tariffs it levied on imports, although exports were also taxed, a right granted to the central government by an 1866 amendment to the Constitution. The custom duties represented a significant proportion of income for several years. Taxes were the principal source of revenue for government spending. These were circumstances that demonstrate a more efficient fiscal regime that would not have to resort to extraordinary revenues.

We may get a glimpse into the public needs of the period and the historical moment generally by analyzing the type of spending the government engaged in. What was revenue from taxes spent on? Until 1880, the largest share of tax revenue was used to finance both foreign and domestic wars and to pay debts on previous armed conflicts. This demonstrates, as we have seen, the high cost of protecting property rights amid generalized violence. Military spending at the beginning of the 1820s represented 44% of all public spending and dropped to 41% in the period between 1830 and 1834.[21] This number increased to 53.9% of the total spending in 1869, as the country was still awash in foreign and domestic conflicts. Following the cessation of these hostilities, military spending dropped to 34% in 1882, to 20% in 1885, and further still to 17% by 1888 (see Figure 1.10).[22]

Beginning in 1880, however, public works received a much greater proportion of public expenditures. This includes what Buenos Aires received when it became the capital in 1880, as numerous buildings and other projects became property of the National Government. Government operations demanded an ever greater proportion of public spending, as did ill-advised subsidies and those based on favoritism, as the governing party

20 Roberto Cortés Conde, "Migración, Cambio Agrícola y Políticas de Protección: El Caso Argentino," in *Españoles hacia América: La Emigración en Masa, 1880–1930*, ed. Nicolás Sánchez-Albornoz, Madrid, Alianza, 1988, p. 247.

21 Tulio Halperín Donghi, *Guerra y Finanzas en los Orígenes del Estado Argentino (1821–1850)*, Buenos Aires, Editorial Belgrano, 1982.

22 Roberto Cortés Conde, *Dinero, Deuda y Crisis*, Appendix.

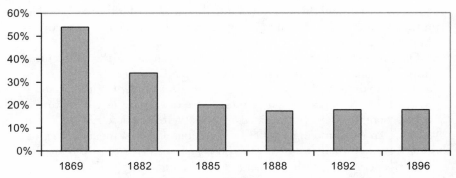

Figure 1.10. Evolution of Military Expenditures as a Percentage of Total
Government Spending, 1869–1896. *Source:* Roberto Cortés Conde, *Dinero, Deuda y
Crisis: Evolución Fiscal y Monetaria en la Argentina. 1862–1890*, Buenos Aires,
Sudamericana, 1989, and Dirección General de Estadística de la Nación, *Extracto
Estadístico de la República Argentina correspondiente al año 1915*, Compañía
Sudamericana de Billetes de Banco, Buenos Aires, 1916.

worked to hold onto power as the decade neared its end. Although the
concession of these subsidies was reprehensible, they represented a smaller
proportion of expenditure than in later years. Public works projects were
financed outside of the ordinary budget, ordered by special laws, but they
still added to pubic debt and had an ever greater effect on payments that
the government had to make on this debt. Debt increased enormously until
1893, and servicing it accounted for a growing proportion of fiscal revenue
(see Figure 1.11).

From 1890 to 1900 the National Government did not incur new debt,
but a significant proportion of expenditures went to service debt from
previous years. Between 1900 and 1910 an extraordinary increase in revenue
spurred an equally significant increase in expenditure on public works. A
large share of public spending also went to payment on the national debt.
The primary fiscal accounts for this period are shown in the table in the
Appendix.

Differences in the methodology of recording data account for the discrepancies in findings between the two primary sources of fiscal information
(see the Appendix for an in-depth explanation). These differences explain
the discrepancies in the years of surplus and deficit.

Differences may be explained by the fact that, on the one hand, the data
analyzed refer to revenues and expenditures and, on the other, they refer to
credits and liabilities (not necessarily received or paid). These are essential
differences that likely translate to higher debits and credits, though not
necessarily in the same proportion (see Figure 1.12).

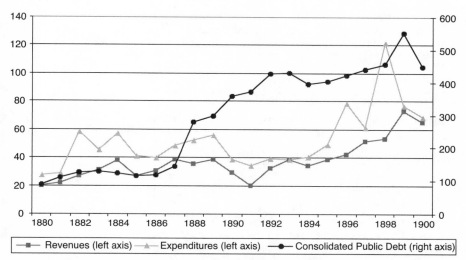

Figure 1.11. Government Revenues and Expenditures 1880–1900 (in millions of *pesos oro*). *Source:* Roberto Cortés Conde, *Dinero, Deuda y Crisis: Evolución Fiscal y Monetaria en la Argentina. 1862–1890*, Buenos Aires, Sudamericana, 1989 and *Anuario Geográfico Argentino*, Comité Nacional de Geografía, Buenos Aires, 1941.

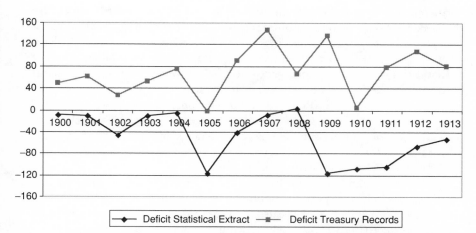

Figure 1.12. Argentine Balance Sheet Comparison: Treasury Balances and Statistical Extract from the Republic of Argentina (in millions of pesos). *Source:* Treasury Yearbooks, 1900–1913, and Dirección General de Estadística de la Nación, *Extracto Estadístico de la República Argentina correspondiente al año 1915*, Compañía Sudamericana de Billetes de Banco, Buenos Aires, 1916, p. 237.

Table 1.2. *Republic of Argentina Consolidated Debt, 1901–1915 (in pesos oro)*

Year	Internal Debt	External Debt	Internal and External Debt	Change in Total Debt
1901	17,863,000	386,451,295.93	404,314,295.93	–
1902	17,403,400	381,082,761.98	398,486,161.98	−1.44
1903	16,626,500	375,844,786.38	392,471,286.38	−1.51
1904	16,544,000	370,772,667.15	387,316,667.15	−1.31
1905	16,468,500	329,167,941.55	345,636,441.55	−10.76
1906	16,400,000	324,333,116.35	340,733,116.35	−1.42
1907	55,505,700	319,512,105.75	375,017,805.75	10.06
1908	38,198,800	314,743,909.06	352,942,709.06	−5.89
1909	87,483,900	311,513,829.33	398,997,729.33	13.05
1910	92,505,000	306,858,729.44	399,363,729.44	0.09
1911	161,367,000	303,719,786.97	465,086,786.97	16.46
1912	159,751,700	297,993,986.97	457,745,686.97	−1.58
1913	157,769,800	308,855,037.47	466,624,837.47	1.94
1914	155,990,000	312,423,556.54	468,413,556.54	0.38
1915	153,844,600	309,301,960.57	463,146,560.57	−1.12

Source: Dirección General de Estadística de la Nación, *Extracto Estadístico de la República Argentina correspondiente al año 1915*, Compañía Sudamericana de Billetes de Banco, Buenos Aires, 1916.

This may explain why the deficits and surpluses on the balance sheets do not correspond to the variations in debt and why the debt looks greater (because it is likely that liabilities outweighed credits). On the other hand, data on debt variation refer only to consolidated and not to floating debt, which in some cases represented a significant proportion of government liabilities. Lastly, payments made with debt were not registered as expenditures in the balances of the National Treasury.

For this reason, it is difficult to reach any conclusions. What is most relevant information for a short-term analysis is the Treasury balance sheet; an analysis of long-term issues requires consideration of variations in indebtedness. Table 1.2 gives an incomplete view of national debt, one that includes consolidated, but not floating, debt.

To some degree, because floating debt is either paid or consolidated, these data give a snapshot of public finances. As debt decreased, as it did until 1906, we had years of surplus. From then on, the record of public finances fluctuates with the debt; during years in which debt increases, we have a deficit, such as in 1907, 1909, and 1911, and during years in which debt decreases, a surplus, such as in 1912 and in 1915.

As for the currency, the monetary regime, since colonial times, was based on the circulation of coins (the *peso plata*, the silver Spanish American hard dollar worth eight *reales*). With national organization the *peso fuerte*, with

17 *pesos fuertes* equal to one Spanish ounce (27 grams) of 0.9 fine gold, or its equivalent in other currencies, was declared legal tender. Until 1882 the *peso fuerte* was not a real coin but a money of account.

But in 1822 provincial (nonconvertible) notes began to circulate in Buenos Aires (bank notes issued by the Discount Bank (*Banco de Descuento*) and then by National Bank (*Banco Nacional*), since 1836, and finally by the provincial mint (*Casa de la Moneda*)). By 1826 this became forced currency, or fiat money. There were a few attempts by other entities to issue paper money directly or through banks of issue, but they had either failed or enjoyed very limited circulation. The *boliviano* coin was also in circulation; this coin was worth less than (around 80% of) a silver Hispano-American peso.

Apart from the previous inconvertible paper currency in 1867, the Bank of the Province of Buenos Aires issued convertible metallic notes that were used as payment for the National Government's taxes. Later on, from the time of its incorporation in 1872, the National Bank also issued convertible *metallic* notes,[23] those circulated in the Buenos Aires province. In the interior generally circulated silver boliviano coins.

In 1881 a new monetary unit was established for the whole country, the gold peso (*peso oro*), worth 1.6129 grams of fine gold, or one ounce of silver. Chartered banks issued notes in this denomination, and these were legally convertible from 1883. This convertibility was of brief duration, because it was suspended from 1885 to 1899.

Monetary fluctuations were often caused by operations carried out by the National Government through the banks. This was the case when the government placed its debt in the Bank of the Province of Buenos Aires in both 1865 and 1876, or when it made a deposit with an 1870 foreign loan in the same bank, and later in the National Bank, producing, thanks to the increase in reserves in those banks, a considerable expansion of notes and loans, and later on a commensurate contraction when it withdrew its deposits from the reserves of those banks. The amount of currency circulated was also affected when in 1862 the government deposited public bonds in the National Bank, which the bank then sold abroad; the sale of bonds abroad increased the bank's reserves, which increased the issuance of bank notes. Notes issue had an extraordinary increase when the government authorized issues through the Guarantee Banks, backed by a new and colossal national debt, which culminated in the severe financial crisis of 1890 (see Figure 1.13).

Lastly, in 1890, the government transferred the right to issue bank notes from the Guarantee Banks to the National Government (in compensation

23 See Roberto Cortés Conde, *Dinero, Deuda y Crisis.*

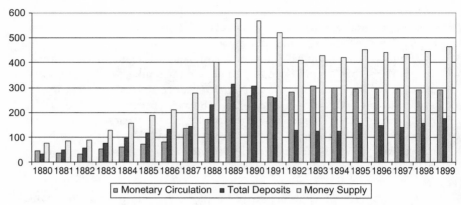

Figure 1.13. Money Supply, Circulation, and Total Deposits, 1880–1900 (in millions of pesos). *Source:* Roberto Cortés Conde, *Dinero, Deuda y Crisis: Evolución Fiscal y Monetaria en la Argentina. 1862–1890*, Buenos Aires, Sudamericana, 1989.

for the debt they were assuming) and by applying restrictions on note issues, as a result of an arrangement with the Bank of England regarding the 1890 Baring crisis. The National Government assumed responsibility for the issue of bank notes starting in 1890, and in 1899 the international gold standard was imposed in Argentina, with the creation of a currency board or a system of convertibility.

Between 1900 and 1913 the monetary system consisted of a fixed exchange rate and currency backed by gold reserves. It issued notes only when it received the corresponding amount of gold, although previous issues did not have gold backing.[24]

With regard to the creation of banking money (deposits), there were no fixed rules on the ratio of reserves to deposits; banks decided for themselves whether or not there were sufficient reserves and then followed seasonal fluctuations, and when reserves increased because of export earnings liquidations, the banks increased the amount of loans and then decreased it when customers withdrew cash. For a few years the Bank of the Argentine Nation (*Banco de la Nación Argentina*) adopted an anticyclic policy and, starting in 1904, managed to rediscount documents from other commercial banks, but only in relatively small amounts from their own reserves, not by issuing currency (see Figure 1.14).

24 For more about the system of convertibility and the Currency Board, see Gerardo Della Paolera and Allan M. Taylor, *Tensando el Ancla*, Buenos Aires and México, Fondo de Cultura Económica, 2003.

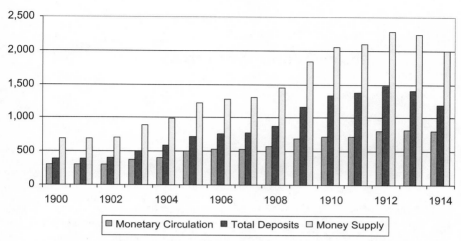

Figure 1.14. Money Supply, Circulation, and Total Deposits, 1900–1914 (in
millions of pesos). *Source:* Dirección General de Estadística de la Nación, *Extracto
Estadístico de la República Argentina correspondiente al año 1915*, Compañía
Sudamericana de Billetes de Banco, Buenos Aires, 1916, and *Anuario Geográfico
Argentino*, Comité Nacional de Geografía, Buenos Aires, 1942.

The End of an Era

In stark contrast to the first half of the nineteenth century, as World War
I approached, Argentina found itself in relatively stable macroeconomic
conditions. The country was an integral member of the economic community of the Atlantic, with strong cultural and demographic ties to Europe,
and was trying to become something similar to the United States of South
America.

Although it played no role in World War I, Argentina suffered its
negative effects in both the short and long run, as Chapter 2 demonstrates.
The consequences of the war were long lasting for Argentina and were
seen in the generalized loss of confidence in world markets, into which the
country had so successfully integrated. This, in turn, changed not only the
way in which Argentines would view their relationship with the rest of
the world, but also how they would view the new institutions created in
response to changing conditions internationally and the way they would
perceive many of the policies that were eventually implemented. The three-
decade interwar period was one of great transformations in Argentina, as
it changed from being an outward-looking country, with its sight on the
world beyond its borders, to an excentric and introspective one.

2

From World War I to the Great
Depression of 1930

The Great War

The years between World War I and the 1930 crisis may be characterized as a period of great transitions. As a response to the extraordinary economic challenges that arose during the crisis, institutions would be forever altered, with policies that would be further elaborated during World War II. The Great War represented a watershed between the world that was open to trade, and to the movements of capital and people, and the world of the closed economies that followed. Yet it was the 1930 crisis that definitively ended *la Belle Epoque* and the "Roaring Twenties" and led to the creation of this different world.

World War I had also left considerable intellectual changes in its wake. The notion of total war led to government intervention in economic affairs. But this intervention was also spurred on by workers and entrepreneurs who demanded it, as they began to realize that they could improve or imperil their respective positions (their relative prices) by doing so. To that point in time, prices had been negotiated on the market.

When the government financed projects by issuing debt or currency, the move had an effect on workers' real earnings and savings, as well as on capital and financial markets. Government intervention in trade and financial and exchange markets, in housing rents, and so on, created a new framework; the government made decisions that had previously been dealt with between the interested parties.

On the other hand, the war had increased the political participation of popular sectors, whose demands had much more influence on governmental policies. This participation intensified when the war ended and millions of men who had made great sacrifices during the conflict returned to their homes with a new sense of their own rights. The most extreme case was the Bolshevik revolution in Russia, as this ideology led to the Spartaquist attempt in Germany and the Bela Kun regime in Hungary. In the West, the demands of the poor bolstered the popularity of leftist parties, which gained political majorities in France and Germany, with programs to tax wealth and not consumption. This created a considerable conflict (war of attrition in France[1] and Germany[2]). In some countries these conflicts led to Fascism and Nazism.

The war inspired the conviction that political power could allow government intervention in markets, affecting prices. This happened indirectly, although not explicitly, when a government issued debt, causing an increase in the interest rate. It also happened when it monetized the deficit and caused inflation and a drop in real wages. But there was also direct intervention through the regulation of prices or through policies regulating tariffs and trade. Thus, government intervention in this sense had not arisen from a romanticized notion of a utopia of collective ownership of the means of production, or of a planned economy, but rather from a series of measures that – implemented during the war – were again applied amid the urgency of the 1930 crisis.

If the war had led the state to intervene in markets, people began to think that intervention could also be used to overcome market failures. Furthermore, the transition toward a new institutional framework was gradual,

---

1 "Disagreement over whose social programs should be cut and whose taxes should be raised resulted in an extended fiscal deadlock. The parties of the Left demanded increased taxes on capital and wealth, those of the Right reductions in social spending. As long as agreement remained elusive, inflation and currency depreciation persisted." Barry Eichengreen, *Globalizing Capital*, New Jersey, Princeton University Press, 1996, p. 52. "The burden of paying for the war was common in the belligerent countries after World War I. For example, in France, Germany, and Italy, the political struggle over fiscal policy was not about the need for reducing enormous budget deficits of the debt overhang, but over which groups should bear higher taxes to achieve that end. Parties of the Right favored proportional income and indirect taxes; parties of the Left proposed capital levies and more progressive income taxes. In particular, France in the first half of the 1920s is a textbook example of a distributional war of attrition. The period 1919–1926 is marked by a high degree of polarization of the political debate and by large swings in the composition of the legislature. After it became clear, in the early 1920s, that the German war reparations would not have solved the French fiscal problem, the Chamber of Deputies was deadlocked for several years because of lack of agreement on feasible fiscal plans. . . . The lack of compromise led to a 18-month period of complete fiscal inaction, which implied a sharp rise in the inflation rate, capital flight, and speculative attacks against the franc." Alberto Alesina and Allan Drazen, "Why Are Stabilizations Delayed?" *American Economic Review*, vol. 8, no. 5, December 1991, pp. 1172–1173.

2 "The fiscal implications of the transfer were accommodated by tax reforms guided through the Reichstag by the finance minister, Matthias Erzberger, over the strident opposition of a Right wing led by Helfferich. Erzberger's tax package featured an emergency levy and transferred the income tax from the states to the Reich in return for a commitment by the central government to redistribute some of the revenues back to local authorities. The tax increase was essential for maintaining fiscal balance in the face of interim transfer. German politicians and their constituencies tolerated higher taxes because they anticipated that the revenue would be transferred abroad for only a limited period of time. Rather than provoking capital flight and other forms of evasion, the tax increase was followed by short-term capital inflows in anticipation of possible stabilization of the mark." Barry Eichengreen, *Golden Fetters. The Gold Standard and the Great Depression 1919–1939*, New York, Oxford University Press, 1995, p. 130.

and only later, especially after the 1930 crisis, did the true magnitude and duration of the changes become evident.

There were certain institutional changes that nearly all countries undertook, so that national differences were a matter of degree. These were the suspension of convertibility, and intervention in markets in the allied countries in order to maintain prewar nominal parities. Besides, to finance the war, governments issued public debt or money, intervened in markets by establishing maximum or minimum prices, and regulated trade and industry. Although some sense of normalcy returned when the war was over, this was not entirely achieved in the 1920s, with the notoriously frustrated attempts to return to the gold standard, and, ultimately, the 1930 financial crisis that led to a new institutional framework.

Argentina, which did not participate in the war, nevertheless felt the negative effects of the conflict. Firstly, following the European countries, in August 1914 the Currency Board suspended peso convertibility. The war had considerable consequences for imports, producing a supply shock: shortage of fuel, raw materials, and industrial parts, which greatly affected the country's economy. The war also proved detrimental to the inflows of capital and labor from Europe, which had been so important in the prewar period.

Although the Argentine government did intervene, early on, in the exchange markets, what was more important for the depreciation and later appreciation of the peso was the suspension and the return to convertibility. Fluctuation in the value of the peso affected the labor market as well. Changes in real wages were a result not only of changes in labor supply and demand but also of governmental measures that led to the rise and fall in the value of the peso.

Two circumstances began to show the powerful role that the government could play in improving remuneration on the factors of production (their relative prices). The first was the possibility of increasing prices for local producers by raising customs tariffs – which made imports more expensive and because of that, consumers seek domestically produced goods. (This could also be achieved by altering official values.[3]) The second was the

---

3 "The cost of imported goods depended on several factors: the international price, the exchange rate and tariffs. The effective tariff was a combination of the nominal tariff and the values which the government fixed on imported merchandise for the purpose of paying the duty – the official or *aforo* value. In general, each year up-to-date lists of *aforo* values were published which might or might not coincide with market values; however from 1906 to 1920 the *aforo* values were not revised. As the prices of imported goods had increased significantly during the war the divergence between both values increased, resulting in a decline in protection. . . . The state used the *aforo values* as an instrument to increase or lower the effective tariff and compensate for changes on the prices of consumer goods and raw materials and, second, fiscal income and protectionist pressures. . . . Villanueva (1972, p. 465) argued that . . . with the increase of custom *aforos* in 1923 . . . 'the protection the industry was doping

increase or decrease of real wages produced by the appreciation or depreciation of the peso. Appreciation benefited wage earners but had negative effects on profits. The repercussions for producers of local goods prompted them to demand increased tariffs for protection.

These inconsistencies were bound to last, although if the increase in the value of the peso benefited wage earners and increased disposable income, and therefore consumption, it decreased profits for entrepreneurs, especially those involved in labor-intensive activities. If both objectives were to be achieved – that is, to benefit workers as well as entrepreneurs – it was necessary to control the exchange rate, as was done later, in order to prevent the increase in income from turning into an increase in imports.

Furthermore, in an attempt to maintain real wages without having to resort to increasing nominal wages, as happened during the Peronist period, the government implemented price controls. Issues such as these led to increasing intervention in various markets. In Argentina – a country with an enormous influx of immigrants – significant social and political changes were occurring that were not unlike the European experience. Political parties such as anarchists, socialists, and communists had a powerful role. At the same time the socialist party influenced legislative reforms that made the labor market less fluid. Nevertheless, the party had always supported monetary stability. Finally, with the passage of the 1912 Suffrage Law, providing for mandatory universal male suffrage by secret ballot, popular participation in voting increased and the radical party[4] gained ground. Just as in Europe, the result was expectations of rising living conditions, which in turn inspired social movements, and with these, violent confrontations with those who felt threatened by them.

Although the conflicts never reached the magnitude and gravity of those of the 1920s in France and Germany, there was a redistribution of income toward wage earners, which would be reversed during the 1930s. However, and most importantly, the tendency to seek government intervention in markets became firmly instilled in the people's economic culture. This development represented a remarkable philosophical shift where economies were concerned. The Roaring Twenties had come to an end.

External Shock in an Open Economy

As Argentina did not participate in the war, the conflict did not cause loss of human life or other material losses for the country, but its consequences

---

for was achieved.' R. Cortés Conde, "The Vicissitudes of an Exporting Economy: Argentina 1875–1930," in *An Economic History of Twentieth-Century Latin America*, ed. E. Cárdenas, J. A. Ocampo, and R. Tropp, New York, Palgrave, 2000, pp. 284–285.
4 Unión Cívica Radical (UCR), a center moderate party.

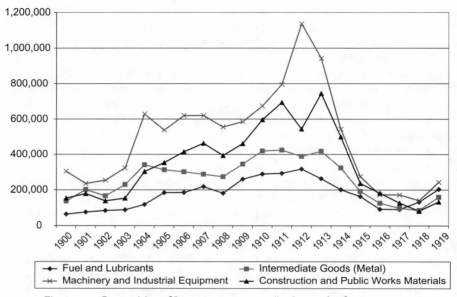

Figure 2.1. Composition of Imports, 1900–1919 (in thousands of pesos at 1950 prices). *Source:* CEPAL, *El Desarrollo Económico de la Argentina*, Santiago de Chile, CEPAL, 1958.

for the economy were nevertheless damaging. However, unlike after the 1930 crisis, the damage was not due to a decrease in world demand for Argentine products, which would have affected exports.

Despite the blockades, the war at sea, the scarcity of cargo ships for merchandise, and the evermore costly shipping freights, Argentina continued to supply grain and meat, especially to Allied countries. The country exported goods to central powers only through neutral countries, but these exports began to taper off almost entirely as the war dragged on and the British Royal Navy created an effective blockade of the central powers.

The main problem for Argentina was on the supply side. The countries involved in the war that had previously provided fuel, raw materials, and manufactured goods to Argentina redirected their resources toward the war effort. Thus soon the difficulties for Argentina began to mount; imports dropped precipitously, where primarily intermediate goods and industrial equipment were concerned (see Figure 2.1).

Coal and coke provided fuel, and both came from Great Britain. As these began to rarify, they were replaced, partially and inefficiently, by wood from the Chaco Forest (Santiago del Estero, norte de Cordoba, and Chaco). The scarcity of fuel, raw materials, and intermediate goods contributed to a surge in local industrial production to substitute imports.

The decline in imports, shown in Figure 2.1,[5] caused a remarkable drop in government revenue, primarily from customs. This resulted in a reduction in investment in public works and in public spending. The war cut off foreign investment, which, by 1910, had represented a significant contribution to the Argentine economy. As a result, trade bore the consequences, and there was a contraction in economic activity overall. But the war was not the only detriment to the country's economy. Two serious droughts, one in 1914 and another in 1917, caused severe harvest loss and provoked a downturn in agricultural output in both years. The result was a sharp drop in GDP, 3% annually between 1912 and 1916, especially in agricultural production.

This external shock came at a moment in which, by 1913, economic growth had reached its peak. This expansion had been spurred on by a strong capital flow, which was reversed in 1913, causing great tension in the banking sector and halting real estate appreciation. Reversion of capital flows was also reflected in a slump in the construction sector, signs of which had begun to appear in 1911, as illustrated in the Figure 2.2.

With an economy that was intricately tied to international flows of production factors and of merchandise, Argentina greatly suffered the impact of the external shock. This would have consequences for the hitherto generally positive perception of the benefits of the country's integration into the world economy.[6]

Suspension of convertibility and the passage of Laws 9479 and 9577, which authorized the issue of currency through rediscounts of commercial documents, sparked a process of institutional reforms that would, in future, have profound repercussions for Argentine life. At the same time, the war in Europe caused a sharp decline in reserves at the Argentine Currency Board. These were circumstances that had arisen because the countries at war, foreseeing eventual emergencies, had to scramble for gold (war chest), anticipating a lack of access to international credit.[7] These

5 Further on in this chapter we demonstrate that the imports data that CEPAL use were, until the 1930s, at official values (*aforos*) and not at market values. Because during the war years there was a significant increase in prices, whereas between 1906 and 1922, the official prices remained the same and the import estimates appeared undervalued in terms of values, although there was indeed a reduction in units purchased.

6 Imports fell in 1913 before the war as a result of the reduction in loan inflows coming into the country from an already tense Europe. See Raúl Prebisch, "Anotaciones Sobre Nuestro Medio Circulante", *Revista de Ciencias Económicas*, year IX, series II, no. 3, 1921, p. 300.

7 Among other measures, the warring countries prohibited gold exports. In Argentina "the closure of the Currency Board decreed by Presidential Edict on August 9, 1914 and sanctioned by Law 9481 was imposed by circumstances and as a result of analogous laws passed by the most powerful nations at the start of the European war . . . to face the need for gold that the warring nations would experience, safeguarding, to the extent possible, the increase in fiduciary circulation which would be imposed due to the enormous expenditures they would have to make." Alfredo Echagüe, "Expedientes de

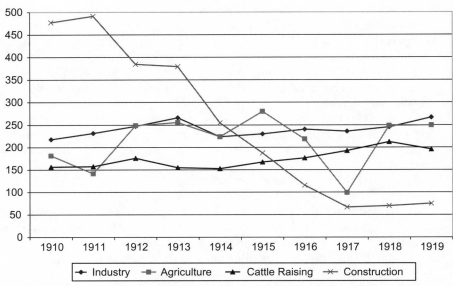

Figure 2.2. Evolution of GDP: Primary Sectors (Base index numbers: 1900 =
100). *Source:* Cortés Conde, Roberto, with the collaboration of Marcela Harriague,
Estimaciones del Producto Bruto Interno de Argentina, 1875– 1935, Buenos Aires,
Universidad de San Andrés, 1994.

countries liquidated their financial assets abroad in order to convert them
into gold. Between July 1913 and July 1914, the withdrawal of gold from
the Argentine Currency Board reached 59 million gold pesos. Under the
gold standard regime it resulted in a reduction of some 134 million pesos
from the reserves.

The Crisis of 1913–1914. Monetary Difficulties during the War Years

The scramble for gold on the part of warring countries that provoked
the reduction of Argentine reserves induced the Argentine government to
suspend convertibility at the Currency Board on August 9, 1914, shortly
after war had been declared. In fact, the withdrawal of a considerable
amount of gold and its concomitant monetary contraction had really begun
in 1913, with the Balkans crisis, when the influx of foreign capital was
interrupted and marked an end to the expansive phase that had begun in
1908. According to Prebisch,

la Comisión Designada para Dictaminar sobre Cuestiones de Carácter Monetario", in "Conferencia
Económica Nacional", *Revista de Economía Argentina*, vol. III, no. 17–18, November–December 1919,
p. 503.

Argentine banks, whose political extravagance is well known, drastically reduce the total sum of their loans: from 812 million paper pesos in 1912, to 728 million in 1913, and to 372 in 1914. Foreign banks also restrict their credit, though to a lesser degree than Argentine ones.... Foreign markets loaned us less money, and we had to export metallic currency in order to pay for financial services, reducing the amount of notes. Credit was restricted and the collapse was felt by those who had previously provided this credit.[8]

The Congress passed a law on August 8, 1914, that authorized the Currency Board to issue currency based on commercial documents discounted by the Bank of the Argentine Nation, provided that a metallic reserve of 40% remained. This act was motivated by a fear that the depletion of reserves and the continued withdrawal of bank deposits, along with a monetary contraction, would have effects that would ripple throughout the economy. The 1914 law stipulated:

The Currency Board, previously authorized by the Executive Power, will carry out all rediscounting of commercial documents at the Bank of the Argentine Nation issuing the necessary amount of notes among the types currently in circulation, provided that the gold backing of the legal tender does not drop below 40%.[9]

This law caused a change in the rigid regime of the gold standard, which had to that time prohibited currency issues unless they were backed by the corresponding quantity in gold. The former had the effect, as we have seen, of impeding the government from simply printing money to finance its deficits. Issues were determined by balances on foreign accounts and by public desire to have their monetary assets either in gold or in paper pesos. If the new rediscounting regime were enforced, the quantity of money would also be influenced by the supply of credit, allowing for greater discretion on the part of currency-issuing agencies. It was precisely this discretion that had been so problematic in the nineteenth century, causing, among other things, the 1890 financial crisis.

However, shortly after, following the European governments' early attempts to hoard gold, the tendency reverted instead to inflows of it, as illustrated in Figure 2.3. Large amounts of capital began to enter the country, which, because it was not involved in the war, offered greater security. Furthermore, Argentina's recent past had been renowned for its stability and order. Nevertheless, as exports increased, imports slumped, leaving favorable commercial balances that made it possible to pay for financial services. Thus, the 1914 law was not to take effect at that time,

8 Raúl Prebisch, "Anotaciones Sobre Nuestro Medio Circulante", *Revista de Ciencias Económicas*, year IX, series II, no. 3, October 1921, p. 302.
9 Law 9479, Art. 2. Passed on August 8, 1914, effective August 9, 1914.

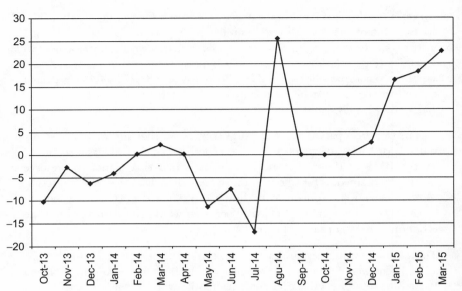

Figure 2.3. Monthly Balances in Gold Flows at the Currency Board (in millions of gold pesos). *Source:* Baiocco, Pedro J., *La Economía Bancaria Argentina a través de sus Índices más Representativos en el Período, 1901–1935*, Buenos Aires, Universidad de Buenos Aires, 1937, p. 50 (see Table A.C.2.5 in the Appendix).

but instead was only enforced in response to the 1930 crisis. Prebisch further points out that "it is for this reason that during the war suspending the Currency Board and prohibiting the export of gold were fruitless and routine exercises, thanks to a series of positive balance of payments."[10]

Instead, issues backed by gold deposited in Argentine embassies abroad were allowed. These deposits remained abroad so as to prevent loss due to the submarine war in the Atlantic and a possible sinking of a transport ship.

Despite the suspension of convertibility between 1914 and 1927, monetary issues were backed by gold deposits at the Currency Board or in Argentine embassies abroad, with the exception of 1914, year in which gold was sent abroad followed by a decline in deposits; in the following years, as a result of a renewed influx of gold the total sum of currency increased. But it is important to bear in mind the effect the issue of currency had on the decision to mobilize the Conversion Fund at the Bank of the Argentine Nation. About 20 million of these gold funds were used to replete gold reserves at the Currency Board, because otherwise, it would

10 Prebisch, "Anotaciones Sobre Nuestro Medio Circulante", p. 306.

Table 2.1. *Gold Stock at the Currency Board, at the Bank of the Argentine Nation and the Total for the Country, 1912–1917 (data from December 31, in millions of gold pesos and in percent variation)*

Year	Entire Country		Banks		Bank of the Argentine Nation		Currency Board		Ratio Gold Reserves in the Bank of the Argentine Nation/Gold Reserves at the Currency Board
1912	291.9	17.42	30.98	22.55	37.8	11.14	223.13	17.87	16.94
1913	287.39	−1.55	21.67	−30.05	32.27	−14.63	233.45	4.63	13.82
1914	270.31	−5.94	17.02	−21.46	28.64	−11.25	224.66	−3.77	12.75
1915	329.6	21.93	13.63	−19.92	10.33	−63.93	305.64	36.05	3.38
1916	347.53	5.44	15.78	15.77	14.91	44.34	316.84	3.66	4.71
1917	370.24	6.53	16.46	4.31	36.93	147.69	316.85	0.003	11.66

Note: Bank of the Argentine Nation is excluded in the category Banks.
Source: Baiocco, Pedro J., *La Economía Bancaria Argentina a través de sus Índices más Representativos en el Período, 1901–1935*, Buenos Aires, Universidad de Buenos Aires, 1937.

have caused a contraction of currency.[11] The funds were also utilized to extract pesos from the Currency Board to loan to the government or to rediscount documents in commercial banks to bolster their reserves. In this case, they affected the expansion of currency.[12]

Variations in gold reserves in the Bank of the Argentine Nation, and to a lesser degree in commercial banks, had an indirect effect on currency issues. If the Bank of the Argentine Nation increased its gold reserves, it restricted issues from the Currency Board, and if the reserves declined, issues increased. This demonstrates the inverse relationship between the gold stock at the Bank of the Argentine Nation and that of the Currency Board. The data in Table 2.1 show that the Bank of the Argentine Nation reduced its reserves in 1914, at the start of the war. When gold reserves

11 In 1918 the bank granted the National Government an extraordinary loan to the amount of 200 million gold pesos in payment for the negative balance that the latter had with France and Great Britain. This was the single largest loan that the Bank of the Argentine Nation had ever given. The previous year the same bank had granted another loan in payment on debt that the National Government had with the United States. See Banco de la Nación Argentina, *El Banco de la Nación Argentina en su Cincuentenario*, Buenos Aires, Banco de la Nación Argentina, 1941, pp. 342–343.

12 With a September 1914 law the Bank of the Argentine Nation was authorized to reduce the Currency Fund by 30 million gold pesos. With Law 9479 now enforceable, 20 million were used, the equivalent of 45,454,541.00 pesos. The 10 million gold pesos remaining were used to pay for service on various debts. Since the government paid back a portion of the debt, 7 million gold pesos remained, and these were converted to pesos, leaving a total debt of 15.9 million pesos as an advance to the government's current account at 5% annual interest rate. Banco de la Nación Argentina, *El Banco de la Nación Argentina en su Cincuentenario*, Buenos Aires, Banco de la Nación Argentina, 1941.

Table 2.2. *Monetary Indicators, 1910–1919 (in millions of pesos)*

Year	Currency (Held by Public and Banks)	Bank Deposits	Ratio Currency/ Deposits	Cash Reserves at Commercial Banks	Ratio Cash Reserves/ Deposits	Bank Multiplier	Bank of the Argentine Nation Rediscounts to Commercial Banks[a]
1910	716.0	1,331.6	0.54	472.4	0.35	2.86	4.44
1911	722.9	1,374.8	0.53	487.0	0.35	2.90	5.82
1912	799.8	1,480.9	0.54	486.5	0.33	2.85	8.91
1913	823.3	1,411.2	0.58	535.0	0.38	2.71	7.68
1914	803.3	1,189.3	0.68	523.4	0.44	2.48	43.20
1915	987.6	1,418.5	0.70	465.7	0.33	2.44	13.40
1916	1,013.1	1,596.1	0.63	608.5	0.38	2.58	15.64
1917	1,013.1	1,891.1	0.54	639.1	0.34	2.87	6.61
1918	1,154.5	2,665.6	0.43	663.7	0.25	3.31	5.04
1919	1,177.2	2,834.2	0.42	775.4	0.27	3.41	32.08

[a] Data from December 31 of each year.

Source: Anuario Geográfico Argentino, Comité Nacional de Geografía, Buenos Aires, 1941 and Banco de la Nación Argentina, *El Banco de la Nación argentina en su Cincuentenario*, Buenos Aires, Banco de la Nación Argentina, 1941.

drained out of the country the bank further reduced its reserves, softening the contraction on issues from the Currency Board and, on the contrary, when more gold entered in 1916 and 1917 it increased its reserves so that the influx of gold in the Currency Board was less than that of the entire country. Thus, it partially neutralized its monetary effect.

Between 1912 and 1914 the amount of the country's gold reserves dropped, and the same applied to the Bank of the Argentine Nation. However, the Currency Board maintained a stable level of gold, thanks to the help of the Bank of the Argentine Nation Conversion Fund condition that helped avert a contraction of currency. In 1915 the amount of gold at the Currency Board increased, as it decreased at the Bank of the Argentine Nation, even more than in the country, which increased the amount of currency.

But the expansion of bank money resulting from the reduction in the ratio between reserves and deposits in commercial banks was also important (see Table 2.2). It is true that with the exception of 1915 the amount of cash in the banks did not decrease, but the ratio of reserves to deposits did. This could be attributed to the Bank of the Argentine Nation rediscounts to the commercial banking system.[13] Nevertheless, the rediscounts that

13 Thus, we can conclude that the Bank of the Argentine Nation enforced a policy of monetary sterilization. The role of Bank of the Argentine Nation rediscounts did not go unnoticed by Ford, and was mentioned in the work of Della Paolera and Taylor, where they refer explicitly to a policy of sterilization, following a Dornbusch model about the British internal drain in 1847. See

the Bank of the Argentine Nation gave were made from their own reserves and were not through rediscount from the Currency Board, which is what happened just after 1930, when the law authorizing the rediscounts came into effect. Between 1910 and 1919 the rediscounts granted by the Bank of the Argentine Nation to commercial banks went from 4.4 to 32.08 million of pesos, reaching the highest proportion in relation to currency in 1914 (5.38%).

During this period the ratio between cash reserves and deposits dropped from 0.44 in 1914 to 0.27 in 1919. The multiplier increased from 2.38 in 1914 to 3.41 in 1919. Deposits increased by 138% during those five years. The public deposited a growing amount of cash in banks and the C/D coefficient (currency to deposits) dropped from 0.68 in 1914 to 0.42 in 1919.

Issues from the Currency Board continued to be tied to the strict regimen of the gold standard with contractive effects when there were gold outflows. The lack of flexibility of the gold standard was compensated with a reduction in gold reserves at commercial banks, which inversely affected the creation of deposits (banking money) mainly in the Bank of the Argentine Nation, where in 1915 it had 3.13% of the country's overall reserves. That inversely affected the amount of reserves at the banks and therefore in the creation of banking money.

When there was a scarcity of currency as a consequence of keeping to the rule that required the Currency Board to issue on the basis of gold inflows, the banks as well as the public simply spent less currency, the banks reducing cash reserves and the public substituting currency for deposits (Table 2.2). Those measures were intended to avert the circumstances that affected the real economy aggravating the recession.

Fiscal Policy

The differing criteria with which the information in the official sources was elaborated (see Methodological Appendix) produced inconsistencies that hinder definitive conclusions. However, we may broadly conclude that because of the war, duties on imports, the primary source of revenue, reduced considerably between 1913 and 1915 (some 60%). From 1916 on,

Gerardo Della Paolera and Alan Taylor, *Straining at the Anchor: The Argentina Currency Board and the Search for Macroeconomic Stability, 1880–1935*, Chicago, University of Chicago Press, 2001 (also the Spanish version: *Tensando el Ancla: La Caja de Conversión Argentina y la Búsqueda de la Estabilidad Macroeconómica, 1880–1935*, Buenos Aires, Fondo de Cultura Económica, 2003). In this important work they point out that the rediscounts at the Bank of the Argentine Nation were a method of shoring up the fragile private banking system, whose situation would become more precarious after the 1929 crisis. The absence of a firmly established financial system in Argentina would be one of the primary reasons for its economic backslide, which had begun in the 1920s.

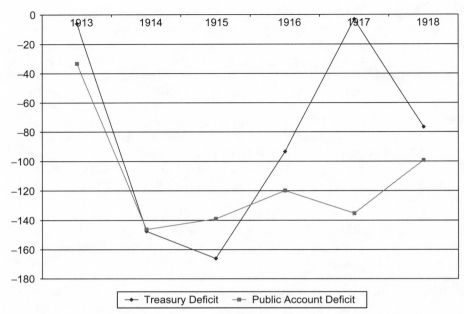

Figure 2.4. Comparison of Balance Sheet from Budget Investment Accounts and National Treasury, 1913–1918 (in millions of pesos). *Source:* Treasury Yearbooks, 1913–1918, and *Anuario Geográfico Argentino*, Comité Nacional de Geografía, Buenos Aires, 1941.

data from the Budget Investment Account on income show an increase that must have been related to nontributary revenues, which do not appear in budget accounts that included only revenue from taxes. The gap becomes greater in both data sources and then constricts again in 1918. With regard to expenditures, though, the sources show amounts that are quite similar, and it appears that what is paid is less than the liabilities assumed. This could be due to the fact that the information from the Treasury refers to payments but not to the overall liabilities, creating the discrepancies with the other source. According to both versions the deficit in each case would be as shown in Figure 2.4.

During the war years, because of a lack of access to international credit, the drop in revenue from duties on imports was compensated in part by an increase in the amount of floating debt. A significant portion of this debt was drawn against the Bank of the Argentine Nation, where the government's negative balances steadily increased, as illustrated in Table 2.3.

At the same time, if we consider the evolution of the total number of loans to the government granted by the Bank of the Argentine Nation, it becomes evident that the number increases sharply during the war years and then decreases. (These loans include other items that were not considered within the "National General Treasury" account; see Figure 2.5.)

Table 2.3. *Balance Sheet "Tesorería General de la Nación" National Treasury (in pesos as of December 31 of each year indicated)*

Years	Balance Debits or Credits	Amount of Change	Legal Limit (20% of Capital)	Surplus
1914	−691,529.37	−	32,220,639	−
1915	−21,638,324.76	−20,946,795.39	32,220,639	−
1916	−52,563,447.29	−30,925,122.53	32,220,639	20,342,808
1917	−49,443,566.92	3,119,880.37	32,653,597	16,789,970
1918	−56,043,842.10	−6,600,275.18	33,995,546	22,048,296
1919	−64,103,715.21	−8,059,873.11	36,440,879	27,662,836
1920	−7,806,088.21	56,297,627.00	38,986,509	−
1921	−54,317,188.31	−46,511,100.10	41,036,217	13,280,971
1922	1,712,832.09	56,030,020.40	41,991,314	−

Source: Banco de la Nación Argentina, *El Banco de la Nación Argentina en su Cincuentenario*, Buenos Aires, Banco de la Nación Argentina, 1941.

Debt. The differences between revenues and expenditures in the two sources cited should really correspond to the increase or decrease in the debt. The existing data regarding consolidated debt, however, do not show a significant increase in those years (Figure 2.6). However, if

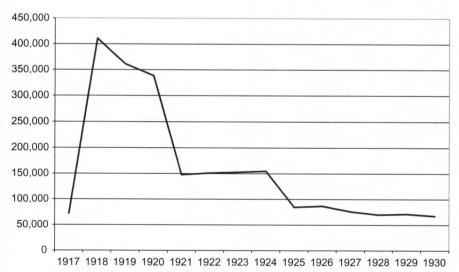

Figure 2.5. Evolution of Official Loans from Bank of the Argentine Nation. *Note:* Official loans include short-term government loans, Treasury Bonds, payments on the baring loan, Ministry of the Treasury (Yearbook) Law 10251, various National Government accounts, monetary exchange loss and interests loan to Great Britain Law 10350, and Loan to Allies Law 10350. *Source:* Banco de la Nación Argentina, *El Banco de la Nación Argentina en su Cincuentenario*, Buenos Aires, Banco de la Nación Argentina, 1941.

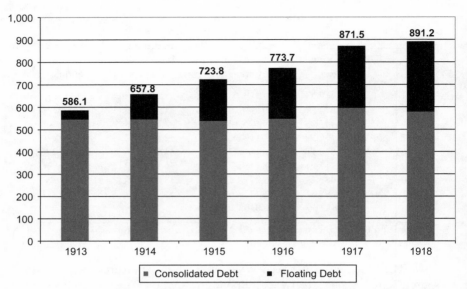

Figure 2.6. Evolution of Debt, 1913–1918 (in millions of gold pesos). *Source:* Peters, Harold, *The Foreign Debt of the Argentina Republic*, Baltimore, MD, The Johns Hopkins University Press, 1934.

we add the floating debt, the picture changes and total debt increases substantially.

The floating debt[14] was financed in part by loans from the Bank of the Argentine Nation, as we have seen, and refers to late payments and accounts filed. Part of this debt, like the banking type, is either paid off (and henceforth appears as payments on the debt at the Treasury) or is consolidated in public bonds, which in turn increases the consolidated debt.

The Postwar Period: Recuperation and Growth, 1917–1927

The restrictions that existed during the war years had finally ended, allowing for a substantial economic upturn beginning in 1918, albeit briefly interrupted by the effects of the 1920 world economic crisis. By 1924, Argentina experienced strong economic growth, fed by a resurgence of imports, which increased from 380 million gold pesos in 1917 to 500

---

14 The only available information about floating debt for the years in question are the data collected by Harold Peters, included in Figure 2.6. The data available from the period 1918–1940 are from *Anuario Geográfico Argentino*, Comité Nacional de Geografía, Buenos Aires, 1941.

million pesos in 1918, and 656 million of the same currency in 1919, sustaining high import levels from that year on.

GDP swiftly showed a strong rebound, as growth nearly doubled in the 1920s. Nevertheless, it is worth noting that this phase of economic expansion did not last long. The cattle sector and a few others began to experience a slowdown during the mid-1920s. On the other hand, grain production never came to recuperate the frenzy of the prewar period. However, it would be another external shock, the 1930 worldwide depression, which would ultimately halt growth. Taking the trend between the two peaks – one before the war, in 1913, and the other in 1929, which preceded the depression – the level of the prewar period had not been achieved.

Although cereal production did not show the dynamism of the previous decades, a change occurred in agriculture so that land use now included industrial crops, especially cotton, which was the sector showing the decade's greatest growth and on which the substantial expansion in the textile industry would depend in the following decade.

Cattle production suffered from 1925 the sanitary restrictions imposed by the United States (foot and mouth disease). Construction, as usual, showed the ample cyclic movements; after a drop of 36% per year during the war (between 1914 and 1917), it experienced 32.5% yearly growth between 1917 and 1923. As far as industry is concerned, for which there are no annual data or census, in tables we elaborated elsewhere, taking imputs as proxies we found a growth of 4.8% annually for the period between 1920 and 1928. As Villanueva asserts, several companies were founded during that decade, many of them U.S. firms. Data on machinery and equipment imports indicate that it was a period of significant investment, which in the 1930s (with closed markets) would allow an increase in production for the internal market and a shift from more important activities, from the foods sector, to the textile sector.

The price of exports increased by 91% between 1913 and 1919, but imports increased even more during this period, 148%. The increase in prices of tradable goods affected the cost of living. Thus, to alleviate the effects of this increase the government effectuated a veiled decrease in tariffs, freezing official values (*aforos*[15]). At the end of the war the trend was reverted: export prices dropped by 41% until 1922, and those of imports 22%. However, export prices spiked between 1923 and 1925 and

---

15 "The 1906 law set an estimated unit value (*aforo*) on each imported item that could be changed only by law. Thus, although the law included duties expressed in both ad valorem and specific terms, so long as the aforo or tariff values were unchanged, all duties were in effect specific" (emphasis added). Carlos Díaz Alejandro, *Essays on the Economic History of the Argentine Republic*, New Haven and London, Yale University Press, 1970, p. 281.

later continued to fall, a trend in imports that continued until 1930. The favorability of the terms of trade changed: they were unfavorable until 1922, became favorable in 1922, and remained that way until 1925, and then a negative trend reigned until 1928. The unemployment rate, which had been significant during the war years (reaching 19.4% in 1917/1919[16]), dropped in the 1920s and remained at 4%.

Rise and Fall in Agricultural Prices in the Postwar Period: Protectionism

Whereas the recession from the war had been due to a shock in supply caused by a drop in imports, the expansion was rooted in a significant demand for foodstuffs and raw materials in Europe. This caused the producer countries to increase the total surface of arable land, the number of cattle stocks, and the production of raw materials. But the European countries recuperated quickly. It is true that in transportation the damage had been great, but it had been restricted to a quite limited war zone in the northeastern part of France and Belgium, although the majority of the conflicting nations had not been affected by the bombs and pillaging. On the other hand, the Central European countries, which had suffered from a lack of foodstuffs and imported raw materials, proposed to achieve self-sufficiency and, to that end, adopted protectionist measures. Even the United States reverted to the favorable trend toward a reduction in tariffs established under the 1913 Underwood Law. Products such as meet and corn, which in 1913 had not been taxed, began to be charged in 1922 and these increased more than 60% with the new 1930 tariffs.[17]

In the world of the 1920s there was a significant increase in the supply of primary products, while the rate of population growth diminished.

This resulted in a decrease in the price of primary products worldwide, causing a strong trend toward protectionist policies, with the purchase of surpluses and accumulation of stocks. These actions led to greater imbalances and, ultimately, to an even sharper drop in prices, which affected the principal primary producer countries' and the United States' agricultural sectors. As prices fell it had an effect that rippled beyond the agricultural sector, leaving regional banks, precisely the banks that tended to extend agricultural credit, extremely vulnerable.[18]

In Argentina the increase in the demand for meat in the period immediately following the war and the concomitant rise in prices caused a sharp increase in cattle stocks. Because cows are not only consumer goods but

---

16 According to A. Bunge, "La Industria Durante La Guerra", *Revista de Economía Argentina*, no. 150, 1930, p. 24.

17 See Table A.C.2.1 in Appendix of Tables.

18 Charles Kindleberger, *The World in Depression, 1929–1939*, Berkeley, University of California Press, 1973, p. 76.

also capital goods, a feature of the cattle cycle is that when prices increase, supply does not, but rather it decreases, because cows, as breeders, are not sold off or slaughtered. Thus, prices further increased, as did cattle stocks, but later, the greater number of reproducing cows created an even greater supply, causing prices to drop even further.[19] This caused a crisis in the cattle industry of such proportions that it led to producers and trade organizations to blame their woes on foreign cold storage plants, demanding state intervention in the market to set minimum prices for meats and establish a national cold storage plant.

It is true that there were very few firms involved in the marketing of meat and grains, and for that reason they were accused of being monopsonistic, having power over the market to influence prices, although in the case of cold storage plants, there was healthy competition between the British, the first ones to establish themselves, and U.S. packet meat firms, who came later. For a short while, this benefited the local producers, although later there were rumors of price fixing among them.

The marketing of grains was in the hands of five companies, but the lack of silos made the producers vulnerable to the cereals intermediary companies, which could regulate sales, having knowledge of the evolution of supply by following the climate conditions in other countries. Again, intermediaries were blamed when prices dropped, creating a climate of discontent and suspicion, and an unfavorable attitude toward foreign capital inflows, which would be repeated during the 1930s and again in the second postwar period. Gone was *La Belle Epoque* and Argentina's open to the world.

Did the 1920s Mark the End of Economic Expansion and Foreign Investment?

The enormous investments during the years leading up to World War I were financed primarily through foreign capital. Foreign investment from more developed countries, which had stalled during the war years, rebounded significantly in the 1920s but never recovered the levels reached during the first decade of the twentieth century. Furthermore, these were no longer primarily British, but rather U.S., investments. According to Taylor,[20] in some of the countries that were recipients of significant British investment,

---

19 Raúl Prebisch, *Obras, 1919–1948*, vol. I, Buenos Aires, Fundación Raúl Prebisch, 1991, p. 236.

20 "Argentina was very dependent on foreign financing: foreign investment comprised about half of all Argentine capital before the war, but less than one quarter of Australian capital. The need for a foreign loan was a direct consequence of the relatively low capacity for Argentine domestic savings. The country saved less than 5% of national revenue before 1929, compared to Australia and Canada, countries that had a savings rate of 15%.... Argentina had a dependency rate that was four or five points higher than the Argentine-Canadian average, and a savings percentage ten or eleven points lower." Alan Taylor, "Argentine Economic Growth in Comparative Perspective," Ph.D. Thesis, Harvard University, 1992, pp. 924–992.

like Australia and Canada, domestic savings replaced British capital. But this was not so in Argentina – sustained Taylor – because the highest dependency rate caused a greater increase in consumption in detriment to savings.

The estimates regarding investment utilized until now came from the ECLAC study on Argentina of 1958,[21] and this source gets its data from the annual influx of imports of capital goods as an indicator of investment levels. Despite it being the most reliable source available, its usefulness is tarnished by the fact that until the 1930s, imports, according to the official source, are listed at official values (*aforos*) and not market prices. During the war years, there was a significant increase in prices, but between 1906 and 1922 the official prices remained unchanged, so that for those years, the estimates are undervalued. The same problem arises when relying on official prices to estimate the balance of payments, which are part of those used in the current account that Taylor utilizes to estimate domestic and foreign savings.

Just as import values slipped, as the work of Bunge suggests (see Figures 2.7 and 2.8), data on official prices (*aforos*) on machinery imports show not less expenditures in equipment but rather that the price that they paid for it was higher. Data at official prices offer a view of the evolution of the physical volume of imports that was, in effect, less, although what was paid for them was greater. Undoubtedly, the country had to save more in order to import a smaller volume because of the increase in the price of imports, something that was not taken into account because only the unchanging official price (*aforo*) was recorded. It is not as though savings decreased, it is just that imported capital goods cost more.

As illustrated in Figures 2.7 and 2.8, Bunge estimates the difference in value of imports considering market prices on the one hand and official prices (*aforos*) on the other. Immediately evident from this estimate is the fact that imports values in the postwar years, taken at market prices, were greater than what is evident from official statistics, which use official prices (*aforos*). It is clear, then, that utilizing official data has the effect of underestimating the value of imports. This affects the ECLAC estimates of capital goods imports, as well as that of the balance of trade, balance of current account estimates.

Figure 2.8 indicates that the balance of the current account at market value is less than at the official value (*aforo*). Yet the positive balance of trade (difference between exports and imports) from these years was primarily to pay financial services on the loans and profit remittances of capital that had come in previous years. That is, these were to pay foreign debt drawn

---

21 CEPAL, *El Desarrollo Económico de la Argentina*, Anexo III, p. 77, Anexo IV, p. 107, and Anexo VII, p. 243, Santiago de Chile, June 1958.

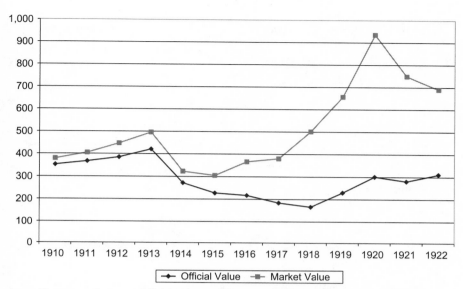

Figure 2.7. Imports: Official Values (*aforos*) and Market Values (in millions of gold pesos). *Source:* Bunge, Alejandro, *Análisis del Comercio Exterior Argentino en los Años 1910 a 1922*, Buenos Aires, Dirección General de Estadística de La Nación, 1923.

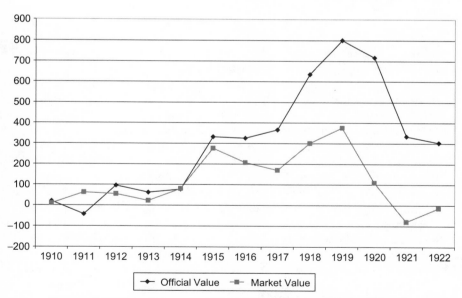

Figure 2.8. Balance of Payments: Official Values (*aforos*) and Market Values (in millions of gold pesos). *Source:* Bunge, Alejandro, *Análisis del Comercio Exterior Argentino en los Años 1910 a 1922*, Buenos Aires, Dirección General de Estadística de La Nación, 1923.

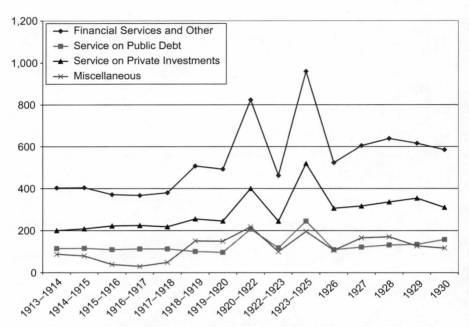

Figure 2.9. Balance of Payments on Debt Services and Remittances (in millions of pesos). *Source:* Manuel Balboa, "La Evolución del Balance de Pagos de la República Argentina, 1913–1950", *Desarrollo Económico*, no. 45, June 1972, p. 152.

from the country in the years leading to the war and the remittances of immigrants' savings that were the labor inputs.

It is clear that a significant portion of gross domestic savings was used to pay service on the debt, and profit on capital investments, and that it was transferred abroad (and because of that, those saving were not invested in Argentina). In this regard, one cannot conclude that there was a lack of savings capacity – gross savings – but rather that a large share of those savings had to be used to pay the enormous foreign investment incurred from the previous period. Thus, what remains was less net savings, which is what is recorded in the current account. Note how, in Figure 2.9, the magnitude of payment on services and, in Table A.C.2.2 in the Appendix, the positive commercial trade balances become a negative current account (except during the war years) because of payments on financial services and remittances.

According to the Beveraggi Allende estimates of the balance of payments in Argentina between 1900 and 1930, it appears that during the prewar period, commercial surpluses and capital inflows more than compensate for the negative balances in the services account. The deficit in the current account was compensated by positive balances in the capital account. In the

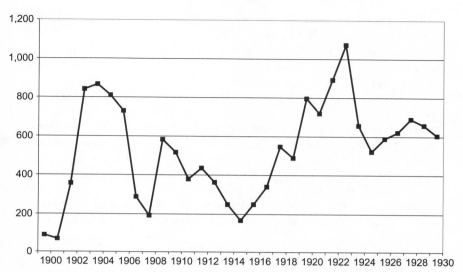

Figure 2.10. Savings Indicators, 1900–1930 (in millions of pesos). *Note:* Savings were estimated by taking the sum of investments in public bonds, mortgages, stocks, corporate bonds, and so on. *Source: Anuario Geográfico Argentino*, Comité Nacional de Geografía, Buenos Aires, 1941.

war years the commercial surpluses were greater (because of the decrease in imports), and although the balance of services was negative there was a surplus in the current account because the positive balance of payments was larger than payments on services, whereas the capital account was negative. However, between 1921 and 1930 commercial surpluses decreased (as imports increased) and the negative balance of services increased, leaving a negative current account balance as well, which was to a large extent compensated for with favorable balances in the capital account (see Table A.C.2.2 in the Appendix).

What is certain is that in the 1920s a high proportion of gross savings was diverted to payment on loans and to profit remittances that reached between 161 and 248 million gold pesos annually, 27% of average exports between 1913 and 1929, a smaller amount of net savings remaining in the country (see Table A.C.2.2 in the Appendix).

Although there are no reliable estimates of domestic investment and savings, other indicators of the evolution of savings in the years following World War I do not suggest that these were declining. Note in Figure 2.10 the evolution of savings invested in public bonds, mortgages, and stocks between 1900 and 1930 and the striking rebound during the later part of the war, with levels similar to those during the years before the war, 1920–1923 (except in the case of the extraordinary years between 1903 and 1906).

Before the war, investments in infrastructure – the most important ones, such as in railroads – had two primary characteristics: the indivisibility of the investment and costs so high so as to be beyond the capacity of local savings. For this reason, this kind of infrastructure was built with foreign capital. It was England that provided the main source of funds, not only because at that time the country was the financial capital of the world but also because it had a greater proportion of adults who saved. Age distribution in Argentina before mass immigration could be illustrated with a pyramid: a wide, youthful base and fewer people as age increased. Furthermore, the majority of direct investment was in the railroad sector, in which Great Britain had been pioneer and world leader and where, because there were economies of scale, its costs were less. Investment in railroads in the periods 1901–1905 and 1906–1910 had represented 15.1% and 20.6% of total fixed gross investment (see Table A.13 in the Appendix).

But following World War I, not only did foreign investment drop off, but the source of this investment, as well as the investments themselves, had changed markedly. British foreign investment began to dry up worldwide, as well as in Argentina, which had been a favorite for British investors. This was most likely related to a change in the age structure, with a British population that was aging and for this reason using up its retirement savings. In addition, the railroad network in Europe and beyond, including Argentina, had been a truly astonishing achievement. It was thus difficult to conceive that the network could continue to expand at the same rate and that Great Britain could somehow continue to be the primary producer of the goods use in the construction and exploitation of the railroads. In the postwar years, the automobile and telephone sectors gained importance, and the United States was the leading manufacturer of these goods. The United States also replaced Great Britain as leader in the manufacture of other consumer goods; with these companies, the magnitude of the investment necessary was different than that needed for infrastructure.

Nevertheless, before World War I, the majority of investments had features of indivisibility and were made during the first decade of the century while the peso was highly valued. This made them less costly. After such extraordinary investments it was not surprising that they would diminish (this is evident in the annual flow of imports of capital goods) especially in the railroad network, which had already covered a vast area. With regard to investment in other sectors, Villanueva has shown that U.S. investments were significant in factories:

[B]etween 1924 and 1933, 23 US subsidiaries opened facilities in Argentina. Between 1900 and 1920 the majority of foreign companies are involved in the branch of foodstuffs and drinks (cold storage facilities). Three of the six investors in this area were American and three from the United Kingdom. 43 large companies begin operations in Argentina in the period between 1921 and 1930 (this compared to 45 that opened facilities in the period between 1931 and 1943)... A large part of the large firms installed in Argentina in the 30's is American, especially in the textile sector. Most scholars agree that in the 1920's and 30's the real number of foreign companies operating in the country, and other businesses financially and technologically tied to them, was much greater than is usually estimated from data from the available sources.[22]

Elsewhere Taylor maintains that the postwar slump was due to the decline in investment caused by the interruption in foreign capital flows.[23] He also asserts that foreign capital outlays were not substituted by domestic savings because the population had a greater dependency rate as a result of immigration, which brought with it a greater number of children who were not part of the labor market. Spending on children would have to replace a part of family savings.

Available data on the purchase of bonds and mortgages (shown in Figure 2.10) do not appear to indicate a decline in savings.

However, if that had been the case, and according to Taylor's argument, the cause was the greater dependency rate because of a greater birth rate caused by immigration, it would appear to contradict the fact that the immigrants who came to Argentina were adults of working age, mostly men, so that the working population increased, which meant just the opposite: a lower dependency rate (see Table 2.4). The population pyramids for 1914 and 1938 show a significant number of foreigners of working age. In Figure 2.11, the foreign population is represented by the darkened portion of each interval.

Although the dependency rate was less in Australia than in Argentina, the rate dropped in Argentina between 1869 and 1947 (see Table 2.4).

The Evolution of Public Finances in the Postwar Period and the 1920s[24]

With the end of the war came normalization of imports and a significant increase in revenue. The Treasury balance shows higher numbers than those for revenues from taxes (Budget Investment Accounts, *Cuenta de Inversión del presupuesto*), but especially since 1923, because of an increase in nontax revenues. At any rate, the increase in spending was even greater.

22 Javier Villanueva, "El Origen de la Industrialización Argentina", *Desarrollo Económico*, vol. 12, no. 47, pp. 463–464.

23 Alan Taylor, "Argentine Economic Growth in Comparative Perspective", Ph.D. Thesis, Harvard University, 1992.

24 It is important to note, first, that there are discrepancies in the official information for this period. However, we can make several observations.

Table 2.4. *Dependency Rate*

Years	Argentina	Years	Australia
1869	0.839	1861	0.610
1895	0.734	1891	0.666
1914	0.688	1901	0.643
1947	0.533	1911	0.520
		1921	0.567
		1933	0.500
		1947	0.496

Note: The dependency rate is the ratio of the population
between the ages of 0 and 15 years plus the population
over the age of 64 to the working age population.
Source: Blanca Sánchez-Alonso, "Labour and Immigration
in Latin America," in *The Cambridge Economic History of Latin
America*, ed. Victor Bulmer-Thomas, John Coatsworth, and
Roberto Cortés Conde, New York, Cambridge University
Press, 2005.

The difference between the Treasury data and that of Budget Investment
Accounts regarding revenue and expenditures is also apparent in the differing balance statements (surplus/deficit). As illustrated in Figure 2.12,
during some years data from the Treasury show a total surplus, but during
those same years public accounts show a total deficit. In 1921, 1922, and

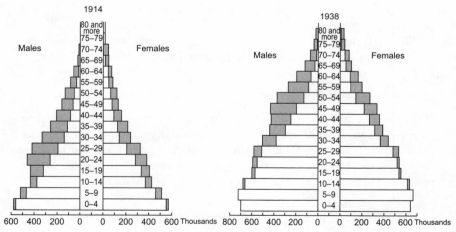

Figure 2.11. Argentina, 1914 and 1938: Population by Age and Sex. *Source:* García
Mata, Rafael, and Emilio Llorens, *Argentina Económica 1939*, Buenos Aires,
Compañía Impresora Argentina, 1939.

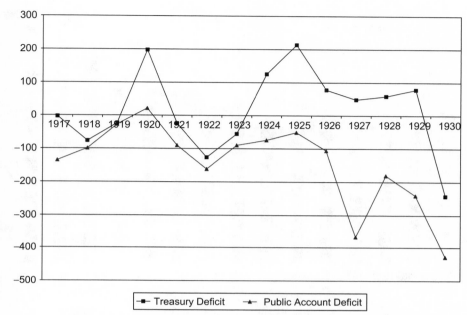

Figure 2.12. Comparison of Balance Sheet from Budget Investment Accounts and National Treasury, 1917–1930 (in millions of pesos). *Source:* Treasury Yearbooks, 1917–1930, and *Anuario Geográfico Argentino*, Comité Nacional de Geografía, Buenos Aires, 1941.

1923, years of European and American crisis, the deficits were small, but they increased substantially after 1926, when the difference between the two sources increased.

As we have seen, fewer Treasury deficits indicate that part of expenditures (or of debt) was not paid. This would have increased the debt issued in bonds (consolidated debt), which is drawn from banks or which is simply not paid (floating debt), whose evolution is shown in Figure 2.13.

As indicated in Figure 2.13, the total debt did not increase until 1921. Consolidated debt remained slightly below 6 billion pesos until 1924 and floating debt increased, albeit slightly. Fiscal stability reigned from 1922 to 1925, because debt did not increase. (Floating debt even decreased because with more access to credit, part of it was consolidated.) A significant increase came only in the years between 1926 and 1929 because debt was placed in bonds (consolidated), thereby decreasing the total amount of floating debt. As of 1928, when international market conditions became more difficult, consolidated debt reached 1 billion pesos and floating debt increased considerably.

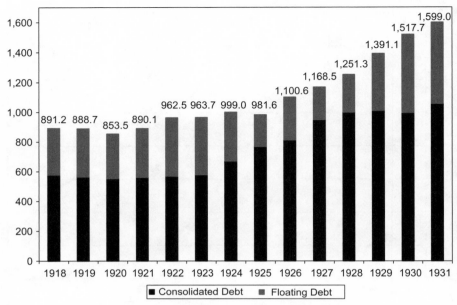

Figure 2.13. Evolution of Debt, 1918–1931 (in millions of gold pesos).
Source: Peters, Harold, *The Foreign Debt of the Argentina Republic*, Baltimore, MD,
The Johns Hopkins University Press, 1934.

Monetary Fluctuations

Under the rigid rules of the gold standard maintained during the years of suspension of convertibility and fully in effect when convertibility was reinstated in 1927, the variations in the monetary base went with the flow of gold reserves. However, as has been shown, gold reserves were affected also by the flows of gold in the commercial banks, and particularly at the Bank of the Argentine Nation. To some degree it would seem that during the war years the Bank of the Argentine Nation was operating under a sterilization policy.

When the Bank increased its gold reserves, which it did in response to inflows of foreign capital between 1917 and 1928, these reserves would not be converted at the Currency Board, so that it restricted by the same proportion an expansion of currency. Likewise, if the increase at the bank was greater than the deposits of gold into the country, a monetary contraction was the result. The opposite occurred if the bank took gold to the Currency Board to convert it to pesos in order to make loans, which it did in 1929, when the monetary contraction was slightly less than the overall sum of reserves that left the country, whereas the bank reduced its reserves even further (see Table 2.5).

Table 2.5. *Gold Stock at the Currency Board, in the Bank of the Argentine Nation and the Total for the Country, 1918–1929 (data from December 31, in millions of gold pesos and in percent variation)*

Year	Entire Country		Banks[a]		Bank of the Argentine Nation		Currency Board		Ratio Gold Reserves in the Bank of the Argentine Nation/Gold Reserves at the Currency Board
1918	430.68	16.32	15.54	−5.59	36.11	−2.22	379.03	19.62	9.53
1919	450.15	4.52	22.16	42.60	38.96	7.89	389.03	2.64	10.01
1920	513.74	14.13	18.41	−16.92	24.73	−36.52	470.60	20.97	5.25
1921	504.98	−1.71	11.21	−39.11	23.17	−6.31	470.6	0.00	4.92
1922	503.85	−0.22	9.96	−11.15	23.29	0.52	470.6	0.00	4.95
1923	492.86	−2.18	9.35	−6.12	12.91	−44.57	470.6	0.00	2.74
1924	469.06	−4.83	8.96	−4.17	8.31	−35.63	451.78	−4.00	1.84
1925	475.26	1.32	8.23	−8.15	15.25	83.51	451.78	0.00	3.38
1926	475.3	0.01	8.31	0.97	15.21	−0.26	451.78	0.00	3.37
1927	559.4	17.69	10.95	31.77	70.86	365.88	477.58	5.71	14.84
1928	640.87	14.56	11.42	4.29	139.79	97.28	489.66	2.53	28.55
1929	460.87	−28.09	11.10	−2.80	30.12	−78.45	419.64	−14.30	7.18

[a] Excludes Bank of the Argentine Nation.

Source: Baiocco, Pedro J., *La Economía Bancaria Argentina a través de sus Índices más Representativos en el Período 1901–1935*, Buenos Aires, Universidad de Buenos Aires, 1937.

On the other hand, if the Bank made a loan to the government, which happened every year during the 1920s,[25] it used pesos from its deposits (of reserves in pesos) or its reserves in gold that it deposited at the Currency Board to convert to pesos. In the latter case, loans the bank granted to the government had an expansive effect on currency (the monetary base).

Banking Money

The other monetary effect – still within the regimen of the gold standard – had to do with the demand for currency on the part of banks (evolution of cash reserves and the public's preference for currency) or bank deposits (the ratio between currency and deposits). As Table 2.6 indicates, there was a significant increase in the multiplier, from 2.58 in 1916 to 4.14 in 1930, as a result of two factors: a public that preferred deposits and banks that reduced their cash reserves.

25 The loans to the government went from 338 million pesos in 1920 and began decreasing in quantity, although new loans were granted every year, until 1929, the year in which the only loan was to the amount of 71 million.

Table 2.6. *Monetary Indicators, 1916–1930 (in millions of pesos)*

Year	Currency (held by public and banks)	Bank Deposits	Ratio Currency/ Deposits	Cash Reserves at Commercial Banks	Ratio Cash Reserves/ Deposits	Bank Multiplier	Bank of the · Argentine Nation Rediscounts to Commercial Banks[a]
1916	1,013.1	1,596.1	0.63	608.5	0.38	2.58	15.64
1917	1,013.1	1,891.1	0.54	639.1	0.34	2.87	6.61
1918	1,154.5	2,665.6	0.43	663.7	0.25	3.31	5.04
1919	1,177.2	2,834.2	0.42	775.4	0.27	3.41	32.08
1920	1,362.6	3,293.9	0.41	744.9	0.23	3.42	29.26
1921	1,362.6	3,177.2	0.43	949.4	0.30	3.33	37.92
1922	1,362.6	3,297.4	0.41	970.6	0.29	3.42	12.90
1923	1,362.6	3,316.8	0.41	923.1	0.28	3.43	106.99
1924	1,319.8	3,319.5	0.40	780.7	0.24	3.52	121.59
1925	1,319.8	3,334.6	0.40	656.6	0.20	3.53	123.00
1926	1,319.8	3,359.1	0.39	708.6	0.21	3.55	147.19
1927	1,378.4	3,545.9	0.39	594.5	0.17	3.57	106.42
1928	1,405.9	3,953.2	0.36	734.0	0.19	3.81	91.58
1929	1,246.7	3,903.2	0.32	878.8	0.23	4.13	156.21
1930	1,260.7	3,956.2	0.32	481.9	0.12	4.14	151.50

[a] Data from December 31 of each year.

Source: Anuario Geográfico Argentino, Comité Nacional de Geografía, Buenos Aires, 1941, and Banco de la Nación Argentina, *El Banco de la Nación Argentina en su Cincuentenario,* Buenos Aires, Banco de la Nación Argentina, 1941.

With the end of hostilities, the demand for foodstuffs increased in Europe and exports followed suit, as did gold flows at the Currency Board, which meant an increase in the amount of currency, but deposits increased and with them the money supply (currency 14% in 1918, deposits 41%, and money supply 31.5%). In 1919, growth was decelerating, but in 1920 there was a sharp spike in the money supply; the postwar boom ended and 1921 was a year in which the expansionist trend reverted (the demand for and price of Argentine exports dropped), and a financial crisis in Europe and the United States ensued. (Argentine GDP rose by 3.7%, due mostly to industry, construction, and cattle raising.) In 1921, reserves at the Currency Board did not increase and no new currency was issued, whereas deposits dropped (there was a greater demand for cash) and the banks increased their reserves.

In 1922, a rise in deposits led to a spike in the money supply, but the monetary base remained constant until 1924, when it fell by 3.1%. Nevertheless, between 1924 and 1927, the annual growth rates of monetary issues were less than 1%. Suspension of convertibility lasted until 1927 but currency issues continued, gauged by gold deposits at the Currency Board. As for imports, during the postwar period, their levels normalized and this

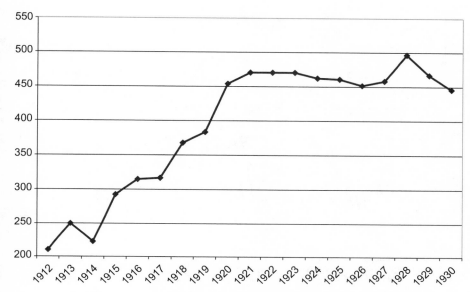

Figure 2.14. Gold Stock at the Currency Board (in millions gold pesos).
Note: Averages for each year. *Source:* Baiocco, Pedro J., *La Economía Bancaria
Argentina a través de sus Índices más Representativos en el Período* 1901–1935,
Buenos Aires, Universidad de Buenos Aires, 1937, p. 54.

led to a less favorable balance of trade (see Table A.C.2.2 in the Appendix).
Between 1917 and 1927 currency issues increased 3.13% yearly, although
at a much lower rate than tax revenue.

The public deposited a greater proportion of their monetary holdings
in banks, which affected the C/D coefficient (currency to deposits), which
dropped from 0.54 in 1917 to 0.39 in 1927. Between 1917 and 1927,
the demand for money (the real amount of money) increased 7% annually.
In the ensuing years gold deposits at the Currency Board did not vary
significantly (most likely because of the increase in imports), the reason
for which, the increase in circulating currency, was minor. During these
years the government made great efforts to return to the gold standard. In
the case of Argentina, because the Currency Board made issues solely on
the basis of the amount of its gold reserves, a strong issue contraction was
unnecessary in order to have sufficient reserves to get back to convertibility.

However, there were short-term capital flows as a result of variations
in the interest rate determined by the Federal Reserve. Reserves at the
Currency Board increased between 1927 and 1928 and then quickly and
sharply decreased around 1929 (see Figure 2.14).

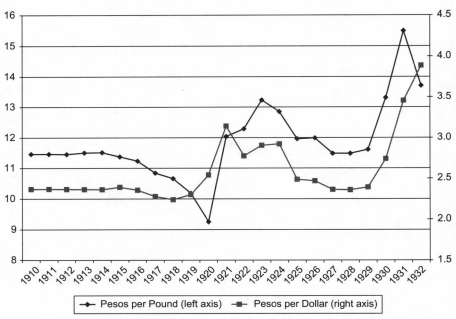

Figure 2.15. Value of the Peso Compared with the Dollar and the Pound.
Source: Anuario Geográfico Argentino, Comité Nacional de Geografía, Buenos Aires,
1941, p. 431.

Monetary Appreciation and Competitiveness

With regard to Argentine economic external competitiveness, it would appear that the peso had been overvalued if we consider the evolution of real wages during the 1920s. Real wages in Argentina should drop 8% in real terms vis-à-vis the British in relation to the prewar levels.

Moderate expansion continued until 1928, year in which significant gold inflows were made at the Currency Board. (These were from U.S. funds, resulting largely from a drop in the interest rate on the part of the U.S. Federal Reserve.) The deposits were in the amount of 12.08 million gold pesos or 27.4 million pesos, representing some 2.5% of the inventory at the Currency Board. Currency increased 2% according to year-end data, but if we compare June 1928 with June 1927, the growth reaches 9%. This is because the gold deposits were greater during the first half of the year, but during the second half, there were gold outflows. Growth was greatest in deposits and money supply. Gold stock at the Currency Board at the end of 1927 was 477.6 million gold pesos, which if multiplied by 2.2727 would be equal to 1,085.4 million pesos. (The discrepancy in the graph is due to the fact that it has annual averages.)

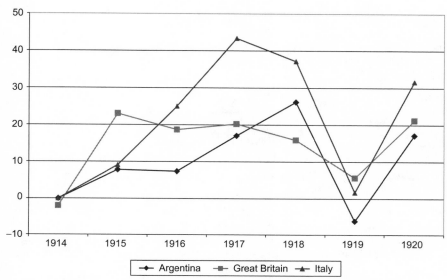

Figure 2.16. Consumer Price Index (percent variation with regard to previous year). *Source:* Roberto Cortés Conde, "The Vicissitudes of an Exporting Economy: Argentina, 1875–1930", in *An Economic History of Twentieth-Century Latin America*, ed. E. Cárdenas, J. A. Ocampo, and R. Thorp, New York, Palgrave, 2000.

Living with Instability; Currency Depreciation: Prices and Wages

With convertibility suspended in 1914 the value of the peso began to fluctuate. Suspension only meant that individuals could not withdraw gold from the Currency Board, but exchange transactions continued at the banks. Exporters could liquidate their foreign exchange, hold it, or sell it to importers or others needing the exchange. Things continued this way until 1920. As in other countries at war, official transactions continued at the official unit of account, the gold peso at presuspension of convertibility rates (1 gold peso = 2.27 paper pesos = $1). But the market value of the pesos fluctuated with regard to foreign currencies (pounds and dollars) with years of appreciation and of depreciation (see Figure 2.15).

The depreciation and later appreciation of the peso had unprecedented effects on real income. Although in the past nominal remunerations had been an issue negotiated by employees and employers, when the gold standard was abandoned, there were sharp fluctuations in the gold value of currency[26] and this had a further dampening effect on the purchasing power of nominal wages. Further, prices increased significantly during the war years (see Figure 2.16).

26 J. Viner, "The Bullionist Controversies," in *Studies in the Theory of International Trade*, New York, Harper and Brothers, 1937, pp. 119–209.

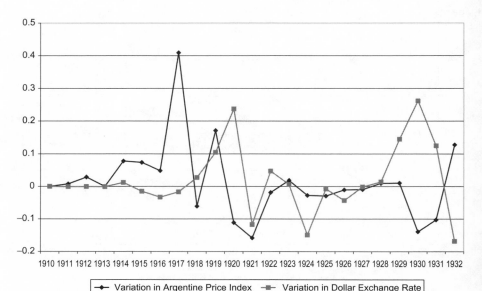

Figure 2.17. Variations in the Dollar Exchange Rate and the Argentine Price Index.
Source: For dollar exchange rate: *Anuario Geográfico Argentino*, Comité Nacional de
Geografía, Buenos Aires, 1941. For price index: Roberto Cortés Conde, "The
Vicissitudes of an Exporting Economy: Argentina, 1875–1930", in *An Economic
History of Twentieth-Century Latin America*, ed. E. Cárdenas, J. A. Ocampo, and
R. Thorp, New York, Palgrave, 2000.

The increase in international prices in the war years – although greater
in the manufacturing sector – affected the foodstuffs and therefore had
negative effects on the purchasing power of real wages. Depreciation of the
peso against the dollar intensified starting in 1920, when open negotiation
of foreign exchange with transactions abroad was prohibited, a trend that
was reverted after 1924. But at the beginning of the 1920s, although
the peso devalued against other foreign currencies, its purchasing power in
terms of goods did not diminish in equal measure, because since the postwar
period, prices of manufactured goods and especially those of foodstuffs had
decreased.

The government made an effort to return to convertibility at prewar
levels. Although this was not achieved at that level, in 1927, two years
after Great Britain, Argentina returned to convertibility at the rate of 2.27
pesos per dollar, or 11.40 pounds (Figure 2.17).

The Currency Board reopened in 1927. It is worth noting that despite
the board having suspended convertibility for thirteen years it kept the
discipline of the currency school, issuing on the basis of gold reserves,
so that the creation of money and its effect on prices were not a result of

domestic, but rather external, factors (gold inflows). The 1914 law allowing emissions by rediscounting commercial documents was never invoked.

As noted previously, the decrease in domestic prices was influenced by the global decline in prices and even more so by the decline in agricultural prices from 1925, just like their previous increase during the war years (see Table A.C.2.3 in the Appendix). The decrease in the international price of foodstuffs was not reflected to the same degree in the drop in operating costs because wages – the most significant component – increased, causing a tense, competitive situation in industry, something that led to pleas for state protection.

When the price of goods increases (exportable foodstuffs and imported manufactured goods), measured in their particular units of measure, general wages do not keep pace, but rather decrease, in real terms. This is related to the nature and terms of labor contracts (see Table A.C.2.4 in the Appendix).

A drop in real wages during the war years caused several conflicts in the labor market. In 1918 alone labor struck 78 times because of wage complaints, and the number increases to 196 strikes if all causes are considered. An enormous railroad strike occurred in 1917, and in 1919 strikes sparked what is known as the *Semana Trágica* (Tragic Week).[27] The way wages had been affected by the depreciation of the Argentine currency had not been lost on the Socialist Party leader, Juan B. Justo, as Raúl Prebisch points out:

He [referring to Justo] provides a lucid analysis of the depressive effects of currency speculation on the quality of working class life: that as the currency further depreciates, the worker feels a reduction in his purchasing power, being incapable of opposing the strength of their organizations against a predatory monetary policy.[28]

However, the effect is different when the price of goods drops. Between 1924–1925 and 1930–1931, the price of wheat, reflected in bread, an essential component of foodstuffs, dropped 39% (see Table A.C.2.3 in the Appendix). In this case, nominal wages did not drop, but rather increased in real terms. Real wages dropped from 1914 to 1918 and later continually increased until 1928, as illustrated in Figure 2.18.

This was a consequence of two separate movements: the cost of living, which had risen until 1920 but later dropped, and that of nominal wages, which in the war years increased at a slower pace than the cost of living. On the contrary, between 1918 and 1920, wages increased more than the cost

27 Academia Nacional de la Historia, *Historia Argentina Contemporánea, 1862–1930*, Buenos Aires, El Ateneo, 1963.
28 Raúl Prebisch, *Obras, 1919–1948*, vol. I, p. 55.

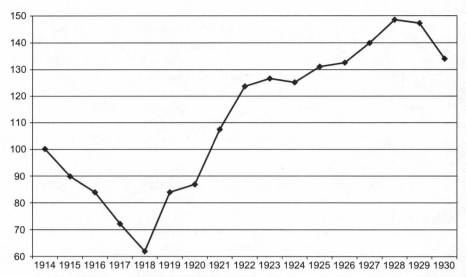

Figure 2.18. Real Wage Index in Argentina (1914–1930). (Base index numbers, 1914 = 100). *Source:* Roberto Cortés Conde, "The Vicissitudes of an Exporting Economy: Argentina, 1875–1930," in *An Economic History of Twentieth-Century Latin America*, ed. E. Cárdenas, J. A. Ocampo, and R. Thorp, New York, Palgrave, 2000.

of living, and from 1920 the latter decreased, which affected the purchasing power of wages.

The increase in political participation by a greater number of people (the 1912 reform brought the radical Irigoyen to the presidency in 1916) and the decrease in immigration during the war years, creating a less flexible labor supply, may have been related to the significant increase in real wages in Argentina in the 1920s. Alejandro Bunge had noted in the postwar period a change in the trend toward population growth,[29] which must have affected the market's labor supply.

Note in Figure 2.19 the comparative evolution of real wages in Argentina, England, and Italy (in index numbers having a common base value 1914=100). Wage hikes during the 1920s were substantially greater in Argentina than in the European countries, which made Argentine business owners complain due to the loss of competitiveness that this implied. The situation was further aggravated by the fact that in the postwar period the industrial structure was dominated by the labor-intensive textile sector, had

29 "In the 14 years between 1902 and 1916 the country's population grew 65%....But between 1916 and 1930 population growth was only 40%." Alejandro Bunge, *Revista de Economía Argentina*, vol. XXV, no. 150, December 1930, p. 400.

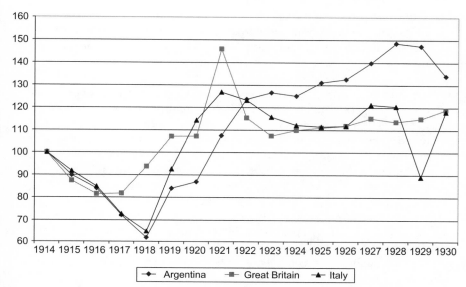

Figure 2.19. Real Wages: Argentina, Italy, and Great Britain. (Base index numbers, 1914 = 100). *Source:* Roberto Cortés Conde, "The Vicissitudes of an Exporting Economy: Argentina, 1875–1930", in *An Economic History of Twentieth-Century Latin America*, ed. E. Cárdenas, J. A. Ocampo, and R. Thorp, New York, Palgrave, 2000.

become more reliant on labor-added value,[30] and was no longer led by food-stuffs that relied on natural resources. Industrialists clamored repeatedly for government protection and expressed forceful opposition to laws that socialist legislators initiated in Congress, which in their opinion increased the cost of labor and made Argentine industry less competitive.

Changes in Income Distribution before and after the War

During the war and its aftermath there were significant changes in income distribution, which would have far-reaching consequences for Argentine society. During the period of great expansion, 1875–1913, real wages had risen 1% yearly, remaining at a higher level than those of the European countries that were homeland to vast numbers of immigrants.[31] However, during those same years, per capita GDP rose more than 3%. Thus, even though wage earners benefited, productivity increased, which had to have

30 Elsewhere I show the comparative evolution of wheat and cotton production between 1913 and 1929. The total area dedicated to cotton crops increased by 257% between 1921 and 1928, and textile production increased by 156% during the same period. See Roberto Cortés Conde, "The Vicissitudes of an Exporting Economy," pp. 271–272.

31 See Roberto Cortés Conde, *El Progreso Argentino, 1880–1914*, Buenos Aires, Sudamericana, 1979.

benefited the owners of the factors of production, land, and capital. Salaries higher than their European counterparts continued to attract immigrants, yet at the same time, the significant flow of investments and demand for employment prevented continued salary increases.

The continued increase in wages at the lower end of the labor force – unskilled labor, a category used here – explains part of the consensus that existed during this period, in which labor conditions improved without negatively affecting entrepreneurs' profitability. During the war years, real wages dropped because they lagged behind prices. Although labor supply diminished, it was compensated by a drop in labor demand.

Completely the opposite occurred after 1920. Now prices dropped but wages remained at previous levels (after a brief spike), which caused a strong surge in real wages. A significant shift in income distribution occurred toward the end of the decade. Although real wages increased 4.4% per year between 1924 and 1928, per capita GDP grew by less, only 0.9% annually during the same period.[32] This had repercussions for entrepreneurs, who lost profits, and caused conflicts regarding taxes, which would also occur in postwar Europe.

Entrepreneurs as well as wage earners began to realize that their income no longer solely depended on productivity, but rather on exogenous circumstances that affected their purchasing power, mainly government policies (fiscal, foreign exchange, and revenue). In sum, they learned that it was worthwhile to pressure the government to effect changes. And this required a different institutional design.

The End of the Decade

The war years had been difficult ones. The country had been surprised by an unexpected shock. The recession continued until 1917, and from that time on, the economy quickly recuperated and all indicators pointed to a return to normalcy. But it became clear halfway through the decade that international imbalances continued. The structural problems were, to some extent, hidden by the speculative fever unleashed by the success of the NYSE (New York Stock Exchange); the boom was evident in the abundant flow of capital to finance trade deficits and also allowed the rhythm of imports to continue unabated. The Roaring Twenties lasted until 1928; when concerned about the speculative bubble, the U.S. Federal Reserve increased the interest rate, which put a stranglehold on capital flows and caused a worldwide contraction.

---

32 See Roberto Cortés Conde, "The Vicissitudes of an Exporting Economy", for real wages, and *Revista de Economía Argentina* vol. XXV, no. 150, December 1930, p. 443, for total GDP.

World War I had far-reaching consequences. Previously, the market of goods as well as factors of production functioned quite well throughout the world under a multilateral system of payments like the gold standard. But *La Belle Epoque* had definitively ended. Argentina was one of the countries that had benefited most from the sensational growth that monetary and price stability allowed, in a world in which there was a free flow of merchandise, capital, and people. The war caused huge fiscal deficits, enormous inflation, monetary instability, and great volatility in the capital markets; it hindered trade and marked the beginning of state intervention in almost all markets. During the postwar period it became impossible to go back to the economic stability that countries had previously enjoyed, and attempts to reestablish the gold standard failed. Yet the lessons learned to prepare the world for the new and uncharted economic circumstances were perhaps more important, albeit subtler. From timid and often gradual responses to these circumstances, new institutional frameworks emerged.

In Argentina, these new frameworks included such important elements as laws that authorized issues based on rediscounts, the first attempts at bilateral trade agreements (the D'Abernon Mission), as well as legal protection for the cattle industry. Interest groups and trade associations finally started to garner power. In the 1930s, Argentina would begin down a corporatist path and then essentially close its doors to the outside world, gradually at first and in a more pronounced manner after World War II.

3

From the 1930 Financial Crisis to World War II

The 1930 Crisis

There is no real consensus regarding when and where the financial crisis began. For some, it is the moment when the New York Stock Exchange crashed, that infamous Black Thursday in October 1929. Others point to the bankruptcy of Credit Anstaldt in Austria, which had immediate repercussions in Germany and the Central European countries, where there was an enormous loss of reserves. The Anstaldt bankruptcy would ultimately exert pressure on the British pound, which in turn would lead England to abandon the gold standard in October 1931. According to Sauvy, the crisis began in France, yet Kindleberger asserts that the origins of the crisis can be found in the agricultural depression of the mid-1920s.[1] In the United States, the stock market crash was followed by a banking crisis in 1930 and bank closures, which froze deposits. These closures were repeated in 1931.

From the mid-1920s, there were serious imbalances in the international goods and capital markets. Protectionist measures not only led to the accumulation of primary product inventories, which created downward pressure on prices, but, in the case of the United States, with passage of the Smoot-Hawley Law, decreased imports from the rest of the world. In response to this, demand for U.S. exports would have logically dropped, but this situation was averted initially because imports from the United States were financed with loans, which in turn increased the world's indebtedness to the United States. This was particularly the case for Germany and Latin America. These circumstances continued as long as the Federal Reserve (the Fed) maintained a policy of cheap credit. For this reason, agricultural protection continued to expand under conditions of severe international trade financial imbalances.

[1] Roberto Cortés Conde, *Historia Económica Mundial*, 2nd ed., Buenos Aires, Buenos Aires, Ariel, 2005, p. 211. Charles Kindleberger, *The World in Depression, 1929–1939*, Berkeley, University of California Press, 1973. Alfred Sauvy, *Histoire Économique de la France entre lês deux Guerrres*, Paris, Economica, 1984.

When in 1928 the Fed increased the interest rate, there was a massive withdrawal of capital deposited abroad. Because of a lack of loans to compensate for the commercial deficits, debtor countries drastically reduced their imports from the United States and had severe difficulty servicing their debts with the United States.

The effect of the U.S. stock market crash was twofold. First, the value of assets plummeted, as demand for them diminished. The second effect was that when the Fed increased the rediscount rate, commercial banks denied credit renewal to their customers. These loans included advances to stock brokers, who, in order to make payments and lacking credit, sold their stocks, causing the prices to fall further. As the public pressured the banks to liquidate, they increased their reserves, aggravating both the monetary contraction and the drop in consumption. All of this was reflected in a significant decrease in domestic commerce, U.S. imports from the rest of the world, and international trade.

Closure of the Currency Board

After a gold withdrawal (70 million gold pesos in 1929 or 14% of the gold stock at the Currency Board in 1928), in response to the interest rate hike in the United States, the administration of President Yrigoyen closed the Currency Board in December 1929. From that point, issues were nonconvertible and individuals could not withdraw gold. In Argentina, the Currency Board's closure averted an even greater loss of reserves, which translated into a reduction in currency (which is what would have happened under the gold standard) and prevented a serious credit contraction. With less currency, the banks increased their reserves without renewing credit to customers, because the initial contraction of primary money (currency, the monetary base) was increased by the banking multiplier, contrary to what happened during World War I. The dramatic drop in export prices created a climate of gloom (see Figure 3.1).

However, the expected drop in imports from a decrease in revenue following the slump in exports was delayed because, lacking convertibility, credit expansion continued unabated. This was particularly the case for bank credit to the government such that the demand for imports dropped less. But the drop in imports ultimately followed that of exports. Thus, fiscal revenue, which was largely dependent on imports, decreased.

With the 1890 financial crisis still a vivid memory, authorities insisted on fulfilling their financial obligations abroad in spite of the multiple suggestions to declare a moratorium on servicing foreign debt. Part of the funds that were frozen at the Currency Board was used by the government to pay foreign debt, and part was spent on intervening in the foreign exchange market, in an attempt to avert the growing devaluation of the peso (which,

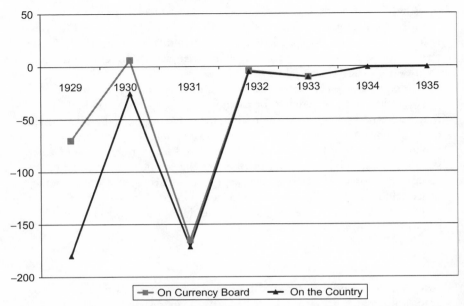

Figure 3.1. Gold Flows Annual Balances: 1929–1935 (in millions of gold pesos).
Source: Pedro J. Baiocco, *La Economía Bancaria Argentina a través de sus Índices más Representativos en el Período, 1901–1935*, Buenos Aires, Universidad de Buenos Aires, 1937.

after the closure of the Currency Board, had depreciated 59% against the dollar between December 1929 and December 1931) (see Figure 3.2).

Partial protection from the drop in international prices was provided by the abandonment of the gold standard with the peso devaluation, which increased export revenue in local money. Note in Figure 3.3 that Argentine prices fell less than international prices. It furthermore gave protection to local industry as imported manufactured goods became scarce. But it was also the means by which the government made sure it had sufficient gold flows to pay its foreign obligations, without having to resort to the market, which would have increased the price.

Although the Currency Board was closed, it still adhered to the rule of contracting currency if reserves dropped; gold withdrawals had fueled the contraction that had begun before its close. But suspending convertibility averted an even greater currency contraction. The drop in international prices, which was not entirely compensated by a depreciation of the peso, only added to the economy's woes, especially in the agricultural sector, and these difficulties spread to other sectors. The extraordinary indebtedness of the agricultural sector to the banks threatened its solvency, a situation that was made more difficult by the fact that the government itself was indebted to the same banks. These circumstances led to an institutional innovation.

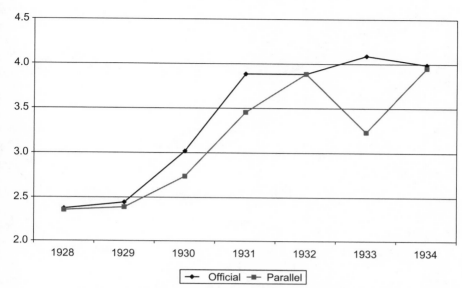

Figure 3.2. Price of U.S. Dollar in Pesos: 1928–1934 (in pesos per dollar).
Source: Carmen Llorens de Azar, with María Inés Danelotti, Antonio Pablo Grippo,
and Dora Delia Puente, "Argentina, Evolución Económica, 1915–1976,"
Buenos Aires, Bank of Boston Foundation, 1977.

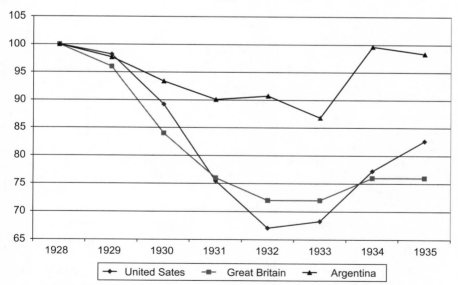

Figure 3.3. Fluctuation of Producer Price Index: Argentina, United States, and
Great Britain, 1928–1935 (Index: 1928 = 100). *Source:* National Statistics U.K.,
Bureau of Labor Statistics, and the Argentine *Dirección General de Estadísticas y
Censos de la Nación.*

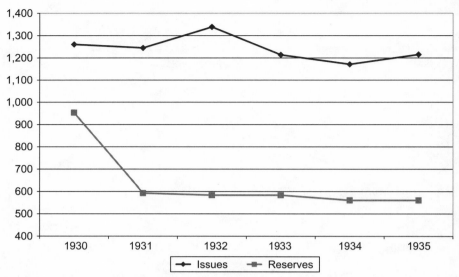

Figure 3.4. Relation between Issues and Reserves at the Currency Board,
1930–1935 (in millions of pesos). *Source:* Aldo Arnaudo, *Cincuenta Años de Política
Financiera Argentina (1934–1983)*, Buenos Aires, El Ateneo, 1987, p. 29.

The New Role of the Currency Board

Rediscounts

After a while, the role of the Currency Board changed, as it took on
new functions, and issues were no longer pegged to gold flows. As of
1931, currency issues based on rediscounts from the Bank of the Argentine
Nation were permitted, relying on a 1914 law that was enforced only
at that time. And later, rediscounts based on government debt (when it
deposited a portion of the bonds from the *Patriótico* Loan) were allowed.
Thus, issues, which were backed by gold, dropped from 953 million in
December 1929 to 592.9 million in 1931 and to 583.9 million in 1932. In
compensation, in 1931, 359 million had been issued through rediscounts,
to which 156.5 million of the *Patriótico* Loan were added in 1931 (despite
the fact that in 1932 issues through rediscounts dropped to 295.3 million).
Gold reserves continued to drop despite the closure of the Currency Board
because the government withdrew gold to pay its foreign debt (see Figure 3.4).

The currency issues that were not backed by gold were moderate and
were only allowed so as to make up for the contraction due to the drop in
reserves following the closure of the Currency Board. The contraction had
been caused by the government's gold withdrawals in order to pay debt and

Table 3.1. *Sources of Monetary Issues at the Currency Board, 1930–1935 (in millions of pesos)*

		Currency Board			Bank of the Argentine Nation	
Year	Gold	Commercial Documents	Patriotic Loan	Monetary Issue	Commercial Rediscount	Loans to National Government
1930	953.7			1260.7	151.5	692.5
1931	592.9	359.2		1245.1	284.8	721.8
1932	583.9	295.3	156.5	1338.7	315.9	713.8
1933	853.9	206.5	153.4	1213.9	292.6	719.9
1934	561	172.2	145.3	1171.5	295.2	729.6
1935	561	216.4	145.3	1215.7	216.4	n.a.

Note: Data for the end of the period.
Source: Aldo Arnaudo, *Cincuenta Años de Política Financiera Argentina (1934–1983)*, Buenos Aires, El Ateneo, 1987, p. 29.

to intervene in the market. Maintaining a fixed exchange rate had caused the closure of the board in the first place. The amount of cash in the hands of the public increased slightly from 1930 to 1932. In 1933 and 1934 the government pursued a more contractive policy, rediscounts at the Currency Board dropped slightly, and currency dropped by 9.3% in 1933 and by 3.5% in 1934.

The Patriotic Loan (Empréstito Patriótico) and the Increase in Rediscounts to the Government

During the difficult period from 1931 to 1933 the government was urged by various entities to suspend payment on the debt or issue money. But it refused to do either. While Minister Hueyo of the Justo administration opposed defaulting on the debt, he proposed issuing a loan to be placed with private investors and in local banks. The proposal was not well received from the public, so the government issued debt for other purposes (perhaps its original intention), in this case to place it in the Currency Board.

The government authorized the issue of a *Patriótico* (Patriotic) Loan, to be used to pay not only back-wages of government employees but also the government's accounts receivable at the Bank of the Argentine Nation, and the State Railroad deficit, all of which amounted to 304 million pesos. The law authorizing the government to issue 500 million pesos in bonds allowed it to place them at the Currency Board, which would issue currency backed by those bonds at 85% of its face value. Another article of the law put a cap on rediscounts from the Currency Board so that the gold backing could not slip below 36%.[2] Note in Table 3.1 how the factors

2 J. Prados Arrarte, *El Control de Cambios*, Buenos Aires, Sudamericana, 1944, p. 223.

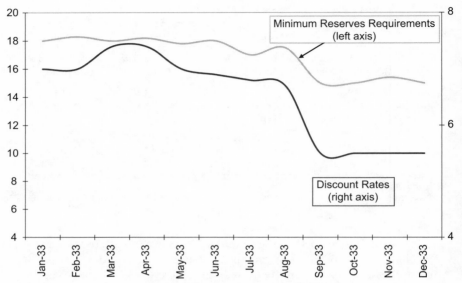

Figure 3.5. Evolution of the Ratio Reserves/Deposits and Discount Rates during 1933 (in percentages). *Source:* J. Prados Arrarte, *El Control de Cambios*, Buenos Aires, Sudamericana, 1944, p. 266.

affecting monetary issues at the Currency Board have changed compared with the previous period, in which the issues depended strictly on gold flows.

The monetary contraction and increase in interest rates were not as great as they might have been. This was because the government monetized a large portion of the Patriotic Loan and prohibited remittances abroad, which prevented people from transferring funds out of the country. Other factors, such as the drop in the ratio reserves/deposits, also played a part in palliating the contraction. Note also in Figure 3.5 the relationship between the decline in the banks' ratio reserves/deposits and the drop in the discount rate.

Among the most important innovations of the period was the rediscount law. Although it was applied judiciously in the beginning, after World War II, its application went beyond the original spirit of the law, which was solving banks' temporary liquidity problems. It became instead a political tool that the Peronist government used as its primary means of financing its operations and social programs.

Thus, another institutional transformation had taken place, one that had strayed far from the strict rules that for half a century had prevented the government from financing its operations by simply printing money. The government had been given enormous discretion.

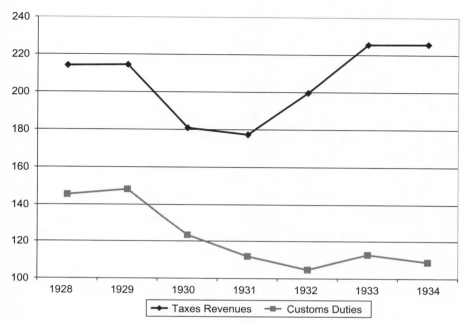

Figure 3.6. Evolution of Revenue from Taxes and Customs Duties, 1928–1934 (in millions of current gold pesos). *Source:* Treasury Yearbooks, 1928–1934.

Tax Reform

As we have seen, the drop in prices and in exports had triggered, after a slight lag, a reduction in imports. This put downward pressure on fiscal revenue, which was based mainly on customs duties. The provisional government that emerged from the coup d'état of September 1930 took measures to try to compensate for the drop in prices and exports. The experience of the previous years had provided a cautionary tale about the difficulties arising from the volatility of fiscal revenue that was tied to fluctuations in foreign trade and crop yields.

In 1931, in anticipation of extremely difficult circumstances, public spending was reduced and new taxes imposed. Among these were an emergency income tax and an additional 10% on imports, which was added to the property tax (see Appendix). Later a tax on transactions was introduced; it was highly criticized for having a cascade effect, and so was replaced near the end of 1934 by a sales tax that excluded basic consumption goods. Although taxes increased, until 1933, these additional contributions could not compensate for the decline in taxes on foreign trade. But a new source of revenue was on the horizon (see Figure 3.6).

Exchange Control, 1931

With the closure of the Currency Board in 1929 it was no longer possible to legally exchange pesos for gold or other foreign currencies at the official rate of 1 peso for 44 gold cents. The frozen gold at the Currency Board continued to be quoted at the official rate.

In October 1931, when Great Britain also abandoned the gold standard (a regimen that it had followed for more than two centuries) and suspended convertibility of the pound, the provisional government decided to control exchanges. All transactions in foreign currency had to been done henceforth through authorized banks in the Federal Capital, at a rate to be determined daily by the Exchange Commission. This rate was fixed at 3.86 pesos per dollar, thus remaining 20% below even the 1931 market rate. This measure allowed for a monopoly on the exchange of foreign currency under the control of a commission appointed by the government. Exchange controls had been tested during World War I, and in 1931, to prevent capital flights, and these were imposed by the German and Austrian governments, which assumed that devaluation would be ruinous. In Latin America controls were imposed by Argentina, Brazil, Chile, and Mexico. Governmental control was an instrument that would have far-reaching consequences for Argentine life and would forever change the role that the state had in it.

As of October 1931 only individuals authorized by the Exchange Commission could sell currency at a fixed rate of 3.88 pesos per dollar. The official exchange rate remained stable until 1933. A January 25, 1932, decree, one that revised the previous decrees of October 10 and 22, 1931, required exporters to present a document showing previous permission in which all currency exchanges by the banks were detailed.

Because the established price was lower than the market price, exchange was rationed. Payments on foreign public debt became the first priority of the government. Then came a list of what were considered indispensable imports: raw materials for national industries, fuel, and so on. At the end of the list were remittances of profits of foreign companies located in Argentina and payment on private financial obligations, immigrants' cash transferences in small amounts, and cash for international travelers. Later on, more transactions were permitted by a March 14, 1933, decree. However, the new norms could not be applied because of a lack of personnel at the commission. For this reason, on November 25, 1933, the Ministry of the Treasury issued a statement declaring the formation of a new commission, the Exchange Control Office (*Oficina de Control de Cambios*), which would operate under the Treasury.[3] Between 1932 and 1933, the commission distributed the currencies it sold into the following sectors, shown in Table 3.2.

---

3 Ibid., pp. 73–89.

Table 3.2. *Data on Currency Sold on the Official Market*

Sectors	1932 (%)	1933 (%)
Imports	53.6	59.4
Service on debt	14.6	17.4
Public service companies[a]	12.4	13.4
Individuals and immigrants	11.9	5.1
Other transfers	7.5	4.7

[a] Includes exchange for fuel imports, rolling stock, machinery, and financial services.

Source: Raúl Prebisch, *Obras, 1919–1948*, Tomo II, Buenos Aires, Fundación Raúl Prebisch, 1991, p. 165.

The government, through the Exchange Commission, intervened in the market, selling gold to prevent further depreciation.[4] Foreign companies understood that it was not the market that was responsible for the exchange loss, but rather the government, which monopolized transactions in foreign currencies. In fact, exchange controls implied a tax on profits that foreign companies, largely British, remitted abroad. This tax was levied by governments that, paradoxically, many accused of being associated with British interests.

On the other hand, foreign companies did their bookkeeping in pesos, which they converted at the official rate and procured foreign currency at market rates. The difference was recorded as an exchange loss. For their headquarters abroad, this was reflected in a loss that caused a significant decrease in profits, which in some cases dropped from 5.7% in 1928–1929 to 1.39% in 1934–1935, as indicated in Tables 3.3 and 3.4.

Because transactions requiring foreign exchange were under the control of the Exchange Commission, the alternative was illegal markets – though as yet there were no enforcement procedures in place. These began to be generally referred to as the black market. Companies of all kinds, railroad, insurance, banks, and so on, particularly British ones, were faced with the dilemma that their profits in pesos could not be converted into pounds to be remitted abroad. The sum of the accumulated funds that remained essentially frozen (they could not get foreign exchange) reached, in the space of two years, remarkable proportions. The holders of so many unwanted pesos deposited a portion of them in banks and another portion in public bonds, which helped to lower the interest rate. The enormous quantity of *frozen* pesos was a permanent bone of contention between Argentina and Great Britain. Furthermore, it was well understood that the Argentine currency would suffer a significant depreciation if this considerable peso

4 Ibid., p. 51.

Table 3.3. *Anglo-Argentine Tranway Company Exchange Losses*

Year	Pound Sterling Quotations in pesos	Exchange Losses Pound Sterling
1929	11.61	21,508
1930	13.27	169
1931	15.39	269,326
1932	13.68	103,168
1933	13.08	113,845

Source: Raúl García Heras, *Transporte, Negocios y Política: La Ccompañía Anglo Argentina de Tranvías, 1876–1981*, Buenos Aires, Sudamericana, 1994.

stock were suddenly converted to pounds. To make matters worse, the government now had to assume obligations that were previously not its domain, because it was the state itself that had imposed its monopoly on the foreign exchange market (see Table 3.5).

The issue of the frozen pesos was an obstacle in the bilateral negotiations that were being carried out with Great Britain, and later Germany and Belgium, after the multilateral system of payments had been abolished. They were an issue in the discussions with Great Britain over Argentine export limits imposed by the Imperial Preference System (which the Ottawa conference would enforce, with quotas, on any meat imports that were not from British producers). In order to recuperate Argentina's position in the beef market and the pending payment problems (the frozen pesos), the Argentine government, with the pretext of returning the visit that the Prince of Wales had made to Argentina, sent a mission to England, led by Vice President Julio Roca (junior). Although, undoubtedly, Great Britain had a strong negotiating hand, being the largest market for Argentine beef

Table 3.4. *Railroad Companies' Balance Sheets*

Railroad Years	Thousands of Current Pesos			
	Gross Profit	Exchange Losses	Net Profits	Capital Returns (%)
1928–1929	186,589	982	185,607	5.71
1929–1930	135,588	8,345	127,243	3.80
1930–1931	124,482	37,863	86,619	2.51
1931–1932	114,109	32,849	81,260	2.36
1932–1933	81,719	15,940	65,779	1.91
1933–1934	95,310	32,473	62,837	1.82
1934–1935[a]	105,000	57,000	48,000	1.39

[a] Provisional values.

Source: Virgil Salera, *Exchange Control and the Argentine Market*, New York, AMS Press, 1968, p. 132.

Table 3.5. *British Company Holdings of Blocked Pesos in Argentina on February 27, 1933*

Company	Pesos	Equivalent in Sterling
Buenos Aires Great Southern Railway	20,000,000	1,503,000
Central Argentine Railway	20,000,000	1,503,000
Pacific Railway	3,333,000	250,000
Buenos Aires Southern Dock Co.	1,850,000	139,000
Bahía Blanca Waterworks	250,000	19,000
Buenos Aires Western Railway	3,105,000	236,000
Shell Mex	9,045,000	680,000
Gath and Chaves and Harrods	13,330,000	1,000,000
British American Tobacco Co.	1,000,000	75,000
Primitiva Gas Co. and Buenos Aires Waterworks	6,000,000	450,000
Anglo-Argentine Tramways	1,700,000	127,500
River Plate Trust Loan and Agency Co.	1,500,000	112,000
Consolidated Waterworks of Rosario	1,150,000	86,000
Drainage Works of Rosario	450,000	34,000
Trust Agency Co. of Australasia	333,000	25,000
Anglo-Persian Oil Co.	700,000	52,000
Argentine Northernland Co.	250,000	19,000
Argentine Land and Investment Co.	4,073,000	306,200
Argentine Southeran Land Co.	220,000	16,500
Río Negro (Argentina) Land Co.	142,000	10,700
Tecka (Argentina) Land Co.	92,000	6,900
Córdoba Land Co.	66,000	5,000
Port Madryn (Argentina) Co.	56,000	4,200
Summers	8,450,000	650,000
	97,095,000	7,310,000

Source: Roger Gravil, *The Anglo-Argentine Connection, 1900–1939*, Boulder, CO, Westview Press, Dellplain Latin American Studies 16, 1985.

exports, Argentina had the leverage of the frozen pesos. And the negotiations centered on this issue, as well as the requirement of certain trade concessions.

The result of these negotiations was the Roca-Runciman Agreement, signed May 1, 1933, which granted Argentina a quota of the British market based on 1932 exports, considerably less than the 1928 level but greater than what was expected. But more importantly, there had been agreement on the issue of payments and a loan to unfreeze the pesos. Paragraphs 3 and 4 of the Second Article of Law 11639 (225), "Commercial Trade with Great Britain and Northern Ireland Agreement and Protocol," signed May 1, 1933, stipulated that the equivalent of 12 million pounds sterling in paper pesos be taken from the exchange of pounds sterling that remain available "for remittances from Argentina to the United Kingdom during 1933, in order to make payments in cash up to a sum to be determined

Table 3.6. *Distribution of Exchange Funds Earmarked for Great Britain*

	In Thousands of Pesos at the Buyers' Exchange Rate		
Destination	Paper	Gold	Percentage
Imports	741,976	376,469	57
Debt services	190,769	83,938	15
Remittances from public utilities companies	335,003	147,401	26
Individual remittances	13,349	5,873	1
Others	20,377	8,966	2
TOTAL	130,474	572,647	100

Source: Vernon Lovell Phelps, *The International Economic Position of Argentina*, Philadelphia, University of Pennsylvania Press; London, H. Milford, Oxford University Press, 1938.

by the government of the United Kingdom and that of Argentina, with regard to each of the cases of balances in pesos that, until May 1, 1933, were waiting to be exchanged to pounds sterling and remitted to the United Kingdom." It held that "the Argentine government would issue bonds in pounds sterling in exchange for balances in pesos that may have remained on May 1, 1933, awaiting exchange in pounds sterling to be sent to the United Kingdom, after the 12 million paper pesos ... have been used up." These bonds were supposed to be issued at the same time, redeemable within five years, and were to accrue 4% interest annually.[5] The conversion rate and other conditions of the bonds were to be negotiated upon by the Argentine government and a commission of the representatives of the holders of the bonds in question. Table 3.6 indicates how the exchange funds obtained from trade with Great Britain were utilized.

The Loan to Unfreeze Funds

As we have seen, companies and individuals who had earned profits and wanted to send them abroad had to either pay debts abroad or buy imports could not obtain foreign exchange. Those amounts had been deposited in banks or invested in public bonds and had reached significant quantities.

---

5 "Provided that there is a system of control over the exchange rate in the Argentine Republic, the conditions under which exchange occurs, during any year, and the availability of foreign currencies, will be such that, in order to satisfy the demands for remittances from Argentina to the United Kingdom, the entire sum of the exchange in pounds sterling from the sale of Argentine products in the United Kingdom will be remitted to the UK, after deducting a reasonable yearly sum for the payment of service on Argentina's foreign public debt (national, provincial, and municipal), owed to countries other than the UK." Article 2, paragraph 1, *Agreement and Protocol on International Trade*, signed in London, May 1, 1933. See also Vernon Lovell Phelps, *The International Economic Position of Argentina*, Philadelphia, University of Pennsylvania Press; London, H. Milford, Oxford University Press, 1938.

As it was impossible to obtain such a quantity of pounds all at once from the trade balances, the problem was essentially getting credit abroad in order to exchange them for the frozen pesos. However, no one in the British market was willing to buy Argentine long-term bonds issued in pounds, after the general crash of the markets caused by the 1930 crisis. Furthermore, because it was impossible to conceive that thousands of those who had debt in the country, in pounds, and creditors of pounds abroad could ever agree on exchanging outstanding obligations for debt instruments, the government, which had created the lack of availability of foreign currency, decided to substitute private liabilities in foreign currency, assuming them in exchange for receiving their holdings in pesos. With that move, the government obtained cash funds in pesos, exchanging them for long-term debt in pounds. It managed in this way to hold onto domestic savings when, following the crisis, local conditions were extremely difficult and the deposit of the 1932 Patriotic Loan had failed. Later, the same process was followed by issuing bonds in dollars, and in French and Swiss francs, to distribute to those who had liabilities abroad in quantities that ended up being greater than the amount of the loan in pounds. From 1932 to 1936 these were deposited in the Treasury: in 1933, 167 million pesos from the "Roca-Runciman" loan and 116 million from other foreign loans; in 1934, 4 million and 149 million, respectively; in 1935, 41 million pesos from foreign loans; and finally in 1936, 4 million pesos from the "Roca-Runciman" Agreement. But this issue was not fully resolved.

It was extremely difficult to sell Argentine bonds on the London market in the wake of the 1930 financial crisis. Could the market absorb the issue of such an enormous sum, the first issue since the crisis, without producing a precipitous drop in prices, which would be detrimental to creditors, debtors, and the Argentine government? To this end, a complicated scheme of financial engineering was hatched. First, a private company, The Argentine Convention Trust, was formed. This company would buy Argentine government bonds from holders of the frozen funds with the issue of certificates, which could then be sold on the London market. At the same time it would buy, with the proceeds of the sale of the other certificates and its own capital, other bonds from the British government at 3% interest. Certificates 98 A, B, and C would have different interest rates and rates of maturity. The Argentine bonds would be bought with 20% in cash and 60% in holding certificates (i.e., 80%) "C, bearing interest up to a maximum of 3%." Table 3.7 shows the assets and liabilities of The Argentine Convention Trust.

This operation was explained in the following terms by the National Government in its publication the Obra Financiera (Financial Yearbook).[6]

---

6 Raúl Prebisch, *Obras, 1919–1948*, vol. 3, 1st ed., Buenos Aires, Fundación Raúl Prebisch, 1991.

Table 3.7. *Assets and Liabilities of the Argentine Convention Trust*

Assets	Liabilities
Cash	Certificates
British bonds 3%	A, B, and C issued by the company
Argentine bonds 4%	

Source: "The Stock Exchange, Argentina and the Investor," *The Economist*, April 28, 1934.

It held that the May 1933 agreement with Great Britain stipulated that the Argentine government would issue documents in pounds sterling, at twenty years' term, 4% annual interest, and redeemable after an initial period of five years, during which time they would yield only interest. These bonds were to be placed in the public at par. Given this provision, the government issued the first loan on October 25, 1933, to unfreeze the funds. Subscriptions were made in Buenos Aires by people or corporations that needed to make remittances in pounds. The government gave them newly issued bonds, at the rate of 12.68 pesos for one pound sterling (£1). These bonds could be collateral for credit in London or be sold if their holders needed to exchange them for cash. In order to prevent massive supply of these bonds from causing a drop in their value, and losses for bondholders, British bankers established a fund into which the newly issued bonds could be deposited. This fund also included British government bonds. One partial payment in cash and a certificate of participation in the comprehensive value of the bonds in this fund were given in exchange for these deposits. This combination, otherwise beyond the scope of the Argentine government, was undoubtedly useful during the days in which any transaction in foreign markets was racked with difficulty. It was, in effect, the first transaction that we could carry out since the crisis. Soon, similar precautions were no longer necessary because Argentine credit acquired high standing in markets abroad.

After the first loan to unfreeze the funds in pounds sterling, others were deposited in various currencies, which cleared the situation in the exchange market. Bondholders abroad could buy the Argentine bonds at what was considered an attractive exchange rate because of the expected devaluation of the peso, which in fact did occur, on November 28, 1933. Furthermore, with these funds the government paid floating debt and bought some of its own bonds; this helped to increase the price of the bonds, a condition necessary for the successful conversion of domestic debt in 1934, with an interest reduction from 6% and 5% to 4%.

The deposit of the loan was enormously successful, as was noted in *The Economist*[7] in a long article it eulogized Argentina, saying that

7 "The Stock Exchange, Argentina and the Investor," *The Economist*, April 28, 1934, p. 933.

Today Argentina stands in magnificent isolation as the only South American borrower who has met 100% of her overseas debt service, throughout the depression, promptly, unquestioningly and with a good grace. Some 7,156,100 pounds of new sterling bonds of the Argentine government have been ingeniously mixed with 5,367,075 of British government 3% conversion loan, 1948–53 and a small amount of cash, to form a basis for three classes of stock in the United Kingdom and Argentine convention trust, and a further 6,370,300 pounds of 4% ("Roca") bonds have subsequently been introduced separately and directly to the London market.

It went on to note that "although the primary object of the 'Roca' issue was to enable British companies in the Argentine to secure sterling for the homeward remittance of frozen peso balances, the Argentine government has been put in possession of a corresponding amount of loaned funds, subscribed in effect by the British investor, which is at liberty to expend at its unfettered discretion." This enables the government to devalue the peso, which allows exporters to "sell their produce freely, but are required to hand over the resulting devisen to the government at a fixed rate." The government can then use these proceeds to meet

its own external debt obligation, and puts the residuum up to Dutch auction among the importing interests. This system is allied to a grain price control. It combines ingeniously Argentina's practical recognition of her necessity, as a primary producing country, to secure the maximum return from exports of agricultural products, and at all costs to avoid heavy accumulation of unsold stocks, with the maintenance of full debt service and the automatic "balancing" of her overseas payments. . . . The bondholders interest are safeguarded for the obtains the equivalent of a first charge, not merely on Argentina's export "surplus" but on the entire proceeds of her export trade.

The article went on to estimate that "the government's total overseas requirements should represent only about 15% of the total available in foreign currencies" and noted that

Argentine government bonds may claim to rank, as regards security, among the soundest stocks in the foreign market. British owned companies in the Argentine, however must bear the full brunt of peso depreciation on homeward remittances, without the immediate assurance of compensation through the stimulation of Argentina's internal trade. . . . The Argentine budget situation is probably the healthiest of any South American State. . . . On the whole the outlook for bond-holders may be brighter than at any time in the last 3 years.

The success was not only due to the mixture of bonds in the holding that had been formed (Convention Trust) but also because the risks of exchange and liquidity had decreased, thanks to the Roca-Runciman Agreement and the 1933 reforms of the exchange system. Article 3 of the agreement committed any commercial surplus that Argentina might obtain from the British beef market to the payment of debts in pounds (for British imports and interest and profits remittances).

Whether Argentina could have gotten better trade conditions or if Argentina suffered discrimination because of imperial preferences are issues that are debated but not at issue here. If concessions were made to Great Britain it was also true that the British Government allowed entry of some Argentine beef into its market (even if at a lower capacity than before the crisis); this was perhaps due, in no small part, to the pressure exerted by British railroad, insurance, and other companies themselves that had to collect dividends, interests, and so forth.[8] In this regard, it is worth noting that a portion of that debt was paid with trade.

Furthermore, the new exchange regime established a spread of 20% between the buyer's and seller's rate, a margin that the government appropriated in order to pay its debts abroad (among them the Roca Loan and other debt in foreign currency). The solution to the problem of the frozen pesos ended with a factor that was exceedingly disturbing in maintaining the value of Argentine currency and allowed progress toward the next stage of exchange controls implemented in 1933 under Minister of the Treasury Federico Pinedo.

The treaty had specific paragraphs regarding the meat trade between Great Britain and Argentina affected by the application of the Imperial Preferences in the Ottawa Treaty. Regarding this, Gravil points out that the Ottawa conference really produced several agreements and that Beaverbrook saw no distinction between the various treaties. As Gravil well understood, there was, however, a crucial difference: "The Dominions were pressing to maximize an advance in the British market, while the Argentines were struggling to minimize a retreat." As a result of the Ottawa agreements the 32% of the Argentine imports continued to be excluded from the payment of duty, whereas before the Ottawa agreements it was 7.3% and before 1930 it was none (in accord with the treaty of 1825); the frozen meat exports suffered a decline of 35%, but the chilled beef products were

---

8 Some years ago an interesting polemic was sparked by an Alhadeff article to which Jorge Fodor and Arturo O'Connell responded, "La Argentina y la Economía Atlántica en la Primera Mitad del Siglo XX," *Desarrollo Económico*, vol. 13, no. 49, April–June 1973. Alhadeff justified the signing of the Roca-Runciman Agreement as a condition of the deposit of the loan. I think the opposite is true. It must have been lobbying on the part of British companies that forced acceptance of conditions that were more favorable to the sale of Argentine meat than the original ones (in the British market), which Imperial Preferences had damaged. As Fodor and O'Connell point out, Argentina was not under any obligation to pay sums that were private obligations but it was a way of obtaining credit in pesos. Alhadeff refers to the loan, though not to the financing mechanism detailed herein. See Meter Alhadeff, "Dependencia, Historiografía y Objecciones a Pacto Roca," *Desarrollo Económico*, vol. 25, no. 99, October–December 1985.

Table 3.8. *Percentage Imports of Frozen and Chilled Beef into the United Kingdom, 1929–1937*

Country	1929	1930	1931	1932	1933	1934	1935	1936	1937
Argentina	77.4	72.9	71.4	74.4	68.8	64.2	65.1	65.8	61.5
Uruguay	8.1	9.8	8.5	6.2	6.1	5.6	5.7	5.4	5.6
Brazil	4.0	6.4	6.5	5.1	5.6	5.1	5.2	5.2	4.9
Australia	7.9	6.9	9.5	8.4	10.5	13.9	14.3	14.9	18.5
New Zealand	1.1	2.7	3.2	5.1	6.4	8.3	7.1	6.3	6.9

Source: Roger Gravil, *The Anglo-Argentine Connection, 1900–1939*, Boulder, CO, Westview Press, 1985, 1985.

saved from this decline, although they suffered a temporary decline of price of 10%. To select June 30, 1932, as the standard end of the trading year, and therefore immediately preceding the conference, may have been natural enough; but it proved to be uniquely unfavourable to Argentina and highly advantageous for the Dominions. The designated "Ottawa year" represented a mere 390,000 tons of Argentine chilled beef exports to Britain, compared with, say, 463,239 tons in 1927. Generally it was the republic's worst trading performance in the preceding five years.[9]

The evolution of the meat trade between Argentina and the British territories is shown in Tables 3.8 and 3.9.

The 1933 Reforms

In November 1933 a decree announced by the Justo government stipulated a significant reform to the exchange regime. It enacted a 20% devaluation of the peso against the French franc, a currency that remained tied to gold. From then on, 18.36 pesos would equal 100 French francs (the new Poincare franc that replaced the germinal one). Parity in pounds remained at 15 pesos buyer's rate and 17 seller's rate on the official market and 20 pesos on the free market; this, according to justifications of the time, was an attempt to prevent overvaluation of the peso, whose parity of 12.85 pesos per pound sterling had remained stable in nominal terms since October 1931, when its parity was fixed to the dollar at 3.8864 pesos per dollar, which remained until the following devaluation in 1933. The peso appreciated while maintaining a fixed rate since 1931, until it again dropped with the 1933 devaluation. Figure 3.7 shows how the real exchange rate evolved.

Once the issue of the frozen pesos was resolved, the exchange reforms divided the markets into two: one official and one free, in which the rate

9 Roger Gravil, *The Anglo-Argentine Connection, 1900–1939*, Boulder and London, Westview Press, 1985.

Table 3.9. *Percentage of Britain's Chilled Beef Imports from the Empire,*
1932–1939

1932	1933	1934	1935	1936	1937	1938	1939
0.1	1.7	2.9	5.6	7	10	11.1	12.4

Source: Roger Gravil, *The Anglo-Argentine Connection, 1900–1939*, Boulder, CO, Westview Press, 1985.

could be negotiated for specific categories of exports. The official market was itself divided in two: one for the buyer's rate and another for the seller's rate. For the buyer officials liquidated traditional exports and for the official seller, official financial transfers, and some imports declared essential. In the free market currencies of other exports were liquidated (nontraditional exports with neighboring countries) that were bought at public auction among those that demanded foreign exchange in order to remit them in payment of financial obligations or for imports. This was an attempt to prevent the problems of arrears in payments abroad due to lack of availability of foreign exchange, a problem dating back to 1931, and to eliminate illegal transactions. However, the government intervened in this supposedly free market, although it maintained that it did so only to

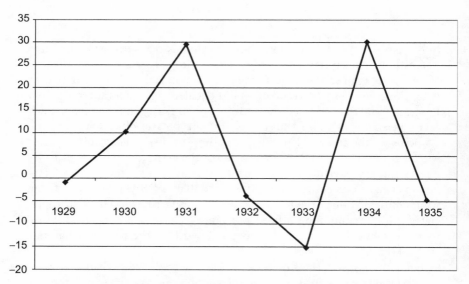

Figure 3.7. Real Exchange Rate (percentage variation from the previous year).
Note: Using cost of living index from Great Britain and Argentina. *Source:* Díaz Alejandro, "Tipo de Cambio y Términos de Intercambio en la República Argentina, 1913–1976," Buenos Aires, CEMA, March 1981.

prevent great volatility and not to modify market trends. In order to make payments abroad and prevent the accumulation of debts due to remittances (and prevent a possible freeze), by law, each and every import had to receive permission from the Exchange Control Commission (*Comisión de Control de Cambios*).

The Exchange Differential

An exchange differential, referred to as the "margin of exchange," contributed to and established a significant source of financial resources for Argentina. This fund was derived from the spread between the exchange rates at which the government bought foreign exchange from exporters on the official market and the price at which they were sold (which went beyond 80%).

The government maintained that this exchange differential would be utilized to pay the increased cost of service on the debt generated by the devaluation (for which the additional 10% tax was insufficient) and to finance the National Grain Commission (*Junta de Granos*), which was established during the same period to purchase, at support prices, grains whose prices had plummeted. Because international prices improved the following year, the margin was primarily used to make payments on foreign debt.

Since the devaluation generated unexpected profits for exporters, the government appropriated a portion of it by means of the so-called margin of exchange. Minister Pinedo declared as much in a congressional debate. The idea of having extraordinary profits generated by the devaluation endured for many years. However, the original bounty did not last long, because once the exchange was established, domestic prices continued to increase to the point that the income vanished and the exchange differential (and later export taxes) came to amount to a tax burden for the export sector (see Figure 3.8).

The Debate over Exchange Reforms

Exchange reforms, which had implications for tax collection, were established by a decree in November 1933. The socialists and progressive democrats (*demócratas progresistas*), both of whom aired complaints about the Congress not having been consulted in these reforms, bitterly opposed the decree. The Minister of the Treasury responded to this opposition by saying that matters of the exchange rate were very sensitive and could not be aired in the congressional venue, justifying the need for devaluation based on an overvalued peso, which had become a subsidy for imports and an obstacle for exports. Criticized by Representative Dickman, a socialist,

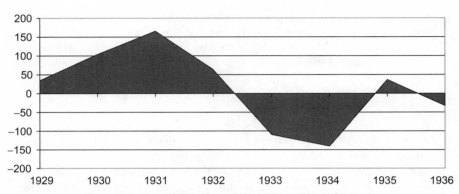

Figure 3.8. Exporters Profits and Losses (in millions of dollars).
Note: Exports in $t(\$)$ (Exchange rate index in t – Exchange rate index in $t-1$)/
(Imports Price Index in t – Imports Price Index in $t-1$). *Source: Fundación FIEL* and
Dirección Nacional de Estadísticas y Censos (Statistics and Census Bureau).

who remembered the defense of peso stability that Dr. Pinedo had made during World War I (when he belonged to that side), Pinedo responded that no country maintained parity with gold and that even the Britain's Labor Government had devalued the currency.

One of the commitments that the Argentine state was eager to fulfill – with the lingering memory of the not-so-distant 1890 financial crisis – was payments on foreign debt, whose total reached some 1,600 million pesos. Services on this debt fluctuated between 2% and 3% of GDP.[10] This commitment was expressed in a speech given by Minister Hueyo, who cites Nicolás Avellaneda, asserting that "domestic credit obligations are always managed by thousands of current creditors; but foreign credit commitments are generally only backed by the anonymous feeling of national honor and by political leaders. Thus, it is the responsibility of these leaders to be ever vigilant of our foreign obligations, when difficulties or conflicts occur."[11]

One of the unspoken reasons for the closure of the Currency Board, in 1929, was to make the gold deposited there available for the government. The board's gold was used not only to pay the debt but also to intervene in the market, in 1932, so as to prevent an even sharper drop in the value of the peso, which would make payment on the debt more costly. In this way, the government did not have to resort to the exchange market to buy

10 M. Balboa, "La Evolución del Balance de Pagos de la República Argentina, 1913–1950", *Desarrollo Económico*, no. 45, 1972, p. 152.
11 A. Hueyo, *La Argentina en la Depresión Mundial, 1932–1933*, "Discursos y Conferencias," Buenos Aires, El Ateneo, 1938, pp. 286–287.

Table 3.10. *Consolidated Public Debt*

Years	Millions of pesos
1929	2,208.1
1930	2,214.0
1931	2,230.7
1932	2,557.2
1933	2,748.7
1934	2,835.1

Source: R. Cortés Conde, "The Vicissitudes of an Exporting Economy: Argentina, 1875–1930," in *An Economic History of Twentieth-Century Latin America*, ed. E. Cárdenas, J. A. Ocampo, and R. Thorp, New York, Palgrave, 2000.

gold in a situation in which the drop in exports and in capital flows had made hard currencies extremely scarce, and the government demands for currencies made their price greatly increase (which had been one of the factors that had led to the 1890 crisis).

Debt

Both the abandonment of the gold standard and the devaluation of the peso made debt in foreign currencies (whose parity had risen after devaluation) more costly. In order to compensate for this, a tax on devaluation economic rent was imposed; this was the exchange differential. Thus, a new experience emerged: the state's role as redistributors of income, generating economic rents and using a portion of those rents. The state began to seek sources of income, intervening in markets and giving, to some, extraordinary profits of which it appropriated a portion. This was the foundation of the same commercial policies that in the past had been employed in Europe,[12] and they would have a much longer-lasting effect in the postwar years, becoming extremely controversial (see Table 3.10).

Conversion of Domestic Debt

The successful conversion of domestic debt was due primarily to the improvement in public finances achieved by renewing access to the debt market and to the income derived from the margin of exchange. The government offered to exchange bonds at par from the years 1907, 1909, and 1910 that were in circulation at 5.5% and 6.0% interest for "various series

12 Robert B. Ekelund and Robert D. Tollison, *Mercantilism as a Rent-Seeking Society: Economic Regulation in Historical Perspective*, Texas, A&M University Press, 1981.

of bonds, issued in pesos, that shall be called *Crédito Argentino Interno* at 5% interest and 1% accumulated annual redemption, by purchase or bid (tender), when the bonds are quoted below par, and by lot when they might be at or above par; and the Patriotic Loan at 5% interest and 1% annual accumulated redemption by lot at par."[13] Similarly, a decree announced on November 21, 1933, ordered the conversion of mortgage loans, to trade those that rendered 6% interest for new ones that rendered 5%.

It was stipulated that the conversion would be voluntary and those who did not accept it had the option of cashing in their bonds at their face value. In order to attempt to decrease the interest rate (and also using the Roca Loan bonds), the government bought its own bonds on the market, thereby increasing their value. In response to the Socialist Representative Dickmann, Minister of the Treasury Pinedo announced before the Chamber of Delegates, referring to these operations:

The right and honorable *representative* Dr. Dickmann, asked: Were the bonds bought before or after the conversion? Yes sir, bonds were bought because it had to be done . . . Bonds were bought; it helped support the Stock Exchange . . . Bonds were bought for as much as 14,000,000 pesos, and then sold for a profit. Today, the market is such that what had to be absorbed at that time could be sold later at prices that, calculated with interests, provide substantial profits.[14]

The operation was intended to increase the value of government bonds, in order to better invest those that were offered in exchange: the old bonds were exchanged for new ones or for cash payment at their face value. In reality, in the parliamentary debate over the conversion of the debt, Minister Pinedo claimed that if there is a modicum of trust in the debtor, nothing scares a creditor more than advanced payment on debt, "because saying that one is going to pay all of what one owes threatens Banks (creditors) much more than asking them for a loan."[15]

The Devaluation and the Obligation to Pay in Different Monies

Ever since 1890, when the National Government seized control over the issue of currency, which made it legal tender, all public and private debts could be settled with legal tender bills at face value. During World War I and the postwar years – as long as the suspension of convertibility lasted – judicial proceedings to demand fulfillment of obligations to pay in other currencies (or gold) had begun.

13 Article 1 of the Conversion of Domestic Debt (*Conversión de Deuda Interna*), November 11, 1933.
14 F. Pinedo, Cámara de Diputados (Chamber of Delegates), Meeting no. 13, June 6, 1934, p. 840.
15 Ibid., p. 842.

Because of the strong devaluation in the wake of the closure of the Currency Board and the subsequent devaluations in 1931 and 1933, several cases were brought to the Supreme Court, which in 1934 handed down a decision reflecting a new interpretation of the value of currency. The court understood currency to be something used for its purchasing power, but when, because of extraordinary circumstances beyond the control of either of the parties, this purchasing power increases or decreases, what it produces is an illegitimate enrichment (or impoverishment) for the bearer, so that obligations should be readjusted. The court held that there was no "judicial definition of value," which meant that

laws implicitly suppose that value is measured by currency, even over time, as though this were a measure in the same way that a liter measures volume, a kilogram measures weight, or a meter measures distance. Faced with catastrophic over-valuation or devaluation of the currency, the Court understands the obligation to address this gap and provide a definition of value. Contractual rights, where currency is concerned, directly conflict with another more fundamental and more general right, which is founded on redeeming a given good and the duty to return a received good.[16]

Foundation of the Central Bank

Although many Central Banks in Latin America, such as in Colombia, Chile, and Peru, were founded in the 1920s as a result of the recommendations of Princeton University Professor Kemmerer's missions, this was not the case for the creation of the Argentine Central Bank in 1935. In the case of the other Latin American countries, the idea was to concentrate monetary functions in a single state bank, instead of having several private banks of issue, with the intention of maintaining monetary stability. In Argentina, however, stability had long been achieved, with the Currency Board in operations since 1899. However, during the 1930s, the functions of the board, having been granted permission to issue currency on the basis of credit, gradually changed, which made the Currency Board more closely aligned to the Central Bank's approach of the Federal Reserve. But several other additional functions, such as exchange control and supervision of the banking system, could be consolidated by establishing a Central Bank.

Ever since Uriburu's presidency, Undersecretary of the Treasury Prebisch began to explore the possibility without actually founding the bank. Later, during the Justo administration a renowned specialist and director from the Bank of England was approached to oversee a project of this nature. In a report from the British specialist Sir Otto Niemeyer to the Minister of the Treasury, he proposed that "immediate measures be taken to coordinate the banking system through the establishment of a Central Reserve Bank, along with parallel legislation that considers other aspects of the banking system in general." At any rate, Niemeyer recognized that the control of the movement of capital and exchange transactions under the exchange control established in 1933 was not the most appropriate for the proper functioning of the new institute: Niemeyer argued that so long as there did not exist a free exchange market, a Central Bank could not properly fulfill its functions, though this was not a reason to not create a Central Bank that was still needed to carry out the important role of guaranteeing a stable currency.

According to Article 35 of Law 12155:

the Bank has the exclusive right of issue of notes in the Argentine Republic, except subsidiary money to which Article 4 of the Founding Law; and neither the National Government, nor provincial, nor municipal governments, Banks or any other institution may issue notes or other documents that could possibly be circulated as paper money.

The bank has the obligation to maintain "as a reserve at all times the equivalent of a minimum of 25% of its bills in circulation and liabilities payable on demand, in gold,"[17] sufficient to insure the value of the peso. But hard currencies and foreign exchange could not exceed 20% of reserves, nor be calculated by more than 10% (Article 39 of Law 12.155). Comercial bank members were penalized by prohibiting them from receiving dividends from their stocks in the Central Bank in the event the latter's reserves dropped below 33% for sixty consecutive days or for ninety days total in one fiscal year. The final version of the law stipulated that gold stocks should be calculated taking into account the peso depreciation that had taken place since the closure of the Currency Board.

Certainly, the primary reason for the creation of the Central Bank was maintaining currency stability, but with much greater flexibility than the Currency Board, without being tied to a fixed exchange rate. Another important factor in the founding of the Central Bank was that by means of the revaluation of its assets, additional financial resources were secured, and these were used to solve Argentine banks' problems – especially those of official banks – with loans and rediscounts that were difficult to redeem and to improve the fiscal circumstances. The revaluation of gold stocks, at the new exchange rate, created an accounting improvement to the order of 663 million pesos, almost as much as the total amount of currency in public hands.

---

17 J. Prados Arrarte, *El Control de Cambios*, Buenos Aires, Sudamericana, 1944, pp. 112–113.

This could have caused an enormous monetary expansion and an increase in prices. Both Pinedo and Presbisch, each on different occasions, asserted that this would not happen, and such was the case, because the money created by the revaluation reappraisal was utilized to replenish banks' dangerously diminished cash reserves (the ratio between reserves and deposits) but did not increase their lending capacity.[18]

When the balance at the closure of the Currency Board is compared with the initial balance at the opening of the Central Bank, what is immediately evident is that there was a significant difference in assets, which corresponded to the revaluation of gold in reserves. However, an increase in currency issues is not perceived on the liabilities side. The accounting maneuver was complex, because it included some assets and liabilities from the Bank of the Argentine Nation (loans to the government and rediscounts to the banks) and was based on what the Central Bank undertook along with the credits from the entities whose documents had been rediscounted. Because they were difficult to collect, they were handed over to the new Mobilizing Institute for Bank Investments (Instituto Movilizador de Inversiones Bancarias [IMIB]) with the purpose of recovering, at least partially, the amounts loaned. The Central Bank, with the surplus from the revaluation, replenished the exhausted reserves of the banks, paying off government loans, and assumed its rediscounts to the banking system cancelled against the submission of credits that went to the IMIB (see Table 3.11).

The funds (from the revaluation) not only provided a solution to the difficult situation in which the Bank of the Argentine Nation found itself but also helped commercial banks that had a substantial amount of nonperforming loans in their portfolio (in credits to the government as well as the private sector) because they were used to replenish reserves, improving the reserves to deposits ratio without increasing their lending power. Thus, the commercial banks' reserves to deposits ratio, which had dropped substantially, began to improve. Gold and foreign exchange reserves increased between 1934 and 1935, in nominal as well as real terms, decreasing in the following years (except in 1939) and then increasing from 1941 on (see Figure 3.9).

Monetary Policy

The law that created the Central Bank established as the institution's objectives maintaining monetary stability and preventing sudden fluctuations caused by external shocks or climatic factors because of their effect on export crops. The law provided for the Bank to lend only limited amounts to the

18 Raúl Prebisch, *Obras, 1919–1948*, pp. 471 and 475.

Table 3.11. *Balance Sheet from the* Bank of the Argentine Nation *and the Argentine Republic Central Bank (opening balance, May 1935)*

Assets		Liabilities	
Consolidated Currency Board and Bank of the Argentine Nation *(millions of pesos)*			
Gold	561.0	Notes	1,004
Bank of the Argentine Nation Foreign Exchange	122.6	Subsidiary money	212
Patriotic Loan bonds	145.3	Official deposits	136
Treasury drafts	254.7	Clearing house deposits	70
Direct government debt	173.4	Deposits in the Bank of the Argentine Nation from the interior banks	73
Loans against the National Government for issues previous to Law 3871	293.0	Rediscounts received by the Bank of the Argentine Nation from the Currency Board	216
Rediscounts from the Currency Board to the Bank of the Argentine Nation	216.4	Government Foreign Exchange Account	123
Loans to the Bank of the Argentine Nation against Bancos	178.4	Other	111
Total consolidated assets	1,945	Total consolidated liabilities	1,945
Initial Balance Central Bank May 1935 (millions of pesos)			
Gold in country	1224.4	Notes	964.4
Gold and foreign exchange agents abroad	122.6	Bank of the Argentine Nation	230.5
Collateral bonds	118.9	Official deposits	136.3
National Treasury consolidated bonds	400.0	Bank deposits	158.7
Subsidiary money	11.0	Pass-throughs (Bank of the Argentine Nation)	76
		Mobilizing Institute for Bank Investments	187
		Pass-throughs (other banks)	124
TOTAL	1,876.9	TOTAL	1,876.9

Note: Because not all balance items are included and there is some rounding, the subtotals do not add up to the totals.
Source: BCRA Yearbook, 1935.

government and restricted rediscounts to short-term banking illiquidity problems.

According to Prebisch, the Central Bank began to utilize instruments that allowed it to make these two objectives possible and consistent: monetary stability on the one hand and smoothing the cycle on the other. Unlike the Currency Board, the Central Bank could issue not only on the basis

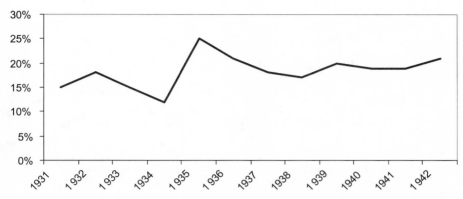

Figure 3.9. Reserves/Deposits Ratio, 1931–1942 (in percentages). *Source:* BCRA Yearbooks and BCRA Statistical Bulletins, 1931–1942.

of gold and currency reserves but also on the basis of credits to the government and to the private sector (rediscounts). Nevertheless, the bank's monetary policy differed little from that of the Currency Board, because during the initial years of its existence it made issues primarily on the basis of its reserves. From 1935 to 1940 gold and currency reserves represented 80% of the monetary base.

The government deposited a proportionally smaller portion of its debt in the Central Bank: between 500 and 600 million pesos (closer to the latter value). The bank's policies resulted in the revaluation of reserves, which had monetary and fiscal consequences. Another consequence was the sterilization of the inflow or withdrawal of reserves, creating absorption instruments (participation certificates), which smoothed the cyclical fluctuations of foreign trade and their influence on money creation, between 1935 and 1939.

Figure 3.10 illustrates that when exports fall the Central Bank buys certificates from the public issuing money, decreasing its nonmonetary liabilities, and that, inversely, when exports increase it sells certificates, contracting the currency in the hands of the public and increasing its nonmonetary liabilities. But during the war years when, because of extraordinary trade surpluses, and because sterilization instruments were not used, there was a great influx of foreign currencies and a significant monetary expansion ensued.

Figure 3.10 also shows that in 1943, despite the Central Bank's intervention, by buying participation certificates that year, the means of payment reached 700 million pesos in 1942 and 1,083 mllion pesos in 1943 because of an increase in government debt in the Central Bank occurring in 1943. That is, the Central Bank sterilized almost all increases in debt that the government placed in its assets.

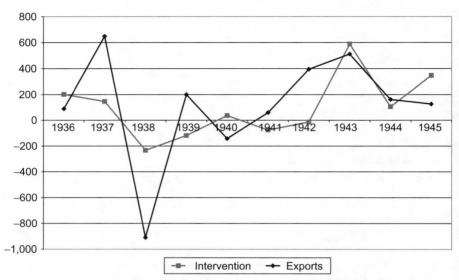

Figure 3.10. Relation between Changes in Participation Certificates in Consolidated Bonds and Certificates of Gold and Foreign Currency Holdings in Central Bank Liabilities and Changes in Export Values (variations in millions of current pesos). *Source:* Aldo Arnaudo, *Cincuenta Años de Política Financiera Argentina (1934–1983)*, Buenos Aires, El Ateneo, 1987, p. 46, and Argentine Republic Central Bank (BCRA), *Series Históricas de Cuentas Nacionales de la Argentina*, Buenos Aires, Gerencia de Investigaciones Económicas, 1976.

All of the Currency Board's assets and liabilities were transferred to the Central Bank. Among the assets were gold reserves and rediscounts to banks that had portfolios tied up in loans, both to farmers, the loans to whom had been rendered nonperforming because of decrease in prices, and to the National Government. Because the closure of the Currency Board was followed by a peso devaluation in dollars of more than 50% between 1929 and 1935, officials decided to reassess the reserves at the new exchange rate, as the United States had done in 1933; thus, reserves went from 560,300,000 pesos in 1934 to 1,353,700,000 pesos in 1935. This allowed for an expansion in the monetary base, which went from 1,174,200,000 in 1934 to 1,660,000,000 pesos in 1935 and allowed the government to help the banks, which were in a precarious financial situation (because of their clients' difficulties and the slump in the price of their guarantees). At the same time, with the funds from the revaluation, the government settled its debt with official banks (particularly the Bank of the Argentine Nation), thereby improving their portfolios. The 41% expansion of the monetary base allowed banks' balance sheets to improve, increasing their reserves to deposits coefficients from 0.12 to

Table 3.12. *Participation Certificates in National
Treasury Consolidated Bonds Deposited in Stock
Holding Banks (in millions of pesos)*

End of 1935	Face Value	Real Value
June	210.85	234.36
July	250.00	264.25
August	250.00	264.25
September	250.00	267.62
October	193.17	210.14
November	172.33	188.02
December	178.65	194.90

Source: BCRA Yearbook, 1935.

0.25 in 1935. Whereas deposits in current accounts dropped, the rest, like fixed-term accounts, remained at previous levels. These values are slightly lower in real terms: the monetary base grew by 33.4% between 1934 and 1935.

The Central Bank sought to prevent the effect of the creation of bank money in periods of gold inflows and did the opposite in periods of outflows. The Financial Report argued that the increase in exports and the inflows of foreign capital in the years 1935–1936 to the first half of 1937 brought an increase in gold and cash, and the Central Bank for the first time had the opportunity to put out "absorption" bonds to prevent the effects that this expansion would have had on credit. When gold inflows increased because of better export prices in 1936, the Central Bank decided to offer participation certificates, which it sold to banks, thereby eliminating excess liquidity in the market.[19]

Because of the relative abundance of funds in credit institutions, the Central Bank initiated cooperative banking operations with consolidated bonds. On June 7, 1935, that is, a few days after it was founded, the bank decided to offer participation certificates in these bonds to stock-holding banks at a face value of 250 million pesos. The Annual Financial Report of the Central Bank added, "With these deposits, the Central Bank can absorb considerable quantities of funds that would have had a negative effect on the money market."[20] It was anticipated that when the inflows of reserves diminished, the certificates would be bought, creating money. Open market policies proceeded in this manner (see Tables 3.12 and 3.13).

In 1936 participation bonds were made available in the amount of nearly 400 million pesos, of which 310 million remained in circulation,

19 BCRA Yearbook, 1935, pp. 17–18.
20 Ibid., p. 19.

Table 3.13. *Evolution of Government Debt in the Argentine Republic Central Bank, 1935–1944*
(in pesos)

Year	BCRA Assets	Government Debt in BCRA Assets	Absorption bonds in BCRA Liabilities	Net Government Debt
1935	1,730,071,171	354,358,015	0	354,358,015
1936	2,086,905,347	536,793,035	399,000,000	137,793,035
1937	2,306,695,320	539,654,503	310,500,000	229,154,503
1938	2,295,320,699	544,731,431	302,350,000	242,381,431
1939	2,500,174,298	560,318,260	114,950,000	445,368,260
1940	2,859,837,403	565,653,419	126,800,000	438,853,419
1941	2,141,436,414	571,255,829	30,000,000	541,255,829
1942	2,771,381,877	578,198,922	26,500,000	551,698,922
1943	4,243,377,898	987,556,998	444,286,897	543,270,101
1944	4,864,322,482	964,248,976	119,934,169	844,314,807

Source: BCRA Yearbook, 1935–1944.

and by 1938 302 million remained. In 1937 came the placement of the Certificates of Custody of gold and foreign exchange that by the end of that year reached 234.6 million. The monetary base, which had reached 1,728 million pesos in 1936, dropped in 1937 to 1,714 million and in 1938 to 1,648 million. With the contraction caused by the declaration of war in 1940, the bank began to buy a portion of these bonds from the public, thereby creating money. The amount of bonds dropped to 115 million in 1939, 126.8 million in 1940, 30 million in 1941, and 26.5 million in 1942; the monetary base increased from 1,648 million pesos in 1938 to 1,829 million in 1940.

However, movements in real terms were less pronounced and sometimes in the opposite direction: the real monetary base experienced an overall decrease of 3.6% between 1935 and 1938 and later a vigorous recuperation of 9% in 1939, reaching a level at which it stabilized in 1940. Rediscounts were used to solve short-term problems of liquidity, and national stocks represented between 20% and 30% of the Central Bank's assets. Again in this case, in real terms was a quite similar behavior.

Reserves increased in 1936 and decreased in 1937 and 1938; they again increased in 1939 and dropped in 1940. However, from 1941 on, reserves experienced a robust increase due to the trade surplus, since, because of the war, exports continued but imports dropped considerably. In 1941 reserves had increased by 16% compared with the year before (from 1,329 to 1,542 million pesos). A great increase occurred in 1942: 36% compared with the previous year, and 53% in 1943, 20% in 1944, and 22% in 1945.

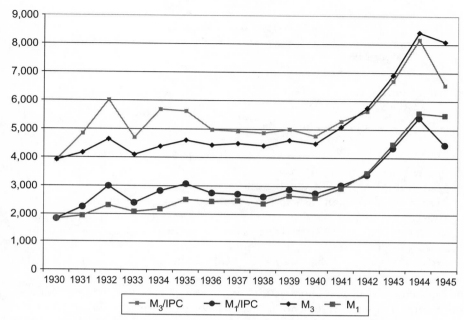

Figure 3.11. Evolution of Monetary Aggregates by the Retail Price Index, 1930–1945 (in millions of 1914 pesos). *Source:* BCRA Yearbooks and *Anuario Geográfico Argentino*, Comité Nacional de Geografía, Buenos Aires, 1941.

This extraordinary inflow of reserves from 1941 corresponded to another exceptional situation: exporters liquidated their currencies, whereas importers did not purchase foreign exchange because, due to the war, there was no supply of imported foreign-manufactured goods. The bank did not use participation certificates in 1942, but did in 1943, depositing 444.3 million pesos. In 1944 and 1945 the bank again declined to use the certificates and bought a portion from the public, thereby diminishing its holdings to 119.9 million pesos in 1944 and 167.6 million the following year. This caused a remarkable increase in the monetary base, which was 53% in real terms between 1942 and 1945 (during the Ramírez-Farrell de facto government).

Monetary Aggregates

Between 1935 and 1940 the nominal monetary base grew by 6.4% by year, whereas the money supply rose by 4.2% per year. These values are less in real terms in which the monetary base remained nearly constant and the money supply increased only by 1% (see Figure 3.11).

Table 3.14. *Reserves (Gold and Foreign Currency) and Monetary Base,*
1935–1940 (in millions of pesos)

Millions of Pesos	1935	1936	1937	1938	1939	1940
Reserves	1,354	1,528	1,422	1,296	1,396	1,329
Monetary base	1,660	1,728	1,714	1,648	1,829	1,850
Ratio R/MB	0.82	0.88	0.83	0.79	0.76	0.72

Source: BCRA Yearbook, 1935–1940.

Deposits in local currency increased by 4.9% per year. Currency rose more than the monetary base, by 3.7% per year. This was a result of the fall in the deposit of private banks into the Central Bank (reserves) by 9%. From 1935 to 1938 cash reserves dropped from 482.4 million pesos to 320.6. On the one hand gold inflows were sterilized (absorption) but on the other the ratio reserves/deposits dropped (expansion). The government controlled the primary expansion but not the banking expansion. The ratio reserves/deposits at the commercial banks in the first years of the Central Bank was not an instrument of monetary regulation and was fixed with the sole objective of providing security for deposits. In the first ten years of the Central Bank (until the end of the war) two stages may be discerned, one from 1935 to 1940, during which time there was a moderate expansion with anticyclic policies, and the other from 1940 to 1945, which was a period of robust expansion.

War and the Pinedo Plan

The outbreak of the war in Europe in 1939 caused the loss of continental European markets and a concomitant drop in exports, a sector that had been continually strengthening since 1935. (Exports in 1937 were 48% greater than in 1930, although less than in 1929; in 1930 they reached $509 million; in 1937, $755 million, its lowest point being in 1932, with $331 million.) With the closure of the continental markets in 1939, a significant portion of crops was in danger of being lost, which would have affected the entire economy. In reality, the fall in exports began in 1938 and had a direct impact on the decrease in gold and currency reserves until 1940, as illustrated in Table 3.14.

Although the immediate measures tended to finance the purchase of crops, for which the Bank of the Argentine Nation was used and received a National Treasury Bond for 400 million pesos that it could discount at the Central Bank, for the long term there was an attempt to promote industrial production that in theory could thrive in the domestic market so as to prevent exclusive dependence on foreign markets.[21]

---

21 See Juan Llach, "El Plan Pinedo de 1940, su Significado Histórico y los Orígenes de la Política Económica del Peronismo," *Desarrollo Económico*, vol. 23, no. 92, January–March 1984.

Industrial activity suffered a chronic shortage of capital and financing in the absence of long-term credit. Unlike the agricultural sector, whose loans for labor work until harvesting followed traditional banking norms, under which there was short-term financing, the industrial sector required longer-term credit, particularly if it was for installation needs and not just for working capital.

There was an undeniable surplus in the supply of short-term credit, whereas demand was primarily for the long-term loans. Banks held more deposits than loans extended. The problem was how to provide long-term credit if savings deposited were for the short term. What would happen if people wanted to withdraw the entire amount of their deposits when the term expired, and this period did not correspond with the term for which the bank had extended credit? Minister of the Treasury Pinedo's 1940 project sought to help banks use their short-term deposits to extend long-term credit. In the unlikely case of a sudden demand for the withdrawal of deposits before the loans matured, the Central Bank would provide the financing by rediscounting bank's portfolios. It was an ingenious, and ultimately dangerous, operation, an attempt to promote industrial development. As Prebisch points out, the measure, conceived of as a response to the financial emergency, was not put into practice because the emergency vanished when, the very next year, exports enjoyed a robust expansion when demand appeared anew. This time, the demand for raw wool and hides came from the United States, foreseeing that the war would spread and other countries would be implicated. At any rate, as is the case with other institutions conceived of for exceptional circumstances, allowing for new, broader rediscounting possibilities led to what would become the usual means of financing during the Perón years.

Wartime Expansion: Increase in Reserves, Monetary Effects

Although continental European countries subject to the blockade remained outside of trade with Argentina, and despite the risks of submarine war, the Allied countries' demand for foodstuffs, hides, and raw wool persisted, and Argentine exports experienced solid growth, which was not followed by a similar increase in imports, because the warring countries dedicated the whole of their production to the war effort. This caused an especially large positive balance of trade, which led to a vigorous inflow of reserves from 1941 on (see Figure 3.12).

Imports that had reached $481.8 million in 1937 dropped to $380.9 million in 1940 (a 21% decrease), whereas exports dropped even further, going from $768.6 million in 1937 to $430.2 million (a 44% drop). But exports would increase substantially starting in 1941, reaching $686.5 million by 1944. Imports, on the other hand, continued to drop, and by 1943 had plummeted to $238.9 million, an amount that is only slightly

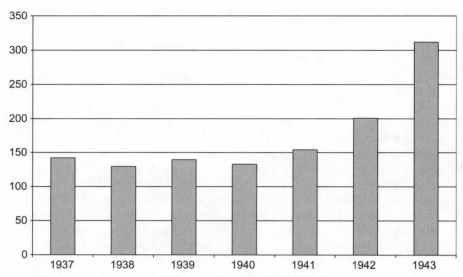

Figure 3.12. Evolution of Central Bank (BCRA) Reserves (in millions of dollars)
Source: BCRA Yearbooks, 1937–1943.

higher than in 1932, at the height of the decade's devastating financial crisis, and even less than in 1914–1915 (see Figure 3.13).

The drop in imports caused a concomitant slump in fiscal revenue – not to the dramatic extent it did during World War I – but to a significant degree. What primarily fell was the margin of exchange, the spread between the price at which the government bought currencies and the price at which it sold them. Because of the increasing inflows of currencies produced by the increase in exports, and lacking a parallel demand for imports, the Central Bank bought foreign currencies from exporters not with the pesos that importers bought foreign exchange but by creating money. The export sector became a fundamental factor in the creation of means of payment from 1941 on.

Indeed, the Central Bank came to hold a surplus of foreign currencies that it bought from exporters, and it could not sell to importers, circumstances that invigorated money creation and generated substantial liquidity. At the same time, government revenue dropped, due to two principal factors, the margin of exchange and import taxes: the margin of exchange plummeted from 201 million pesos in 1940 to 43 million in 1943, and from 270 million pesos to 127 million, in the case of import duties, during the same period. Because revenue dropped from 1,907 million pesos in 1940 to 1,621 million pesos in 1942 (in 1914 pesos) the government took advantage of the liquidity and deposited debt on the market to cover the contraction in

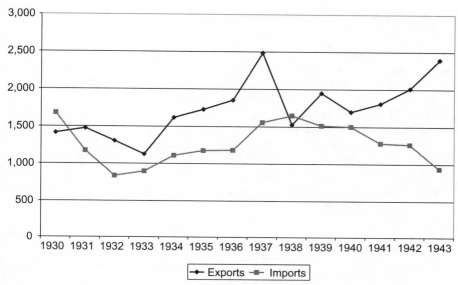

Figure 3.13. Evolution of Foreign Trade (in current dollars). *Source:* INDEC
(National Bureau of Statistics and Census).

revenue. But this very situation prevented the Central Bank from sterilizing the inflow of currencies, placing participation certificates on the market, as it had done between 1935 and 1937. As revealed in the Treasury Yearbook for that year, as long as the government had to resort to the market to deposit its debt, the Central Bank could not do the same with its bonds, which would compete with the government debt, because if the market could not absorb it, the government would have to bring it to the Central Bank, causing an increase in money issues.

According to the 1942 Central Bank Annual Report, it was

[t]he obstacle which prevented the placing of all the Treasury Bills which the market asked for has been removed by the latest Budget Law and as it has been decided to offer medium – term Treasury Bonds for public subscription, it will be possible to meet fully the requirements of the financial market, thus giving it the elasticity which it formerly lacked. The greater the volume of this class of paper placed among the public, the less the Treasury will have to resort to bank credit. This explains the monetary as well as financial importance of these notwithstanding the authority granted to it, has deemed it advisable to give preference to such operations over those involving its own absorption certificate. Otherwise, the Treasury would have to make more use of bank credit, and purchasing power could continue to expand, in the measure in which the placing with the public of Central Bank Certificates might prevent that of an equivalent volume of Government paper.

The absorption of media of payment would thus be immediately offset by a further expansion.[22]

The foregoing extract explains why sterilization instruments were not used despite their success in the thirties and why there was a significant monetary expansion. Because government revenue dropped, the government used the monetary liquidity to place its debt in the market. The Central Bank did not follow an absorption policy during the years 1941 to 1942 in which there was a significant inflow of reserves, causing substantial monetary expansion and affecting prices that had already been affected by the increase in the cost of imported goods. Actually, monetary policy was subordinate to the fiscal needs of the government. The external sector generated enough liquidity to allow easy access to credit for the government to offset the drops in revenues.

The Fiscal Evolution, 1930–1945

The drastic decline in world trade and the demand for foodstuffs in the thirties caused a fall in exports and in imports, and thus in the most significant source of income for the government. The main aspects of tax reforms that were aimed at compensating for the drop in tax revenues have already been previously addressed. What is important to remember is that other nontax financial resources emerged, especially the margin of exchange.

With regard to revenue, there was a positive trend until 1937, a slump in 1938, and a clear upturn in 1943. As noted in the previous chapter, there are discrepancies between the Treasury Accounts and that of the Budget Investment Account (*Cuenta de Inversión del Presupuesto*). (See the methodological note in the Appendix for further details.) One of the reasons for this discrepancy is that in the data from the Treasury there is an item for special resources, which is what came from the revaluation of gold reserves at the Central Bank for a sum that was greater than a year's revenue: 331 million pesos of paper money and subsidiary money issued, plus 773 million that went to aid the financial sector and the recently constituted Argentine Republic Central Bank.

There is no clear trend with regard to the total surplus or deficit; some years showed a surplus and others a deficit. The successful financing, negotiated especially after 1933, seemed more a measure to cover the substantial payments on public debt, domestic debt (which was successfully restructured in 1933), and foreign debt (whose payments were strictly adhered to) (see Figure 3.14).[23]

---

22 BCRA Yearbook, 1942, pp. 20–21.
23 In the case of payments, there was a reduction in indebtedness to the Bank of the Argentine Nation, which allowed it to leave the agreed-upon credits to the National Government in the hands of

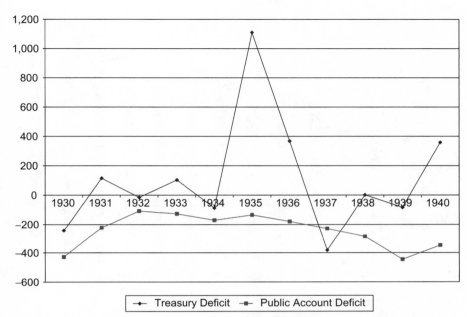

Figure 3.14. Data Comparison of Balance Sheet from Budget Investment Accounts and National Treasury, 1930–1940 (in millions of pesos). *Source:* Treasury Yearbooks, 1930–1940, and *Anuario Geográfico Argentino*, Comité Nacional de Geografía, Buenos Aires, 1941.

Starting in 1935 there was a significant expansion in public outlays, made possible by the increase in revenue but also by a greater access to credit. Probably, the expansion would be much greater with the onset of the war, not so much because of an increase in revenue but because the government resorted to ever greater deficits (probably expecting a greater recuperation of revenue and imports at war's end). Furthermore, the increase in reserves caused a monetary expansion, which allowed the state greater access to credit, as we mentioned before.

Nevertheless, the Argentine Geographical Yearbook shows detailed information of the debt only starting in 1928, in which enormous floating debt accumulates from 623,700 pesos in 1928 to 1,341,800 in 1931. This debt slowly diminished, until it nearly disappeared in 1936, following the

the Central Bank. Government debt to the Currency Board decreased considerably, and the new sum remained as a debt to the Central Bank in the form of a Guaranty Bond. In short, the gold reappraisal helped to finance government accounts from previous fiscal deficits and to pay for the banking system's misguided maneuvers by means of the Bank Investment Mobilizing Institute (*Instituto Movilizador de Inversiones Bancarias*). See Aldo Arnaudo, *Cincuenta Años de Política Financiera Argentina, 1934–1983*, Buenos Aires, El Ateneo, 1987, pp. 23–26.

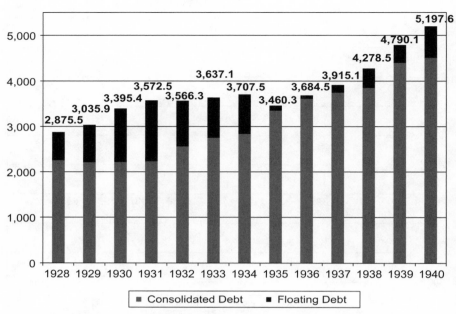

Figure 3.15. Evolution of National Consolidated and Floating Public Debt (in millions of pesos). *Source: Anuario Geográfico Argentino*, Comité Nacional de Geografía, Buenos Aires, 1941, p. 409.

inflow of financial resources from the Central Bank gold reappraisal. At any rate, total debt between 1931 and 1937 increased only slightly and only after 1938. During this period it is clear that some spending was covered by bond revenue (see Figure 3.15).

Economic Activity

The 1930 crisis was a result of a fall in foreign demand for goods and the catastrophic decrease in export prices, which between 1929 and 1933 slipped by some 41%. Thus it was quite different from World War I crisis, which resulted from a contraction in imports, affecting the industrial, transportation, and government sectors from investments and from the loss of crops.

Between 1929 and 1932 the physical volume of agricultural production dropped by only 3% but prices dropped precipitously. The physical volume of cattle production did not drop in any significant way either, but because agricultural prices fell by 42% during those same years, the dramatic fall in revenue from the agricultural sector had a ripple effect throughout the economy. Construction, which always has an ample response to cyclic fluctuations, dropped by 27% between 1929 and 1932, whereas industry saw only a 2.3% decline. In terms of physical volume, GDP dropped by 3.1% between 1929 and 1932, whereas the decline in revenue was much greater, because prices had plummeted. Despite the fact that the closure of the Currency Board prevented the effects of the fall of revenue in foreign currency and of reserves, these factors caused a monetary contraction that aggravated the recession.

The economy rebounded starting in 1934 – as O'Connell[24] has pointed out – spurred on by an increase in export prices, which that year increased by 39.8% and between 1934 and 1937 by 36%. The upturn in agricultural prices, due to the 1934 drought, "the Dustbowl," in the United States, was furthered by the 20% devaluation in November 1933, allowing greater profits for producers. From 1929 the peso had depreciated, but in 1931, when exchange controls were established, it kept constant at 3.80 per dollar until the end of 1933. In the meantime, as the exchange rate remained fixed, there was a slight increase in domestic prices.

With the increase in agricultural income and the financial situation improving because of measures previously outlined (and with a significant increase in the monetary supply – when part of the Patriotic Loan was monetized), the economic recovery heightened and spread to industry grew by 10.2% in 1934 with respect to 1933 in physical volume. Industrial activity continued to increase by 17.5% between 1935 and 1938 (in volume), but it was the war that gave it the greatest impetus. Between 1938 and 1945 the volume of industrial activity grew by 31%. It was the high point of import substitute industrialization. Prices dropped until 1937, remained steady, and then began to climb from 1939 on (see Table A.C.3.1 in the Appendix). Between 1939 and 1940, due to a climate of distrust from the war, construction declined by 11.5%, but later steadily rebounded until it reached previous levels around 1943.

Agriculture suffered a decline in 1938, affected by marketing problems following the closure of the Central European markets during the first years of the war, which led the government to intervene by purchasing the 1938/1939 wheat crop, but the following year growth returned. Investment dropped in 1930 and recovered in 1933, but at a level slightly higher than 20% of GDP. Later, during the war years, it remained below that, being proportionately higher in construction than in machinery and equipment (65% and 35% of investment, respectively, as an average during the war years).

It was undoubtedly a period of expansion that employed all of the industrial capacity put in place before 1930 and, for this reason, was limited.

---

24 Arturo O'Connell, "La Argentina en la Depresión: los Problemas de una Economía Abierta," *Desarrollo Económico*, vol. 23, no. 92, 1984.

That is, there was a sore need for investment in infrastructure and capital goods, both of which had been neglected during the war years due to limits on imports. Between 1929 and 1932, nominal wages plummeted, by 40%, but as a result of the drop in prices, the real decrease was much less severe: 9% between 1929 and 1930. They recovered but remained 4% below 1929 levels during the forties, while GDP increased. The trend of the 1920s had changed course, this time against wage earners. The terms of trade became negative until 1933, because prices of manufactured goods dropped less than those of foodstuffs. They later increased until 1937 as a result of the rebound in agricultural prices, and from then until 1944 the trend was negative, because despite the increase in export prices, import prices increased even more.

Conclusions

As in other parts of the world, in Argentina some of the more remarkable economic innovations of the decade had to do with the monetary and exchange regimes. The abandonment of the gold standard in 1929 allowed the economy to isolate itself from drastic fluctuations abroad. Currency issues no longer depended on net balances of external transactions (inflows and outflows of gold at the Currency Board). Argentina was one of the first countries to abandon the gold standard. Uruguay and Brazil followed suit in 1929, New Zealand and Australia in 1930, and the rest of the countries, including Great Britain, in 1931, except for France, which would hold to the standard until 1936. Germany did not devalue currency but established an exchange control. In this regard, the economy was henceforth not affected in the same way by external shocks. The peso was devaluated at the rate of 3.86 pesos per dollar and remained at that rate until 1933.

The depreciation improved income from exports, which had suffered a precipitous decline in international prices. Additionally, it was a benefit for local producers who competed with imports: because of their greater import prices in pesos, they could increase their own. The government, which had closed the Currency Board, could withdraw gold from it to pay its obligations abroad at the official exchange rate of the period of convertibility (2.2727 pesos for 1 gold peso), which prevented the government from having to resort to the market. In short, depreciation averted deeper deflation, and in this sense it aided the agricultural sector, protected local production, and most importantly, helped the government through the margin of exchange.

Following the abandonment of the gold standard, the second innovation was the establishment in September 1931 of an exchange control, a means by which the state gained control over all foreign exchange transactions. During World War I, the countries involved experimented with exchange controls, and these were put in place following the 1930 crisis in Germany, and in the Austro-Hungarian Empire. In Latin America, Brazil, Mexico, and Chile implemented exchange controls. Exchange transactions could take place only in authorized banks at the rate that the respective commission dictated. The obligation to liquidate foreign exchange at a rate that remained at 3.81 was below market rate, which, in addition, had to be rationed. Banks sold currencies at the rate determined by the commission following the priorities determined by the government, the first of which was public debt and after that the import of essential goods (industrial inputs). The government had access to cheaper foreign currency, which it got from exporters, allowing it to avoid taking more gold from the Currency Board. Until 1933 the exchange rate stayed near the same level, but because domestic prices continued to increase, albeit slightly, this adversely affected exporters, as seen in Figure 3.8.

In 1933, there was a 20% devaluation (which was greater than the increase in domestic prices) and two rates were established, buyers' and sellers' rates, and it was stipulated that the spread – the margin of exchange – would go to the government coffers. Thus the government openly began to benefit from the profits of devaluation. This was favorable for local producers to the extent that the devaluation increased the price of imported goods, which allowed them to raise their own prices and improve profitability. It was also favorable for those who accessed foreign currency at official exchange rates for imports because the exchange rate was substantially less than that of the open market. But it was even more favorable for the government, which, through the margin of exchange, appropriated a portion of the devaluation profits. It was a framework in which all sectors attempted to protect themselves from the damages that the crisis had caused. They sought the *socialization* of losses.

The Monetary Regime

The other innovation began with the granting of the right to issue currency on the basis of Currency Board credit and with the creation of the Central Bank in 1935, which not only allowed for greater monetary flexibility but also helped with a significant contribution of financial resources. During its first decade, the Central Bank adjusted the creation of the monetary base to reserve flows, but by being very innovative by smoothing fluctuations with sterilization measures until the war began.

Protectionism: Industrialization through Import Substitution

In addition to exchange policies, there were trade policies. These included policies ranging from the increase in duties, devaluation in 1929 and 1933, and quantitative restrictions (previous permits) that produced a significant portion of the demand for consumer goods that previously came from abroad would not be filled. This allowed local producers to supply goods at a higher price than their imported counterparts. Furthermore, a currency contraction, which would have been the result of the outflow of reserves, was averted by means of issues on the basis of credit.

Outlays contraction did not continue, because new sources of revenue were found, and in 1934 the agricultural sector rebounded, and this spurred an increase in consumption. In response to increased domestic demand, significant industrial growth ensued. The greatest growth was seen in the textile industry, where the expansion that had begun in the twenties continued because from that point the industry could rely on domestic raw material (cotton) at low transportation cost and could import machinery, enabling it to respond to an unmet demand. The expansion spread to other items, domestic products, pharmaceutical, and so on. Direct investment from the United States also played a critical role, because in this way the United States avoided trade discrimination against it, something established by the Roca-Runciman Agreement (because its imports were liquidated on the open market).

American firms finished the product in the country, importing the majority of raw materials at a very favorable exchange rate, while the final product remained protected by an even higher rate. This strategy had a political benefit compared with importing goods, because it demanded labor locally.

Domestic Migrations

An elastic labor supply, this time from the interior regions of the country, also contributed to economic growth. The domestic terms of trade, which were unfavorable for agriculture, drew workers from rural sectors to urban ones, where real wages were subsidized with cheap food. Between 1935 and 1945 more than a million people migrated to Buenos Aires, changing the urban working class and settling in the suburbs of large cities, or in the new and distressingly numerous ghettos or *"villas miserias."* In this sense, the displacement of the population from the agricultural sector, characterized by low productivity, to the manufacturing sector, where productivity would supposedly be greater, could have been another of the reasons for growth. However, the changes to the industrial structure shifting to more labor-intensive activities (e.g., from foodstuffs to textiles) do not show a significant increase in productivity.[25] It is not clear just how productive were the numerous small shops with little capital that carried

---

25 See Roberto Cortés Conde, *La Economía Argentina en el Largo Plazo (Siglos XIX y XX)*, Buenos Aires, Sudamericana, 1994, pp. 213–214 and 223–225.

out industrial activities during the war. According to Katz, it is possible that this migratory influx caused by the contraction of medium-sized industries, particularly in those in which the capital and technical knowledge necessary for startup were low, led to a diminished average industrial efficiency.[26] There is ample evidence to conclude that the industrial activity of the period was characterized by low productivity. However, in a country rich in resources (land), the productivity of work in the agricultural sector could be greater than in the industrial sector, which is quite different than what Lewis theorized.[27]

The Economy Isolated from External Shocks

Whereas during the depression years there was great pressure from the external difficulties of debt payments, with the outbreak of World War II everything changed. Although imports dropped drastically – since production in the warring countries was dedicated entirely to the war effort – Argentine exports, despite the risks of the war at sea, continued to reach Great Britain, which was desperate for foodstuffs. Argentina did not experience the same supply limitation as during World War I because the industries had matured and were partially supplied by local raw materials, as was the textile industry. Energy problems were serious, although the local supply of petroleum and the new Chaco deforestation allowed wood to replace coal for fuel for rail transportation. Furthermore, since 1930, the state no longer depended only on import taxes for its operations and had obtained new sources of revenue. Investment was no longer centered on the railroad, because the government had invested greatly in other infrastructure, like roads. Despite the fact that for several years GDP dropped, growth continued until the immediate postwar period.

26 Especially during the 1940s. Jorge Katz, "Una Interpretación de Largo Plazo del Crecimiento Industrial Argentino," *Desarrollo Económico*, vol. 8, no. 32, 1969.

27 See W. Arthur Lewis, "Economic Development with Unlimited Supplies of Labour," *Manchester School of Economic and Social Studies*, vol. XXIII, no. 2, May 1954, and Juan Llach, *Reconstrucción o Estancamiento*, Buenos Aires, Thesis, 1987.

4

The Political Economy of Peronism

Introduction

There is very little about which all Argentines agree, but there is a general consensus that Peronism brought a fundamental change in the life of the country. Although the 1914 war marked the end of the *Belle Epoque*, certain institutions, and much of the culture of that period, endured until World War II, albeit in a somewhat altered form. Nothing would be the same after Colonel Perón stood in front of the Town Hall (*Consejo Deliberante*) building, now converted into the secretary of labor, and harangued the workers. Who would have thought that a military government would promote a movement that supported political participation of the workers and the defense of their rights? Given that the government had been imposed by a military clique called the Group of United Officials (the *GOU*[1]) and had Nazi sympathies and a desire to repeat Franco's Spanish experiment (even, like Franco, appealing to the notion of a glorious Hispanic past), this brand of populism came as a surprise.

By no means did Perón have a vision from the beginning for the movement that kept him in power, and that lasted the entire twentieth century. Initially, although he was not the leader of the revolutionary Junta, he managed to achieve key positions in the June 4 coup d'état military hierarchy. Although Perón agreed with many nationalist principles – having personally experienced Italian fascism and being favorably impressed with Mussolini – he had risen the professional ranks under the protection of the moderate right-wing President Justo. But because this was a military government, Perón took advantage of his numerous friends within the military and his great professional prestige as professor of the War College (*Escuela Superior de Guerra*). After becoming head of army personnel, he requested a position that no one cared much about: head of the labor department,

---

1 For more information on the GOU (*Grupo de Oficiales Unidos* – Group of United Officials), the military freemason group that directed the June 4, 1943, coup d'état, see Robert Potash, *Perón y el G.O.U.*, Buenos Aires, Sudamericana, 1984.

which enforced labor standards and compiled statistics about such issues. There he met a Catalonian named Jose Figuerola, who would become his most capable advisor.

With the decisive help of Lieutenant Colonel Mercante, who organized the secretary of labor's regional delegations in the interior provinces (future base of his party's structure), he began looking for a post in the military government to maintain contact with trade union leaders, many of whom had previously been sent to jail. Although this initiative was intended to secure the continuation of the current order (likewise the contacts with other political leaders), it was not entirely indicative of the movement to come.

Perón was a brilliant opportunist; he nimbly changed positions on the problems that divided the 1943 government (among others, breaking off relations with the Axis powers). He also understood that he had to abandon the anachronistic rhetoric employed by the June 4 coup participants and opt instead for a populist tone, which was becoming increasingly comfortable for him. To convince his military colleagues of the appeal of this approach, he relied not only on his professional prestige but also on the conviction that there had to be an alternative for the working class to the political left, which was gaining momentum in the West. It was a paternalistic vision in which the state responded to workers' concerns, and was therefore not among the notions of classical economy. Furthermore, it partially coincided with the principles expressed in the papal encyclicals – and although many were opposed to this philosophy (especially expressed in fiery populist terms), it could serve to prevent the spread of communism, the importance of which cannot be overemphasized.

Peronism did not begin out of power, as an organized political party fighting to attain office through the popular vote, but rather it began in the seat of power and doled out its favors as one of its distinctive characteristics. With Perón in the presidency, and a majority in the Congress and in the provincial governments, he had attained almost absolute power. With this power he managed to build the framework of the movement, along with two branches of the party – male and female – and the CGT (*Confederación General del Trabajo*, General Confederation of Unions), which became the structure of the *organized community*.

Some of Perón's ideas about the economy were clear from the very beginning, and others developed in response to the circumstances in which he found the country. The military government supported the notion of full employment – with which both the entrepreneurs, who became established under protectionism, and labor leaders agreed – because nothing scared the government more than the prospect of social unrest like the clashes that had erupted after World War I. Another of Perón's ideas was to improve real wages, to counteract the wage erosion experienced during the 1930s, which in turn had been a response to the significant wage increases of the 1920s. Perón also proposed extending social security to everyone, which was an idea that proved to be a stabilizing feature of postwar Germany, and promised to provide the state with an important source of financial resources. These notions also reflected the intellectual climate worldwide in the immediate postwar period.

Perhaps what most influenced Perón's ideology was his military education. He believed that politics was not the art of negotiation but rather of commanding, and during his long career his rhetoric was dappled with countless military terms. Perón did not have a very well developed or sophisticated economic ideas. During both of his administrations he put the treasury in the hands of men who knew how to get rich, demonstrating his exaggeratedly simplistic view of economic phenomena. This is an indicator of the importance the economy had for Perón. But he doubtless believed that there was something like a market failure and that state intervention – to differing degrees – was, if not a necessary, at least a convenient alternative. This was a commonly held belief during the postwar years, especially in the wake of the 1930 crisis. The military had had the examples of Germany, which had achieved remarkable economic recovery in the 1930s, to the extent that it could become a war power, and of the Soviet Union and its planned economy, even if the regime seemed reprehensible.

Having been trained in the military, Perón also shared the military notion of industrialization, which included the development of heavy industry in order to provide the country its own supply of arms.[2] This became even more necessary when Brazil procured military supplies from the U.S. government, which had disrupted the delicate arms balance in the Southern Cone.

Isolationism was widely accepted because following the war, people expected that international trade restrictions would continue and believed they were a reasonable response to economic conditions. Many of his messages were written by intellectuals and writers with nationalist and Christian socialist tendencies. The authoritarian tendencies of the 1943 government distanced Perón from liberals (of whom he furthermore had a negative opinion). On the other hand, he welcomed the marginalized and some provincial conservative parties, which had been antiliberal. It was within this framework, which changed shape throughout the years, that Perón's economic policies were implemented.

Argentina's fertile ground for isolationism was the result of a convergence of still other circumstances. First, a de facto autarky had existed since World War II, and the public had grown used to (economic isolation and) a nonexistent international capital market. The remarkable accumulation

2 See Juan José Llach, "El Plan Pinedo de 1940, su Significado Histórico y los Orígenes de la Economía Política del Peronismo", *Desarrollo Económico*, vol. 23, no. 92, 1984.

of trade surpluses caused by the restriction on imports during the war had also created the impression that the accumulated currencies were a sign of a significant increase in wealth, but it was actually the result of decapitalization (because of the obsolescence of machinery and equipment). The public perception of increasing wealth was also created by the enormous demand for foodstuffs in Europe, which put upward pressure on prices in the two years following the war. In addition, there was a generalized pessimism regarding the evolution of world trade. Thus, the public responded with nationalist rhetoric against foreign investments, but the government later came to regret its own discursive tactics when, in 1955, it signed a contract with Standard Oil of California for oil exploitation.

It was in this political context that Perón enunciated policies to achieve his primary goals: full employment, industrialization with state support and intervention (state associated capitalism), and an increase in real wages. However, these goals required substantial financing. The initial policies of the government stemmed from a mistaken impression of future worldwide economic and political trends. As we have seen, the experience of the previous two decades had created a pessimistic view of international trade, but the measures adopted in this climate of gloom were wrong. If because of protectionism in the world, it was difficult to sell products on markets in which Argentina had a comparative advantage, this was no reason to punish and discourage the production of goods in sectors in which costs were less, to promote those whose costs were greater. Australia, also a foodstuffs exporter, had a different response in the postwar period. It too was mistaken in believing that it could truly negotiate with the large world powers and that it would have even better leverage in the case of an eventual third world war. Not only did this not happen but the bilateralism toward which the government tended would have negative effects on the economy, especially since Argentina exported commodities and imported manufactured goods.

The government assured full employment by subsidizing activities that would not be profitable in competitive markets. This was achieved by means of customs tariffs and quantitative restrictions on imports, with an overvaluation of the peso, which reduced the costs of food and local labor. In this way an implicit tax on exports was imposed, and this helped to keep real wages high. This all seemed possible thanks to the productivity of the agricultural sector, which could supposedly be taxed without affecting its production, because land was considered a fixed resource whose supply was not elastic. But the Pampas had alternative uses,[3] and so, with unfavorable prices, agricultural exports suffered a long, slow decline. The cost of living

---

3 As the price of a product falls, there is a drop in the income from the assets that produce it, and therefore investment is made in the production of an item that is less costly to produce. Such is the case with land use, because if agricultural prices drop, the land can be used for cattle raising.

did not increase because food prices and the cost of public services (provided by state enterprises running a deficit) were kept artificially low. Capital formation was also subsidized with loans at a negative real rate of interest. These policies created one of the most successful and lengthy coalitions in history, but they also created one of longest and most difficult conflicts.

Institutional Changes and Economic Policy

The government used a series of instruments to achieve its objectives, which shifted over time. Some of these measures had been tested during the previous decade, many were being further elaborated, and others were entirely new. As Prebisch[4] indicates, the state is not an abstract entity but rather a real one, run by civil servants, real people, who have specific self-interests. It is for this reason that many of the objectives were being redefined, to attend to the demands of the members of the governing coalition and mollify the complaints of those who had been excluded.

The exchange control mechanisms became increasingly complex, contrary to those of the rest of the world, which had gone about simplifying theirs. Various rates were established, among them the official rate, the preferential one, and a free market rate, for buyers and sellers. Profits from operations depended more on the particular Central Bank regulation, or *circular*, of the currency exchange than the actual operations. Importation required permits granted according to the government's preestablished priorities. Exchange regulations were determined by an administrative entity granted broad discretion, which allowed for considerable corruption. (Thus, auto imports at official rates, which were prohibited for years, were negotiated on the black market with large profits). Furthermore, if any particular was issued an import permit, this did not mean that there was previous confirmation of availability of the currency necessary, often causing long waiting lists of clients to which the Central Bank then delayed or denied access to currency, causing financial and trade problems.

Overvaluation of the peso was used to keep prices on primary products low and in this way – it was thought – prevent an increase in the cost of living. Overvaluation punished exporters but failed to make imports more affordable, not only because they were sold at a different exchange rate but also because there were quantitative restrictions and they required a permit that was often not granted if the good was also produced locally. Whereas imports of industrial inputs were cheaper, imports of finished products were practically prohibited, and capital goods became much more costly.

---

4 Raúl Prebisch, *La Crisis del Desarrollo Argentino: de la Frustración al Crecimiento Vigoroso*, Buenos Aires, El Ateneo, 1986.

Following the 1951–1952 crises, in order to compensate for the over-valuation of the peso and improve agricultural conditions, support prices by which the IAPI[5] bought crops were established. Because these prices were higher than market prices (which was the price abroad multiplied by the official exchange rate, but not at the free exchange rate), subsidies were paid to the producers with rediscounts from the Central Bank, which was one of the primary causes of inflation. The government that had imposed a tax by means of the exchange rate later partially compensated for it with a subsidy, just one of many inconsistencies with these policies.

Supply Problems: Balance-of-Payments Crisis

Industries still needed to import fuel, raw materials and intermediate goods, but substitution of consumer goods, which in the beginning saved curren-cies, did not compensate the need for imports of industrial inputs. There were repeated problems in the balance of payments because as manufactur-ing increased, imports did the same but, exports – primarily agricultural and livestock – did not increase at the same rate. In order to balance the payments account, the government should improved agricultural and live-stock prices. To do that, the peso was devalued, which in turn increased prices on food and caused real wages to fall and industrial production and employment opportunities to wane. Unions demanded salary raises and entrepreneurs accepted, provided either that the same was done with prices or that they were granted loans at subsidized rates. Fuel supplies had reached a critical low; imports came to represent almost a quarter of the total fuel supply and were essential for maintaining the pace of production (see Table 4.1).

Capital Formation Problems

As we have already seen, at the beginning of the twentieth century and during a period of strong growth, fixed gross investment as a portion of GDP was greater than 30% for some years.[6] The Great War caused a significant drop in the investment rate as a result of two interrelated factors: the drop in foreign investment flows and the contraction in imports because

---

5 Argentine Institute for Trade Promotion (*Instituto Argentino de Promoción del Intercambio*).

6 Investment estimates are from CEPAL, *El Desarrollo Económico de la Argentina*, Appendix III, p. 77, Appendix IV, p. 107, and Appendix VII, p. 243, Santiago de Chile, June 1958. As shown in Chapter 2, the estimates from CEPAL were made by taking the yearly flows of imports of capital goods as indicators of investment. Although the most reliable available, the estimate is problematic because in the official source, imports are registered until 1930 at official prices (*aforos*) and not market prices. From 1906 to 1922 the estimates are undervalued because official prices remained unchanged during those years, whereas during the wars there was a sharp increase in market prices.

Table 4.1. *Fuel Imports, 1940–1955*
(in percentage of total)

Year	Fuel Imports
1940	16.0
1941	14.5
1942	8.6
1943	9.6
1944	8.1
1945	8.4
1946	12.2
1947	7.4
1948	11.2
1949	10.5
1950	12.3
1951	14.9
1952	21.0
1953	24.3
1954	18.5
1955	17.3

Source: Carmen Llorens de Azar, with María
Inés Danelotti, Antonio Pablo Grippo, Dora
Delia Puente, *Argentina, Evolución Económica,
1915–1976*, Fundación Banco de Boston,
Buenos Aires, 1977, pp. 76 and 121.

of constraints resulting from the war (difficulties of shipping in the Atlantic and the fact that industrial countries that exported capital goods directed their production to strictly war needs) (see Figure 4.1).

At the end of the war, with the return to normalcy, despite the fact that foreign investment dropped off considerably, as Alan Taylor[7] has pointed out, investment recuperated (although it was affected by the highest prices of capital goods). Furthermore, significant investments in infrastructure, railroads, and ports had reached remarkable levels before the war and investment needs were different in sectors that required less substantial investment. As we have seen, these investments were greatest in the industrial sector (machinery and equipment).

The 1930 crisis caused a renewed contraction of investment (and also proportionate with regard to GDP) although, despite difficult conditions, this investment rebounded after 1935 (as can be seen in Figure 4.1). A remarkable drop in investment resulted from World War II. Again, a

7 Alan Taylor, "Argentina and the World Capital Market: Saving, Investment and International Capital Mobility in the Twentieth Century," NBER Working Paper W6302, 1997.

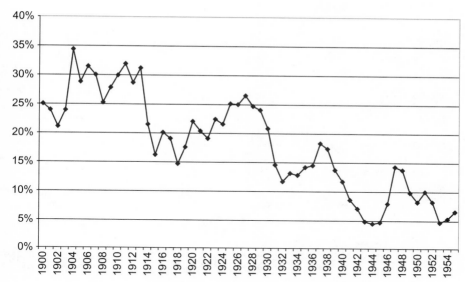

Figure 4.1. Fixed Gross Investment as a Percentage of GDP at Factor Costs, Holding Prices Constant, 1900–1955. *Source:* BCRA until 1949, and between 1950–1955, CEPAL.

supply shock was caused by industrialized countries producing strictly for war consumption and impeded Argentina's access to imported capital goods for more than six years, adding to the difficulties that had begun with the 1930 crisis. With the end of World War II, Argentina found itself, contrary to the eve of the World War I, or even during the 1920s, with modern stock and at the cutting edge of technology of the period with regard to infrastructure, machinery, equipment, and transportation. In the decade and half since the 1930s, much of this machinery had become obsolete or needed to be renewed.

Amid the enormous supply restrictions endured during the war years, Argentine technicians, who had specialized in repairing imported machinery, had achieved a maintenance miracle, making obsolete machinery work by refitting, repairing, or modifying it to be applied to light manufacturing on which the significant industrial growth of the war years was based. Despite the difficulties faced by manufacturers during the conflict, between 1939 and 1945, industrial production, measured at constant prices, increased to a rate of 3.6% annually.[8] Thus, industrial growth of the period was characterized by lack of capitalization and technology, and

8 Victor Bulmer Thomas, *The Economic History of Latin America since Independence*, Cambridge, Cambridge University Press, 2003, p. 244.

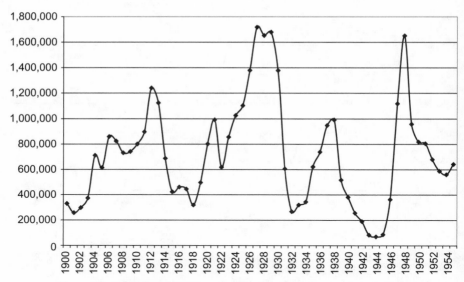

Figure 4.2. Evolution of Machinery and Equipment Imports, 1900–1955 (in thousands of 1950 pesos). *Source:* CEPAL, *El Desarrollo Económico de la Argentina*, Santiago de Chile, CEPAL, 1958.

its notorious inefficiencies. Transportation, energy, and infrastructure suffered the greatest deficiencies. With the return to normalcy, investments were expected to rebound considerably, reaching even higher levels than usual because for years the country had been sorely in need of capital investment.

This situation was further aggravated by the fact that the United States prohibited exports of strategic goods to countries it believed were sympathetic to the Axis powers, and Argentina was considered one of them. These restrictions continued immediately following the war and gave a considerable advantage to Brazil (the Volta Redonda steel mill was constructed with U.S. help) and discriminated against Argentina.[9]

At any rate, with a substantial amount in reserves, imports rose starting in 1946, reaching 8.1% of GDP. Restrictions on imports, imposed during the 1930 crisis, had been lifted during the war because there was nothing to import anyway. So in the end the demand for imports increased significantly, which was determined without estimating the evolution of the future availability of currencies (see Figure 4.2).

Because Argentina is not a producer of capital goods, imports of machinery and equipment represent a very high proportion of gross fixed

9 Carlos Escudé, *Gran Bretaña, Estados Unidos y la Declinación Argentina 1942–1949*, Belgrano, Buenos Aires, 1983.

investment (GFI). This is seen in Figures 4.2 and 4.4 on gross fixed investment, where the peaks in GFI coincide with those of heavy machinery
imports. But the recovery in investment was short lived. In 1949, after
signing the agreements with Great Britain (accepting the British proposal
to pay debt with its assets in Argentina) and using most of its available currencies, which had reached the remarkable sum of 2,539 million pesos, the
country was faced with something that would reoccur in subsequent years,
its first balance-of-payments crisis. While reserves dropped substantially,
import commitments assumed were not sufficiently backed by foreign currencies (1949 imports reached 48.5% of reserves that year). Thanks to a
loan from Eximbank of the United States, the country was able to overcome
the balance-of-payments crisis.

The years of abundance had come to an end, and the country had to ration
its diminished availability of foreign currencies. Restrictions on obtaining
foreign exchange were generally the result of a policy that discriminated
against exports and specifically designed somewhat in accordance with
the strategy of industrial development. This strategy protected industries
which produced consumption goods by prohibiting the import of those
goods, providing favorable exchange rates and subsidized loans, thereby creating a protected domestic market. Although traditional exports stagnated,
the industrial strategy that protected consumption industries did not solve
two serious problems that would soon arise. Whereas import substitution of
finished goods initially saved foreign exchange, growth in light industries
increasingly required raw materials and intermediate goods that had to be
imported. Paradoxically, net substitution turned out to be negative. Faced
with this restriction, government measures, which prioritized the assignment of currencies for raw materials and primary products, were discriminatory with respect to capital goods imports, which caused the contraction
in GFI, especially in machinery and equipment and transportation material.

Multiple Exchange Rates

The 1933 reform of the exchange control regime had established several
different exchange rates. In 1946 the system became much more complex,
with buyer, seller, preferential, and free rates. Whereas raw material and
primary goods imports had preferential rates, the same was not true for
capital goods. Furthermore, quantitative priorities to grant exchange permits favored raw materials and primary products (see Tables 4.2 and 4.3).

Actually regulations tended to favor existing industries that needed to
import inputs in order to continue production, but that also were the
industries that provided the greatest number of jobs. The priority – as in
other parts of the world – was to maintain full employment. The temporary
trade off, however, was negative because at the end of the Peronist period

Table 4.2. *Exchange Rates at Which Various Products Are Negotiated*

Date	Product or Article	Type of Exchange Rate
January 09	Cow's ear (hair)	Preferential
January 16	Whole cow spleen, powdered	Preferential
February 18	Cheese, lard, and casein	60% Preferential
		40% Open market
February 27	Frozen and cooked beef	Preferential
April 24	Industrial ethyl alcohol, arms and spare parts, bullets and lead munitions	Open market
July 10	White cement	Open market
July 16	Frozen chicken and hens	Open market
July 21	Raw or scoured wool	50% basic, 50% preferential
July 23	Virgin wool and pulled wool	50% basic, 50% preferential
September 02	Conserved meats, conserved tongue, meat prepared pastes, meat prepared with vegetables, other canned meat products prepared in various ways	Open market
September 09	Shredded or ground bone, including calcined bone, in 2.5-in. tubes, bone meal and ash, shredded or ground bone splinters and hooves	Open market
September 16	Cured or salted beef	50% open, 50% preferential
October 14	Quebracho tree and urunday extract	60% preferential, 40% open market
November 21	Essences or essential oils of mint and lemon	Open market
November 21	Uncovered sheep hides	50% basic, 50% preferential

Source: BCRA Yearbook.

the bottlenecks, particularly in transportation and equipment, had negative repercussions for growth (see the *Prebisch Report* in Chapter 5).

The result of these circumstances, and of the vested interests involved, ended up favoring the development of labor-intensive industries that were small scale and had obsolete, low-tech equipment. It was no longer a question of catching up, as in the years before World War I. Between 1945 and 1955, the manufacturing industry remained closed to external capital and technology flows and "given the paucity of internal technological development, capital accumulation during those years included relatively outdated technologies and processes. This was particularly notorious in sectors in which technology was experiencing an explosive transformation internationally."[10]

10 Jorge Katz, "Una Interpretación de Largo Plazo del Crecimiento Industrial Argentino", *Desarrollo Económico*, vol. 8, no. 32, 1969, p. 25.

Table 4.3. *Exchange Rates*

		1943–1948	1949	1950–1952
Buyer	Basic	3.36	3.36 (1)	5.00 (dev 49%)
	Preferential	3.98	4.83 (A)	7.5 (dev 42%)
			5.73 (dev 33%)	
Seller	Basic	4.23	6.09 (dev 44%)	7.5 (dev 23%)
	Preferential	3.73	3.73 (A)	5.00 (dev 10%)
			5.37 (B)	
Open		4.12	5.87	14.2 (2)
Corporation for the	A	4.55		
Promotion of	B	4.85		
Exchange		4.94		
Bids				

Note: (1) Meat products, some grains, and oil seeds. Buyer preferential (B) Various agricultural and cattle and manufactured products. Seller preferential (B) Combined. Raw materials and popular consumption items. (2) In 1950, 10.72; in 1951, 14.2; and in 1952, 14.03.

Sources: FIEL, *El Control de Cambios en la Argentina:Liberación Cambiaria y Crecimiento*, Buenos Aires, Manantial, 1987. Open exchange rate in Rafael Olarra Jiménez, *Evolución Monetaria Argentina*, Buenos Aires, Ed. Universitaria, 1968, p. 108.

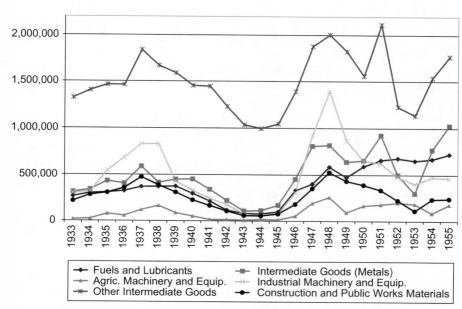

Figure 4.3. Import Categories (in thousands of pesos at 1950 prices). *Source:*
CEPAL, *El Desarrollo Económico de la Argentina*, Santiago de Chile, CEPAL, 1958,
p. 109.

Table 4.4. *Prices of Capital Goods in Argentina Relative to Prices for All Nongovernment Expenditures, June 1962 and 1935–1938, Compared with U.S. Prices (Houston and Los Angeles = 100 in June 1962)*

	Buenos Aires, June 1962	Buenos Aires: Estimate for 1935–1938
Construction	112	94
New transport equipment	326	109
New machinery and other equipment	254	176

Source: Carlos Díaz Alejandro, *Essays on the Economic History of the Argentine Republic*, New Haven and London, Yale University Press, 1970, p. 525.

The prohibitively high cost of capital goods, at times three times those of the United States, explains the low level of investment in them, according to Carlos Díaz Alejandro. In one of his earlier works, Díaz Alejandro points out: "The extraordinary increases in relative prices of capital goods resulted first from the war and afterwards, from those government policies that also led to low rates of capital formation and technological change."[11]

The same author cites a work by CONADE, in which he shows that prices of capital goods are much higher in Argentina than in the rest of the world. "Besides CONADE calculation of the Argentine GNP for 1960, *measure in current U.S. dollar prices*, shows gross domestic fixed capital formation of only 14% of GNP, in contrast with a share of 23% when all GNP components are measure at 1960 Argentine prices."[12]

Alan Taylor more recently pointed out that the high cost of capital goods was one of the factors involved in the industrial stagnation during the second half of the twentieth century: "The postwar turn toward inward-looking trade policies . . . had accumulation (and growth) implications as they distorted the domestic cost of capital goods. . . . Such price distortions diminished the incentives for accumulation, and, thus, the motivation for foreign capital inflows."[13] Taylor echoes what Díaz Alejandro had already asserted: "Real capital formation in the form of new producers' durable equipment during 1935–61 was determined mainly by supply conditions, which were heavily influenced by post-war public foreign trade policies."[14] Given the distortions caused by exchange and customs mechanisms, a unit of production required greater effort than in developed countries because producing large output requires greater savings than in those countries.

11 Carlos Díaz Alejandro, *Essays on the Economic History of the Argentine Republic*, New Haven and London, Yale University Press, 1970, pp. 310–311.
12 Ibid., pp. 319–320.
13 Alan Taylor, "Argentina and the World Capital Market", pp. 13–14.
14 Carlos Díaz Alejandro, *Essays*, p. 310.

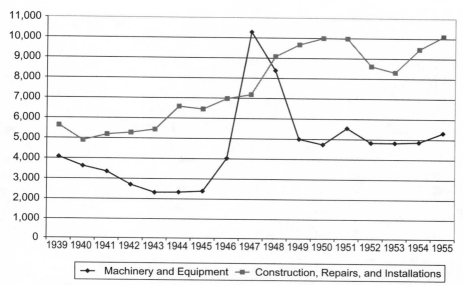

Figure 4.4. Gross Fixed Investment (by Type), 1939–1955 (in millions of 1950 pesos). *Source:* CEPAL, *El Desarrollo Económico de la Argentina*, Santiago de Chile, CEPAL, 1958, p. 82.

The Components of Investment: Machinery, Equipment, and Construction

In addition to investment estimates, it is important to point out that, when referring to the total GFI irrespective of its particular items, we must separate investment in reproducible goods, like machinery and equipment, from those that are not, like construction goods. In the case of Argentina, the GFI in construction, repairs, and installations was greater during each of the years in question (except 1947) than GFI in machinery and equipment, as illustrated in Figure 4.4. This affected the extent to which the GFI influenced growth of GDP and of productivity (the K/O ratio) over the total GFI stock. On this, see Figure 4.5.

Capital Productivity

In his groundbreaking work, Díaz Alejandro also maintained that capital productivity was greater in the United States than in Argentina, but that this was not a result of only investment estimates with a domestic price structure in 1951 completely distorted by regulations. At international prices, or using the 1935 price structure, investment in capital goods would have been much less. According to Díaz Alejandro, "there is little doubt that capital goods prices rose substantially relative to the GNP deflator after 1935–38. . . . As a result, Argentine prices of capital goods have reached

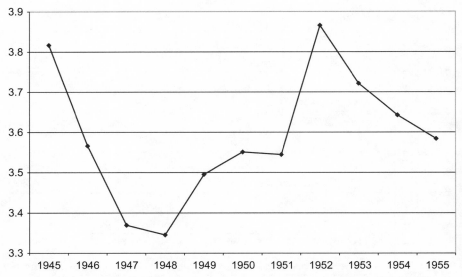

Figure 4.5. Capital–Product Ratio, 1945–1955 (at 1955 prices). *Source:* CEPAL, *El Desarrollo Económico de la Argentina*, Santiago de Chile, CEPAL, 1958, p. 103.

levels that are much higher than those of most other countries."[15] This can be seen in Table 4.5. This affected the extent to which the GFI influenced growth of GDP and of productivity (the K/O ratio) over the total GFI stock.

Capital productivity in the manufacturing sector was also low compared with other countries, as seen in Table 4.6.

Labor Productivity

As previously indicated, Katz has studied the technological lags of the industrial structure under a closed economy between 1950 and 1955.[16] The industrial structure was characterized by low labor productivity; it was not capital intensive, often running on obsolete machinery, and still functioning thanks to Argentine creativity. On average, labor productivity at the stage of industrialization of import substitutions was around 40% of that of the United States.[17]

The decision to assign resources to modern or traditional activities also affected possibilities for growth. Probably the most serious problem during

15 Ibid.
16 Jorge Katz, "Una Interpretación de Largo Plazo del Crecimiento Industrial Argentino," *Desarrollo Económico*, vol. 8, no. 32, 1969.
17 Alejandro, *Essays*, p. 254.

Table 4.5. *Composition of Apparent Domestic Absorption during 1950–1951 (percentage of total)*

	New BCRA Current Prices	Old Series Current Prices	New BCRA 1960 Prices	Estimates 1935 Prices
Private consumption	70.4	65.6	73.6	74.5
Public consumption	9.9	12.1	9.4	13.4
Private construction	9.1	8.4	7.0	4.0
Public construction	4.5	5.5	3.3	3.1
Transport equipment	0.8	1.4	1.2	0.4
Other new machinery and equipment	4.6	4.9	4.8	3.3
Repairs	0.8	2.0	0.7	1.3
TOTAL	100.0	100.0	100.0	100.0
All construction	13.6	13.9	10.3	7.1
All new machinery and equipment	5.4	6.3	6.0	3.7
All gross fixed capital formation	19.7	22.3	17.0	12.1

Source: Carlos Díaz Alejandro, *Essays on the Economic History of the Argentine Republic*, New Haven and London, Yale University Press, 1970, p. 314.

Table 4.6. *Technology: Power by Equipment in Manufacturing Sectors, 1948*

	Power Consumption per Employee			Difference in Technology[a]	
	Argentina	Australia	Brazil	Australia/ Argentina (%)	Brazil/ Argentina (%)
Foodstuffs, soft drinks, and tobacco	2.52	3.55	2.56	40.9	1.6
Textiles	1.25	2.03	1.54	62.4	23.2
Manufacture goods	0.26	0.32	0.37	23.1	42.3
Wood and furniture	1.47	4.94	2.19	236.1	49.0
Paper	2.85	5.86	6.4	105.6	124.6
Presses	1.2	1.63	0.68	35.8	−43.3
Leather	1.51	2.25	1.89	49.0	25.2
Rubber	3.56	6.03	4.1	69.4	15.2
Chemicals, petroleum	3.17	5.01	2.47	58.0	−22.1
Nonmetallic minerals	1.99	6.02	1.31	202.5	−34.2
Basic metals	2.67	8.77	3.42	228.5	28.1
Other metal products	1.29	2.27	1.79	76.0	38.8
Other manufactured goods	0.97	1.63	0.81	68.0	−16.5
TOTAL	1.92	3.12	2.01	62.5	4.7

[a] Difference in technology: percentage quotient of power consumption per employee in Brazil and Australia compared with the same ratio in Argentina.

Source: Guillermo Vitelli, *LosDos Siglos de la Argentina: Historia Económica Comparada*, Buenos Aires, Prendergast, 1999.

Table 4.7. *Comparison of Labor Productivity by Sector*

Year	Industry			Rural Sector		
	Employees	Product	Product/Employee	Employees	Product	Product/Employee
1913	410,201	3,022,300,000	7,367.85	–	–	–
1914	–	–	–	619,811	2,838,600,000	4,579.78
1937	642,901	7,629,200,000	11,866.83	205,460	5,232,600,000	25,467.73
1946	938,387	11,716,000,000	12,485.25	–	–	–

Source: National Census (*Censos Nacionales*), and Orlando Ferreres, *Dos siglos de economía argentina (1810–2004): Historia argentina en cifras*, Buenos Aires, El Ateneo y Fundación Norte y Sur, 2005.

the war years and the postwar period had to do with shift of labor from agriculture to the industrial and service sectors (see Table 4.7). In countries in which the marginal labor productivity in the rural sector is nearly zero (Lewis[18]), any rural to urban demographic labor shift increases GDP. This was probably not the case for Argentina.[19]

With regard to the first case, perhaps because there never was a surplus of labor in the rural sector, from early on, the need for labor was obviated with intensive investment in machinery. Thus, it was unlikely that Argentina would experience a notable increase in labor productivity when this labor supply was transferred from an agricultural sector, which was not very labor intensive, to the manufacturing sector, scarce in capital goods and outdated in technology.

On the other hand, labor shifted to the service sector that was, unlike in other parts of the world (still in the 1980s), not modernized but rather involved in traditional activities such as domestic service, small businesses, and public service.

The Argentine Position in International Trade

Those economic policies resulted in strong antiexport bias and were reflected in a stagnation and decline in exports. Except for the brief postwar boom, Argentine exports never again reached in current dollar values their 1928 levels until the 1960s. The decline in exports had its counterpart in import limits that forced rationing of foreign exchanges according to the criteria discussed in this chapter.

It is true that toward the end of the war and following the fall in international trade after the 1930 crisis a gloomy outlook prevailed, but it is also

18 See W. Arthur Lewis, "Economic Development with Unlimited Supplies of Labour," *Manchester School of Economic and Social Studies*, vol. XXIII, no. 2, May 1954.

19 Juan Llach, *Reconstrucción o estancamiento*, Buenos Aires, Thesis, 1987.

true that from the start of the 1950s worldwide trade showed a remarkable expansion, which continued until the 1970s. While gross world product grew, between 1950 and 1970, 4.9% annually, trade grew still more, by 7.9%.[20] However, the greatest expansion was seen in industrial production, and agriculture suffered because of protectionist trends, particularly following the establishment of the European Community and their formulation of a Common Agricultural Policy.

At any rate, the primary agricultural and livestock exporting countries like Australia, which did not have a particularly remarkable economic performance during the postwar years, could enjoy greater participation in exports. Although in Australia a similar policy of industrial substitution was applied, it did not discriminate against agricultural and livestock exports, but rather, these exports had support from the government through trade and tariff policies and other measures.[21] With industrialization policies similar to Argentina's, Brazil's performance was also better, because it adopted policies that were more favorable to exports.[22] Argentine participation in world trade dropped from 0.7% in 1950 to 0.25% in 1973, during the years of booming foreign trade.[23]

Trade Deficits, Balance-of-Payments Crisis and Growth

The fall in demand and in the value of exports in the 1930s caused repeated trade deficits and imposed severe restrictions on imports. Everything changed when the war broke out in 1939, and, on the contrary, there were continuous and growing trade surpluses and legal restrictions on imports were lifted.[24] Trade surpluses from 1939 until 1946 reached historic levels. (The greatest surplus was seen in 1946, $499.4 million.) The years 1946 to 1948 were exceptional both in volume and in prices; exports increased 18% annually and prices 17.6% annually (see Figure 4.6). However, because once the war ended, imports rebounded heftily and the trade gap began to shrink, these were actually an indication that normalcy had returned.

---

20 Data from Angus Maddison, *The World Economy: Historical Statistics*, Paris, OECD Development Centre, 2003, pp. 127–128.
21 Carlos Díaz Alejandro, "Argentina, Australia and Brazil before 1929", in *Argentina, Australia and Canada: Studies in Comparative Development, 1870–1965*, ed. D. C. M Platt and Guido Di Tella, London, Macmillan/St. Anthony's College, 1985, p. 106.
22 Ibid.
23 Ibid.
24 See the corresponding law in the Appendix.

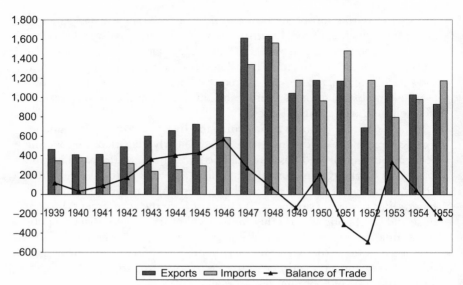

Figure 4.6. Exports, Imports, and the Balance of Trade, 1939–1955 (in millions of current dollars). *Source:* INDEC, www.indec.gov.ar.

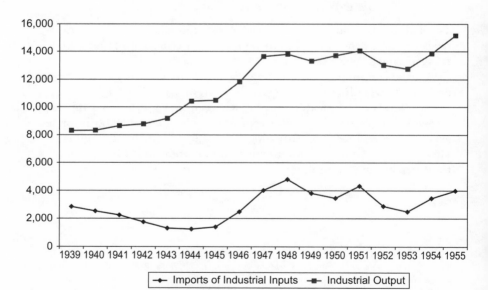

Figure 4.7. Relation between Industrial Inputs Imports and Gross Industrial Output (in millons of 1950 pesos). *Note:* Industrial primary product imports include fuel and lubricants, intermediate goods (metals), machinery and industrial equipment, and other intermediate goods. *Source:* CEPAL, *El Desarrollo Económico de la Argentina*, Santiago de Chile, CEPAL, 1958.

Starting in 1948 exports plummeted because of a downward trend of international prices caused by the upturn in European agricultural production, which increased supply. Two circumstances affected external accounts and inhibited economic growth: one was the desperate need in 1948 for equipment – the supply of which had been frozen during the war; the other was, paradoxically, that as local industries grew, they required more industrial inputs (raw materials and intermediate goods), but lacked the currency with which to buy them, despite having managed to save currency by substituting imports of consumer goods (negative net substitution). Not only did Argentina have to import capital goods, but industry also urgently needed imports of raw materials and intermediate goods (see Figure 4.7).

The need to maintain the steady pace of imports in order to continue to grow was at odds with the stagnation in exports. Furthermore, the industries that had come into being under protection were in no condition to compete in international markets. Contrary to the rhetoric of the period that blamed external factors, these limitations sprang from misguided domestic policies in the postwar period. Nevertheless, the terms of trade had an undeniable effect on the Argentine economy because they had been dropping since 1948, and when they improved, as in 1953, import capacity increased, although they continue falling until 1955 (see Table 4.8). Thus, overall, domestic policy had a greater effect on economic conditions.

While the economy grew, and so did the aggregate labor income earned with it, domestic consumption of exportable goods increased, leaving less surplus for export abroad (see Table 4.9).

At the start of the Perón period, there was a general assumption that a future war would place Argentine exports in a privileged position and because of the enormous quantity of reserves accumulated, the government allowed these reserves to be spent not only on assets and repayment of the debt but also on importing the greatest amount of goods possible. Although the threat of another war loomed, the war never materialized. So, when in 1949 the reserves were all used up, Argentina had its first payment crisis (see Figure 4.8). The crisis was to be repeated during successive stop-and-go cycles, with very negative consequences.

The government resolved the problem of the near cessation of payments with a loan from the Eximbank (even though the president had said he'd sooner cut his hands off than resort to foreign credit). In any case, the *fiesta* was over. Although severe restrictions were imposed on imports, whereby intermediate goods (industrial imported inputs) were given priority over capital goods, using foreign exchange rates, tariffs, and limits on quantity, foreign exchange permits also represented a change in economic management. Alfredo Gomez Morales, a respected professional who replaced Miguel Miranda, a wealthy and extravagant entrepreneur, as leader of the economic team, took measures to correct the imbalance.

Table 4.8. *Evolution of Exports, Grain and Seed Oil Crops, and Terms of Trade index (exports in millions of dollars, crops in thousands of tons, and percentages; index: 1938 = 100)*

Year	Exports	Percent Change	Crops	Percent Change	Terms of Trade
1939	478.2	–	17,630	–	96.1
1940	430.2	–10.04	22,383	26.96	89.9
1941	458.3	6.53	19,036	–14.96	92.8
1942	505.3	10.26	11,473	–39.73	84.3
1943	611.4	21.00	20,786	81.18	86.8
1944	686.5	12.28	11,079	–46.70	80.6
1945	737.6	7.44	11,667	5.30	89.6
1946	1175.3	59.34	15,950	36.72	125.4
1947	1614.3	37.35	16,146	1.23	132.3
1948	1626.8	0.77	12,098	–25.07	151.9
1949	933.8	–42.60	8,863	–26.74	135.6
1950	1167.6	25.04	12,622	42.42	127.5
1951	1169.4	0.15	6,570	–47.95	121.2
1952	687.8	–41.18	16,691	154.06	95.9
1953	1125.1	63.58	14,431	–13.54	111.7
1954	1026.6	–8.75	14,255	–1.22	95.9
1955	928.6	–9.55	13,147	–7.78	95.9

Sources: Orlando Ferreres, *Dos Siglos de Economía Argentina (1810–2004)*, Buenos Aires, Fundación Norte y Sur; and El Ateneo, 2005, Secretaría de Estado de Agricultura y Ganadería, Junta Nacional de Granos, *Estadísticas de Área Cultivada, Rendimiento, Producción y Exportación de Granos: Totales del País, 1900–1975*, Buenos Aires, 1975; M. Balboa, "La Evolución del Balance de Pagos de la República Argentina, 1913–1950", *Desarrollo Económico*, no. 45, April–June 1972; CEPAL, *Estadísticas Económicas de Corto Plazo de la Argentina: Sector Externo y Condiciones Económicas Internacionales*, Buenos Aires, 1986.

One of these measures was a slight devaluation of the peso in 1950, following Great Britain, where the pound was devalued in 1949. Public expenditures were reduced by postponing the second five-year plan for public works projects on infrastructure. Further cuts were required when, to make matters worse, there were serious droughts that wreaked havoc on the 1951–1952 crops and caused exports to drop in 1952 by 26.7% compared with the previous year.

Perón himself declared that the years of abundance belonged to the past, and called a Productivity Congress, before freezing salaries from 1952 to 1954. Workers protested the implementation of those measures, behavior that unleashed the government's severely repressive policies under the state of "internal war," which was declared in 1951 and which suspended constitutional guarantees. Many workers and opposition leaders were imprisoned. Nevertheless, these adjustments helped to improve the domestic and external sectors of the economy. The annual inflation rate, which had reached an exorbitant 38.8% in 1952, was reduced to 44.0% and its effects on

Table 4.9. *Evolution of Aggregate Wage Earnings and Exports (real wages in constant pesos, exports in millions of dollars)*

Year	Industrial Wage	Employees	Aggregate Wage	Change	Exports	Change
1939	1,085.32	5,066.8	5,499,099.38	–	478.2	–
1940	1,095.38	5,164.9	5,657,528.16	2.88	430.2	−10.04
1941	1,098.86	5,275.1	5,796,596.39	2.46	458.3	6.53
1942	1,129.94	5,394.2	6,095,122.35	5.15	505.3	10.26
1943	1,187.54	5,509.7	6,542,989.14	7.35	611.4	21.00
1944	1,285.34	5,606.6	7,206,387.24	10.14	686.5	12.28
1945	1,211.69	5,703.9	6,911,358.59	−4.09	737.6	7.44
1946	1,166.35	5,818.4	6,786,290.84	−1.81	1175.3	59.34
1947	1,408.13	5,970.4	8,407,099.35	23.88	1614.3	37.35
1948	1,769.60	6,124.9	10,838,623.04	28.92	1626.8	0.77
1949	1,785.96	6,257.3	11,175,287.51	3.11	933.8	−42.60
1950	1,732.10	6,438.1	11,151,433.01	−0.21	1167.6	25.04
1951	1,581.43	6,497.7	10,275,657.71	−7.85	1169.4	0.15
1952	1,446.55	6,477.6	9,370,172.28	−8.81	687.8	−41.18
1953	1,513.04	6,419.6	9,713,111.58	3.66	1125.1	63.58
1954	1,668.82	6,517.1	10,875,866.82	11.97	1026.6	−8.75
1955	1,619.68	6,632.5	10,742,527.60	−1.23	928.6	−9.55

Source: Orlando Ferreres, *Dos Siglos de Economía Argentina (1810–2004): Historia Argentina en Cifras*, Buenos Aires, El Ateneo y Fundación Norte y Sur, 2005.

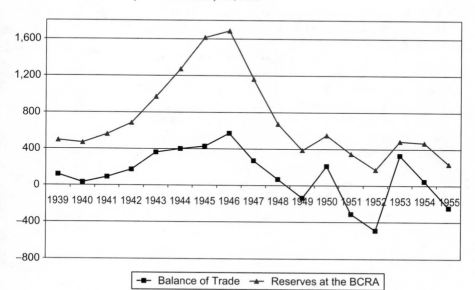

Figure 4.8. Evolution of Exports and Reserves at the Argentine Republic Central Bank (BCRA) (in millions of dollars). *Source:* INDEC, www.indec.gov.ar, and BCRA Yearbooks, 1939–1955.

public finances and the balance of payments – coupled with the improvement in international prices in 1953 – allowed the government to relax the quite nearly orthodox measures it had imposed. Starting in 1953, a recovery ensued and continued through Perón's defeat in 1955, leaving lingering problems that were a permanent source of conflict in subsequent decades and that worsened when he returned to power eighteen years later, culminating in a severe financial crisis after his death in 1975.

The industrial model that had been adopted led to a dead end; the demand for industrial imports increased to a point where it outpaced that of exports, and when the imbalance had exhausted reserves, they were left with no other alternative than to take measures to curb imports and encourage exports in order to acquire foreign currency. This required devaluing the local currency to increase the earnings, and with it the production of exportable goods, while simultaneously reducing consumption of imports as well as of domestic products that were part of the exportable goods supply. These same circumstances were to repeat themselves in the following decades (see Chapters 5–8). A severe recession followed, but these were the measures that international financial organizations – the IMF – recommended throughout the world (whether Chile or Great Britain). It was believed the measures would diminish internal absorption, decrease public spending, and curb monetary expansion (reducing subsidized credits), as well as increase fares for transportation and tariffs of public services. Although Argentina was not affiliated with the IMF until 1956, somehow the country managed to follow its policies, approaches that were quite nearly orthodox.[25]

Applying these policies affected entrepreneurs, workers, the public sector, and a huge urban population that lived on subsidized services and resulted in a long-feared recession; in 1952 GDP fell by 5%. Of course facing the consequences of these series of measures would be a nightmare for any government, threatening its very existence. Although the concept that people cannot spend more than they produce is simple, they often feel that the remedy is worse: to work more, only to consume less – a remedy that had previously only been accepted in extremely serious circumstances. This explains why the measures implemented had only limited effects and ended up failing. As for Perón, his economic framework had already begun to reveal problems during his regime, problems that he failed to resolve in his last tenure in office. And he did not even live to see the worst of these consequences.

25 Eprime Eshag y Rosemary Thorp, "Las Consecuencias Económicas y Sociales de las Políticas Ortodoxas Aplicadas en la Argentina Durante los Años de Postguerra", *Desarrollo Económico*, vol. 4, no. 16, April–June 1965.

Policy Instruments

The Central Bank

As we have seen, many of these measures, which were more limited in scope, had begun to be implemented in the 1930s. Exchange control and rediscounts had been used at the reformed Currency Board, but Prebisch points out that the rediscounts had originally been conceived with different objectives. He claimed that the government in 1931 applied the old rule of rediscounting commercial documents, which it had not done prior to this date because of the feat of inflation. For the first time the Currency Board issued money backed by these documents. He notes that "rediscounts were used sparingly to replenish cash in the banks and not to make new loans."[26] There was a change in 1932, and an emergency law permitted the board "to issue new bills backed by public debt to pay urgent commitments that were exhausting the Treasury. With all of these changes, the primitive system of the Currency Board disappears," and the way was thus prepared for the creation of the Central Bank.[27] These tools were created during a crisis, and it was assumed that they would only last as long as the crisis.[28]

What made Peronism different was not the introduction of these new institutions, but rather that he elaborated and broadened existing ones and made them a permanent feature of the economy. Furthermore, he conceived of them explicitly as instruments that the state should utilize to achieve the goals of maintaining full employment, spreading industrialization in the country and improving workers' real wages.

In 1947 the government outlined its political objectives. In the BCRA Yearbook it argued that the war forced it "to intervene more actively in the economy" and forced it to create a central command of the monetary-economic policy, and this could only be achieved by the creation of a "nationalized Central Bank," among whose functions were both a regulator and a promoter of economic growth.[29]

Nationalization of Deposits; Reform of the Organic Law of the Central Bank, 1946; 1947 Reforms. Most likely at the request of Perón himself and to avoid delays in Congress, in April 1946, shortly before it assumed office, the Farrel government reformed the 1935 Central Bank statutes, changing

---

26 Raúl Prebisch, "La Experiencia del Banco Central Argentino", en *El Banco Central de la República Argentina en su 50 aniversario, 1935–1985*, Buenos Aires, Banco Central, 1986, p. 32.
27 Prebisch, "La experiencia," p. 20.
28 Ibid., p. 50.
29 BCRA Yearbook, 1947.

the bank's functions. Not long after, all of the deposits were transferred from the banking system to the Central Bank that was nationalized and was no longer a mixed capital company (both private and state owned), although it maintained some autonomy from the executive branch. The commercial banks became agents of the Central Bank, which not only maintained the monopoly on monetary issues and the role of supervising the financial system but also controlled all of the deposits in the commercial banks, lending those funds wherever it wanted.

It was argued that the government's constitutional monetary powers over the monetary base were not limited to currency but also encompassed bank deposits, so that it had full control over all monetary instruments (adding deposits to the monetary base), which were consequently guaranteed by the National Government. By means of rediscounts, the Central Bank supplied banks with funds for lending, so that they could continue to perform their commercial functions. The amount of these rediscounts was not tied to the volume of deposits of each. The Central Bank had full discretion in this regard. Certain banks, especially official ones, got preferential treatment, and it was industry that was primarily favored. Individuals with closed ties to official circles were also likely to be favored. The Central Bank paid private banks for the deposits transferred to it, and it charged them for the rediscount granted, but at a negative real interest rate. The banks perceived a fee for administrative its costs. That is why, for many, these operations were not entirely risky but in fact frequently profitable, causing few complaints.

The Central Bank established an interest rate that remained unchanged for a long time of 5–6%, which was well below the rate of inflation.[30] Because the demand for credit was greater than the supply, it was rationed according to supposedly objective criteria, but the bank had enormous discretion. In the past the Central Bank accounts listed gold and currencies as assets, along with loans to the official sector, and under liabilities, notes in circulation and individual bank deposits in the Central Bank (cash reserves). Now Central Bank accounts included rediscounts granted to individual banks in the assets column and under liabilities, the sum total of deposits in the banking system (see Table 4.10).

The rediscount rate used for loans to the banks fluctuated between 2% for credit with collateral to 3.9%, as seen in Table 4.11.

In 1949 the bank's charter was altered, confirming its relative autarky and placing it directly under the executive branch. Its president would be the secretary of finance and the board would be made up of members of the executive cabinet and presidents of official banks. The clause that

---

30 A. Arnaudo sustained that the rate fluctuated between 5.5% and 6.5%. From A. Guissarri was 4% in 1946–1949, 7.5% in 1950–1951, 8% in 1952, and 8.5% in 1953–1956.

Table 4.10. *Changes in Assets on the Central Bank Balance Sheet, 1945–1946*

1945	1946
Assets	Assets
Gold in the country	Gold and foreign exchange
Buyers of foreign exchange in forward markets	Guarantee bonds
Guarantee bonds	National securities
National securities	Real estate, furniture, and machinery
Subsidiary money	Temporary advances to the National Government
Real estate	Bank accounts – Operations
Various	Secure bank loans
	Rediscounts and advances on debtor current accounts in other banks
	Advances on mortgage loans
	Various
Liabilities	Liabilities
Capital	Capital
General Reserve Fund	General Reserve Fund
Reserves	Reserves
Bills in circulation	Monetary circulation
Bank current accounts	Bank current accounts
Official current accounts	Official current accounts
Various current accounts	Various current accounts
National securities participation certificates	National securities participation certificates
Foreign exchange sold in forward markets	Central Bank (BCRA) deposits in other banks
Losses and gains	BCRA mortgage bonds
Bank deposits: new accounts from abroad	Losses and gains
Various	Various

Note: The most relevant accounts have been listed and new accounts have been underlined.
Source: BCRA Yearbooks, 1945–1946.

required a currency reserve of 25% of issues (Law 13571, September 23) was eliminated.

The provisions of the new charter were the following. The Central Bank's new Organic Law eliminates the article that limited the holding of foreign exchange to 20% of total reserves that back currency issues and its inclusion in the ratio of reserves to bills and on demand deposits, by no more than 10%. It also eliminates the article that requires that the Central Bank have enough reserve in gold and foreign exchange to back the value of the peso, that is, at least 25% of notes and demand deposits; exchange control functions and regulation of the securities market, part

Table 4.11. *Rediscount Rates*

Year	Rate until 12–31	Note
1946	From 2% to 3.9%	The lower rate was for credit with collateral by banks requiring collateral.
1947	From 0.25% to 3.9%	The rate is lowered for loans with collateral from banks requiring collateral (drops to 1% and later to 0.25%).
1948	0.5% average increase	Rediscount rates vary, during the second half of the year owing to the Executive Decree # 33425/48. System changes from 10 rates to 3.
1949	No changes	BCRA distinguishes between rediscounts of general public loans and official loans.

Source: BCRA Yearbooks, 1946–1949.

of the Central Bank's purview, have been incorporated in its new charter; the bank's capital has been altered (raised to 100 million pesos), as has its system of profits distribution; the Central Bank is charged with resolving individual bank conflicts regarding distribution of market share in a given area or zone; regarding the Central Bank's buying public bonds, exclusively for the purpose of regularizing the market, authorization is broadened to 15% of the average of total deposits for the last three years. Likewise, the margin of agreement of advances to the National Government to cover seasonal or temporary deficiencies in the budget is raised to 15% of the average of cash on hand raised in the past three years.

Exchange Control. The 1931 exchange control system was created in response to a financial crisis, when Great Britain abandoned the gold standard in October 1931. It was also conceived in order to separate currency emissions from the volume of foreign reserves, preventing buying power boosted by monetary issues from being directed toward imports. The system was altered in 1933 (when a free market with some intervention was added to the official buyers and sellers' rates) and a permit was required for importing goods, so that the volume of imports was linked to the availability of currency. These were attempts to prevent the accumulation of unpaid debt from imports, which had happened in previous years. In the 1930s and during the war, the exchange control became more flexible and restrictions were eased just when these were a function of the warring countries' limited supplies anyway. From its inception, the exchange control regime was seen as a temporary measure in response to a financial emergency.

At the end of the war, in 1946, imports resumed and an exchange permit was again required. These permits endowed the government bureaucracy with enormous power, as they were granted according to the whim of the authorities at hand. Exchange permits were also useful to transfer resources from exports of natural resources and to imports of goods that were considered necessary. The regime became more complicated and, during the Perón government, increasingly discriminatory. Several sellers' rates were established: basic, preferential A and preferential B, and a free market rate that went from 5 pesos per dollar for grain and meat exports to a special rate of 14 pesos per dollar for those products that needed protecting. Doubtless company profits varied substantially, depending on whether the export was made at the official rate (much lower) or at the special one (180% higher).

Starting in 1950, imports received a basic sellers' rate that was greater than that of exports (7.50 pesos per dollar), which provided a profit margin for the government and a lower preferential rate. The import regime had been changed several times since 1946. The existence of basic buyers' and sellers' exchange rates created a spread that, as we have seen, provided fiscal resources that reached 3.7% of GDP from 1946 to 1948, and 0.5% of GDP from 1949 to 1955. These estimates are somewhat high because some of the exports could be made at a rate that was higher than the basic buyers' rate and some of the imports were authorized at rates that were lower than the sellers' basic.[31]

These multiple rates were eliminated in 1956, when, still under the exchange control regime, at the insistence of the IMF – to which the country had adhered – a single exchange rate of 18 pesos per dollar was adopted. Between 1950 and 1952, this brought a 188% devaluation of the peso with respect to the average official rate for exports and imports (during the 1950–1952 period the average exchange rate was 6.25) and a devaluation of 140% with respect to the basic sellers' rate or of 260% with respect to the preferential sellers' rate.[32] Exchange spreads, with a fixed official rate, spurred the emergence of a parallel or black market. Figure 4.9 shows the spread between the official and black market rates.

When reserves increased at the Central Bank, it earned profits because it bought them at a low official exchange rate. Later, between 1946 and 1947, when reserves dropped to some 2,121 million pesos, those who profited were those who could buy them at the official rate. This can be seen in Figure 4.10.

Those who were lucky enough to import at basic or preferential rates (as opposed to free rates) earned a profit paid by the exporters. But the best circumstances were those of exporting at a high exchange rate (not traditional exports) and buying imports at a lower rate (if permits could be obtained). One of the features of the system was that officials periodically changed the goods included on each list, which meant that individuals

31 FIEL, *El Control de Cambios en la Argentina: liberación cambiaria y crecimiento*, Buenos Aires, Manantial, 1987, p. 69.
32 Ibid., p. 75.

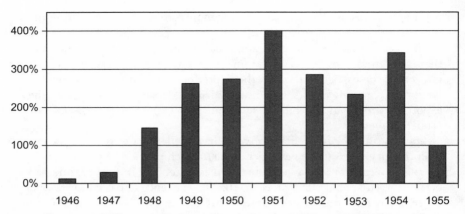

Figure 4.9. Difference in Exchange Rates in Percentages. *Source:* FIEL, *El Control de Cambios en la Argentina: Liberación Cambiaria y Crecimiento*, Buenos Aires, Manantial, 1987.

with vested interests dedicated substantial resources to place themselves in the most favorable circumstances possible, looking to increase their profits.

A noncompetitive business culture emerged because of the absence of risk involved in obtaining a license to import goods. Entrepreneurs could earn handsome profits simply by getting an exchange permit to import at a low rate, so as to later sell the imported goods at higher prices in captive markets. Civil service officials, friendly politicians, and military officers on whose support the president relied were generally those who obtained

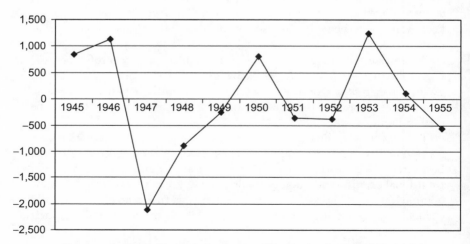

Figure 4.10. Yearly Change in International Reserves at the Central Bank of Argentina (in millions of current pesos). *Source:* BCRA Yearbooks, 1944–1945.

permits to import cars; the automobile industry was literally devoid of supply since the war had broken out.[33]

Exchange control caused a substantial drain of capital from the country. Because exporters had to liquidate their goods at a lower-than-market price, many began to undervalue their sales, leaving the difference abroad. Importers, on the other hand, started to overvalue them, doing the same with the difference. After a few years this was a way of diverting foreign exchange abroad – more so during periods of insecurity. This caused a capital flight that would later have very serious repercussions. With the advent of exchange control two markets were formed. Everyone wanted to sell their foreign exchange on the free market and buy them on the official market, which led to numerous deals that were very costly and left an enormous trail of corruption.

Currency Depreciation and the Profitability of Capital. Because of arbitrage, flows of capital move from where it is abundant and its returns lower to where it is scarce and its returns higher. Argentina benefited from this situation during the last decades of the nineteenth century and the first thirty years of the twentieth, as enormous flows of capital moved from more industrialized countries to newly developing areas like Argentina, where returns were higher.

Earning in one currency instead of another was never an issue while the gold standard regime lasted, because domestic money had a fixed value in gold. However, because the foreign investors wanted to bring their earnings back into the country where they lived, once the gold standard was abandoned, the stability of the exchange rate became a fundamental problem in calculating actual profits. After decades of stability, foreign investors assumed more of the same and had estimated the differences in profitability between one country and another without taking into account changes in the exchange rate. Later investors found that they had been mistaken and that upon converting profits at fluctuating and depreciated exchange rates, particularly after 1930, results could differ considerably from original estimates. Returns on capital could change according to the discretion of the government under whose jurisdiction the capital was located. Because the government had coercive power, it could prevent a free market for transactions, monopolizing the exchange market.

The governments' exchange regime measures also affected profits and losses of foreign companies that had to absorb the losses that the peso devaluation caused when they sent their profits abroad.[34] The difference

---

33 See Jorge Antonio's memoirs, *Y ahora qué*, Buenos Aires, Ediciones Verum et Militia, 1966, where the process of auto imports first to Aguirre Mastro and later from Mercedes Benz is outlined.
34 See Chapter 2.

Table 4.12. *British Investment in Argentina*

Year	Investment Face Value (in millions of pounds)	Average Rate of Return
1880	20.0	
1890	157.0	
1900	207.0	
1910	290.6	4.8
1913	357.74	4.9
1928	420.38	5.6
1939	428.52	2.6
1949	69.43	3.4

Source: J. Fred Rippy, *British Investments in Latin America, 1822–1949: A Case Study in the Operations of Private Enterprise in Retarded Regions*, Minneapolis, University of Minnesota Press, 1959.

between estimates and profits and losses based on past or actual events was one of the factors that affected the reduction in the flow of British capital. See the return rate on British investments in Table 4.12.

The Central Bank became the primary and most significant instrument for financing political goals. Other tools included profits from the exchange differential and public debt placed in pension funds. In fact, the Bank's important role in making policy was recognized, and touted by authorities as representing unified action to promote the expansion of the economy,[35] which included the official banks, the National Postal Savings Bank, and IAPI, which were also under its control.

By issuing money, the Central Bank financed operations at the IAPI. The Bank redeemed mortgage loans and rediscounted the loans of the Mortgage Bank, bought public service companies that became nationalized, such as Unión Telefónica, and met fiscal needs, all of this costing enormous sums of money, as seen in Table 4.14. With the nationalization of deposits in commercial banks that went to the Central Bank, and by means of rediscounts credit was reoriented according to government preferences. Money from deposits went back to the banks, but not necessarily to the same banks. Official banks (Bank of the Argentine Nation, Bank of Industrial Credit and National Mortgage Bank) received the largest share of the rediscounts; the Central Bank paid interest on deposits, but at a rate that in real terms ended up being negative.

The 1946 BCRA Yearbook indicates that rediscounts would no longer be limited to their previous functions but rather would be the primary

35 BCRA Yearbook, 1947.

Table 4.13. *Creation of Means of Payment*

Years	Yearly Change in Millions of Current Pesos				
	1945	1946	1947	1948	1949
Internal factors					
Loans to the public and others	322	708	2,384	2,394	1,468
Regulating the stock market	−90	173	232	84	−189
Mortgage activity		1,440	297	1,011	1,262
IAPI	−35	−35	1,395	811	1,339
Nationalization and financing public services		351	314	1,695	651
Fiscal needs	318	890	763	805	1,065
Total internal factors	515	3,830	5,385	6,800	5,596
External factors					
Foreign exchange used to nationalize services	−1	−331	−52	−52	−13
Foreign exchange used to repatriate foreign debt		−442	−334		
Exports on credit		232	553	373	−209
Gold and foreign exchange from regular operations	1,121	895	−1,351	1,060	−224
Total external factors	1,120	354	−1,184	−638	−446
TOTAL	1,635	4,184	4,201	6,162	5,150

Source: BCRA Yearbook, 1947 and 1949.

instrument in credit policy for fomenting economic activity: "By rediscounting bank portfolios [the Central Bank] can now efficiently regulate the volume and direction of credit, to the extent necessary for the orderly development of the economy."[36] As can be seen in Tables 4.13 and 4.14, credit helped primarily the public and industrial sectors. In the official sector, credit was given primarily to finance IAPI operations, to finance the government, and to nationalize foreign public service companies and the repurchase of mortgage loans.

During the entire Perón period these loans appeared in the assets column of official banks and of the Central Bank, which had rediscounted them, though they were actually defaulted. This fact was officially recognized in 1957, when a debt restructuring bond was issued to substitute the unrecoverable loans at the Central Bank. The official banks' debt originated in rediscounts was cancelled by ceding their credit against their clients'.

The debt that the state assumed in 1957 was not registered at the Treasury, because in the banks they were listed as debts from decentralized government agencies (and companies and the government to IAPI) rediscounted by the Central Bank, which because they were uncollectible (or partially so) were financed with monetary issues. This provisional restructuring bond, as government debt, covered the deficit incurred by companies,

36 BCRA Yearbook, 1946, p. 18.

Table 4.14. *Credit Recipients (in millions of pesos adjusted for inflation)*

Year	1945	1946	1947
Total loans	3,662	5,424	10,348
National Government	409	1,461	4,294
Agriculture	281	281	369
Industry[a]	571	935	1,826

[a] Includes transportation, communications, and construction companies.
Source: BCRA Yearbook, 1947.

decentralized entities, and so on. Operations were financed with credit that was never repaid, and for which the Central Bank issued money. Yearly totals were registered neither in the budget nor in the investment account, but had to be added to the government's annual deficit. Table 4.15 shows the yearly debt that was incorporated into the restructuring bond. This debt, which became part of the country's overall debt, was reduced through inflation. Table 4.16 shows what the debt would have been in constant money (with the same purchasing power). The debt incorporated in the restructuring bond was 27.6 billion pesos, but if it were adjusted for inflation it would have been 73.7 billion, which means that inflation eroded government debt by 46 billion pesos.

Table 4.15. *Debt Included in the Provisional Restructuring Bond (in millions of pesos)*

	1948	1949	1950	1951	1952	1953	1954	1955	Restructuring Bond
Bank of the Argentine Nation	2,960	4,101	3,807	4,632	5,160	8,482	13,281	17,798	19,489
Bank of Industrial Credit	2,744	3,787	4,345	4,310	4,421	4,693	5,098	5,138	7,471
Bank of the Province of Buenos Aires	421	581	572	556	560	541	623	655	639
Total three banks	6,125	8,468	8,724	9,498	10,141	13,717	19,002	23,591	27,599
Percentage of GDP	14%	16%	13%	10%	9%	11%	13%	14%	10%
Flow of annual financing		2,343	255	774	644	3,575	5,286	4,589	4,008
Percentage of GDP	4.5%	0.4%	80.0%	60.0%	2.8%	3.7%	2.7%	1.4%	
Percentage of public spending	32.1%	3.1%	6.2%	4.5%	23.7%	31.5%	25.1%	14.5%	

Source: BCRA Yearbooks, Bank of the Argentine Nation, Bank of Industrial Credit, and Bank of the Province of Buenos Aires, 1948–1957.

Table 4.16. *Inflationary Erosion (in millions of current pesos)*

Accumulated inflation, 1948–1957	50,500.0%
A. Value of existing debt in 1948 indexed to 1957	37,058
Percentage of GDP	1,090.0%
B. Value indexed in 1957 from accumulated flows since 1948	36,636
Percentage of GDP	1,290.0%
C. Value of the debt from 1948 plus incorporated flows indexed to 1957 = A + B	73,694
Percentage of GDP	2,590.0%
D. 1957 Provisional Restructuring Bond	27,599
Percentage of GDP	970.0%
E. State Inflatory Financing: Difference between debt and bond = C−D	46.0995
Percentage of GDP	1,620.0%

Source: BCRA Yearbooks, IAPI, Bank of the Argentine Nation and Bank of Industrial Credit.

Rediscounts and Money Creation. Rediscounts were considerably greater than deposits (see Figure 4.11), and thus substantial money creation resulted. Between 1946 and 1948 the nominal money supply[37] increased by 49% despite the fact that gold and currency reserves dropped by 52%. The primary sources of money creation were rediscounts and other loans to banks, which increased during the same period by 127%, of which some 58–59% went to the government (and of that, almost 60% went to IAPI).

In 1948, the BCRA received new deposits totaling 3,484 million pesos, while it granted rediscounts and bank loans to the amount of 6,162 million pesos. Total loans increased by 5,889 million, of which the public sector received 3,564 million, whereas the private sector got 2,325 million, which means that the public sector absorbed all of the growth in deposits. Thus, it was inevitable that the policy of financing the government with credit would lead to money creation.

In sum, the Central Bank was the instrument employed to generate enormous monetary resources. As long as the public, which had grown accustomed to half a century of monetary stability, continued to have faith in the value of the peso, it seemed that a clever and easy financing mechanism, for a host of purposes, had been discovered. As illustrated in the 1957 balance sheet, the results were ruinous. Once people began to perceive that prices were increasing faster than the interest rate, the illusion of monetary backing dissipated and people began to withdraw their deposits.

---

37 Monetary supply is the currency in the public's hands plus total private deposits (checking accounts, installment loans, and savings accounts).

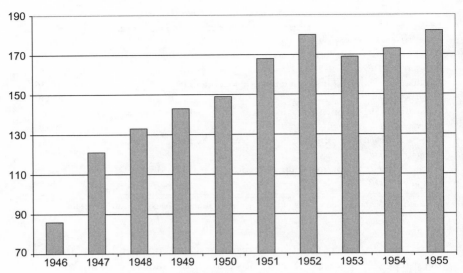

Figure 4.11. Rediscounts and Other Loans to Banks Relative to Total Deposits (in percentages). *Note: The following categories were included under* Rediscounts and Other Loans to Banks: Bank accounts-operations, In escraw loans, Bank loans with varying forms of collateral or guarantees, Rediscounts and Advances on debtor current accounts, and Advances on mortgage loans. *Source:* BCRA Yearbook, 1946–1955.

Furthermore, the government had created a large amount of purchasing power, which because it could not be used to purchase foreign imports or financial assets (because they were not preserved against inflation) was spent on domestic goods, promoting inflation. The money supply, deposits, loans, and currency increased in real terms, as illustrated in Figure 4.12.

On the other hand, nationalizing deposits and redirecting credit to banks and privileged sectors – with rates that became negative in real terms – caused an enormous income transfer from savers to debtors. Table 4.17 shows the subsidies debtors received and the implicit tax imposed on savers.

A portion of the enormous amount of government spending was directed toward the purchase of railroads and other public services as well as paying back the external debt to Great Britain. In effect, to pay the external debt to Great Britain and purchase railroads, export earning from those years was used, leaving the accumulated reserves to be used for buying imports from Great Britain. Although because money is exchangeable, and this being a simple fact of accounting, it shows, on the other hand, that importing material and equipment from England was a possibility. Foreign exchange earned from exports could no longer be used to import goods precisely because it had been used for debt repatriation and the nationalization of

Table 4.17. *Indicators of Financial Stagnation*

Year	Real Liability Rate	Real Asset Rate	Implicit Tax on Deposits/GDP	Implicit Subsidy for Loans/Private Investment
1950	−16	−12	2.1	21.6
1951	−32	−28	2.8	35.0
1952	−14	−9	1.3	20.1
1953	4	9	−0.2	−4.8
1954	−11	−7	1.3	17.7
1955	−4	0	0.6	6.7

Source: A. J. Canavese, V. J. Elías, and L. Montuschi, "Sistema Financiero y Política Industrial para la Argentina en la Década de 1980," Buenos Aires, *El Cronista Comercial*, 1983.

railroads, when it would have been possible to use those reserves to import more machinery and equipment from Great Britain itself (see Table 4.18).

Furthermore, the reserves were owned by the Central Bank and the government could have bought them with the tax surplus or with debt place on the public, but none of these measures was followed; instead it was done by means of Central Bank rediscounts to official banks to finance the IAPI (that is, by creating money). Thus, the majority of the purchase of reserves from the Central Bank were financed through money creation by means of rediscounts granted by the Central Bank. It is true that this

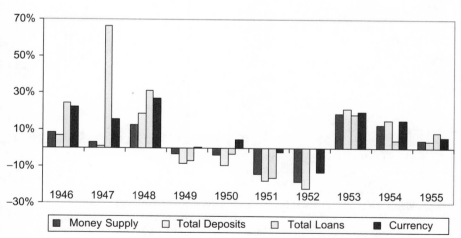

Figure 4.12. Real Yearly Growth Rate. *Note:* Changes in value adjusted for inflation by the Consumer Price Index 1955 = 100 (*Source:* INDEC). *Source:* BCRA Yearbook, 1946–1955, and BCRA Statistical Bulletins, 1948–1958.

Table 4.18. *Balance of Payments, Debt Repatriation,*
and Public Spending (in millions of current pesos)

Year	Total BP	Public Spending	Public Debt Repatriation
1944	1,047	33	174
1945	1,143	33	7
1946	1,363	60	442
1947	578	116	334
1948	201	125	–
1949	–633	168	–

Source: BCRA Yearbooks, 1945, 1947, 1949, and 1950.

expansion was offset by the absorption produced to pay external debt with
reserves, but the initial expansion of the 1940s derived from commercial
surpluses was not neutralized. (What would have happened if the fiscal
surplus were used.) Lastly, as we have seen, having accumulated reserves
due to the restriction on imports caused by the war, they were not used to
import enough capital goods to overcome the supply shortages of the war
years. The drop in reserves in the Central Bank's assets was compensated
by a parallel increase in rediscounts, as shown in Figure 4.13.

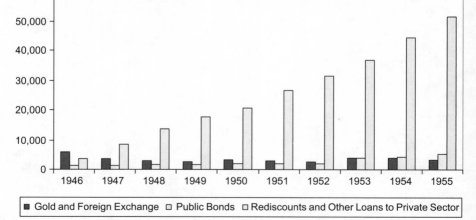

Figure 4.13. BCRA Assets (data in millions of current pesos). *Note: The following*
categories were included under Rediscounts and Other Loans to Banks: Bank
accounts-operations, Secure bank loans, Bank loans with varying forms of collateral
or guarantees, Rediscounts and Advances on debtor current accounts, and Advances
on mortgage loans. *Source:* BCRA Yearbook, 1946–1955.

It was expected that when the war ended, imports, which had been extremely limited while the hostilities lasted, would increase more than exports because of the need for capital goods and industrial primary goods, and so on, the purchase of which had been postponed. Thus, the amount of reserves was expected to diminish. But ignoring the fact that the country would require foreign exchange to normalize imports, the government spent those reserves, causing significant shortages of equipment, machinery, and industrial inputs, which would become evident with the 1949 balance-of-payment crisis and would continue during the entire Perón administration. Thus, when the trend during the war years reversed and the amount of currencies that importers and the government needed exceeded what exporters could sell, the government began to compete with private industry for available foreign exchange.

National Mortgage Bank (Banco Hipotecario Nacional). As part of the 1946 reforms, operations at the National Mortgage Bank were modified. Mortgage loans had played an important role in savings. These loans were given by the bank to debtors who mortgaged their rural or urban dwelling for a portion (50%) of its appraisal, usually at 6% interest, and then brought it to the stock market to find an investor who would buy it. The bank acted as an intermediary, backing the loan, but the funds were provided by private investors. This market had seen significant volume of sales, although it declined after the 1930 crisis. In 1946 the government used the Central Bank to redeem the mortgage loans still on the market, replacing them with mortgage bonds issued by the Central Bank that would be placed on the public. However, subscription to these bonds was unsuccessful. To recover these loans more than a billion pesos were issued, whereas the bonds were sold for only 384 million pesos, so that the recovery was financed principally through rediscounts at the Central Bank. According to the 1946 BCRA Yearbook, the redemption of mortgage loans caused a partial liquidation of stocks. Of the 1,497 million in recovered loans, only 2.5% were reinvested in the new mortgage bonds. This amounted to 384 million as of December 31, 1946. This means that "by financing operations at the National Mortgage Bank with funds supplied by the Central Bank *it was not necessary to sell the new issues, but rather, it was preferable to wait, thus avoiding interest payments*"[38] (emphasis added). A significant increase in liquidity resulted from these operations. From this point on, rediscounts were the primary source of funding for the National Mortgage Bank (see Figure 4.14).

38 BCRA Yearbook, 1946, p. 102.

Table 4.19. *BCRA Assets (in millions of current pesos)*

Year	1946	1947	1948
Advances on mortgage loans (A)	1,480	1,741	2,746
Gold and foreign currency (B)	5,807	3,686	2,795
Rediscounts (private sector)	3,720	8,639	1,3896
Bank accounts – Operations	1,529	1,919	1,585
Loans (private sector)	2,806	3,178	3,414
Government (Public Securities, National Treasury Bonds and Securities)	1,311	1,301	1,786
Other	268	521	66
Total BCRA assets (C)	16,921	20,985	26,288
A/B	25.5%	47.2%	98.2%
A/C	8.7%	8.3%	10.4%

Source: BCRA Yearbooks, 1946–1948.

According to the Central Bank (BCRA) Yearbook, changes in the composition of assets (including advances for mortgage loans) were as shown in Table 4.19.

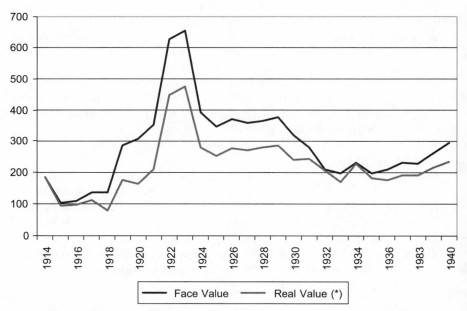

Figure 4.14. National Mortgage Loans (in millions of current pesos) * at 1914 constant prices. *Source: Anuario Geográfico Argentino,* Comité Nacional de Geografía, Buenos Aires, 1941, pp. 365–366.

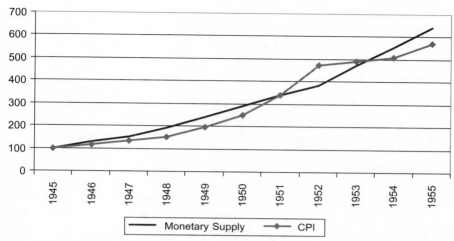

Figure 4.15. Monetary Supply and Consumer Price Index (Index: 1945 = 100).
Source: "Serie Histórica del Índice de Precios al Consumidor (IPC) en el Gran Buenos Aires," INDEC, www.indec.gov.ar, and BCRA Yearbooks, 1945–1955.

These operations caused a generalized increase in prices, as illustrated in Figure 4.15.

Hoarding. The loss of purchasing power of monetary assets is not immediately perceived at the beginning of an inflationary process (monetary illusion). But later, as it becomes more evident, people look to shift from domestic monetary assets to others that protect them from inflation. These may be in real assets whose prices increase in nominal money, or in foreign currencies that prevent the loss in value that domestic currency incurs. Whereas the purchase of durable consumer goods was an incentive to invest in these activities, the purchase of foreign currency sent savings out of the country and was not an incentive to invest domestically (i.e., although the level of domestic investment dropped, the level of savings did not necessarily do the same.) The dollar – which, as Perón had said, had not been seen in Argentina before 1947 – became the most common refuge. Despite the fact that during that period transactions in foreign currency were unlawful, the value of the dollar on the black market began to increase.

The Monopoly on Foreign Trade: The IAPI

Among the many policies of the Perón government, one of the most significant was the monopolization (nationalization) of foreign trade. This measure may only be understood in the context of war, when trade was interrupted for a number of reasons. On the one hand, the Allied powers'

Agricultural Advisory Board had depressed the price of food in order to aid in the war effort, an intervention policy that continued after the war ended. On the other, whereas there were thousands of agricultural producers, intermediaries in grain exports and meat packing companies were few. The state substituted a private oligopoly for a state monopoly in order to confront a single source of demand (a monopsony). Foreign trade had lost its multilateral nature starting with the 1930 crisis and continuing into the war years. Negotiations would be made as a part of bilateral agreements by which, with the war's end, countries from Western, Central, and Eastern Europe were incorporated under Soviet control.

The government gave two main reasons for this method: first, that the only way to get better prices was to concentrate the supply,[39] and second, that some of these operations were carried out with credit, which only the government could offer. The IAPI set a purchase price for producers and negotiated crops on markets abroad. During the war, prices dropped (in 1933 the *Junta de Granos* – Grain Board – was created to maintain prices, and subsidies would come from the margin of exchange). Between 1946 and 1948 prices on foodstuffs increased considerably because of an increase in demand from countries that had been at war. During these years the IAPI bought domestically directly from producers at a lower price than that at which they sold these goods. However, this trend reversed because of the reconstitution of foodstuffs production, and the IAPI suffered losses when it bought at prices that were greater than that at which it sold them. Producers received a subsidy because the domestic price was higher than the international price, but they too suffered losses when they liquidated their currencies at the official rate, with the peso considerably overvalued. Buying from producers at a lower price than the international one prevented the international increase in prices from having an impact on internal ones, which was probably one of the government's goals, although it hurt producers.

---

39 BCRA Yearbook, 1946, p. 24: "The creation of the IAPI was essential to deal with the manner in which countries that bought our products operated. After a period in which purchases were made directly by the governments of these countries, a further step was taken midway through 1945 with the creation of joint international controls. In order to prevent competition among the countries in question which would have resulted in a greater value on the products that Argentina could supply, these countries agreed to make their purchases together through international entities, such as the Junta Combinada de Alimentos (Foodstuffs Collective) and later the Consejo de Alimentación Internacional de Emergencia (International Counsel on Emergency Food Supply). In order to confront the creation of an exclusive official purchase organization, as well as an agreement or consortium that forced supplier countries (among them, Argentina) to deal with a single buyer, with the concomitant effect on prices, the country had to react with appropriate measures in order to prevent a serious detriment to its interests, coordinating sales on the part of Argentina."

Table 4.20. *IAPI Participation in Total Exports (in millions of current pesos)*

Year	Total Exported	Total Exported by IAPI	IAPI Participation (%)
1949	3,741	3,679	98.3
1950	5,427	3,822	70.4
1951	6,711	4,607	68.6
1952	4,392	2,656	60.5
1953	7,189	5,056	70.3

Source: Susana Novick, *IAPI: Auge y Decadencia*, Buenos Aires, Centro Editor de América Latina, 1886.

The IAPI as a Secondary Treasury. Article 17 of the 1946 de facto president Farrel decree law – which created the IAPI (to which it gave a monopoly on foreign trade) – stipulated that its resources would come from the difference between the purchase and the sale of foreign exchange. In effect, these included not only foreign exchange but also funds from the difference between purchase prices (domestic) and sale prices (abroad) for exports and of import purchase prices (international) and sale prices (domestic).

However, not only the IAPI did this for the market abroad, but in some instances (as in the case of wheat), it also extended these operations to the domestic market. These imported between 60% and 90% of the value of exports[40] (see Table 4.20).

Central Bank Financing to IAPI. The IAPI financed operations not only with its own resources but also, to a great extent, with loans obtained from the official banking system, the Bank of the Argentine Nation and the Bank of Industrial Credit, through rediscounts from the Central Bank (see Tables 4.21 and 4.22).

This was a significant source of funds, which allowed the government a wide margin of discretion because these resources were not subject to congressional control. With these funds the government financed the nationalization of various public services. The government was also able to purchase capital goods for the central administration and some provinces, finance state public enterprises, finance current public sector expenditures, and finance industrial subsidies (among them, most significantly [cooking] oil and meat packing companies) and farm and cattle production subsidies (in order to keep prices of foodstuffs low) (see Table 4.23).

40 See Federico Todeschini, "el BCRA y el IAPI en la política económica Peronista: 1946–1955", *Documento de Trabajo*, no. 68, Universidad de San Andrés, 2004.

Table 4.21. *IAPI Bank Debt (in millions of current pesos)*

Year	Crop Sales	Commercial Operations	Public Services	Government Financing	Total
1946	281.0	313.1	351.4		945.5
1947		2,445.4	666.6	77.6	3,189.6
1948	437.6	3,022.8	2,360.3	247.6	6,068.3
1949	1,157.8	3,382.2	3,011.1	297.6	7,848.7
1950	406.2	3,770.9	3,352.0	328.8	7,857.9
1951	560.3	3,689.6	3,555.6	344.2	8,149.7
1952	1,426.6	3,636.1	3,684.4	353.2	9,100.3
1953	4,536.5	3,624.0	3,762.8	339.6	12,262.9
1954	7,816.1	4,862.5	3,893.4	358.4	16,930.4
1955	9,837.8	6,460.8	4,059.5	366.5	20,724.6
1956 (July)	9,999.0	5,987.2	4,112.0	368.8	20,467.0

Source: Eugenio Blanco, *La Política Presupuestaria, la Deuda Pública y la Economía Nacional*, Buenos Aires, Ministerio de Hacienda de la Nación, 1956.

Table 4.22. *IAPI Revenue (in millions of current pesos)*

Year	Trade Revenues	Financial Revenues	IAPI Revenue/Tax Revenues (%)
1949	545	552	36.2
1950	812	292	27.8
1951	1,046	213	20.4
1952	408	257	9.2
1953	2,106	237	32.9
1954	4,310		52.6

Source: Federico Todeschini, "El BCRA y el IAPI en la Política Económica Peronista: 1946–1955", *Documento de Trabajo*, no. 68, Universidad de San Andrés, 2004.

Table 4.23. *Financing Granted by IAPI (in millions of current pesos)*

Year	Public Sector	Net Financing Private Sector	Subsidies to Private Sector	Net Financing	Total/ GDP (%)
1948	3,959.1	330.0	n/d	373.0	10.6
1949	1,239.4	164.0	143.5	210.0	3.3
1950	828.2	147.6	332.4	−124.8	1.7
1951	−6.9	198.7	159.5	−113.7	0.2
1952	536.1	60.1	295.8	−65.7	70.0
1953	−29.7	1,544.9	363.2	73.5	1.5
1954	100.3	5,062.4	541.2	−35.4	3.9
1955	206.8				0.1

Source: IAPI Yearbook, 1948–1955.

Table 4.24. *National Treasury: Use of Credit (in millions of current pesos)*

Years	Net Bond Placement	Ratio to Cash Income (%)
1944	950.4	59
1945	1,053.1	61
1946	1,538.2	67
1947	1,008.7	25
1948	2,287.6	42
1949	2,852.0	45
1950	3,367.3	41

Source: Eugenio Blanco, *La Política Presupuestaria, la Deuda Pública y la Economía Nacional*, Buenos Aires, Ministerio de Hacienda de la Nación, 1956, p. 11.

Social Security as a Source of Financing. Because there was no market for debt, and trying to prevent the inflationary effect of placing government bonds in the Central Bank, the government placed them in the social security system. The system had a surplus because the law, which broadened the scope of coverage to almost all workers, increased the number of contributors, whereas the number of people reaching the retirement age was small in comparison (see Table 4.24).

According to the Central Bank,

In 1948 the net absorption of national bonds (Bonds and Treasury Bills) for the different investment sectors, increased to 1,497 million pesos, double the amount recorded for 1947. The most important source of these funds was the increase recorded in net investments from Retirement Savings in the Instituto Nacional de Prevision Social; from the Financial Aid Institute (*Instituto de Ayuda Financiera*) for the payment of Retirement and Military Pensions and of the Federal Police Retirement and Pensions Accounts (1,714 million pesos), which amply neutralized the liquidation of bonds in public hands.[41]

However, in the future, when a significant portion of the population reached the age of retirement, the surplus from the social security system would disappear (see Figure 4.16 and Table 4.25).

The Perón administration used new ways of creating savings. Instead of using market incentives, savings were forced. These methods included nationalizing deposits, using Central Bank rediscounts, appropriating funds from Retirement Accounts to place government debt at rates that

41 BCRA Yearbok, 1948, p. 73 (emphasis added).

Table 4.25. *Evolution of Income and Ordinary Spending per Family (in millions of current pesos)*

Year	Consumer Spending	Retirement Contributions	Savings
1950	478.8	42.3	66.8
1951	694.9	56.5	76.3
1952	831.0	66.9	78.0
1953	899.0	83.8	146.0
1954	1,027.7	103.5	147.8
1955	1,236.9	116.6	167.8

Source: BCRA, *Gerencia de Investigaciones Económicas, Sistema de Cuentas del Producto e Ingreso de la Argentina,* vol. 2, 1975.

were lower than inflation, and utilizing foreign trade taxes as a source of revenue. Table 4.26 summarizes how rediscounts were used.

Furthermore, starting in 1949, in response to the balance-of-payments crisis, the government adopted restrictive measures that affected not only

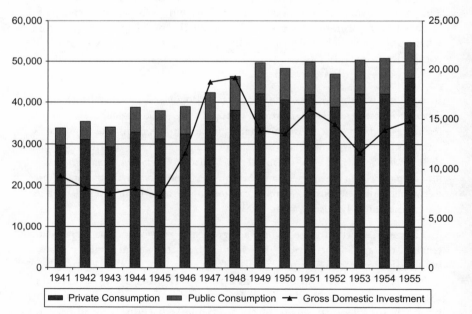

Figure 4.16. Evolution of Consumption and Investment (in millions of pesos at 1950 prices). *Source:* BCRA, *Gerencia de Investigaciones Económicas, Cuentas Nacionales de la República Argentina,* vol. 3, 1976.

Table 4.26. BCRA *Financing of the Government and the Private Sector (rediscounts, in millions of current pesos)*

	1946	1947	1948	1949
Government	5,339.6	8,979.0	12,741.1	17,560.7
IAPI (included in government)	4,893.0	6,288.0	7,470.1	8,439.0
Private sector	3,719.5	8,639.3	13,896.3	17,773.9

Source: BCRA Yearbooks and BCRA Statistical Bulletins, 1946–1949, and Federico Todeschini, "El BCRA y el IAPI en la Política Económica Peronista: 1946–1955", Documento de Trabajo No. 68 de la Universidad de San Andrés, 2004.

credit but also economic activity. People invested only when these investments were subsidized. Note the inverse relationship between the interest rate and investment in Figure 4.17.

Canavese, Elías, and Montuschi have calculated the implicit or hidden tax on deposits as the loss incurred on deposits using an average real interest rate of 2% annually. The implicit subsidy on loans has been calculated as the transference received on loans, supposing an average real interest rate

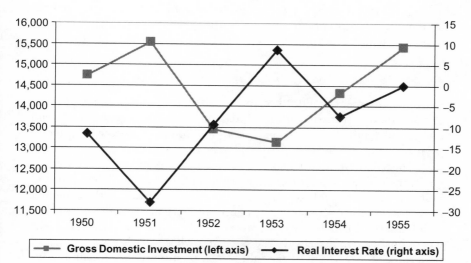

Figure 4.17. Evolution of Gross Domestic Investment and the Real Interest Rate for Loans (in millions of 1955 pesos, in percentages). *Source:* A. J. Canavese, V. J. Elías, and L. Montuschi (1983), *Sistema financiero y política industrial para la Argentina en la década de 1980*, Buenos Aires, El Cronista Comercial, 1983, and *Series históricas de cuentas nacionales de la Argentina*, BCRA, Gerencia de Investigaciones Económicas, Buenos Aires, 1976.

of 5% annually.[42] These subsidies also distorted the financial calculation of entrepreneurial projects because without them, very often profitability would likely have been negative.

Thus two distinct markets for credit emerged. The first was the official one, with a subsidized rate, and the other was for companies that did not have access to the official rate and for whom loans were more costly. Those who did not have the benefit of the official rate, generally small businesses, had to fight to survive in a savagely competitive world, whereas the favored companies had privileged access to subsidized markets. This led to the black market (underground) economy.[43] However, not everyone was protected; small businesses involved in agriculture, commerce, and services generally did not have access to captive markets and had to survive in extremely difficult circumstances. These businesses most often relied on (tax) evasion in order to stay afloat.

Sometimes the companies' own profits were the source of investment income, although these companies tried to invest by borrowing from the financial system and sending their profits out of the country to protect them from inflation and the government's attempts at confiscation. Under these circumstances the financial market was nonexistent, nor was a capital market, whereas before the 1930 crisis it was substantial. Furthermore, investment was overestimated, because estimated at 1960 prices it was 17% of domestic absorption (consumption, investment, and public spending), whereas calculated at 1935 prices, it reached only 12.1%.[44]

Trade Policy, Imports Restriction, Bilateralism

In this environment, imports became increasingly reduced, quotas were set, certain products were simply prohibited, and there was a generalized trend toward bilateral agreements and providing compensation with deferred payment plans for uncovered balances. The oldest bilateral agreement was with Great Britain and it had begun in 1933. Under the Perón government, trade agreements with neighboring countries and with Western and Eastern Europe multiplied. These accords were not always to the benefit of Argentina, because although the country produced commodities at prices set internationally, in exchange it received manufactured or capital goods whose quality was not always the same and whose prices could be higher than those of, or the products could be of a quality inferior to, alternative products in other markets.

---

42 See Figure 4.3.
43 See Adrián Guissarri, *La Argentina Informal: Realidad de la Vida Económica*, Buenos Aires, Emecé, 1989.
44 Carlos Díaz Alejandro, *Essays*.

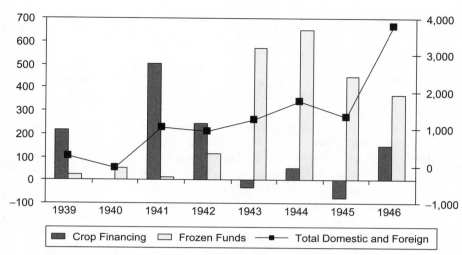

Figure 4.18. Creation of Means of Payment (change in millions of pesos). *Source:* BCRA Yearbooks, 1942, 1944, 1945, and 1946.

Frozen Pounds Sterling. Among other bilateral agreements was the one signed in 1933, which was undoubtedly the most important and most controversial. Known as the Roca-Runciman Agreement, this trade agreement resolved the problem of the pesos frozen (made nonconvertible) by the Argentine government. The accord dealt with remittances of British companies' profits, stipulating that the excess balances in pounds from trade with Great Britain would be used to this end and to pay for British imports (at the official exchange rate). The agreement furthermore granted preference to British imports and quotas on Argentine exports of meat to the United Kingdom, which had been in decline due to imperial preferences.

The Roca-Runciman Agreement was renewed in 1936, but in 1940, already at war, Great Britain decided not to convert the balances in pounds sterling. During the following five years a significant quantity of pounds from the sales of Argentine exports had accumulated in the Bank of England, and Argentina could not convert them to other currencies. In 1945 there was a balance of 1,541 million pesos in the Bank of England.[45] The frozen pounds were part of an enormous trade surplus that the country had accumulated because the war restricted imports. Until 1941, the frozen funds, along with crop financing, were a significant factor in money creation (see Figure 4.18).

---

45 At the buyers exchange rate, foreign exchange is nonconvertible to gold, but with a gold clause. BCRA Yearbook, 1945. See clauses in the Appendix.

Financing Debt Repayment and the Nationalization of Railroads: Monetary Effects. Those in the export business receive foreign exchange for their sales, which they deposit in their banks. The banks, in turn, buy the foreign exchange from exporters with pesos and sell it to importers who bought it with pesos. The difference becomes part of the reserves that are deposited in the Central Bank. (To simplify matters, only foreign exchange coming from traded balances is discussed here.) The Central Bank, for its part, creates money with the flow of reserves. Under the exchange control regime, the Central Bank monopolized all operations involving the purchase and sale of currencies by means of authorized banks. Later, if the balances were positive, reserves in the Central Bank increased, and there was an expansion in money issues, or if they were negative, reserves decreased and issues constricted. The bank mainly issued the monetary base with the difference between the inflow and outflow of foreign reserves. Thus, the pesos used to pay exporters – in circumstances of balanced trade – came from the pesos with which importers bought foreign exchange, and only the differences were covered with expansion or contraction of reserves and creation or contraction of the monetary base. Just like individuals had to do, if the government wanted to acquire reserves, it had to buy them from the Central Bank. It could do this with cash (fiscal surplus) or placing debt in public hands or with credit from the Central Bank.

During the war, because of restrictions on supplies in the warring countries – production was dedicated exclusively to war needs – so that there was a wide gap between imports and exports. When exporters sold their foreign currency to the Central Bank in exchange of pesos, because demand for imports was greatly reduced, the Central Bank did not receive a sufficient amount of pesos from those who wanted to import goods, and thus it had to issue money. The flow of foreign exchange from exports that was not compensated by a parallel outflow from imports caused an enormous increase in reserves and in monetary issues. It is important to note that a significant quantity of pounds had remained frozen (nonconvertible) at the Bank of England in the account of the Argentine government, which, for its part, bought the foreign exchange from exporters through the Central Bank issuing money.

In 1946 the first of two agreements, known as the Eady-Miranda Agreement, were signed. This agreement allowed access to the pounds sterling that Argentina received in exchange for its exports, in order to pay for current transactions, even though these pounds were only convertible to gold or U.S. dollars. Regarding the frozen balances (or those that could not be converted due to technical problems) a gold clause was established in order to guarantee their value. The Accord also established conditions for the sale of meats and for the establishment of joint companies involving

British capital for railroads that until that time had been mainly British (see the Appendix).

The agreement was cancelled when in 1947, Great Britain, following a significant run on reserves, abandoned its attempt to return to convertibility, which had lasted scarcely two weeks. Thus, that very same year a new agreement was signed that resolved the remaining problems. Argentina paid its debt to Great Britain and bought railroads from Britain. How the purchase of railroads affected Argentine national wealth is debatable because much of the equipment was obsolete or had to be updated, something that had not been done since 1930. Although the payment of the debt was reflected in a decrease in foreign liabilities, the trade surplus should have been used for buying imports (allowing the liquidity in public hands to be used to refill inventories and equipment). The Central Bank, with reserves nearly depleted, had to immediately assume other, private sector liabilities, and in 1949 when faced with a payment crisis that left the country without commercial credit abroad, the Bank lacked foreign exchange to pay for imports.

The State and the Economy

State as Producer

Because the state assumed that the private sector did not have enough capital – to finance important projects or because they were considered strategic sectors – the government took over a great number of companies. Some of these enterprises already existed, such as the YPF, and others were nationalized, such as railroads, telephone company, the merchant marine, power companies, and so on. Still others were created, such as Aerolineas Argentinas, Somisa, YCF, and so forth; these included not only public services but also extractive and industrial production. Table 4.27 shows the companies, the year of their founding, and their purpose.

State enterprises became the country's most important companies, because of volume of sales and production, and though they should have been managed like private ones, with the goal of maximizing profits, this was not the case. Their objective was not always the production of goods and services (to supply demand at minimum cost) but rather they had other goals, namely, to provide employment, to subsidize consumption at prices at times lower than the cost of production, and so on. Furthermore, state enterprises differed in the areas of financing and risk. If they were running at a deficit, they recurred to the government instead of going bankrupt. In fact, with such a confusing and complex system, political favors and corruption in management were rampant. Oddly, some companies bought

Table 4.27. *State Enterprises*

State Enterprises	Year Founded and Purpose
Bank of Industrial Credit/*Banco Industrial*	1943. Finance industrial sector
National Fruit Market/*Mercado Nacional de Frutas*	1944. Control fruit supply in the capital
Merchant Air Force/*Flota Aérea Mercante Argentina (FAMA) – Zonda – Alfa – Aeroposta Argentina*	1945. Control of air traffic
State Airlines/*Líneas Aéreas del Estado*	1945. On the baseline military air transport LANE y LASO. Develop Patagonian Zone
Solid Mineral Fuel Management; Coal Mines/*Dirección General de Combustibles Sólidos Minerales – Yacimientos Carboníferos*	1945. Direct coal mining YPF
State Gas Company/*Gas del Estado*	1945. Nationalize the Buenos Aires *Compañía Primitiva de gas*
Argentine Institute for the Promotion of Trade/IAPI	1946. Promote foreign trade
Telephones and Telecommunications/*Empresa Mixta Telefónica Argentina (EMTA) – Empresa Nacional de Telecomunicaciones (ENT l)*	1946. The government bought Unión Telefónica (ITT) and in 1948 eight more companies. ENTel was created in 1956
Real Estate Investment Institute/*Instituto Mixto de Inversiones*	1947. Promote public and private real estate market
Argentine Iron and Steel Joint Venture (SOMISA)	1947. Redeveloped in 1958. Produces rolled iron, etc.
Water and Electric/*Agua y Energía Eléctrica*	1947. Continuation of the ex *Dirección General de Agua y Energía Eléctrica*
National Industries Management Co./*Dirección Nacional de Industrias del Estado (DINIE)*	1947. Manage a group of enemy-owned properties (German and Japanese). In 1953 the government decided to begin the restitution of these companies
National Fruit Distributor/*Distribuidora Nacional de Frutos*	1947. Nationalize the industry; it harvested fruit in the Río Negro Valley Zone
Alcohol Distilleries/*Destilería de Alcohol Anhídrido*	1948. Expropriated by the state and transferred to the DINIE
Chemical Industry/*Atanor – Compañía Nacional para la Industria Química, Sociedad Anónima Mixta*	1949. Produce methanol and sodium chloride, etc.
State Railroad/*Empresa Ferrocarriles del Estado Argentino (EFEA)*	1949. Nationalization. In 1969 its legal name becomes Ferrocarriles Argentinos
High Seas and River Fleet/*Flota Argentina de Navegación de Ultramar (FANU) – Flota Argentina de Navegación Fluvial (FANF)*	1949. The government acquires *Compañía Argentina de Navegación Dodero*
Argentine Airlines/*Aerolíneas Argentinas*	1950. Control air traffic
National Energy Company/*Empresa Nacional de Energía (ENDE)*	1950. Create a holding company to join national energy companies (YPF, Gas del Estado, YCF, Agua y energía). Failed to achieve its objective. Dissolved in 1957

(continued)

Table 4.27 *(continued)*

State Enterprises	Year Founded and Purpose
National Transportation Co./*Empresa Nacional de Transporte*	1952. Same as previous but for transportation companies
Airplane Factories/*Industrias Aeronáuticas y Mecánicas del Estado (IAME, DINFIA, IME)*	1952. Successor of Fábrica Militar de Aviones. Became and automobile manufacturer
Munitions and Naval Factories/*Astilleros y Fábricas Navales del Estado (AFNE)*	1953. Two plants, Astillero Río Santiago and *la fábrica de Azul* (gun powder)
Provincial Enterprises	*Year Created and Purpose*
Victoria Fruit Market/*Mercado de Frutas "Victoria"*	1947. Bahía Blanca railroad market, where raw wool and hides, and so on, are traded
Buenos Aires Prov. Energy Co./*Dirección de Energía de la Provincia de Buenos Aires (DEBA)*	1947. Small private companies are expropriated
Cordoba Provincial Energy/*Empresa Provincial de Energía de Córdoba*	1952.

Regarding legislation, in 1946 Executive Order 15.349 was issued, creating joint ventures (Sociedades de Economía Mixta) and thus establishing the first judicial system that regulated direct state intervention in the economy. In 1949 Executive Order 13.653 was issued, establishing a legal framework for state enterprises that therefore were known as "State Enterprises."

Source: Alberto Ugalde, *Las Empresas Públicas en la Argentina*, Buenos Aires, El Cronista Comercial, 1984.

primary products from other state companies at prices higher than market ones, not surprisingly resulting in a negative balance statement. The deficits were partially financed with bank loans that the Central Bank rediscounted.

State as Regulator: Price Controls

The day after war was declared in Europe, September 4, 1939, the executive sent a bill to Congress that established maximum prices on various products and materials and a complex mechanism meant to discourage speculation and *agio*. The law swiftly passed both chambers of the Congress and signed by the executive on September 8, 1939. During debate on the bill the minister of agriculture maintained that there was no doubt "that the war had caused great concern, unscrupulous concern . . . and that was something the State could not accept as it had to defend the public interest from those who wished to enrich themselves by taking advantage of difficult circumstances." The minister also pointed out that all modern legislatures had seen fit to "adopt severe measures" to combat the speculation and *agio* that were at the root of the price increases.[46] He added that the Supreme Court had found that the extent of the need for regulation was directly correlated to the public interest affected. The law was established as an emergency

46 *Anales de Legislación Argentina*, p. 652.

measure because the exceptional restrictions imposed on the freedom to do business had been a concern to all of those involved in the sanction; this was a "special and temporary law" according to the executive, "originating from the dramatic circumstances experienced throughout the world."

Article 1 of the law established initial maximum prices on consumer items – these included food, clothing, housing, construction materials, heat and electricity. It took the average prices from the first half of August, determined by the executive, and these could be periodically adjusted for each region. Article 5 stipulated that the executive would also determine price caps for manufacturers, intermediaries, importers, and wholesalers for sales to retail outlets. The law authorized the creation of registries, inventory controls, cost controls, the imposition of penalties for infractions, and prison sentences and immediate closure of businesses for repeat offenders. Article 14 granted the executive the power to restrict the exportation of merchandise that the country needed. Article 16 declared the goods included in Articles 1 and 2, raw materials required for their manufacture, and public utilities subject to expropriation. On the same day as passage of the law, September 8, the Supply Control Commission (*Comisión de Control de Abastecimiento*) was formed by decree as an addendum to the law.

During the debate in Congress the extraordinary powers that would be granted to the executive branch by means of this law were recognized and only justified as a way to confront the economic emergency that the country was facing. Although it was agreed that the law should only be applied for the duration of the conflict, the legislature chose not to put a precise date of expiration.

A year after the war ended, on June 3, 1946, a day before Colonel Perón assumed power, the still chief executive General Farrel, along with his cabinet, issued Decree 16.216 modifying Law 12.591, prolonging maximum prices. This time the decree was justified because of the "urgent nature of the defense of the public interest to prevent an unfair increase in prices." It authorized the executive to modify prices of the goods and services included in Articles 1 and 2, adding the procedure to be followed by provincial and territorial governments. These included price fixing for intermediary manufacturers and wholesalers, with procedures and sanctions, giving the Ministry of Industry and Commerce the role of a tribunal to intervene in the process concerning infractions of the law as well as the decree that modified it.

Subsidized Loans. With prices reaching double digits and much lower fixed nominal interest rates (around 5%), real interest rates were nearly permanently negative. This forced rationing credit. The phase of increase in investment tended to coincide with negative real interest rates, and when because of circumstances the real interest rate was positive, investment

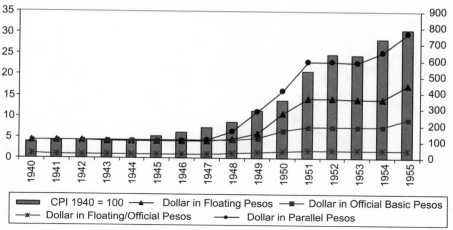

Figure 4.19. Consumer Prices and the Value of the Dollar, 1940–1955. *Source:* Rafael Olarra Jiménez, *Evolución Monetaria Argentina*, Buenos Aires, Universitaria de Buenos Aires, 1968, p. 184. IPC: Until 1942, Dirección Nacional de Estadísticas y Censos, Costo del Nivel de Vida en la Capital Federal, March 1968. From 1943, Instituto de Estadísticas y Censos (INDEC), Índice de Precios al Consumidor (IPC) GBA, www.indec.gov.ar. Consulted in May 2005.

decreased. Obtaining loans from banks at negative rates allowed a source of capital formation from borrowed funds, something that everyone wanted to take advantage of. Many of these investments were only profitable with negative interest rates and would not have rendered profits at market rates. People began businesses only if they could access subsidized credit, which could even sometimes be used for other purposes. This allowed entrepreneurs to agree to pay better salaries (when devaluations eroded the purchasing power of wages) as long as the government helped to provide loans at negative real interest rates.

Peso Overvaluation. Devaluations improved exporters' earnings because they received foreign exchange. However, some time later, when domestic prices continued to increase and the exchange rate stabilized, the situation reversed. In fact, the supposed exporter extraordinary profits (from achieving greater local purchasing power due to events beyond their control) disappeared and the official exchange rate for exports was significantly overvalued. Figure 4.19 shows the evolution of prices and of the dollar between 1940 and 1955.

In this way, legal stipulations taxed exporter income and were reflected in even more unfavorable terms of domestic trade between agricultural and manufactured products, as Díaz Alejandro has pointed out (Figure 4.20).

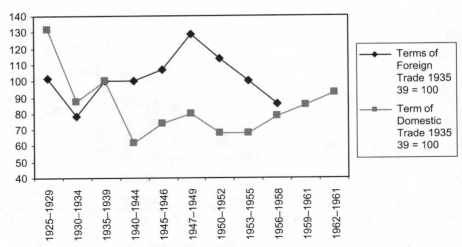

Figure 4.20. Terms of Domestic and Foreign Trade. *Source:* Carlos Díaz Alejandro, *Essays on Economic History of the Argentine Republic,* New Haven and London, Yale University Press, 1970.

These circumstances caused a continuous and prolonged decline in exports and a struggle for income distribution that would continue during the decades to come. Figure 4.21 shows that after the postwar boom exports dropped and remained around a billion dollars. Thus, Argentine exports dropped considerably on the world market (see Figures 4.21 and 4.22).

Fiscal and Monetary Policy, 1946–1955

Fiscal Policy

Official records of revenues, expenditures, and financing during the Perón period reflect only a portion of the operations carried out through the government. Official statistics hid expenditures, as was seen in 1956, a year during which contributions to state companies such as Water Supply and Drainage (*Obras Sanitarias*) recorded as assets but, because they were nonrecoverable, should have been recovered as government expenditures. Furthermore, as noted previously, a considerable portion of state companies' deficits, decentralized entities, and even government expenditures were financed with loans that were never recovered. This is the case of the loans to the IAPI that were not repaid and that the government recognized placing a provisional restructuring bond in the amount of 27,598.77 million pesos in the Central Bank to substitute them. The annual flows of those nonrecovered loans that were part of the bond and are shown in Table 4.15 should be added

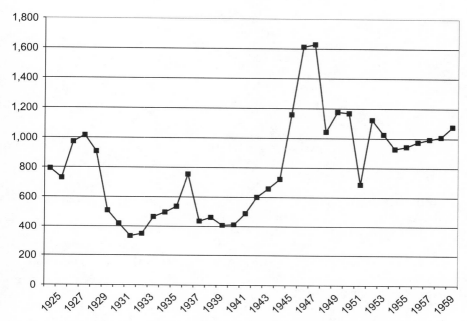

Figure 4.21. Argentine Exports, 1925–1960 (in millions of current dollars). *Source:* INDEC, www.indec.gov.ar.

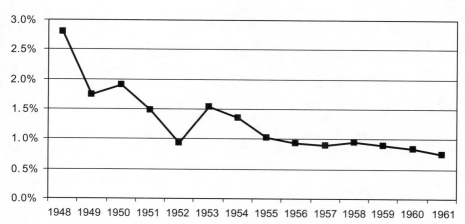

Figure 4.22. Argentine Exports on the World Market. *Source:* J. Fornero and A. Díaz Cafferata, *Tendencias y Quiebres del Grado de Apertura Exportadora de Argentina, y el Marco Internacional, 1884–2002*, IEF and University of Córdoba, 2004.

Table 4.28. *Argentine Total Debt as of December 31, 1955 (in millions of current pesos)*

National public debt	57,576.30
Provincial and municipal debt	8,367.50
IAPI and Bank debt	20,482.20
Foreign debt	13,626.00
	100,052.00

Source: Eugenio Blanco, *La Política Presupuestaria y Otros*, Ministerio de Hacienda de la Nación, Buenos Aires, 1956.

to the deficit during each of the years indicated, increasing government debt.

Taking the expenditures that were not registered, Blanco[47] concluded that public debt had increased from 6,183 million pesos to 57,576 million by the end of 1955 (without including the IAPI debt). Total public debt reached 100,052 million pesos in 1955. Table 4.28 indicates how this debt was broken down.

Compare Blanco's estimates of public expenditures for that year; they reached 11,666 million pesos, with the data from the foregoing table. That is, the debt was 8.6 times the expenditures for one year. Furthermore, according to Blanco, in 1946 revenue covered only 58% of expenditures, and in 1955, 66.7% of expenditures. Ted Reutz[48] took into account undeclared expenditures in the budget and the different means of financing to cover disparities between revenues and expenditures (real and simulated loans, the latter through monetary issues) and found that in 1946 the expenditures included in the budget were 3,241 million pesos, whereas the expenditures not included were 2,406 million, making total expenditures 5,647 million. Subtracting 1,892 million pesos in revenue from this number, the total amount to be financed reached 3,755 million (revenue was only 33.5% of total expenditures). In 1955 budgeted expenditures were 19,892 million, and nonbudgeted expenditures 8,224 million, reaching a total of 28,116 million, which, minus 12,551 in revenue, required 15,565 million in financing. Thus, revenue covered 44.6% of expenditures. Note that if out-of-budget expenditures is included, the disparity was enormous and was partially financed with debt and inflationary tax (the 27,600 million covered in the provisional restructuring bond).

47 E. Blanco, *La política Presupuestaria y Otros*, Ministerio de Hacienda de la Nación, Buenos Aires, 1956.
48 Ted Reutz, "Ilusiones Fiscales, Dimensión y Método de Financiamiento del Déficit Fiscal del Gobierno 1928–1972", *Ciclos*, Ministerio de Economía, 1991.

Table 4.29. *Public Expenditure outside of the Ordinary Treasury Budget (in hundreds of million current pesos)*

Year	IAPI	National Mortgage Bank	State Railroad	Total
1946	9.5	14.6	–	24.1
1947	22.4	3.1	–	25.5
1948	28.8	9.9	–	38.7
1949	17.6	12.8	7.4	37.8
1950	0.1	13.3	7.3	20.7
1951	2.1	12.7	12.8	27.6
1952	9.5	18.7	11.1	39.3
1953	31.6	22.1	12.5	66.2
1954	46.7	35.2	18.5	100.4
1955	38.9	44.3	–	83.2

Source: Ted Reutz, "Ilusiones Fiscales, Dimensión y Método de Financiamiento del Déficit Fiscal del Gobierno 1928–1972," *Ciclos*, Ministerio de Economía, 1991. Extract of Table 4, p. 135.

Advances and subsidies to the IAPI, the National Mortgage Bank and the State Railroad were the main out-of-budget expenditures items. These are shown in Table 4.29.

In 1946, 61% of financing went to the National Mortgage Bank. But between 1947 and 1949 the IAPI was the primary recipient, as this period was characterized by massive nationalization of public services. Again, between 1950 and 1952 the National Mortgage Bank received a large part of financing, but railroads began to require substantial financing. Later, starting in 1953, the IAPI was again the main recipient of government funding. According to Reutz, 4,000 million pesos were issued in 1946 to finance the government and 44,600 million in 1955 (see Table 4.30).

The OAS/IDB/ECLA study, *Estudio sobre Politica Fiscal en la Argentina*, referred to herein for data for 1961, uses a different methodology, showing revenues, expenditures, and financing that differ from previous estimations of Treasury balances. Thus, it shows data that differ from the tables of Treasury revenue and expenditure that appear in the Treasury Yearbook that we followed in the first three chapters.

From here on, given the magnitude of inflation, we've put the data in constant money from 1974. Although budget investment accounts, as opposed to Treasury balances, incorporated revenues and expenditures from the retirement system for state personnel, the OAS/IDB study incorporates revenues and expenditures from the entire social security system from 1945 on. This distinction is a very important one, as mentioned previously, given

Table 4.30. *Monetary Issues for Government Financing (never recovered, in thousands of million of current pesos)*

Year	Issue
1946	4.0
1947	6.7
1948	9.6
1949	13.6
1950	15.4
1951	16.9
1952	19.7
1953	27.0
1954	35.3
1955	44.6

Source: Ted Reutz, "Ilusiones Fiscales, Dimensión y Método de Financiamiento del Déficit Fiscal del Gobierno 1928–1972", *Ciclos*, Ministerio de Economía, 1991. Extract of Table 6, p. 138.

the scope of the retirement system, and it resulted in a considerable increase in revenues, which until 1958 was substantially greater than outlays.

In 1945 revenue to social security was 19.9% of expenditures, and in 1955, 29%. More importantly, the social security net surplus was 7.6% of revenue, and in 1955 it was 10%.

Revenues and expenditures rose sharply during this period, and more or less at the same rate, slightly more than 8% yearly in real terms. However, from the beginning expenditures were greater than revenues, 17.5% greater in 1946 and 16.7% in 1955. Given these circumstances, the primary as well as the total deficit was permanent. Outlays of debt payment decreased once foreign debt was converted to domestic debt and placed in the Central Bank.

Nevertheless, two main periods may be discerned. Revenues increased until 1949, then dropped in 1950, increasing somewhat in 1951 and dropping once again in 1952, then steadily increasing until 1955. Expenditures increased substantially until 1948, 40.7% annually, and decreased until 1952, 43.8%, but much more moderately, 13.4% yearly, and later increased again. What does not appear in these accounts is expenditures financed with rediscounts from the Central Bank with money issues that were partially reduced by inflation in real terms, and in nominal terms were not recovered, necessitating the emission of the provisional restructuring bonds mentioned previously.

With two new and significant sources of revenue, retirement system and contributions and Central Bank rediscounts, and having monetized the foreign debt, the government, at least until 1948, believed it had a very

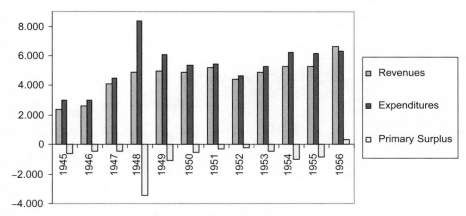

Figure 4.23. National State's Revenues and Expenditures 1945–1956 (in millions of 1945 pesos). *Source: Programa Conjunto de Tributación: Estudio sobre Política Fiscal en la Argentina*, OAS/IDB/CEPAL, 1963.

wide margin for spending. And so it did. This profligate spending lasted only until 1949. Afterward, circumstances changed and required spending cuts until 1953, and later expenditures grew, albeit more moderately (see Figure 4.23).

The government established several new (coparticipatory) taxes – on extraordinary profits, on occasional earnings (*ganacias eventuales*) – and the tax on what was the free transference of goods increased the sales tax rate from 1.25% to 8%.[49] Tax collection continued to rely more heavily on indirect taxes. Although the government maintained that expenditure policy was intended to promote work on infrastructure anticipated in the five-year plan (among other projects, the construction of the Comodoro Rivadavia–Buenos Aires oil pipeline), Blanco maintained that a very significant part of it was for government operations, including the expenditures registered as public works, which partially paid for the growth of an enormous bureaucracy. Furthermore, according to Blanco, what was spent was insufficient to cover the capital erosion of the infrastructure system, including the railroad, energy, and transportation.

Monetary Policy

The postwar years of great expansion. In 1946 reserves increased because of a hike in export prices, and terms of trade improved considerably. However, in 1947 reserves dropped substantially because of the payment of debt in Great Britain and of railroads. But the drop in reserves was not reflected in a contraction of currency and credit, because it was compensated with an

49 E. Blanco, *La política*, p. 24.

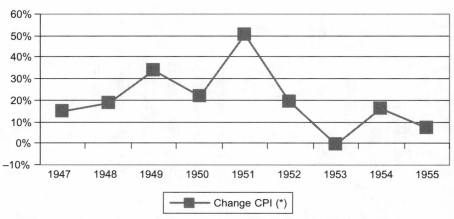

Figure 4.24. Inflation (in percent average annual change of CPI). *Source:* INDEC,
www.indec.gov.ar.

increase in domestic credit (rediscounts). In the following years, the same
mechanism would be used each time reserves fell.

During 1947–1948 reserves dropped, but the Central Bank carried
out a policy of expansion, increasing the money supply. GDP continued to
increase until 1948, but that year there was a negative balance of payments.
The real money supply and credit continued to increase, although more
slowly, as seen in the deposits indicating the beginning of a demonetization
process. Not only did the Central Bank attenuate the drop in reserves but it
also took a more expansive and less prudent posture, reflected in an increase
in inflation (see Figure 4.24).

1949–1952. From 1949 to 1952 reserves continued to drop, except in
1950, when they increased. But the Central Bank increased domestic credit
and the money supply. However, in real terms the money supply decrease,
something that also happened with domestic credit and even more with
deposits. The demonetization process was in full swing. The policy of
monetary expansion was unsuccessful. The economy became demonetized,
showing that the Central Bank did not control the real amount of money,
which was determined instead by demand.

1953–1955. After the devaluation, the fall in GDP, and the monetary contraction, reserves increased in 1953 and remained stable in 1954. However,
the Central Bank began a policy of expanding domestic credit in 1954. In
1953 and 1954 nominal expansion of the money supply was 23.2% and
17%, respectively, whereas the real expansion was considerably less, 18.5%
and 12.6%.

Here too, monetary policy had little effect on the real money supply.
In 1954 the public accepted, though to a lesser degree, the real increase

Table 4.31. *Expansion/Contraction of GDP and Net Balance of the Balance of Payments*

Period	Growth in GDP (%)	Accumulated Net Balance of Balance of Payments[a]
1945–1948	27.7	−1,846
1948–1953	1,5[b]	−2,054
1953–1955	8.9	1,571

[a] In millions of current pesos.
[b] GDP drops more than 6% in 1952 with respect to 1951.
Source: *Cuentas Nacionales de la República Argentina: Series Históricas*, vol. III, Buenos Aires, BCRA, Gerencia de Investigaciones Económicas, 1976, and BCRA Yearbook, 1945–1956.

in the amount of money, probably after the real contraction that happened during previous years. This was also accepted because, starting in 1953, the contractive effects of the real fall in the money supply and the improved harvest of 1953 helped to equalize the balance of payments, creating greater expectations. Thus, what ensued was a greater demand for money (less fear of peso devaluation) (see Table 4.31).

The Perón government did not follow an anticyclical policy that the Central Bank had used, but instead continued to expand in periods of growth as well as periods of contraction, although more moderately, and in 1952 in a more contractive way. This was different from the period of the gold standard, which had been procyclical expansive in good years and contractive in bad ones, and promised to provide the best of both worlds; when there were reserves they were monetized without fear of expansion, and when reserves were reduced, money was created by means of credit in order to compensate its decline. But as has been seen, monetary policy had a different effect on the increase in the money supply in real terms. Figure 4.25 show the evolution of money creation factors in the three periods discussed and Figure 4.26 its components. (Also refer to Tables A.38, A.39, and A.40 in the Appendix.)

Evolution of the Economy

Period of Expansion, 1946–1948

Between 1946 and 1948 the economy experienced a considerable expansion caused by a substantial increase in volume and prices of exports. European countries, whose markets were closed during the years of the blockade, desperately needed foodstuffs at the end of the war, and this demand spurred an increase in the price of Argentine grain exports. This increase was intensified by a significant rise in consumption due to salary increases,

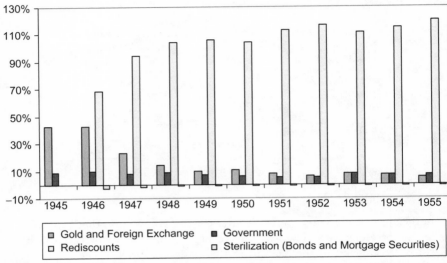

Figure 4.25. Money Creation Factors (as percentages of the money supply). *Source:* BCRA Yearbooks, 1945–1955.

as obligatory Christmas bonus was established. During these years there was also a significant increase in imports, after the long period of war rationing, which affected investment. Construction was an important factor, as it increased by 30.4%; public works grew by 55.7%, whereas private projects grew by only 15.6% (see Table 4.32).

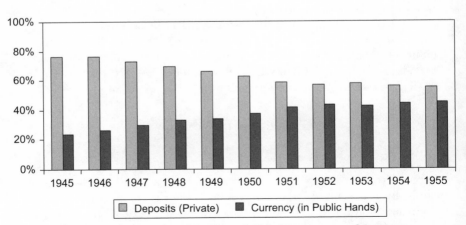

Figure 4.26. Components of the Money Supply (as percentages of the money supply). *Source:* BCRA Yearbooks, 1945–1955.

Table 4.32. *GDP by Sectors, 1946–1948*

	Growth (%)	Annual Rate (%)	Contribution to Total Change (%)
GDP by factor cost	17.30	8.30	–
Agriculture	18.80	9.00	10.20
Fishing	20.50	9.80	0.20
Mining	2.70	1.30	0.20
Cattle	−2.40	−1.20	−1.40
Manufacturing industries	16.70	8.00	22.80
Construction	30.40	14.20	10.10
Transportation	25.10	11.80	11.50
Trade	25.10	11.90	24.80
Public services, personal and housing	13.70	6.70	16.60

Note: Data calculated at 1950 prices, by cost of factors.
Source: Cuentas Nacionales de la República Argentina: Series Históricas, vol. III, BCRA, Gerencia de Investigaciones Económicas, Buenos Aires, 1976.

Agricultural production increased by 18.8%, reflecting an increase not in land cultivated, but rather in productivity. Exports increased by more than 100% as a result of an extremely sharp increase in prices, although import prices also increased. The terms of trade favorable to the country increased by 21%. The manufacturing industry increased by 16.7%, reflecting growth in electro domestics, machinery, and textiles. Import increases favored the industrial sector, providing it with machinery and industrial primary inputs (see Figure 4.27).

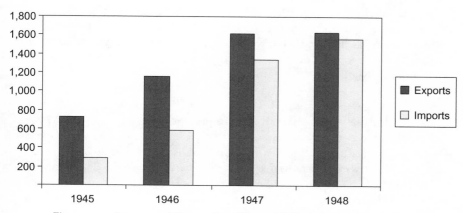

Figure 4.27. Imports and Exports (in millions of dollars). *Source:* FIEL, Online database. Consulted in May 2005.

Government public expenditures, employment, policies, and loans to the official banking system through rediscounts from the Central Bank, not only to the government but to the private sector as well, among other reasons, to face salary hikes, raised the purchasing power of the population and intensified the expansive trend begun during the war. However, this expansive phase very quickly revealed limitations, primarily in the external sector. Within the exchange control system, individuals could only import goods with a permit that assured availability of foreign exchange; when these permits were granted, the Central Bank backed them against foreign creditors giving foreign exchange for the corresponding sale of pesos. When the war ended, demands of importers increased, and they obtained permits and carried out purchases abroad, usually on credit.

During this period, Argentine foreign trade operated in two markets: convertible market foreign exchange[50] (principally concerning the dollar) and trade agreement foreign exchange (primarily with the United Kingdom and later with other European countries). When the war ended, many imports were made on the free exchange market, where availability of foreign exchange quickly dried up. In 1949 the country faced a severe payment problem because it had accumulated a significant debt to creditors, which caused a suspension of the merchandise supply on credit, and from that point could only make with payments in cash. The difficulties were finally overcome thanks to a loan from the Eximbank of $125 million, to a consortium of local banks, with the collateral of the Central Bank. But the first balance-of-payments crisis of 1949 was an indicator that the easy Perón years were coming to an end.

On the other hand, from trade with Great Britain, there were substantial balances in pounds sterling that were largely nonconvertible. It was not entirely true that these balances were spent on the repurchase of the debt and the purchase of Argentine railroads, but rather in 1947 and again in 1949 they were used to finance imports from Great Britain. The debt and the railroads, as has been seen, were bought with trade surpluses from the years 1944 to 1946, and the trade surplus from 1948 was used to pay exports in advance.

The Fiesta *Is Over.* In 1949 GDP fell by 1.3% and the terms of trade changed for the worse. Even though import prices dropped by 15%, the expansion, fomented by an increase of 28% in current nominal government spending and a 29.7% growth in BCRA rediscounts and advances, continued, albeit with substantial signs of an inflationary trend. Thus, toward the end of 1949 the economy began to demonetize. Also M_3, an indicator of financial deepening, declined from 55.8% of GDP in 1945 and 54% in

---

50 In fact, it was not free because the Central Bank intervened in the market.

Table 4.33. *Changes in GDP by Sector, 1948–1952*

	Growth (%)	Annual Rate (%)	Contribution to Total Change (%)
GDP by factor cost	−3.9	−1.0	–
Agriculture	−29.6	−8.4	72.8
Fishing	20.2	4.7	−0.8
Mining	15.5	3.7	−3.7
Cattle	−5.4	−1.4	11.6
Manufacturing industries	−5.7	−1.4	34.4
Construction	−3.0	−0.8	5.0
Transportation	2.4	0.6	−5.3
Trade	−18.0	−4.8	84.8
Public services, personal and housing	14.5	3.5	−76.2

Note: Data calculated at 1950 prices, at factor cost.

Source: Cuentas Nacionales de la República Argentina: Series Históricas, vol. III, BCRA, Gerencia de Investigaciones Económicas, Buenos Aires, 1976.

1949 to 45.7% in 1950 and 37.3% in 1951.[51] This began to have a negative effect. In addition, crop failure during the 1948/1949 season, followed by another during 1949/1950, affected other activities, such as construction, trade, and so on, and caused a complete change in the economy (see Table 4.33).

The fall in exports caused an additional restriction on import capacity, which affected industries while they were still able to import industrial primary inputs. The net substitution became negative and no longer had unlimited expansion capacity. In sum, the Perón *fiesta* had ended. This situation forced the government to make policy changes, causing a minor devaluation and providing subsidies to the agricultural sector. Even though credit, in nominal terms, grew by 8% in 1950 (the IAPI reduced it by 1%), in real terms it dropped by 6%, whereas government expenditures fell by 10.7%, also in real terms (see Table 4.34). At any rate, when with the changes, the economy overcame the most critical period and harvests improved with the 1954 recovery, the expansion policy of credit and loans returned, albeit now at more moderate pace.

Income Distribution

Between 1914 and 1929 the economy had grown 1.5% per capita per year while real wages grew 2.6% per year. The appreciation of the peso during

51 M_3 includes currency in public hands + deposits in pesos and dollars in current accounts + deposits in pesos and dollars in savings accounts + time deposits in pesos and dollars.

Table 4.34. *Changes in GDP by Sector, 1952–1955*

	Growth (%)	Annual Rate (%)	Contribution to Total Change (%)
GDP by factor cost	14.9	4.7	–
Agriculture	54.0	15.5	25.2
Fishing	3.5	1.2	0.0
Mining	13.5	4.3	1.0
Cattle	7.5	2.4	4.1
Manufacturing industries	16.0	5.1	24.7
Construction	8.1	2.6	3.5
Transportation	13.2	4.2	8.0
Trade	16.0	5.1	16.7
Public services, personal and housing	3.3	1.1	5.3

Note: Data calculated at 1950 prices, at factor cost.
Source: Cuentas Nacionales de la República Argentina: Series Históricas, vol. III, Buenos Aires, BCRA, Gerencia de Investigaciones Económicas, 1976.

the second half of the 1920s had been one of the determining factors of the wage increase, which had been greater than in European countries. During the 1930s real wages lagged behind growth in productivity, reversing the trend of the previous decade, when they had increased significantly. Devaluation negatively affected real wages, because the fall in international prices was compensated to some degree by the peso devaluation (in relation to other currencies) and wage earners saw their positions slip, in relation to their gains during the 1920s. However, they were affected to a lesser degree than the depreciation in relation to other currencies because international prices fell during the beginning of the decade of the 1930s. During that decade, whereas the economy grew by 4% per year per capita, real wages declined slightly, by 0.07% per year.

Real wages increased substantially in 1947 and 1948, and this phenomenon is rightly considered the result of Perón's policies, which were favorable to the working class. Although this rate of growth did not continue, during the Perón government wages increased by 51% from 1946 to 1950 and by −2% from 1950 to 1955 (because of reversals in 1950 and 1952), whereas GDP grew by 17.1% and by 10.6% during the same periods. Doubtless, improvements in the beginning were significant, but circumstances abroad, which forced the devaluations, negatively affected real wages, which could not be maintained over time (see Figure 4.28).

During these years there was a positive correlation between the appreciation of domestic currency and increases in real wages. However, there was a negative correlation between the exchange rate and real wages:

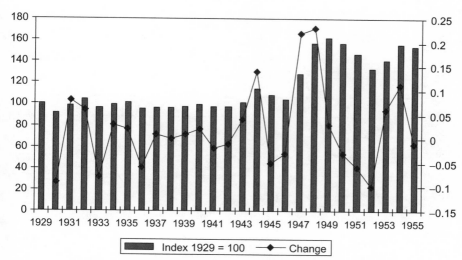

Figure 4.28. Real Wage Index. *Source: Anuario Geográfico Argentino*, Comité
Nacional de Geografía, Buenos Aires, 1941, and Juan Llach, "Los determinantes del
salario en Argentina: Un diagnóstico de largo plazo y propuestas de políticas",
Revista Estudios, Instituto de Estudios Económicos sobre la Realidad Argentina y
Latinoamericana (IEERAL), Córdoba, Año VII, no. 29, 1984.

a high exchange rate meant lower real wages, and vice versa (see Figure 4.29).

The Political Economy of Populism: Mercantilism

It is probably an overstatement to say that Perón had an elaborate long-
term plan expressed in his government's policies. In fact, many policies
that appear in official reports, even the five-year plan (*Plan Quinquenal*)
among others, at times reflect speech writers' opinions more than Perón's.
Perón let them write on policies, and if they turned out well, he supported
them. If not, he did not hesitate to discard them. Perón was also a product
of his time; exchange control and the nationalization of the banking and
transportation systems were not an Argentine invention, because they were
tried in other countries as well. Nationalizing banks and public services
were part and parcel of Great Britain's Labour Party and were implemented
by the first French government coalition headed by General De Gaulle.[52]
But in his milieu and circumstances, he responded with his own particular
perspective, in a very pragmatic way, intending to consolidate political

52 Herman Van der Wee, *Prosperity and Upheaval: The World Economy, 1945–1980*, Berkeley and Los
Angeles, University of California Press, 1986.

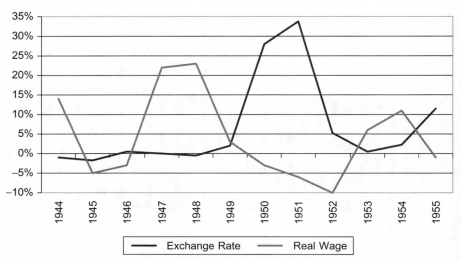

Figure 4.29. Real Wages and the Exchange Rate (annual percent change). *Source:*
Carlos Díaz Alejandro, *Tipo de Cambio y Términos de Intercambio en la República
Argentina, 1913–1976*, Buenos Aires, CEMA, 1981, *Anuario Geográfico Argentino*,
Comité Nacional de Geografía, Buenos Aires, 1941, and Juan Llach, "Los
Determinantes del Salario en Argentina. Un Diagnóstico de Largo Plazo y
Propuestas de Políticas," *Estudios*, no. 29, Córdoba, IEERAL, 1984.

support, something that granted him enormous power. In a country where
many of these methods had been used, and in a favorable ideological world
climate, from the 1930 crisis to state intervention, Perón added his particular view of ruling the country, acquired during his military career. He
was also convinced that his base of support was the new unions that had
emerged from the labor organizations, which had been conceived of by the
state, like the *Carta del Lavoro*. But unlike Vargas, Perón did not take the
further step of a corporate constitution like that of the *Estado Novo* in 1937
in Brazil. Nevertheless, this did not get in the way of his employing all of
the means at his disposal to make institutional changes that would have
long-term effects.

In the beginning, Perón acted as if he had limitless sources of financing
the government to which he added numerous new functions. It is important
to note that after the end of World War II, there were no flows of international capital, on which Argentina had relied in the past, and although
this was a negative restriction, it allowed Perón great autonomy, because
he was free from concerns about confidence abroad and international financial repercussions. What was most important was this degree of autonomy,
which was much greater than in other countries (e.g., Australia), during
the postwar period. At the end of the war, he had an enormous supply of

reserves, although the country could not use in other markets the pounds that were frozen in the Bank of England. He exchanged these reserves in payment of long-term debt and to buy real assets that, to a great extent, were already obsolete (railroads), when he could have used them even to increase imports from Great Britain itself.[53] Furthermore, the substantial amount of reserves available had become depleted after these operations. However, he had at his disposal the Central Bank as an instrument for financing his projects.

If to all of this we add, for a time, the margins of exchange and the funds from the social security system (*Caja de Previsión Social*), the government had an enormous amount of resources that it used to provide favors to several industries without concern for the budget equilibrium. But its main objective was to try to keep real wages high, without regard for productivity, something that in the long run was impossible to sustain. In order to do this, the government intervened in prices it could control[54]: foodstuffs by means of the exchange rate, housing by means of rent control, tariffs on public services, fuel, and sometimes directly setting maximum and minimum prices. The instruments used by the Perón government had a negative effect on exports, because in the long run, the unfavorable exchange rate kept them stagnant. There was no investment in housing because of rent control, and various subsidies, among them, those to companies that were financed by monetary issues. All of these factors made the inflation rate begin to grow. These sources of financing began to dry up, especially when the economy demonetized and the inflationary tax rendered less.

With the nationalization of railroads, telephones, urban transportation in the Federal Capital, and gas, nearly all public services (electricity was excluded for a while) were under state control. The cost of these services had a powerful effect on the consumer basket for the working classes. During the Perón period, from 1946 to 1955, such utility prices lagged in real terms by 35%, as shown in Figure 4.30. This caused repeated losses to companies that operated with prices that did not cover costs for prolonged periods. The differences were covered in part by subsidized loans that were rediscounted by the Central Bank. The losses also affected the financial health of the companies and the quality and efficiency of the services rendered and its investments. Throughout the years equipment was neither replaced nor maintained.

In these conditions, energy was not the only sector where there were shortages. As we have seen, the measures adopted tended to result in an

53 Catherine R. Schenk, *Britain and the Sterling Area: From Devaluation to Convertibility in the 1950s*, London and New York, Routledge, 1994.
54 Adolfo Canitrot, "La experiencia populista de redistribución de ingresos", *Desarrollo Económico*, no. 59, 1976.

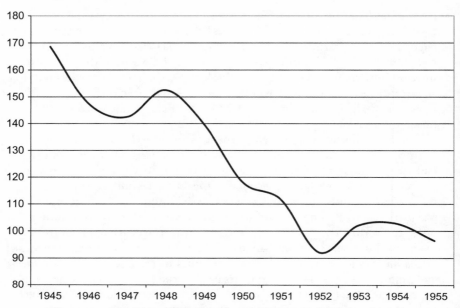

Figure 4.30. General Level of Public Companies' Prices and Tariffs, 1945–1955 (at 1960 prices held constant). *Source:* H. Nuñez Miñana and A. Porto, "Inflación y Tarifas Públicas: Argentina, 1945–1980", *Desarrollo Económico*, vol. 21, no. 84, January–March 1982.

enormous commercial deficit. Imports should have been severely rationed, and the government instead chose to privilege imports of inputs for industries that created employment: raw materials and semifinished goods. Imports of capital goods and transportation material lagged, causing a notorious decapitalization and obsolescence not only in infrastructure – where until World War I enormous investments had been made – but also in machinery and industrial equipment, where significant investments had been made. But still, although technologically outdated and under-capitalized industries could not reach international markets and traditional exports remained stagnant, the current needs of industrial inputs were greater than the availability of foreign exchange; a crisis in the balance of payments began in 1949, was repeated in 1951–1952, and would be repeated during the decades to come, and forced devaluations with changes to relative prices and unpopular adjustments. Thus, the devaluations did not have the expected effects or were abandoned and became a factor in the growth of inflation, which became uncontrollable. Inflation was caused by deficits that were financed by money issues and worsened by the loss in monetary illusion with the drop in deposits.

As has been shown, one of the Perón government objectives was to keep real wages high for the working class. But this went contrary to the economic framework based on protectionism and subsidies to the industrial sector, which, by definition, supposed that these industries were less productive than those with which they competed in international markets. In these circumstances industrial entrepreneurs found themselves in a situation in which they could not increase nominal wages without affecting profits. The government's response was to provide captive markets and credit, as well to control prices using the exchange rate, loans, and fees, so that nominal wages would have greater buying power.[55]

A new Leviathan emerged, one that could control powerful instruments that affected the everyday behavior of economic agents, favoring some and hurting others. It was a new kind of capitalism. With a mass of new institutions, the nominal property of one factor continued to belong to its owner, but profits depended to a large extent not on productivity but on the government. Manipulating profits also affected wealth, and unintentionally, property rights. It is likely that many mixed economies saw the same results, but not to the depth and extent of the case of Argentina.

Furthermore, the varied, complex, and interminable series of laws and regulations made the system quite confusing, and the utilization of the system was very costly in time and resources (and only those who were clever and rich enough could manage it). And this also unleashed a subtle but ferocious competition in the following decades for favors from the government.

The entrance of new factors to the market, in the case of capitals, occurred when special conditions had been achieved (new foreign investments with special tax privileges from the Perón period on). The labor also sought a monopoly and political influence in the unions as a way to increase wages. Growth conditions depended on the efficiency and viability of mercantilist policies. In a framework of growing illegitimacy, reinvestment of profits was not favored, nor were eliminating conflicts of income distribution and political stability. How could this complex system of laws and institutions be overcome? This was a problem that would affect Argentines for the remainder of the twentieth century.

---

55 Ibid.

5

A Divided Society, 1955–1973

Introduction

The title of this chapter is meant to highlight the turbulent political circumstances that surrounded economic activity during the eighteen years that began with the fall of Perón and ended with his return to power in 1973. The serious conflicts that the Argentines experienced happened under an international framework characterized by the Cold War, which, although it was a cohesive factor for Western Europe – under the Pax Americana – had negative effects on Latin America. Added to the chronic instability of the region were military interventions that were supposedly intended to prevent civil governments from falling under communist influence, perceived as an imminent threat once Cuba became part of the Soviet bloc.

The division among Argentines did not begin in 1955, however. There were already deep societal schisms beginning during World War II, more specifically when a military junta from the GOU (*Grupo de Oficiales Unidos*), sympathetic to the Axis powers, took over the government in 1943. When the Allied powers experienced military success, a broad swath of society intensified its opposition to the government hoping that with victory against the Nazis, the strong Allied pressure would help return Argentina to democracy. However, the 1943 military junta, which was the closest thing to an authoritarian government that the country had known, was not overthrown. There were two essential ingredients of the military government's continuity: First, the United States preferred solid, anticommunist governments, as in the case of Spain. And second, Perón distanced himself from the rhetoric of his ex-partners from the GOU, building instead a different coalition that allowed, for the only time in the twentieth century, the continuation of a military government through popular vote. The division between Perón's supporters and the opposition intensified during the ten years of his administration, not only because he stifled opposition but also because in the process of solidifying his absolute power, he took over nearly all of the media, imprisoning his most vociferous critics, severely repressing all dissident voices, and governing, starting in 1951, with the suspension of constitutional rights under a supposed state of internal warfare.

When Perón was overthrown, societal division continued during the following eighteen years, but this time under the proscription of Peronism, which out of power experienced a substantial resurgence, thanks to trade unions, known as "The 62 Organizations" (*Las 62 Organizaciones*). Union leaders fought to defend privileges (not only of union members, but their own), and their increasingly extreme Peronist resistance was severely repressed. Although proscribed, Peronism remained the strongest electoral base, one that could not be ignored; allying with various different groups, it became the decisive factor in elections (as with that of Arturo Frondizi in 1958). Union organizations played a determining role in the destabilization of civil governments, promoting repeated general strikes, even allying themselves with the military when President Illia was overthrown.

The minority army group, which together with a part of the air force and the entire navy had overthrown Perón, was firm about not allowing him to return. This was because they knew they would lose their military careers and, worse, they would end in jail. They were suspicious of any political candidate who showed sympathy for Peronism, and whereas some (the *Colorados*, or Reds) attempted to definitively prohibit Perón's political movement, others were in favor of attracting his followers while distancing themselves from Perón (the *Azules*, or Blues).

This gave a very slim margin of freedom to weak civil governments, like those of Frondizi and Illia, which for some time were dominated by the presence of the military. Any measure that attempted to reestablish a framework of economic stability was considered by the working classes to be antipopular, anti-Peronist, and reactionary. Furthermore, economic policies were severely restricted, and military interventions were justified as a way of legitimating the military in order to overcome these policies.

But Perón was not the only threat. Within the framework of the Cold War, and given the U.S. position regarding Latin American governments suspected of communist sympathies, as in the case of Goulart in Brazil (made manifest at the Punta del Este summit), some in the Argentine military assumed it was their role to control governments so as to prevent communist influence. The case of the turbulent Frondizi government can only be understood in the context of the thirty two attempted military coups, the last a successful one, which overthrew the government in 1962. The same may be said of the Guido provisional presidency and the "supervision" of the Illia government, outlined in a speech given by Onganía at West Point.

Even the military itself faced armed conflicts in 1962 and 1963. And during neither General Onganía's (*Blue*) government nor that of General Levingston could they reach a consensus about what to do with Perón's political movement. Thus, with nowhere else to turn, General Lanusse attempted to allow Peronists to compete in elections, which handed them an electoral victory in 1973.

Fundamental economic changes were impossible to achieve within the context of this political conflict. Even minor changes were nearly impossible, as they inevitably affected vested interests that formed coalitions to ensure the failure of economic teams and even governments. Amid these impossible circumstances – a veritable civil war – successive governments attempted a number of measures to resolve the most pressing problems. Although each of these problems is discussed separately herein, they were intricately connected one to the other and had to be dealt with together, which made the task even more difficult.

As Prebisch noted in 1955 and Frondizi in 1958, the most urgent problem was the decapitalization of the country, especially in the energy and transportation sectors. The industrial sector also had obsolete technology and lacked capital to renew it. Increasing the capital stock not only required increasing the level of investment to gain access to domestic and foreign capital markets, but also required having the necessary foreign exchange to purchase the urgently needed imports. For this, a change in relative prices with real devaluations favoring agriculture (like those proposed by Prebisch in 1955) was needed, which clearly did not benefit the working classes, as it reduced real wages and also diminished the profits of urban entrepreneurs. It also required attaining monetary and fiscal balance – as in the case of Frondizi – palliating uncontrollable inflation. But this was advantageous to neither politicians nor bureaucrats nor those who had access to subsidized loans.

A return to normalcy had become a monumental task, which was partially attempted at different points in time, with very limited success because of the interests at stake. But no one dared propose a clean break or a radical change in the role of the state. Except for the measures taken by Frondizi in 1959, complete measures were never taken. Even Frondizi did not attempt to open the economy or change the state's role in it, and the measures he did take were resisted and had repercussions in the form of political instability. But they did open up access to foreign credit and improve investment and imports of capital goods. These measures, as it turned out, were a precondition to the growth experienced during the decade between 1963 and 1974.

As a result of the strong resistance to the economic reforms during 1959 and 1962, successive governments attempted programs that would not cause recessions and that sought stability with expansion and full employment. These attempts generally failed because of their inconsistent nature. Except during the Illia years, during which Keynesian measures, implemented after two severe recessions, rendered positive results, governments that followed attempted a series of programs, including stabilization without recession, investment without diminishing consumption, and an increase in exports, again without sacrificing domestic consumption.

The most successful of these programs was undoubtedly the Krieger Vassena one, which took advantage of the appropriation of the devaluatory rent. It achieved capital flows and intensified the favorable trend in exports, which during the 1960s experienced a significant spike. This was due to changes in relative prices and technological improvements in agriculture with hybrid seeds promoted by INTA (*Instituto Nacional de Tecnología Agropecuaria*), an organization formed during the government of General Aramburu. Each of the measures is analyzed in this chapter.

The 1955 Provisional Government

After the fall of Perón and the short-lived government of General Lonardi (September–November 1955), the General Aramburu administration (November 1955–April 1958), which had the support of traditional political parties represented in an advisory board, a *Junta Consultiva*, had to face a series of problems. Among the most urgent were the reconstruction of the energy and transportation systems and renewing obsolete capital goods (by increasing investment and imports of machinery and equipment that had been severely restricted during the previous decade). Of equal importance was undoing the enormous regulatory system and the system of state intervention, both of which had grown to unprecedented proportions during the previous administration. Every government after the overthrow of Perón saw it necessary to regain some measure of fiscal and monetary equilibrium and to balance foreign accounts. This was to overcome the reiterated cycles of inflation, devaluation, and recession and to create a stable macroeconomic environment, all necessary conditions for sustained growth.

Although state intervention was still considered necessary for the economy, post-Perón governments sought to limit the excesses of the Perón government, which were furthermore a source of generalized corruption. A few significant reforms were effectuated, despite the different and at times contradictory opinions of various military leaders and their supporters in the political parties. However these reforms could not change the substantial state role in the economy, the closed nature of the economy, or the restricted role of the market.

The Economic Reforms of the Provisional Government

The revolution spurred significant changes in the political economy of the country. Despite the lack of a clearly defined program, and the coexistence within the government of groups with divergent interests, there was a consensus that updating infrastructure was an urgent problem, as was seeking equilibrium in the external sector and in public finances, so as to prevent waste, abuse, and corruption.

The *Revolución Libertadora* had a number of economic objectives, albeit never entirely defined as such. First, it had to obtain sources of capital in order to make necessary investments to get the country on its feet. It had to stabilize currency and stimulate agricultural production, and consequently agricultural exports. The "revolutionary" government also had to overcome the foreign chokehold on the economy and deregulate it by limiting state intervention in areas that had previously been the domain of private industry (and here is where there was the greatest disagreement within the government).

The provisional government faced numerous problems, the most serious and urgent of which had to do with the crises in the energy and transportation sectors. Up until World War II energy was supplied mainly by coal and coke, which were imported from Great Britain. Ever since the discovery of oil deposits in Comodoro Rivadavia, YPF (*Yacimientos Petrolíferos Fiscales*), the state oil company, had a monopoly on oil exploitation, but its production was insufficient to supply domestic needs. As coal was replaced by oil, the need to import fuel increased. Oil was imported at the official exchange rate in order to keep fuel prices low. This had negative consequences for YPF exploitation.[1] Because the government subsidized prices, oil consumption increased even more. By the end of the Perón government, fuel imports reached nearly one quarter of total consumption.

The great need for fuel imports led Perón in 1955 to strike a deal with Standard Oil of California for an exploration and exploitation contract. This deal was stymied by public opinion at the time, which firmly supported only Argentine state exploitation, and which was a significant factor in the growing opposition to Perón, culminating in the 1955 revolution. Energy rationing limited industrial and commercial development. The blackouts in Buenos Aires at the end of the Perón decade gave the impression that it was the capital of a country under siege.

But energy was not the only problem; the transportation crisis was also quite serious. Railroad material, which was already obsolete at the beginning of the war, was not replenished, and it was increasingly difficult to obtain foreign currency to renew wagons and rails. The bottlenecks that put a chokehold on transportation made it very difficult to deliver merchandise. The rolling stocks and rail trucks as well as public works on infrastructure deteriorated over the years because of a lack of maintenance and investment.

[1] Peronist officials claimed that significant work had been done to supply oil (oil and gas pipelines) as part of the five-year plan. See Hugo Gambini, *Historia del Peronismo (1943–1951)*, Buenos Aires, Planeta, 1999.

The significant capitalization efforts lasted until the 1930s, at which point the country misspent its capital. This process was accelerated with the advent of the war and its aftermath. Owing to the crisis, the restrictions on the supply of capital goods during the war, and especially the restrictions on imports, at the end of the war, the country was left with infrastructure in need of repair and outdated industrial capital goods (see Chapter 4, Figure 4.1, regarding the fall in investments during the war years and after 1949).

Starting in the 1930s, restrictions on imports resulted from the fact that exports did not increase except during the first few years following the war. Exports, which had reached a billion current dollars, did not rebound until the 1960s, again, except for the early postwar period. Traditional exports were discouraged by fixing a low exchange rate (the official rate of 5 pesos per dollar, and later 7.5 pesos per dollar until the end of 1955). At the same time, industrial production was protected (by tariffs as well as quantitative restrictions on imports), had a captive domestic market, and was never able to compete in international markets. Furthermore, the substantial accumulation of reserves was mainly due to a drop in imports, and the government proceeded as though these extraordinary circumstances were permanent. In fact, the reserves, which were a byproduct of decapitalization during the war years, were spent as though they were a miraculous gift in unlimited supply.

The extraordinary trade surplus, celebrated at the time and even afterward, hid an ugly truth: the decapitalization of the country, the result of the impossibility of importing goods during the war. Thus it was expected that when the war was over and normal trade resumed, demand for imports would outstrip current export levels. But because the government had purchased the foreign reserves (the trade surplus) and spent them, starting in 1949, imports had to be rationed. The *fiesta* years were short lived, and even Perón had to change his economic policy, with measures that were more favorable to exports. But vested interests would prove to be a formidable obstacle to economic reform, so that during those years and during many to follow, these interests would manage to keep the same inefficient and restricted economy in place.

President Frondizi's dramatic speech in December of 1958 was a clarion call to the nation that urgent problems plagued the economy. Besides, as noted previously, the government had used money creation as a way to finance a substantial portion of its expenditures. Another portion was covered with forced savings, seizing bank deposits, and with the social security fund. The placement of treasury bonds in the Central Bank was not a significant factor in money creation, but government and business expenditures were directly, and indirectly, financed through Bank of the Argentine Nation loans and other official banks that were rediscounted through the Central Bank. Because rediscounts were almost always greater than deposits, they were an important factor in money creation and in the ever-burgeoning inflationary process. The Peronist *fiesta* was over, and Central Bank financed government debt was finally revealed when, on December 2, 1957, a restructuring bond (*Bono de Saneamiento*) was issued in the sum of 27.6 billion pesos. This amounted to 10% of GDP and 45% of the monetary base.

Still in place were the same complex government regulations, dating back to the war years. These included controls on prices, on the flows of capital, and on foreign exchange. The government had also monopolized foreign trade and nationalized bank deposits and public services and had come to control productive enterprises in sectors that were considered strategic. One of the government's main objectives was to keep real wages high. If this could not be achieved with greater productivity (which is not possible in a protected economy), it could be accomplished by controlling factors that affected the cost of living: the prices of food, public services, and housing. To this end, the government kept the exchange rate low for food exports, and when this was no longer possible, it subsidized rates for public utilities, transportation services, and froze housing rentals for a substantial period of time.

Any policy that led to free market pricing, which seemed inevitable if inflation were to be contained and the collapse of the economy prevented, inevitably led to adjustments. These adjustments included price hikes in some areas (changes in relative prices, especially in food and public services), which affected the real income of the working classes. This would be a decades-long problem for Argentina and tended to affect particularly prices for public services. In an attempt to maintain popular support, prices for public services lagged behind costs; this situation persisted, becoming more entrenched and leading to inevitable readjustments, which caused resistance from sectors that once supported price controls. The problem was equally grave for a revolutionary government that had overthrown a populist *caudillo*, and came to highlight the income distribution conflict that had begun during the Perón years and would continue through to the present.

Shortly after taking over the government, the provisional authorities asked Raúl Prebisch to write a report on the economic situation in Argentina and to provide recommendations for policies he deemed necessary. Prebisch was then executive secretary of ECLAC and a former general manager of the Central Bank. In what became known as the *Plan Prebisch*, titled "Healthy Money or Rampant Inflation: Economic Recovery Plan" ("Moneda sana o inflación incontenible: Plan de reestablecimiento económico"), the presidential advisor stressed the stagnant state of the Argentine economy, which, according to his estimates, had grown only by 3.5% in the previous decade (1945–1955). The recommendations were intended to increase import capacity in order to supply urgently needed capital goods and to close the trade gap. To improve the terms of domestic trade for agriculture, Prebisch proposed devaluation of the peso without concomitant wage increases. He also proposed eliminating the state monopoly on trade (the IAPI) and prohibiting inflationary financing.

According to Prebisch, because the nation had "to keep pace with a consumption rate that was greater than GDP, Argentina was in the midst of a grave decapitalization process." He argued that it was necessary to impose "a social obligation on economic production." He claimed that "there has been excessive consumption at the expense of basic capital investments" and noted the negative features that were an obstacle to growth. These included the inability to increase necessary imports of raw materials, fuels, and capital goods to get the needed increase in production, and the decapitalized nature of the transportation infrastructure. The cause of this crisis, he held, was due to the "unnecessarily compromising efficient agricultural production and by bringing export levels to a perilously high level, where they currently remain, thus aggravating the negative consequences of an unfavorable reduction of foreign trade prices." He claimed that negative government policies were to blame for this. Government policy "does not follow a correct policy for import substitutions, nor have we created indispensable basic industries that would strengthen the economy." Finally he called for investments in oil exploration to relieve the high costs of fuel imports.

Prebisch also criticized policy implementation. Despite having considerable influence over capital investments, the government "has not been able to direct or implement [these investments] to accelerate the pace of the country's development and attenuate our external vulnerability." Argentina's postwar resources have been squandered "on failed or nonproductive investments." It would have been better to use these resources "to make investments primarily in agriculture, transportation, energy, and housing." The report highlighted the fall in per capita income, which by 1948 had reached, according to Prebisch, a maximum of 4,041 pesos (in 1950 pesos), dropping to 3,581 pesos in 1955.

Argentine prospects for foreign trade were not favorable during the years that followed.[2] The report stressed that the main obstacles to overcome in order to achieve a sustained increase in production were the slow growth of

2 The BCRA shows a net (provisional) balance of payments total of −153 million pesos but in U.S. dollars it was scarcely 8.5 million (at an exchange rate of 18 pesos per dollar). However, the final amount, published in 1957, shows a net balance of −$151 million. In the case of foreign exchange, if we take BCRA gold and foreign exchange (assets) in December 1955, 3.409 billion pesos, and divide it by 18, the amount is less, $189, but the amount is quite accurate.

domestic oil production, of which local industry required ever-increasing amounts; the energy crisis (at least 30% growth in installed capacity was needed to minimally fulfill industrial demand); and the chokehold caused by the monstrous transportation deficit. Inflation, another cause of economic stagnation, was also mentioned as a complicating factor for investment. With regard to housing, Prebisch recommended reducing loans based on rediscounts, proposing a return to the old method of placing mortgage loans on the market.

Prebisch warned that the devaluation would be followed by an increase in agricultural prices and that these should not be accompanied by salary hikes. He noted, "If wage increases are permitted, these would increase the cost [of production], creating a higher level of domestic prices and diminishing the desired effect of the devaluation." With regard to the more urgent need for equipment, Prebisch added that it was a question of making the necessary investments to increase oil production, because foreign oil was an ever-increasing portion of imports. He recommended construction of gas and oil pipelines and proposed investments in energy and transportation so as to break the most costly and notorious bottlenecks. Foreign credit, negotiated at reasonable rates, was the only resource at Argentina's disposal (once previous debts were paid or settled), because the precarious foreign exchange situation prevented making necessary imports. At the time, just the mention of negotiating foreign loans sounded like treason against the country.

The 1956–1957 Devaluation

In October of 1956, the provisional government created a new exchange regime that caused a sharp devaluation; the official exchange rate went from 5 pesos per dollar to 18 per dollar. (In 1955 the parallel was nearly 30 pesos.) Additionally, on recommendations from the International Monetary Fund (IMF), the exchange regime was simplified by eliminating multiple rates, which were dependent on the discretion of administrative authorities and thus a source of rampant corruption. The new exchange regime also permitted greater import flexibility.

Eliminating the substantial exchange gap would allow a reduction in subsidies for cereal and meat production, which had reached considerable proportions during the final years of the Perón government. In order to boost imports, the provisional government eliminated quantitative restrictions, made import permits unnecessary, and established a free market in which foreign exchange was provided for anyone seeking to import goods. Returning to the free market reforms of 1933 allowed foreign companies to make remittances, which previously had to be channeled through the official market, so that they would be postponed in the waning years of the first Perón government. Furthermore, the 1957 devaluation allowed the reserves in the Central Bank to be revalued at some 5,996 million pesos, although the effect was small compared to the 1935 revaluation because reserves were significantly less. The IAPI, which acted as an intermediary in negotiating sales abroad, was eliminated, as was the government agency that promoted investments in equities (*Instituto Mixto de Inversiones Mobiliarias*).

The policy changes were more difficult than expected, and the recovery less evident; during the first year after the overthrow of Perón, there were no signs of a real improvement in the economy. Harsh climatic conditions were a complicating factor as well, because a drought destroyed many crops, thereby negating the effect of the increase in overall land cultivation produced by exchange reforms. This resulted in a decrease in exports, negatively affecting precisely the economic conditions that the proposed measures were intended to improve. Another cause of the reduction in exports was a decline in grain prices, product of a surplus of this commodity in the United States.

Toward Multilateralism: The Paris Club Agreements

With the worldwide crisis in 1930, the multilateral system of payments, operating under the gold standard, was replaced by bilateral agreements. At the end of World War II, the European Union Payment System was created, thereby initiating a return to multilateral regimes.[3] During the Perón years, Argentina had signed numerous bilateral trade agreements with various European countries, including Germany, Italy, and the Netherlands. These agreements stipulated that advances would be deposited in current accounts to finance purchases from the country that had credit balances; these had to be settled with either imports or creditor money or convertible currencies (foreign exchange).

During the last years of the Perón administration, Argentina repeatedly had negative balances in trade with some of these countries because of the growing need to import industrial inputs, whereas exports remained stagnant. The accumulated debt associated with these negative balances was estimated to have reached $500 million. At the end of 1955, these large sums threatened a near cessation of payments and an imminent interruption of remittances from European countries. The first attempt was made at a partial return to multilateralism with eleven European nations (see Table 5.1).

---

3 As a result of the decision on the part of a group of European countries, the bilateral system used in the postwar years was replaced with a multilateral one for the region; this system allowed arbitrage in negotiating foreign exchange among participating countries.

Table 5.1. *Debt to Paris Club Countries (in millions of dollars)*

Fiscal Year	Germany	Italy	United Kingdom	Japan	France	The Netherlands	Total
1	18.44	11.58	6.57	6.52	3.13	3.77	50
2	16.03	12.62	7.16	7.11	3.41	3.67	50
3	17.43	13.73	7.78	7.73	3.71	4.63	55
4	17.11	13.48	7.64	7.59	3.64	5.55	55
5	18.89	14.88	8.44	8.28	4.02	5.39	59.9
6	20.76	16.35	9.27	9.21	4.42	–	60
7	20.76	16.35	9.27	9.21	4.42	–	60
8	20.76	16.34	9.27	9.21	4.42	–	59.99
9	7.25	18.23	9.85	11.27	2.83	–	49.43
10	1.15	–	–	–	–	–	1.15
Total	158.57	133.56	75.24	76.11	33.99	23.01	500.47
Interest	10.58	19.95	10.82	12.24	3.29	2.07	58.94
	147.99	113.61	64.42	63.87	30.7	20.94	441.52

Source: BCRA Yearbook, 1957, p. 120.

Income Distribution Conflicts

Once the system of multiple exchange rates was eliminated, the government created an Economic Recovery Fund (*Fondo para el Restablecimiento Económico*), which it financed with a tax on traditional exports (*retenciones*). Contributions from exports on the margin of exchange would be replaced, from then on, and for many years to come, with export taxes. In 1956, pressured by trade unions conflicts and various types of resistance, wage increases reached roughly 35%. As these were much greater than productivity increases and were not absorbed by profits, a new phase of price increases ensued, diminishing the redistributive effect of the devaluation intended for the agricultural sector. Later, in order to compensate, the export taxes were reduced and lower official prices (*aforos*) (the portion of foreign exchange that had to be liquidated on the official market) were set. With the increases, although to a great extent industrial workers and entrepreneurs managed to balance the effect of the devaluation, people with less power in society did not have the same luck. Government, commerce, and banking employees, as well as retired people, experienced a drop in real income.

Furthermore, as a result of the devaluation, higher costs of imported primary goods induced entrepreneurs to demand loans from the banking system (because the banks' real interest rate was negative). Those that were granted, with reluctance, caused a greater expansion of means of payment. Because grain prices continued to drop, in 1957 export values showed no signs of rebounding, staying below 1954 levels. However, between 1956 and 1957 export volumes had increased by 6.8% while values showed an increase of only 3.3%.

As we have seen, although the new domestic price levels eliminated part of the incentives of the new trade system, this was compensated by the steady reduction in export taxes, which were ultimately eliminated in 1957. However, production was far from increasing to the levels desired. As for the external (export) sector, not only did the new price levels not result in a reversion of the difficult juncture, but the deficits worsened. Fuel and machinery constituted the great majority of imports.[4]

The balance of payments continued to be unfavorable, partially compensated in 1957 by IMF loans. Fuels were a negative factor because prices had increased due to the Suez Canal crisis, and with them maritime freights. In response to policies recommended by the IMF in 1957, there was a contraction of credit and of the money supply, but because the general level of prices outstripped growth in the money supply, there was a shortage of liquidity. After an inflationary period at the beginning of 1957, which followed wage increases stipulated in amendments to labor agreements, the government decided to freeze them for one year. The drop in real wages caused labor protests that gave way to conflicts during the first months of 1958.[5] By early 1958, it seemed that the stabilization projects had achieved very few of their intended objectives.

The incentives through devaluations and the elimination of export taxes directed at the agricultural sector did not immediately translate into an increase in production that would compensate for the drop in international prices (nor for the poor climatic conditions). Nor was their much success in containing inflation, despite the measures adopted in 1957 following recommendation from the IMF. Despite the wage freeze that year, prices rose by 24.7%. Furthermore, after a period of what seemed like severe measures, the government gave in to the pressures of different sectors, allowing a policy of more flexible loans and a wage increase. These pressures became more intense at the end of the period, when, on the eve of elections, political factors took center stage.

In 1958 the number of trade unions conflicts increased substantially. After various alternative measures and, in some cases, long periods of protest, new wage increases were granted, followed by an increase in prices,

4 Llorens de Azar, Carmen, with the collaboration of María Inés Danelotti, Antonio Pablo Grippo, and Dora Delia Puente, *Argentina, Evolución Económica, 1915–1976*, Buenos Aires, Fundación Banco de Boston, 1977.
5 Between February and August there are high rates of inflation, accumulated inflation of 23% in seven months. The annual inflation rate is 24%.

Table 5.2. *Economic Opening Index*

Years	(Exp+Imp)/GDP (%)
1954	11
1955	12
1956	22
1957	21
1958	18
1959	23
1960	21
1961	19
1962	23

Source: BCRA, *Cuentas Nacionales de la República Argentina*, vol. III, 1976.

with the assumption that a general wage hike would follow the elections. Industrial production saw a slight increase, especially in the mining sector, thanks to an increase in domestic oil production following the enforcement of the YPF Reactivation Plan (*Plan de Reactivación de YPF*).

One of the most successful measures of the provisional government was the YPF Reactivation Plan initiated in August of 1956. The plan provided for the construction of a gas and oil pipeline network to transport oil from its production sites to consumer markets, and the broadening of the Cuyo and Campo Durán refineries, expecting to achieve an increase in production capacity of 60% for the state company.

By 1958 deficits in the balance of payments had intensified. At midyear a difficult trade situation was seen in the depreciation of the peso on the free exchange market, where it reached 42 pesos per dollar. An attempt was made, albeit feeble, to open the economy. The economic opening index (the sum of imports plus imports as a ratio of GDP) was 18% in 1950 and reached 22% in 1956 (see Table 5.2).

The fiscal deficit and financing by means of monetary issues decreased considerably until 1961; the latter experienced a small upward trend starting in 1962. In 1958 the deficit grew by nearly a point to 4.8% of GDP, although rediscounts had ceased to be the customary instrument of financing.

Reform of the Central Bank Charter

The Central Bank Charter was reformed so as to put an end to the system of nationalization of deposits. It was understood that the banking business must be left to the private sector and that regulation of monetary policy could be done with stipulations regarding bank's minimum reserve requirements (*encajes*).[6] The executive decree stipulated that, starting December 1, 1957, banks would receive funds for their account, instead of receiving them by order of the Central Bank, as occurred starting in 1946. It argued that the idea that the banking deposits should be transferred to the Central Bank, thus permitting a more efficient monetary policy, would in fact have been wrong and would only result in a proliferation of regulations that would have inhibited the development of monetary policies and adequate credit.

Stipulations regarding deposits received on the part of banks by the Central Bank were eliminated. Instead, the Central Bank was given the power to set minimum private banks' reserves requirements and to use other instruments for monetary and credit regulation, namely, qualitative and quantitative control over bank loans and investments, setting rediscount rates, determining minimum and maximum interest rates to be charged on loans, issuing absorption documents, and carrying out operations on the open market. Limits on loans to the government were also established. The quantity of temporary advances would be subject to the availability of resources perceived at the Treasury and would be granted for a period of twelve months. Fixed limits were set on government debt that the Central Bank could place in its portfolio.[7] The declaration accompanying the law further argued that the regime of 1946 did not assure the necessary control of the Central Bank over the financial system, but instead permitted the bank to use the deposits as resources to cover the financial necessities of the government and of the IAPI, with a consequent inflationary effect. It was

---

6 The BCRA Yearbook states, "The transference of private deposits to the Central Bank is a mere fiction. Official and private banks receive deposits and the entire sum is registered in an accounting procedure at the Central Bank. At the same time, from this amount the banks receive, also as a total sum, the resources needed for operations. It is truly a very primitive notion of banking regulation to think that money from deposits must be appropriated in order to in turn send them in an official way to the banking system so as to determine how loans are distributed, by activities, and to determine the constraints on possible expansion of operations. The evolution of the central bank in industrialized countries has created more subtle and appropriate instruments to control this expansion: the power of the Central Bank to establish the level of cash it deems necessary, until it reaches 100% of the increase in deposits; the power to establish limits globally, or by category, on loans, on the expansion of credit; the means the Central Bank can control by buying and selling stocks on the open market with the purpose of monetary and credit regulation; the change in interest rates, even if, in this case, with less effect in some countries with large financial markets."

7 The limit was up to 15% of the amount in circulation in the case of investments for the Bond Regulation Fund; this limit can be extended by a unanimous vote of the Governing Board. However, article 49 allows the bank to have in its portfolio up to 35% of the total of existing deposits in all banks. This total does not include the bank restructuring bond, or the regulation fund, or the bonds that the bank had previous to the reform. This, according to Olarra Jiménez, was a mechanism that allowed monetization of the deficit after 1957. Rafael Olarra Jiménez, *Evolución Monetaria Argentina*, Buenos Aires, Universitaria de Buenos Aires, 1968, p. 115.

Table 5.3. *IAPI Bank Debt (in liquidation process) (in millions of current pesos)*

For crop acquisition (Quebranto) losses	10,115
For financing state enterprises	3,561
Railroad (purchase, materials, etc.)	2,154
State telephone company acquisitions	548
YPF (state mining co-op.) acquisitions	412
State gas company	447
For financing and acquisitions of equipment	1,156
Meat subsidies	1,879
Sugar production deficit	720
International agreements	989
For the acquisition of general merchandise and minerals marketing	1,283
TOTAL	19,703

Source: BCRA Yearbook, 1957, Appendix.

well known that the official banks provided credit to the government by funds received through rediscounts.

Thus, what was needed was restructuring of official banks, which was made placing the Restructuring Government Bond in the Central Bank, which would then replace the amount of these rediscounts on nonperforming loans in its portfolio. After eliminating the assets and liabilities of the Central Bank, a government agency would try to collect on outstanding loans granted by official banks (see Table 5.3).

Just a few figures are sufficient to give an idea of the origin of IAPI debts, currently being liquidated, which to date have reached some 19.7 billion pesos. These debts will be consolidated in one or more government bonds and will be registered as assets at the BCRA, which will allow official banks to simultaneously cancel their debts with the IAPI and the related debt to the Central Bank. The frozen official loans to be consolidated currently represent 44% of the Bank of the Argentine Nation's loan portfolio and 30% of that of the Bank of Industrial Credit.[8]

The BCRA Yearbook stated that the Industrial Bank had not fulfilled the functions for which it had been created. Of the sum of 14.8 billions it had on its books, 5.2 billions were in frozen accounts and another 2 billions were uncollectible loans to the private sector.

When the new system was implemented, the government ceased to use rediscounts as a customary instrument of financing. Interest rates were still controlled and remained below the inflation rate, at 7.5% in 1956 and 10% in 1957, compared with inflation rates of 13.4% and 24.7%.

---

8 BCRA Yearbook, 1957, Appendix.

Table 5.4. *Balance Sheet of the BCRA Financial System as of December of Each Year (in millions of current pesos)*

Assets		Liabilities	
1. Principal Accounts in the BCRA Balance Sheet and in the Financial System, December 1956[a]			
Gold and foreign exchange	4,317	Currency	42,802
Rediscounts and advances to banking entities	94,019	Nationalized deposits	61,528
Bank accounts (operations)	10,825		
Financial System Balance Sheet, December 1956			
Loans to the public	66,701	Rediscounts and advances from the BCRA	94,019
Official loans	25,903		
2. Principal Accounts in the BCRA Balance Sheet and in the Financial System, December 1957[b]			
Gold and foreign exchange	5,996	Currency	50,449
Rediscounts and advances to banking entities	6,362	Cash reserves	10,021.6
		Official deposits	1,346
Restructuring bond	27,599	Deposits in special accounts	3,184.8
Real estate titles	29,861	Other obligations (in foreign currency)	5,210
Financial System Balance Sheet, December 1957			
Official loans	11,119	Deposits	74,125

[a] *Source:* BCRA Yearbook, 1956.
[b] *Source:* BCRA Yearbook, 1957.

Monetary Effects of the 1957 Reforms on the Central Bank Charter

The provisional government's decision to give private banks back their deposits was supposed to resolve two problems. One was the accounts balance between the Central Bank and private banks, which, taken as a whole, had become debtors to the Central Bank. In 1956 they had rediscounts in the amount of 94,019 million pesos in their portfolio, whereas the Central Bank owed deposits totaling 61,528 million (see Table 5.4). The other problem was monetary policy. Having returned deposits to the banks, what instrument could the Central Bank use to regulate monetary policy?

The 1935 Charter had established as a precautionary measure a minimum reserve requirement of 8% of time deposits and 16% of on-demand deposits. During periods of economic growth, the banks had a surplus of these reserves, but the Central Bank could only act on the monetary base with sterilization instruments. With regard to banking money, the only instrument available to enforce sound money management was persuasion and moral imperative over the banks. Prebisch noted in this regard that "the Central Bank's policy was to remind banks that they are not merely a

commercial enterprise but that they are also an integral part of the monetary system, with corresponding responsibilities, and that, when the Central
Bank recommends prudent credit policy it does so for the collective good,
for which banks should strive, and not be led solely by their private interests."[9] With respect to instruments created for sterilization of monetary
effects of the flow of reserves, Prebisch noted that "the participation certificates of consolidated bonds were an imperfect instrument and thought
there was no way to prevent bank lending certificates maturing after 90
days."[10]

During years of significant gold inflows (1943, 1944), the Central Bank
did not adopt sterilization measures as it had done in 1936 and 1937, in
order for the flows not to negatively affect the placement of government
debt in the public. This allowed great monetary expansion during the war
years. Table 5.4 shows the BCRA balance statement once nationalization
of deposits was eliminated.

The 1946 law requiring the nationalization of deposits used rediscounts
and selective rationing as monetary instruments. Once the deposits were
returned to the banks, they were then faced with the problem of deciding
what instruments to use in order to regulate the creation of bank money.
Starting in 1957, the legislation allowed banks to grant loans, depending
on the volume of deposits they had received and on the minimum reserves
requirements to remain frozen; the Central Bank would determine any
change in banks' loan capacity so as to prevent sharp fluctuations in the
quantity of money, as well as to direct credit to privileged sectors.

The variable minimum reserves requirement mechanism had been introduced by the Thomas Amendment of the 1933 U.S. Banking Act and was
used by the Central Bank during the years following the Perón administration (see Table 5.5). "Beginning in 1957 the monetary strategy consisted
of adjusting the multiplier in order to supply the economic system with a
sufficient quantity of monetary assets."[11] For fixed installment deposits, a
minimum cash supply of 10% was stipulated, and 20% for sight deposits
but with a 30% minimum on marginal increases with respect to balances
as of November 30, 1957. Arnaudo believed that system was not entirely
efficient: "Fixing basic and marginal cash minimums for deposits while
ignoring their cumulative effect obscured the perception of upward and
downward trends. . . . A fluctuating minimum reserve requirement was not
efficient or was insufficient for the purposes of monetary control, such

9 Raúl Prebisch, "La Experiencia del Banco Central Argentino en sus Primeros Ocho Años", *Cincuente-
    nario del Banco Central de la República Argentina*, Buenos Aires, 1985.
10 Ibid.
11 Aldo Arnaudo, *Cincuenta Años de Política Financiera en la Argentina*, Buenos Aires, El Ateneo, 1987,
    p. 76.

Table 5.5. *Minimum Reserves Requirement and Total Deposits (in millions of current pesos)*

Year	Minimum Cash Reserves (A+B)	Minimum Reserve Requirements at BCRA (A)	Available in Cash (B)	Total Deposits	Ratio Cash Reserves/ Deposits (%)	Minimum Reserve Requirements/ Deposits (%)
1957	21,706	13,070	8,637	71,893	30	18
1958	26,258	15,184	11,074	102,261	26	15
1959	34,090	18,795	15,296	132,833	26	14
1960	38,091	15,835	22,256	176,648	22	9
1961	21,022	3,167	17,855	199,375	11	2
1962	17,503	0	17,503	203,985	9	0

Source: BCRA Statistical Bulletins, 1962–1965.

that [the Bank] relied on the direct concession of rediscounts for specific purposes."[12]

Except for 1959, prices changed at roughly the same rate as growth in the money supply (as shown in Figure 5.1 and in Tables A.19 and A.C.5.3 in the Appendix), whereas real wages (as can be seen in Table 5.6) showed weak growth from 1955 to 1959, during which time they dropped precipitously, by 25.5%.

Development and Stabilization: Frondizi

In 1958 the trade situation had reached a critical juncture. In response to this crisis, shortly after assuming power, the Frondizi administration suspended all imports until it could establish a list of priorities and grant permits. This required a reversal of the previous policy of timid acceptance of market liberalization and appeared to foretell economic intervention-ist intentions on the part of the new government. This impression was understandable, considering its record and political platform. The same tendency was seen in the decision to grant a general wage hike of more than 60% with respect to 1954 levels. At the same time Congress approved the Professional Association law, which helped reorganize the CGT, a General Confederation of Labor.

During the following months, despite the fact that the cost of living continued to increase, industrial production rose slightly and export sec-tor payments improved a bit, signs of change in official policy could be perceived. These were significant changes that further on had deep-lasting consequences. One of them was the decisive support for foreign investment in oil production, which, although some insiders knew even before the

12 Ibid., p. 77.

Table 5.6. *Change in Real Wages*
(in percentages)

Year	Change
1955	−1.4
1956	4.0
1957	0.4
1958	5.6
1959	−25.2

Source: J. Llach, "Los Determinantes del Salario en Argentina. Un Diagnóstico de Largo Plazo y Propuestas de Políticas," *Estudios*, no. 29. Córdoba, IEERAL, 1984.

elections what would happen, came as a surprise to those who supported the state monopoly on oil production, among whose ranks not long before had been the incoming president. Frondizi, in a dramatic gesture, had assumed personal control of the YPF, the state petrol agency that emerged as the last line of defense of Argentine national interests. With no less drama, he announced the start of a significant foreign investment flow (in which he called service contracts) to promote oil production in the country and eliminate what he called dependence on international fuel exporters. Although actual investments turned out to be less than those promised in letters of intent, their very existence had two important effects. First, they caused significant internal strife because Argentines felt strongly that foreign capital would infringe on a sector that should be controlled by

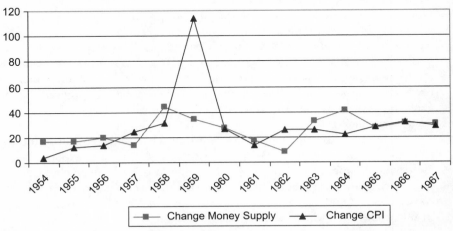

Figure 5.1. Annual Change in the Money Supply and Consumer Price Index (in percentages). *Source*: BCRA Yearbooks, 1954–1967, and INDEC.

Table 5.7. *Monthly Exchange Rate Average in the Free Market (in pesos per dollar)*

Month	Monthly Average
July	42.71
August	45.16
September	49.56
October	61.21
November	71.77
December	66.11

Source: BCRA Yearbook, 1958.

the state, and second, they gave a new image in the international financial market of possibilities for investment in Argentina.

After a brief honeymoon following the law of Professional Associations, union unrest began anew. At the beginning of 1959, they turned violent. Although oil production continued to increase, fuel and lubricants still represented a considerable portion of imports. The slight increase in exports and the pronounced limitation in imports managed to reduce slightly the significant balance-of-payments deficit, which in 1958 was still more than $200 million. At the end of 1958 the gravity of the situation was evident. With both reserves and the possibility of new loans exhausted, the country was nearing a cessation of payments.

Cumulative debt reached $1 billion at the end of 1958, whereas gold and foreign exchange reserves dropped by 36% between July and October 1958, becoming nearly entirely exhausted. The crisis in the export sector was reflected in the quotation of the peso on the so-called free market, which in the second semester of 1958 evolved in the following way (see Table 5.7).

The balance-of-payments crisis in mid-1958 was an important factor in the government's decision to negotiate a new IMF loan. The first, in the amount of $75 million, was negotiated relatively easily. After that, all additional aid was subject to the application of an economic program determined by traditional IMF policy.

The two-year Stabilization Plan announced by the president on December 29, 1958, in agreement with IMF recommendations – although it is known that it was the government that emphasized the severity of the program – marked a change not only in anticipated policy but also in the policies implemented to date during nearly three decades of increasing interventionism. The measures attempted to achieve fiscal and monetary balance and, to some degree, let market forces lead the economy by reducing government intervention in price setting.

Stability and Development Plan

Even before the elections, a group of politicians, entrepreneurs, and journalists that supported the candidacy of Arturo Frondizi – contributors all to the magazine *Que*, with Rogelio Frigerio as their leader – promoted a program of industrial development and strong economic growth. They proposed continued industrialization while intensifying substitution of imports producing intermediate goods and capital goods. They understood that this required enormous investment and had identified the greatest obstacles to the industrialization process. These were lack of capital, inflationary financing, and the balance-of-payments crisis. Thus, correcting these problems necessitated intense capital investment, and because the country lacked sources of capital it should come from abroad. This group agreed with Prebisch's 1955 diagnosis of decapitalization of the country and the deficit in energy and transportation that limited growth. But in order to achieve that they appealed for capital investments, distinguishing themselves from Peronism, which had attempted growth through forced savings and monetary issues.

The administration, which called itself "pro-development" (*desarrollista*), believed that the restrictions on growth and industrial expansion were due to the inability to generate foreign exchange for imports of intermediate and capital goods, which in turn was caused by the agricultural sector's lack of capacity to reach adequate exportation levels for industrial import needs. To overcome the external gap between imports and exports, what was required was greater industrialization and domestic production of intermediate and capital goods. The government thought that by extending import substitution beyond consumer goods to intermediate and capital goods the recurrent payment crisis would be solved. But greater industrial development required significant capital investment beyond what domestic savings could cover. This investment could not come from forced savings either, which had caused rampant inflation with such negative consequences during the Perón administration. What was new about this "pro-development" philosophy was its call for foreign capital savings to expand the most critical manufacturing sectors would come from abroad. The state would guarantee extraordinary profits (economic rents), from the exploitation of natural resources (mainly oil) where the state monopoly had been inefficient, and from restricted access to the domestic market, with a demand bolstered by more than two decades of severe restrictions (such as the case of the auto industry).

The policies, in which some perceived the philosophical influence of Albert Hirshman, seemed to be geared toward a strategy promoting industrial activities with backward linkages, as in the auto industry, whose primary inputs would be provided initially by imports, but gradually

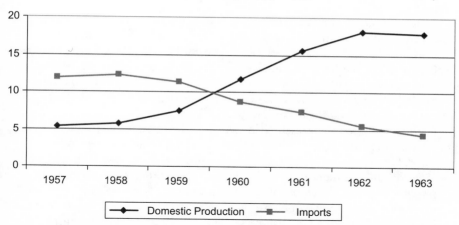

Figure 5.2. Domestic Oil Production and Oil Imports (in millions of tons). *Source: Relevamiento Estadístico de la República Argentina, 1900–1980*, Banco de Análisis y Computación, Consultora de Investigaciones Económicas y Estadísticas, Buenos Aires, 1982. *Primary source*: Office of the Energy Secretary.

these would be substituted by domestic production that would respond to incentives created by new demand. During the following weeks, a series of exploration contracts with foreign companies were announced. Not all of the contracts publicized were actually finalized, but the Frondizi administration's greatest success was a result of precisely these contracts. Oil production increased substantially, whereas oil imports decreased (see Figure 5.2).

However, the government, which tried to respond to problems of the real economy, had to deal with a country that had serious imbalances. Creating a difficult terrain for investments were public enterprises' fiscal deficits, lags in prices of public utilities, arrears in tariffs, and a multitude of subsidies. Frondizi wanted to spur development, but this required stability and consequently the imposition of harsh budget cuts as well as a reduction in the number of public employees. To this end the administration sought an IMF standby loan and in December of 1958 announced a series of measures to be taken. These measures would curb inflation, balance fiscal accounts, limit credit expansion, eliminate subsidies on public utilities that negatively affected public enterprises' balance sheets, and reform the exchange regime. The measures were also meant to open the economy to the mechanisms of the market. This economic liberalization plan did not affect interest rates, which would continue to be regulated by the Central Bank. Export taxes and surcharges persisted, as well as special regimes and quantitative restrictions. Furthermore, the peso was allowed to float, which caused a sharp devaluation that in May 1959 led to an exchange of more than 80 pesos per dollar. The exchange of goods was free from remaining controls, whereas rates for public services increased: electricity by 50%, the price of oil by 200%, and services in general by between 50% and 60%. Credit to the private sector, housing, and industry was drastically reduced. The increase in public utilities rates and the freezing of salaries and of the number of state employees tended to reduce expenditures and the fiscal deficit. Nonprofitable rail lines were closed as well.

President Frondizi presented Argentina's main economic problems and the measures to be taken in this regard in a radio address on December 29, 1958. On presenting his various measures to avoid the devastating effects of inflation and the moratorium on payments, he stressed that a stabilization program without development measures would only provoke impoverization of the population, which was why he proposed a program of economic expansion based on the intensification of the production of petroleum, coal, steel, and energy together with the stabilization measures. He argued that in the recent years the country had spent more than it had produced, without realizing the necessary investments and thus accumulating external deficits and losing millions in the state enterprises, especially with the railroads. Inflation, he added, brought decapitalization, impoverization, and irrational expenditures. Frondizi also announced:

The price of oil and its derivatives will increase substantially in order to adjust it to the real cost of production. The low domestic price [of fuel] spurred by imports at an exchange rate of 18 pesos per dollar, which implied a hidden subsidy, has provoked a waste of fuel. It has also prevented the YPF from obtaining the resources necessary to intensify domestic production.... From now on ... rates for urban transportation and railroads will be increased, so as to reduce the overwhelming losses.[13]

The press summarized the measures that the government adopted for the implementation of this program: As of January 1, 1959, quotas, import permits, certificates of need, and other bureaucratic procedures are eliminated. Imports of essential goods will be purchased at the free-floating exchange rate. Other surcharges for imported merchandise will be established from 20, 40, and 300%, according to the degree of need for these goods, notwithstanding the application of appropriate previous deposits. The national peso will float freely on the market and its fluctuating value will be determined by supply and demand. The Central Bank will oversee the exchange of the peso to eliminate unnecessary variations, thereby guaranteeing relative stability. Exports will be sold at the free floating exchange

---

13 Extract from the radio address given by President Arturo Frondizi, broadcast on December 29, 1958, by the National Radio Network, in BCRA Yearbook, 1958, Appendix I.

rate, with export taxes of 10% to 20% of the value of the exported products. (Like imports, they were exchanged at several different rates.) Credit will increase to the degree that industrial capacity and the availability of goods effectively increase. Credit will not be used to fuel speculative activity or usury or economic parasitism. With regard to prices, the government will create propitious economic conditions for fomenting greater production of goods within a system of open competition, which will reduce costs and profit margins. Monopolies and any arrangement whose purpose is to keep prices artificially high will be forcefully prohibited. The public administration deficit will be drastically eliminated, reducing the bureaucracy to manageable proportions with the steady elimination of excess personnel. Taxes will not be increased. More taxes will be collected and tax evaders pursued. State enterprises will not receive any more direct and indirect subsidies. Transportation fares will be increased so as to reduce the industry's serious operating losses. Oil and coal exploration policy will remain strong and the iron and steel industry will receive a considerable support. Other industries to be promoted are the chemical industry, plastics, metallurgy, paper, vehicles and machinery.[14] Wage negotiations became the domain of entrepreneurs and workers, with the proviso that if increases were not met with improvements in productivity, the government would not grant loans (subsidies) to these companies.

The measures to contain inflation and the current account deficit that had led to near exhaustion of Central Bank reserves (falling from $333 million in 1957 to $179 million in 1958) definitively consisted of not spending more than the country had. The elimination of the public utilities subsidy, which seemed to be a reasonable measure in preventing the deficit of state enterprises from falling to tax payers, would cause a drop in real wages of both lower- and middle-class wage earners and thus lead to strong opposition. That each person would pay the cost of what he or she consumed, which seemed inevitable, sparked enormous political resistance. Of course, eliminating subsidies on consumption affected real wages. The only way to improve them was to increase nominal wages, but this was possible only if productivity increased, because otherwise it would subtract from company earnings. Income from employment in sectors characterized by low productivity could not cover the level of consumption to which workers had become accustomed, so there were state subsidies to maintain the level of employment in sectors that had high costs reflected in prices that demand was not willing to pay. Urban industrial sectors, protected with tariffs, quantitative restrictions, and loans with negative interest rates, needed

14 *El Economista*, Año X, 3 de enero de 1959, p. 1.

that protection precisely because of their low productivity. Such was the dilemma of populism. Macroeconomic equilibrium was impossible with the measures taken to keep prices on foodstuffs and public services low so as to maintain elevated real wages, and it was impossible to increase nominal wages with the protectionist measures that allowed activities characterized by low productivity to continue.

The country would continue to have the same dilemma for decades to come. The Central Bank later explained the measures. It argued that economic policies based on monetary stability and the development of productive resources were complementary, and that stability would not only permit the orderly development of the markets but also promote investment, whereas inflation only led to speculation. It maintained that

orderly economic development is helpful to stability because: 1) the increased productive capacity available, due to long – term investments, allows a regular expansion of demand without causing price increases; 2) the growth in productivity of labour, both through improved production techniques and through the transfer of resources to more productive activities, renders it possible to absorb normal increases in wage rates and consequently to improve real wages without cost inflation; and 3) the greater flexibility of the productive structure, derived mainly from investments in basic sectors of the economy, serves to avoid price increases originating in the existence of bottle necks in production."[15]

Further actions were taken as obstacles to imports were removed and the Central Bank ceased to intervene in the foreign exchange market. With a free-floating currency, devaluation ensued, causing the pesos to reach new levels. The dollar, which was traded for 65.85 pesos in January 1959, was worth 90.30 in June; at the year's end the peso stabilized at 82 per dollar. The other recommended measures were gradually implemented. In January, the Argentine Meat-Producers Company CAP (*Compañía Argentina de Productores de Carne*) privatized one of the state meat-packing plants, Lisandro de la Torre Meatpacking (in Liniers). This caused union unrest, followed by military intervention and a state of emergency. Regarding price policy, subsidies were completely eliminated, and new public utilities rates based on real costs of exploitation were set in order to curb the public service companies' deficit. At the beginning of the new year (1959), which promised to be a difficult one for the majority of residents in urban areas, public utilities rates were increased: transportation by 100%, oil by 200%, electricity by 50%, and for the rest of public services by 50–60%. There was still price control of certain basic items, diminishing the effect of market forces. Drastic restrictions on housing loans were ordered

15 BCRA Yearbook, 1960.

in February, with the stipulation that banks could not grant loans by a margin that was greater than 25% of deposits in portfolio. These measures severely reduced liquidity in the marketplace. The plan recommended a 60% reduction in government sector current expenditures and an 80% reduction in investment, so as to shrink the 1959 deficit and balance the 1960 budget. The reduction in investments was more successful than that of government's current expenditures.

In order to bolster state revenue, the minimum income tax rate went from 7% to 9% and the maximum rate from 47.9% to 42.5%,[16] with fines of up to 250% for tax evasion. However, although there was an increase in income tax revenue, spending was still greater, and as on other occasions, the recession presented a serious obstacle to normal tax collection. Thus, fines and other threats could not prevent taxpayers, who were suffering from a lack of liquidity, from delaying payment, or from evading taxes altogether. When the situation became generalized, threats and judicial actions were insufficient in improving tax collection, because the cost of enforcement against thousands of people would have been larger than the income perceived. Another measure to increase state revenue was implemented in 1961, as the sales tax went from 8% to 10%.

In 1959 the cost of living doubled in relation to the previous year. The price increases were a consequence of the devaluation that had incurred greater costs on imported primary goods. The increase in prices was also a result of the elimination of subsidies due to the previously mentioned increase in prices for services and transportation. Unions exerted significant pressure to recuperate real wage levels; they were successful to some degree, as nominal wage hikes were achieved, promoting inflation in an upward spiral once again. However, wages lagged behind prices, meaning that real wages had fallen, circumstances that led to numerous protests, which became violent during the final months of 1959. In fact, some 73 million man-hours were lost due to strikes, according to estimates from the period. Both demand and production decreased, as unemployment rose, especially in the industrial sector. GDP dropped in relation to the previous year, and gross industrial product dropped even more. The construction and durable goods sectors were most affected, reflecting a reduction in private consumption caused by the drop in employment and income.

The drop in demand and the peso devaluation caused a reduction in imports of more than $200 million, whereas abundant harvests allowed exports to increase. Stabilization measures and a more favorable attitude toward foreign investment were reflected in an increase in investments. In

16 These are effective rates. *Source*: OAS/IADB, 1963.

fact, direct investments reached $245 million, due primarily to investment in the oil industry.

These circumstances managed to reverse the balance of payments, which, for the first time, since 1954, was positive by an amount of $123 million. This affected the value of the peso, which by the second semester appeared to stabilize. Near the end of 1959, when an IMF mission came to study the application of the policies it had recommended, it was largely satisfied with the results achieved. It recommended more severe measures on the part of the government in order to reduce the 1960 deficit and balance the 1961 budget. It also recommended that the state not increase wages. With regard to the private sector, salaries would be determined by bilateral negotiations between workers and management, keeping in mind that if wages were increased there would not be any banking loans forthcoming.

Alvaro Alsogaray joined the cabinet during the first months of 1960 because, among other reasons, he had long defended policies favoring the market. He became, in effect, almost a "premier," heading up the economy and labor departments and all of the government agencies under them. That same year, economic liberalization measures intensified; tariffs on imports were reduced, and those on machinery and equipment were eliminated altogether. Bilateral agreements were no longer sought, and those already signed with nine Eastern European nations were not renewed when they expired. The same was done in 1961, when three more bilateral agreements expired. On the so-called free market the peso remained relatively stable, although with Central Bank intervention.[17]

After the 1959 recession, economic activity rebounded in 1960, and more so in 1961. Foreign capital flows in direct investments and machinery and equipment imported with loans from suppliers was an important factor in the recovery, allowing an increase in the pace of economic activity. Direct investments were largely in the oil industry, although the chemical and auto industries received a significant amount. Industrialists also received loans from suppliers for equipment, which allowed a considerable increase in imports and industrial recovery. For the same reasons, this recovery was most significant in capital-intensive sectors such as petrochemicals and durable goods. There was rapid development in the auto industry, bolstered by a demand that had been repressed for many years.

During these years there was a substantial recovery in the volume of fixed investment and of personal consumption. Fixed investment was directed primarily at updating and modernizing equipment with loans granted by

17 The BCRA Yearbook, 1960, p. 3 states, "Supply exceeded demand in the foreign exchange market, almost, throughout the year. . . . The Central Bank absorbed almost all the surplus exchange available with a view to preventing fluctuations unconnected with the fundamental trend of costs and of the rate of output."

foreign suppliers. Significant investments were also made in public works and electrical energy, largely by finances as well by foreign capital. The increase in consumption was mainly due to industrial sector wages. The industrial real-wage index, which dropped from 100 in 1958 to 80 in 1960, rebounded in 1961, reaching an index of 90. Private consumption was stimulated by the redistribution of income in favor of the urban population caused by stabilization of the exchange rate in 1961. Price levels rose by 26.6% in 1960 and by 13.7% in 1961, albeit more slowly than wage increases. This, in turn, had a negative effect on the terms of domestic trade in the agricultural sector.

The rebound in real wages improved the sociopolitical climate, and the number of strikes decreased in 1960 and during the first months of 1961. However, labor again showed signs of unrest during the second half of 1961; there were three general strikes in July, October, and November. Among them was a railroad strike, the union's response to the Railroad Restructuring Plan (*Plan de Restructuración de los Ferrocarriles*), which was abandoned in part after the conflicts.

After 1959, the year in which the drastic reduction in imports was reflected in a positive trade balance, the trend again turned negative in 1960 because of an increase in prices of imports (by 25% in constant pesos) and in 1961 because of crop failure. However, this was compensated, to a great extent, in the capital accounts.[18] The 1960–1961 recovery could not be maintained over time. During the last trimester of 1961 production stagnated, and in 1962 it began to decline. The downward trend continued throughout the year and during most of 1963, when a drop in GDP of 2.4% was registered. The slump in GDP was related to a decrease in gross fixed investment and varied according to sector. It affected mainly the industrial sector, especially durable goods industries. The agricultural sector fluctuated, whereas mining saw an increase in oil production.

In 1961 there was a trade balance deficit compensated in the capital account. A large amount of loans became due in 1962; these were from capital flows to import machinery and equipment. The balance of trade did not improve; in 1962, despite the increase in exports that reached $1,216 million, there was a negative balance of $268 million. The economic crisis and growing political instability (fall of the constitutional government, clashes with the military) provoked capital flight, which reached critical levels.

During the first months of 1962 the economic team of the new president Guido (former provisional president of the senate) made a drastic devaluation of the peso; in July the dollar reached 120 pesos. The devaluation

18 BCRA Statistical Bulletin, March 1962.

Table 5.8. *Exchange Rate, by Month, 1962 (in pesos per dollar)*

Month	Exchange Rate	Month	Exchange Rate
January	83.04	July	122.14
Febuary	83.04	August	123.6
March	82.76	September	127.43
April	95.38	October	135.75
May	105.44	November	146.93
June	117.55	December	141.65

Source: BCRA Yearbook, 1962.

brought with it further complications. The extremely limited capacity for external payments made it difficult to fulfill short-term commitments. Furthermore, those who imported goods when the dollar was worth 82 to 83 pesos had to buy them at a much higher rate in order to pay debts abroad. This led to bankruptcy for numerous companies, which lacked the recourse of credit that was severely restricted when the rigorous measures recommended by the IMF were implemented. The exchange rate increased in 1962, as seen in Table 5.8.

The IMF declared the standby agreement broken in early 1962, because the government had not made good on its commitments, having used the loan for its own current operations. However, a new agreement was signed with the IMF when the new Guido government chose as leaders of its economic team first Federico Pinedo and then Alvaro Alsogaray, both of whom expressed the conviction to follow policies toward more economic orthodoxy. The government committed to a restrictive policy regarding expenditures and monetary issues, as well as the intention to contain inflation by keeping wages stable and eliminating the remaining obstacles to free markets. At the same time all restrictions on foreign trade, including export taxes, were eliminated. In the beginning reducing the fiscal deficit was extremely difficult because of the decrease in revenue caused by eliminating export taxes, so a hiring freeze on government jobs was declared. The imbalance was financed in part with floating debt, particularly postponing payment to suppliers and issuing certificates of debt that could be used to pay taxes and back-wages, which were ultimately paid with July 9 Bonds (with gold clause). Also, as in 1959, the devaluation and the increase in rates for public utilities resulted in higher costs. Demands for higher wages became ever more vociferous.

Although the government tried to obtain resources by various means, as in the additional sales tax and an emergency tax levy (2 per thousand) on capital, the deficit remained. In 1962 the general sales tax increased from 10% to 13%, and the tax base broadened when the list of exempt items was reduced, though these goods were taxed at 3%. The sales tax was reduced to 10% in 1963, but for certain goods it remained at 13%. An import surcharge of 20% on all merchandise and increases of 30% to 33% on fuels were established. Many of these measures were not entirely implemented. Additional plans were made for the payment of customs taxes, the consolidation of provisional loans, taxes on undeclared assets (*blanqueo de capitales*) in mid-1962, and a tax moratorium at the year's end. The contraction in demand was followed by a drop in production and in commercial activity. The recession also affected employment levels and resulted in underutilization of industrial equipment.

The foreign investment law was changed, becoming more favorable to investors.[19] In reality, foreign investors were favored if they could import at the official exchange rate in and the product was finished in country. The majority of costs (imported inputs) were liquidated on the official market while the final product could compete favorably with imports that had greater duties.

Monetary and Fiscal Policy under Frondizi and Guido

Monetary Policy

Central Bank policies were conditioned by the difficulties in the external sector and by the stabilization measures adopted, which ordered the restriction on loans to the government and to the private sector. The period between 1957 and 1962 was generally characterized by monetary contraction. Between 1957 and 1958 reserves dropped from 4,239 to 1,733 million pesos, which meant a reduction in the monetary base, which from 23% of GDP dropped to 21.5%. This was compensated by an increase in the placement of bonds and of temporary advances to the National Government. Reserves recuperated in 1959 and 1960, thanks to improvements in external accounts and the stabilization policy.

A negative balance of payments that translates into an outflow of reserves has contractive effects on money creation. However, this can be compensated with an increase in other Central Bank assets. The outflow of reserves in 1958 was compensated with an expansion of domestic factors. But in 1959, under and IMF agreement, this was no longer possible. After the rebound in reserves between 1959 and 1960, reserves again dropped in 1961 and even more so in 1962. During these years the monetary base remained constant, although under liabilities, bank cash reserves fell substantially. This drop was compensated by an increase in currency.

---

19 Law 14780 of the investment of foreign capital regime.

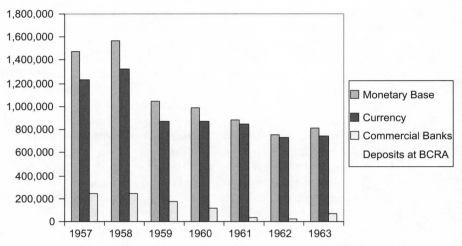

Figure 5.3. Evolution of the Monetary Base, Currency, and Bank Deposits at the Central Bank, 1957–1963 (in millions of pesos, at 1970 prices). *Source:* BCRA Yearbooks, 1957–1963.

The government prevented credit contraction, allowing banks to drop their cash reserves, thereby increasing loan capacity, so that it was commercial banks that compensated for the contraction. When bank deposits decreased at the Central Bank, monetary base levels were maintained by increasing currency issues. Figure 5.3 and Table A.42 in the Appendix show these changes.

Fiscal Policy

Public expenditures grew considerably in 1958, largely due to wage increases. Total expenditures increased in 1958 by 44% in constant terms.[20] There was an increase in income, albeit considerably less, 6.3%, as tax contribution increased only 2.2%. This caused a heavily deficited first-quarter balance statement for 1958. The following year, when the stabilization plan was implemented, expenditures (in constant terms) dropped by 21.4%. In 1960 primary expenditure grew by 6.4%, mainly as a result of capital expenditures, which grew by 30%. In 1959 revenue dropped in real terms, caused by a decrease in domestic taxes, on income, sales, and property, which together dropped by 27%. Export taxes on the other hand increased substantially, such that total revenue dropped by 14%. In 1960 current income increased by 19% in real terms, 20% in tax contribution, and 7% in nontax revenue. Because the increase in spending was smaller, this helped

---

20 Although statistics for 1957 cover only ten months, making the comparison not entirely equal.

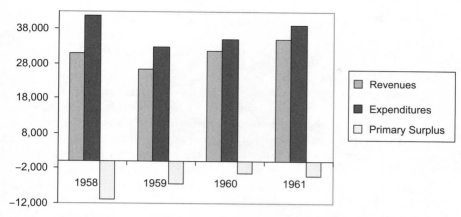

Figure 5.4. Revenues and Expenditures, 1958–1961 (millions of pesos, at 1955 prices). *Source: Programa Conjunto de Tributación sobre política fiscal en la Argentina,* OEA/BID/CEPAL, 1963.

to improve the primary balance, although it continued to be negative for 1961 and 1962 (see Figure 5.4).

The fiscal balance sheets improved, although the primary deficit remained during 1960 and 1961. But the fiscal accounts deteriorated with the increase in spending and the drop in income in 1962–1963, reaching nearly 5% of GDP. Following the previous years of uncontrolled expenditures, the effort to decrease spending was generally short lived. There was some effort during 1957 and 1959, but with the return to a constitutional government in 1958 there was a substantial increase in spending, by 46% in real terms (although data on 1957 covers only ten months, as explained in the Methodological Appendix of fiscal accounts). The following year, 1959, when the readjustment plan was implemented, expenditures also dropped by 22.5% in real terms. At the end of the period, 1961, expenditures were slightly above the levels reached in 1955, increasing by an average of 1.4% per year. Revenues also decreased in 1957 and 1959 and ended in 1961 slightly above 1955 levels, with average growth, during the period, of 2.1% per year.

Another important circumstance was the fact that the retirement system no longer had the positive effect on fiscal accounts that it had during the Perón years. Starting in 1958, the system that until that time produced surpluses and was an important source of fiscal income ran a deficit. A cycle had ended. From that point on, benefits paid out to the retired people were greater than income collected for the future beneficiaries, with the concomitant negative effect on the social security system and on fiscal balances.

Decade of Growth, 1963–1974

Recovery and the Beginning of the Growth Period: The Illia Years

In 1963 the recession that had begun during the second trimester of 1962 continued. This was a consequence of the external sector crisis and stabilization measures. In mid-1963 a recovery phase began. It became more intense when in October the new government of Arturo Illia implemented a policy of increased public spending. This policy, along with other factors, spurred recovery. However, even in 1963 the economic picture remained grim. As in 1952 and 1959, the 1962–1963 stabilization plan sparked a recession, causing GDP, employment levels, and global demand to decrease. Per capita GDP had dropped, with respect to the previous year, by 2.4% in 1962 and by 3.8% in 1963, due mainly to a manufacturing slump. The durable goods sector suffered an even greater decline, because demand was more elastic to income.

The auto industry was a special case because after covering several years of long postponed demand, it had reached satisfactory levels, but would now have to compete in less favorable conditions. The private construction sector saw a drop in production (by 12.2%). In the public sector, however, it increased by 3.25% due to the construction projects paid for by foreign loans. Production in the construction sector as a whole dropped by 5.8%.

In 1963, a positive balance-of-payments situation was achieved for the first time since 1960 because the stabilization measures had brought a reduction in imports by more than $300 million with respect to the previous year. But the reduction in imports was not the only factor; there was also a significant increase in exports as prices improved, reaching a sum that at the time seemed extraordinary: $1,216 million in 1963. But in mid-1963 the balance-of-payments situation had already begun to deteriorate. Central Bank estimates indicate that short-term external debt between the 1960–1961 period and 1964 reached $1,295.6 million, that is, the equivalent of an entire year of exports.

One of the new government's first measures (by decree dated November 8, 1963) was to prohibit imports of capital goods, justifying its actions because of the balance-of-payments deficit. The same argument was used when indirect intervention in the foreign exchange market was declared, which would amount to regulating, by various means, the supply and demand of foreign exchange. All of these measures indicated a trend toward a stronger government role in the economy.

Other measures tended to generate an increase in public expenditures. Government employee's wages and retirement pensions were updated, and debts to suppliers were liquidated, correcting irregular circumstances that had occurred during the previous two years. This fact alone caused greater market activity, and was accompanied by an expansion in credit to individuals.

Public spending produced economic expansion. The 1963 increase in exports also contributed to bolstering growing consumption, by providing greater liquidity. These were mostly agricultural exports, despite the weather, which resulted in a 23% decline in quantum. But given the rise in prices for these exports, exports rose 12.3%.[21] Grain production was bolstered in 1963–1964 by a good harvest and was outstanding the following year, and though 1965–1966 production was quite a bit lower, it again increased for the 1966–1967 crop year. The sustained trend in grain production had a significantly positive effect on international trade, showing perhaps for the first time since the end of World War II positive balances for several consecutive years.

The increase in agricultural production was the most significant factor affecting economic activity as a whole. It was also an important aspect of economic recovery, along with the government's monetary policies. There were also external factors spurring recovery: better international prices and a broadened demand into new markets. Another factor was an increase in productivity, as a result of the improvement in the utilization of resources, and implementation of new technologies, among others hybrid seeds. The work of the National Institute of Agricultural Technology (INTA) spreading technological improvement and better agricultural practices, created in 1956, also aided in the recovery. Lastly, climatic factors must not be underestimated, although they were not the only factor in creating these halcyon years.

The increase in real income in the labor sector bolstered consumption, and due to an upturn in global demand, growth in manufacturing was greater than in agriculture, with nondurable consumer goods leading this growth. Those sectors that were most sensitive to income fluctuations showed the greatest expansion. Although there was a restriction on imports of capital goods, for which there was not great urgency because machinery and equipment had been updated in 1960, imports of raw materials and semifinished products were allowed, which provoked expansion of industrial activity.

The short-term solution consisted of trying to recuperate income levels to sustain aggregate demand while the inflation rate would gradually be reduced. Periodic adjustments were made in the variation in the quotation of foreign exchange, so as to keep its price in step with domestic prices (crawling peg), without extraordinary measures that would cause deep adjustments in income distribution, which would not only cause political tension, but spark considerable speculative activity.

21 BCRA Yearbook, 1963, p. 22.

The capitals market and the flow of investment were no longer normalized to a large degree because of a series of negative measures on the part of the government. Among these measures were the rescission of oil contracts, monetary instability, the pressures from different sectors to capture a larger part of income, and especially the fiscal deficit and the deficit of state enterprises. After a new period in which capital invested in previous years was used, the future need for renovation, modernization, and equipment replacement could be predicted, which meant additional import demands. Lastly, it was clear that growth implied greater pressure on imports, but for that it was necessarily a proportional increase in the value of exports.

What would happen if there were any changes in climatic conditions or in international markets? The government proposed a national development plan with long-term objectives, aiming to confront problems that had plagued the Argentine economy since the postwar period and to combat persistent inflation that had lasted for more than two decades. Although the development plan did not guarantee results and did not clearly define the measures to be taken to carry it out (financing, resources, etc.), there was little opportunity to implement any measures because of a military coup d'état. The government of President Arturo Illia was overthrown in July 1966 by a junta of the commanders of the armed forces in violation of the law, assuming a role that the Constitution did not grant to them. This violation of the Constitution began a very bleak period in the history of Argentina.

Political and Monetary Policy during the Short-Lived Illia Administration

Just as the Frondizi and Guido administrations were characterized by the need for severe economic adjustments, due to stark imbalances dating from the postwar period, to some degree the Illia administration was benefited by measures that had already been taken. As has been noted, the adjustments had created an adverse climate for efforts of this kind because they caused recessions that negatively affected industrial entrepreneurs as well as wage earners. Furthermore, the significant investment in industrial capital goods in 1960 and 1961 and the improvement in relative agricultural prices helped credit expansion and allowed the Illia government to spend without serious inflation because of the existence of idle capacity after the recessions of 1962 and 1963 and it was a stimulus to economic recovery that would continue during the entire decade and part of the next.

Monetary Policy

A change in the trend of international prices improved an external position for Argentina and produced monetary expansion spurred by an increase in

Table 5.9. *Growth Rate Financing Inflow to the Government (annual percentage over current values)*

	1962	1963	1964	1965	1966
Advances	27	88	−12	50	14
Public bonds at the BCRA	24	10	111	16	54
Bank loans to the government		51	58	108	10
Public bonds at banks		86	102	4	6

Source: Treasury Yearbooks and BCRA Yearbooks, 1962–1966.

reserves, which at the same time allowed for an increase in banks' cash reserves. Furthermore, the Central Bank, through the minimum reserves requirements, increased banks' lending capacity, which it directed to certain regions and sectors. The money supply increased, but the monetary base did not. The government requested more funds in advances and loans from the Central Bank and in 1964 issued bonds, but in 1965 it relied more on private banks, and in 1966 it requested fewer funds from the Central Bank (see Table 5.9).

Beginning in 1959, by Decree 11916/58, the exchange difference account appears as a new item under government liabilities. But the main instrument of monetary policy was variable minimum reserves requirements (*encajes variables*). When, with the 1957 reform, deposits were returned to private banks, a new problem emerged: how to regulate the money supply generated by bank loans. The 1946 reform made all deposits available to the Central Bank, which, through rediscounts, had the possibility to expand and contract credit and to make it selective (see Table 5.10).

Table 5.10. *Financial System Required Minimum Cash Reserves, Loans, and Deposits (in millions of current pesos)*

Minimum Reserves	1963	1964	1965	1966	1967	1968	1969	1970
Total	79,800	167,800	223,200	292,200	420,600	511,600	592,800	716,500
With monetary function	53,500	91,400	124,400	137,700	192,200	160,500	183,500	213,500
Required on-hand	26,300	76,400	98,800	154,500	228,400	351,100	409,300	503,000
Deposits	283,109	415,928	539,000	692,362	980,809	1,316,959	1,504,759	1,855,066
Loans	279,672	384,121	526,622	649,875	929,800	1,291,100	1,611,200	1,920,400

Source: BCRA Yearbooks, 1963–1970.

Total minimum reserves were composed of minimum monetary reserve requirements and minimum available reserves. The former were bank deposits in the Central Bank and the BCRA's own reserves, and the available reserves varied according to the Central Bank's regulations (*Circulares*). There was inconsistency between monetary and fiscal policy because during some years available reserves were used not only to increase credit to the private sector (as during the 1960s) but also to place government debt. In these cases, the government did not try to obtain financing by increasing the monetary base, as when deposits were nationalized, but rather by increasing private banks' lending capacity in order to place debt in them.

Furthermore, during some years it made less frequent use of placing bonds in the Central Bank and instead recurred to temporary advances that had a limit of 15% of government reserves inflow during the previous twelve months,[22] and that had to be returned within a period of one year, although the government renewed the advances and, as we have seen, placed debt in private banks.

Fiscal Policy

Revenue increased more than 10% in constant terms during the first years of the administration (1964 and 1965), and primary expenditures increased at a slower rate, but in 1964 payment on the debt incurred increases of 46%. Spending on consumer goods increased 20% in real terms in 1964 due to expenditures on wages, which increased 38% that year. Wages later decreased, but its share went from 35% of expenditure to 40%. Central government transfers to public enterprises were around 2% of GDP and were an even smaller proportion in 1965. In an agreement between the Guido government and the IMF, export duties were rescinded in 1962, and only in 1964 did they begin anew, although initially export taxes represented barely 1% of total income.

Stability without Recession: Onganía and the Krieger Vassena Plan

Growth. The statements of the *military junta* of the self-denominated Argentine Revolution affirmed that its objectives were long-term and that deep societal reforms were necessary, but it is far from true that the junta had a clear economic strategy from the beginning, except the intention of pursuing long-sought external and internal equilibrium by preventing both inflation and the recurrent external payments crisis, without specifying the

---

22 Article 27 of the 1957 BCRA Charter, Law 13126, of October 22, 1957, BCRA Charter (B.O. 29/X/579), Annals of Argentine Law 1957, Buenos Aires, La Ley, Tomo XVII-A, p. 849.

means for such a goal. Some military officers involved in the coup had the simplistic notion that politicians were incapable of imposing order on an administration that was continually stymied by unions and that this job was best left to the military.

It was not until Krieger Vassena assumed the Economic Ministry in January of 1967 that the most important policies were defined in a March 13 announcement. Although it seems paradoxical, it may be said that the policies implemented by the new minister and subsecretary Folcini, who had come from the National Counsel on Development (CONADE), to some degree were influenced by recommendations that the Harvard Institute for International Development consulting group had been making to the Unión Cívica Radical administration.

In fact, the Onganía government's objective was to stabilize the economy without shrinking demand, so as to prevent the recessive effects of the previous stabilization plans and, from there, to spur an economic expansion process based on stability. What was necessary – they thought – was a social agreement between different sectors of society, which in the long run would allow select political institutions to function once again.

The *program*, as Maynard[23] later explained, established that the government would set standards by which money growth would be less than that of bank credit and wage increases would be less than that of inflation. These price and wage controls were achieved thanks in part to military power and the scarcely concealed pact with unions. Thus, after an initial increase, wages were frozen until the end of 1968 and price agreements were made with the most powerful enterprises, which in return received access to subsidized banking loans. Because credit to the private sector had to increase more than the money supply, the government had to obtain genuine financing.

The peso was devalued, going from 245 to 350 per dollar. This was in part compensated by a 25% tax on exports, diminishing the benefits of devaluation, while import duties were reduced. Export taxes levied were 5% on meats, 16% on dairy products, 20% on cotton and linen, and 25% on grain and raw wool. The effects of the new exchange regime on prices of imported goods can be seen in Table A.C.5.1 in the Appendix. Export taxes helped to increase fiscal revenue, which was further aided by a more orderly and efficient management of tax collection at the Dirección General Impositiva (national tax collection agency), as seen in Figure 5.5.

But export taxes had a negative effect on the cattle industry, which was experiencing a period of low prices. This spurred liquidation of cattle

---

23 Gilles Maynard, "Argentine Macroeconomic Policy, 1966–73", in *The Political Economy of Argentina, 1946–1986*, ed. Guido Di Tella and Rudiger Dorbusch, London, St Antony's/Macmillan Press.

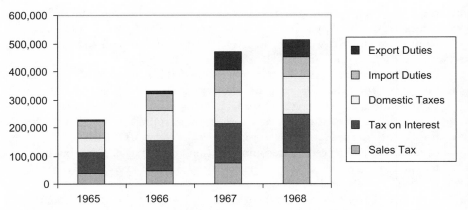

Figure 5.5. Tax Revenues, 1965–1968 (in millions of current pesos). *Note:* The category *Import Duties* includes customs and port taxes. *Source:* Treasury Yearbooks, 1965–1968.

stocks, which also caused beef production to diminish, offsetting the upturn in other sectors. It was also a considerable factor in initially curbing inflation in 1967 and 1968. The most successful component of the Krieger Vassena plan was achieving an 8% annual reduction in inflation (measured by the Consumer Price Index), something that had never before been accomplished (see Table A.19 in the Appendix).

The climate of economic stability was a propitious one for attracting foreign capital inflows. In the 1970s, for the first time Argentina had easier access to international sources of public capital (World Bank, Inter-American Development Bank), which financed large-scale public works projects. These programs included projects in El Chocón, Salto Grande, Zárate Brazo Largo, and so on. In some cases, bond issues abroad aided in monetary expansion and fiscal balance.

Economic expansion in this case was based on an increase in expenditure and in public investments. The initial fall in nominal interest rates produced contradictory results because an even greater reduction in inflation caused positive real interest rates for two years in a row. This situation diminished the political support for Krieger Vassena on the part of entrepreneurs, because in 1968 and 1969 the reduction in inflation led to positive real interest rates (see Table 5.11).

Around 1970, in the fourth year of the Gral. Ongania government, the anti-inflationary plan was exhausted. A continued, though moderate, increase in prices had forced a gradual elimination of export taxes, diminishing fiscal inflows. At the same time, companies that had become accustomed to high amounts of debt while real interest rates were negative began to suffer instead the consequences of positive real interest rates from 1969.

Table 5.11. *Nominal and Real Interest Rates*
(in percentages)

Year	Annual Nominal Rate	Annual Real Rate (with respect to the WPI – Wholesale Price Index)
1965	15	−7.2
1966	15	−4.1
1967	15	−8.5
1968	15	5.1
1969	14	7.5
1970	14	−0.1

Source: Adrián Guissarri, *La Argentina Informal: Reali-dad de la Vida Económica*, Buenos Aires, Emecé, 1989.

The downward inflationary trend reversed course while international beef prices increased. Inflation intensified because a new cycle of not selling breeding ensued causing a period of liquidation. This reduced the supply of cattle for slaughter and caused beef prices to increase, which, given the current mechanisms of propagation, led to the increase of prices generally.

With President Onganía, amid ever-increasing military clashes, a new aspect of Argentine life, lasting nearly two decades, would come to plague the country: terrorism. A terrorist organization, whose name would become associated with tragedy in the following years, assassinated ex-President Aramburu. He was a respected figure who accomplished his promise to have handed over power in 1958 to a constitutionally elected president. After the assassination, the current government, whose very existence rested on the pretense of imposing order, found itself nearly entirely bereft of authority. The de facto President Onganía, who had been brought to power by a military junta, was replaced by another, on the evening of June 8, 1970.

With the demise of this government, although inflation and other recurrent social problems had returned, the only sustained period of economic growth of the second half of the twentieth century had come to an end. This period, characterized by 4.1% annual growth in GDP, had begun with the Illia administration in 1963 and lasted until 1974.

Fiscal and Monetary Policy of the Onganía Government

The Onganía government's fiscal and monetary policies were conditioned by a number of circumstances. Although Onganía's economic ideas had not been clearly articulated, it was clear that he wished to put an end to the cycles of inflation, devaluation, adjustments, and recession that the country had experienced since the end of World War II. But because the adjustment made on credit restrictions and a reduction of public expenditures had caused a recession, the junta that brought Onganía to power demanded that stabilization measures not spark a recession, in an attempt to prevent the negative political and social repercussions seen in 1959 and 1962.

Another important aspect to keep in mind is that the Onganía government took power following those recessions, during a period of expansion begun under the Illia administration. Despite the fear that this expansion could be cut short by inflationary pressures and by the social upheaval experienced during the previous year, it was thought that if order could be restored to the country – averting conflicts over income distribution – with time, growth could be sustained. Those who had proposed this alternative in 1966, including entrepreneurs and union leaders, thought that only the military was capable of acting as arbiter in these conflicts and imposing order from the outside, something that seemed of utmost importance for the country's growth.

The Onganía administration had a different perspective than the 1959 and 1962 governments about the causes of inflation, believing that inflation was rooted in cost pressures (wage hikes), which in turn provoked price increases. Thus, the Onganía government attacked the problem with a fixed exchange rate and a system of wage and price controls, with the support of business leaders. Therefore, there were no measures aimed at reducing credit to the private sector; on the contrary, the credit supply burgeoned with the money supply, but not on the basis of an increase in government financing, but rather on an increase in reserves (result of the renewed confidence of foreigners and of the Argentine people). This resulted in inflows of foreign exchange and an expansion of secondary liquidity through a reduction in bank reserves. Deposits increased at a greater pace than currency and the M3 multiplier (an indicator of financial deepening), which was 1.7 in 1967 and which grew to 1.97 in 1968 and to 2.17 in 1969.

Moreover, the government obtained international financing for public works, issuing foreign debt that brought an inflow of foreign currency that allowed for increased monetary issues. These were justified with the argument that monetary issues were a result of an increase in reserves and not of government debt, which in fact they were.[24] At any rate, except for this not insignificant factor, there was a reduction in Central Bank financing of the government. The policy of diminishing the minimum reserve requirements that allowed for greater lending capacity allowed the government to be able to finance operations with public debt placed in the private banking system (see Table 5.12).

---

24 J. C. De Pablo, *Política Antiinflacionaria en la Argentina 1967–70*, Buenos Aires, Amorrortu, 1970.

Table 5.12. *Required Minimum Cash Reserves (in millions of current pesos)*

Year	1970	1971	1972
Total	716,500	684,400	1,170,700
With monetary function	213,500	238,800	484,300
Required on-hand	503,000	445,600	686,400
Deposits	1,855,066	2,526,800	3,984,800
Loans	1,920,400	2,798,800	4,345,700

Source: BCRA Statistical Bulletins, 1970–1972.

Central Bank financing of government operations and of commercial banks are shown in Table 5.13.

Lastly, there were attempts to place public debt in foreign and domestic capital markets with clauses that protected debtors from inflation. Fiscal policy improved until 1969. This was achieved, thanks to the increase in revenue, due mainly to export taxes and diminished expenditures, which in 1967 was mostly the result of a slump in public employee wages following the devaluation. It was also due in no small measure to the real improvement in real revenues caused by lower inflation (the Olivera–Tanzi effect).

Both factors, export taxes and the drop in wages, would not have the same effect in the medium term, and regardless of the political factors that interrupted the program, they were not long lasting. Yet it was, until that point, the most successful attempt to control inflation, so that in 1969, for the first time in many years, there was only single-digit inflation: 8%. But the repeated utilization of currency devaluation as a source of government revenue was ultimately ineffective in achieving long-term fiscal balance.

The years between President Frondizi and the return of Perón in 1973 were characterized by generally unsuccessful attempts to achieve monetary

Table 5.13. *Financing of Government (in millions of 1967 pesos)*

	1967	1968	1969	1970	1971
Government bonds	326,634	307,429	295,280	385,657	433,564
Under BCRA control	272,534	256,408	242,895	332,423	391,960
Under bank control	54,100	51,021	52,385	53,285	41,605
Loans from BCRA[a]	218,024	138,947	154,941	58,732	46,853
Total loans from banks	929,800	1,110,844	1,288,601	1,352,272	1,418,432
To the public sector	163,100	145,835	149,079	154,211	113,577

[a] Includes advances, exchange differential, and contributions from government-controlled agencies.
Source: Treasury Yearbooks and BCRA Yearbooks, 1967–1971.

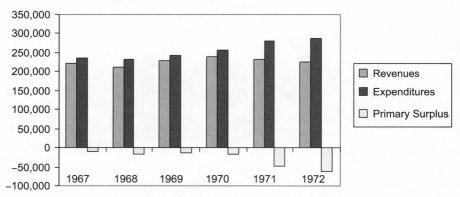

Figure 5.6. Revenues and Expenditures, 1967–1971 (in millions of 1961 pesos).
Source: Ministerio de Economía, *Sector Público Argentino no Financiero. Cuenta Ahorro-Inversión-Financiamiento*, Buenos Aires, Secretaría de Hacienda de la República Argentina, 2004.

and fiscal equilibrium and that of the external accounts. Despite the differences in the policies adopted, in nearly all the administrations public finances were more prudently managed, with varying degrees of decision making in achieving these results or finding long-term solutions to the problems that had plagued the Argentine economy since the end of World War II. Policies were largely influenced by changes in the external sector. The continued incongruence between import needs and export earnings repeatedly resulted in foreign reserves reaching a critical low at the Central Bank. This was no minor factor in the adoption of fiscal and monetary constraints that, as unpleasant as they were, were inevitably a necessity. The enormous mess left behind by the Perón administration, which the 1955 "revolutionary" government did not manage to fix, showed its effects during the following years. It led to severe fiscal and monetary adjustments in search of equilibrium effectuated in December 1958, which in turn were unable to ward off a renewed recession that began during the second semester of 1961 and became more severe in 1962, lasting until mid-1963.

The adjustments during those difficult years not only had the short-term effect of allowing expansive measures during the Illia presidency, but they also had a long-term effect: the modernization of the industrial structure, with the purchase of new machinery and equipment, during the Frondizi presidency, and a change in relative prices that was more favorable to agriculture. These would be some of the determining factors in the significant increase of economic growth in Argentina during the 1960s, the only decade characterized as such during the entire second half of the twentieth century.

The changes in relative domestic price, which, since 1956, were intended to promote the agricultural sector, finally rendering fruits when combined with changes in foreign terms of trade and the incorporation of new technology (the green revolution). In 1962, these changes helped the country to exceed the billion current dollar level of exports that had been reached in 1928. This level was exceeded during the postwar years but had dropped back during the 1950s. From $1.2 billion in 1962, export levels grew to $1.4 billion in 1964 (more than a 40% increase with respect to 1962).

Whereas the Frondizi and Guido governments had to confront the negative effects of the structural adjustments, and the 1959 and 1962 crises, the problem confronting the Illia administration was insufficient demand (complicated during the first year of the administration by private foreign loans becoming due, loans that had paid for machinery imports). With an underutilized industrial sector, the Unión Cívica Radical government managed to increase global demand with expansionist policies without initially causing a significant increase in inflation, which decelerated between 1963 and 1966 with respect to that of the period between 1958 and 1962 (from 42% to 27%). Following the recessions of 1959 and 1962, and spurred by expansionist policies, a recovery began and would continue throughout the 1970s and the first years of the following decade.

It is true that the limitations of the initial recovery measures and the concomitant inflationary pressures were already evident in 1966. Although these factors did not cause the military coup that overthrew Illia (who was justified claiming an economic stagnancy that was nonexistent), the Onganía administration, which did not express a clear policy during the first months, with the appointment of Adalbert Krieger Vassena as minister of economy, however, implemented a stabilization plan. This plan kept past experience in mind and was nonrecessive in nature, because it tried to promote growth on the basis of public works and domestic and foreign investment, with monetary stability and an initially overvalued fixed exchange rate.

It was the considerable social and political resistance that unleashed the measures that led to the 1959 and 1962–1963 recessions that kept Krieger from resorting to the usual adjustments, namely, contraction of credit and a reduction in expenditures. Krieger had a different explanation for the causes of inflation than what underlay the Frondizi and Guido governments' agreements with the IMF. The plan for stabilization without recession assumed that inflation originated in expectations and cost pressures. In order to carry out the plan Krieger proposed altering expectations by creating a fixed exchange rate after an important devaluation that would create confidence in that this would be – as the government affirmed – the last devaluation that the country would have, and maintaining price levels with price and wage controls. The measures that offset the devaluation,

Table 5.14. *Export Taxes*

Year	Export Taxes (millions of pesos)	Official Exchange Rate (peso per dollar)	Value of Exports (Index: 1965=100)
1965	4,979	171.6	102
1966	8,159	209.4	105
1967	65,484	333.5	103
1968	57,469	350.0	100
1969	43,950	350.0	105
1970	51,386	379.2	108

Note: Seller's exchange rate for financial transfers; yearly average.
Source: Boletín Informativo Techint, no. 250; CEPAL, *Documento de Trabajo,* no. 20, and Treasury Yearbooks, 1965–1970.

export taxes, and reduction of import surcharges would ameliorate the effects on the cost of living and prevent large income transferences that the previous evaluations had caused, and also avert their recessive effects and the resistance of the affected sectors (mainly wage earners). As previously mentioned, the undervaluation of the peso and economic stability were important incentives for capital inflows, from Argentines as well as foreigners. These investments increased reserves at the Central Bank and brought a concomitant monetary expansion on the one hand and an increase in investment with foreign savings on the other.

The Onganía government benefited from the previous reforms (with a more concentrated and modern industrial sector), and especially from a greater inflow of international credit (which started with international agencies such as the World Bank and the Inter-American Development Bank), which were decisive in promoting improvements in infrastructure as well as several large projects in the private intermediate goods sector. Furthermore, the compensatory devaluation allowed the government to benefit from its proceeds that resulted by an increase in export taxes, which was an important factor in the improvement in public income. Export taxes that were conceived of since the 1930s as the government's partial appropriation of the economic rent coming from devaluation (the extraordinary profit received by exporters) no longer functioned as such when domestic prices increased more than international ones and the exchange rate remained stable, which regime that the export taxes should be reduced (see Table 5.14).

In the long run export taxes could not be considered regular income for the government, and this was probably its greatest handicap as well as that of other programs that allowed the state the possibility of enjoying the creation of extraordinary profits coming from the devaluation. Besides, there was a significant increase in real terms in domestic taxes until 1968

Table 5.15. *Revenue from Domestic Taxes*

Year	Millions of Current Pesos	Millions of 1960 Pesos
1965	38,117	13,412
1966	47,776	14,052
1967	72,330	16,876
1968	111,310	23,729
1969	111,555	18,448
1970	125,727	18,306

Source: Treasury Yearbooks, 1965–1970.

as a result of an improved tax-collection system on the part of the Internal Revenue Department (DGI, *Dirección General Impositiva*) and also because as inflation decreased, real tax peso appreciation increased it (the Olivera–Tanzi effect) (see Table 5.15).

With regard to expenditures, the country was enduring difficult circumstances it had inherited, and despite drastic measures taken in 1958 and 1962, the lag in prices for pubic services behind production cost could not be overcome due to a desire to keep real wages high by means of a decrease in the price of goods and utilities of popular consumption. This policy, essential to the populist Perón strategy, had continued, although with interruptions and severe adjustments during the governments that followed. The fact that prices did not cover costs was the primary, although not the only, cause of the state enterprises' deficit, which reached between three and four points of GDP.

Growing deficits led to the need for adjustments, but because the measures necessary to reduce them were completely unpopular, every government tried to postpone them so that they would occur during the following administration (what befell Frondizi in 1958). The reduction in GDP and these postponements exacerbated the cost–price imbalance of public services. All of these problems limited the government's ability to control the deficit. For instance, Frondizi began with a railroad restructuring plan, whose application was mostly stymied by strikes, which led the president to call the military to run the railroads companies (see Table 5.16).

The other factor that strongly impacted financing and government spending was the surplus deficit of the social security system. When retirement benefits were broadened to include wide sectors of workers, income from participants was greater than payments to beneficiaries, because, at the beginning, there were a great number of contributors and a smaller number of people eligible because of age and seniority, people who could receive the benefit. Until 1958 the system ran a surplus, which the government used to place debt at an interest rate that was much lower than inflation,

Table 5.16. *Deficit of State Enterprises (as a percentage of GDP)*

Year	Deficit	Government Subsidies	Financing by BCRA
1960	3.95	3.06	
1961	4.58	2.85	0.06
1962	4.39	2.33	0.36
1963	3.98	2.15	0.02
1964	2.87	1.97	0.07
1965	1.91	1.42	
1966	1.43	2.23	
1967	1.28	1.72	
1968	1.04	1.42	
1969	0.86	0.99	
1970	1.36	0.89	
1971	2.33	1.21	
1972	2.55	0.93	

Source: FIEL, *El Gasto Público en la Argentina 1960–1985*, Buenos Aires, FIEL, 1987.

so that the system became decapitalized. In the sixties, on the other hand, the retirement system began to run a deficit and required financing from the Treasury. Net expenditures for the social security system represented around three points of GDP. As will be shown in Chapter 6, the Central Bank did manage, however, to reduce its financing of the government (see Table 5.17).

Conclusions

The governments that followed Perón's overthrow were faced with a difficult dilemma: how to return to relative normalcy without affecting hard-won popular support and confronting as well-vested interests that had joined in an important coalition during the Perón administration. The greatest initial concern, as Prebisch pointed out, was obtaining foreign exchange to keep the production infrastructure from collapsing, because it was in a severely deteriorated state from long yeas of neglect and decapitalization. Investment required not only savings but also foreign exchange, and for that relative prices had to be changed in order to spur agricultural production and increase exports. Prebisch had recommended devaluation without a concomitant increase in wages in order to increase real earnings from the rural sector. But this ran contrary to urban entrepreneurs' and labors' interests.

Table 5.17. *Social Security System Deficit (as a percentage of GDP)*

Year	Deficit
1960	2.71
1961	2.77
1962	3.13
1963	3.34
1964	2.36
1965	2.39
1966	3.36
1967	2.52
1968	3.31
1969	2.91
1970	3.21
1971	3.26
1972	2.78

Source: FIEL, *El Gasto Público en la Argentina, 1960–1985*, Buenos Aires, FIEL 1987.

The struggle against inflation that had lasted for a decade and that was becoming less and less manageable implies the pursuit of fiscal and monetary balance and certainly on the expectation that production would increase and spending would decrease. But this meant reducing state expenditures, state enterprises' deficits increasing rates to the level of costs, and eliminating subsidized loans, which would be resisted by many who stood to suffer its negative effects. Finally, improving productivity meant eliminating inefficient producers from the market. The recessive effects of some of these plans appeared to demonstrate that the remedies were much more harmful than the malady. Any administration that implemented them would be sure to face a formidable opposing political coalition. Thus, attempts were meager and, made reticently, generally failed. The plans could have varying degrees of technical sophistication but invariably ended up being abandoned, followed by a devaluation when faced with the political resistance of several sectors that did not want to pay more for public services, fuel, and food.

But utilizing the state help to keep sectors with low rates of productivity operating condemned the country to low growth. Because adjustments to improve productivity caused insurmountable political resistance, the route of least resistance was devaluation. This not only liquidated state and private debt but also improved competitiveness abroad by decreasing wages internationally. This way of governing was a pendulum that some called populism:[25] periods of monetary and expenditure expansion followed by a balance-of-payments crisis and later, when external equilibrium had been achieved, severe cutbacks continuing the cycle and then a return to the expansionism favored by the "populists."

The government of the 1955 revolution could do very little in terms of reform, although it did manage to partially undo the enormous regulatory apparatus. Deposits in the Central Bank were no longer nationalized, the IAPI suppressed the foreign trade monopoly, bilateralism was increasingly abandoned, beginning with multilateral payment agreements with several European countries that made up the informal Paris Club, and the country joined the IMF. President Aramburu's decision, despite the opposition of several military factions, to call for elections and give up power exacerbated political problems, and little progress followed.

Against all expectations, Frondizi was the one who made the most severe adjustment plans during that time. As has been demonstrated, the president believed that further industrial development and escaping repeated balance-of-payments crises (stop-and-go cycles) required replacing inflationary financing of capital with foreign investment in critical areas: oil, chemicals, iron and steel, for which monetary and price stability were essential. He was partially successful in some aspects and strongly opposed by several sectors in a climate of social upheaval in addition to a political one that was just as severe, which in the midst of the cold war led leaders of the armed forces to overthrow him. The following years were also characterized by attempts at orthodox adjustments that sparked strong reactions in a climate of military confrontations (the *azules* and the *colorados*) and that concluded with a new call for elections.

The radical President Illia benefited from the recessive process that preceded him, and he managed to promote Keynesian policies, greater spending, and so on, without causing significant inflation. He was removed from power following several union conflicts by a coup led by the head of the army, and the presidency of General Onganía was installed.

The plans that followed attempted to overcome inflation by preventing recessions that had so plagued the Frondizi presidency. This seemed more politically viable. It was sustained that inflation was the result of distributive conflict in a conflictive society, such that it should be solved with income policies that could only be implemented by a strong arbiter. General Onganía, with the backing of the leaders of the armed forces, appeared to be just that person. Price and wage agreements were made, and compensatory devaluations, with an overvalued exchange rate to remain

---

25 Federico Sturzenegger, "Descripción de una Experiencia Populista: La Argentina, 1973–1976", in *The Macroeconomics of Populism in Latin America*, ed. Rudiger Dornbusch and Sebastian Edwards, Chicago, University of Chicago Press, 1991.

fixed, were implemented. Because the rate did not change for two years, while domestic prices continued to increase, although at a slower rate, the extraordinary earnings obtained by the devaluation diminished and the program ended amid other, no less difficult, political complications that led to ousting the president and ultimately to another military coup with a new call for elections. This time Perón was not excluded.

At any rate, the 1959 and 1962 adjustments had caused important transformations in the industrial apparatus. The relative price changes had improved agriculture, and exports, after several decades, were increasing. There was also a less balanced management of public accounts and a greater reticence to use the Central Bank as a financial resource. Yet, there was never any attempt to eliminate the protective barriers in which the country had cloaked itself nor were state interventions in public enterprises and the economy stopped.

6

The Long Decline

Introduction

If there is one aspect of the difficult years that characterized the period from 1974 to 1989, it was that Argentina experienced negative per capita growth for the first time in history. The societal impact of this negative growth was easy to understand, considering that the population had suffered ever more extreme and terrifying political experiences. It is true that during these years, the golden age of growth and the stability of the dollar standard in Western countries had ended,[1] as discussed in the introduction of the present book; however, this was not a matter of a decline in per capita GDP but rather a deceleration. This difference caused the growth gap in Argentina begun during the postwar period to broaden, and the country's position on the international stage began to slip. The case of other Latin American countries, such as Mexico and Brazil, was different from that of Argentina. Even though those countries experienced a substantial deceleration during the 1980s, during the 1970s they maintained a respectable rhythm of growth. (Between 1973 and 1980, while per capita GDP in Argentina grew at a rate of 0.48%, in Brazil it was 4.26% and in Mexico 3.8%.)[2]

The events of Argentina's past provide the basis of a plausible explanation for these bleak circumstances. It is important to consider these events in order to go beyond a simplistic treatment of the situation; assigning blame is rather easy because nearly everyone was guilty to some degree. The most immediate of these events was the repeated failures in achieving economic stability, eliminating external and internal restrictions that limited investment and growth.

Great social changes swept through all areas of economic activity in the postwar period; having strong impact in public finance, money, and relative prices, new balances were sought, requiring broad support that was never quite achieved. Each failed attempt raised the level of conflict in

1 Angus Maddison, *The World Economy: Historical Statistics*, OECD Development Centre, Paris, 2003.
2 Ibid., p. 153.

a veritable war of attrition.[3] The so-called *Argentine Revolution* stabilizing program's failure in the more immediate past had negative repercussions, despite appearing successful initially, unleashing rampant inflation that was much more difficult and uncontrollable than what the military found when it had taken control. These were years of extreme political upheaval. By 1989 three economic plans had been attempted. The three had the common characteristic of relying on strong political authority in order to obtain social consensus.

With the first of these plans, it was believed that with the return of Perón to power, the government would reach an agreement with corporate groups and therefore end the wasteful fighting among different sectors. But the so-called social pact, agreed to so as to control prices and wages, disintegrated very quickly when changing circumstances modified relative prices and no one was willing to resign. Perón's scant interest in economics, evidenced by the appointment of the newly rich businessman Gelbard, underscored the neglect of fiscal and monetary factors. While the deficit and money creation increased, economic authority – which maintained the illusion of price controls – centered on greater state intervention in the economy. The government attempted to solve balance-of-payments problems by developing more bilateral trade agreements with Soviet bloc countries.

When the fiscal and monetary nightmare was undeniable, Isabel de Perón (*neé* Estela Martinez) called on Gómez Morales to lead the economy, although amid the chaos he could not achieve even minimal fiscal order in the country. Finally, another minister, Celestino Rodrigo, attempted to implement a severe orthodox plan. This plan also ended in resounding failure, so that by July 1975 the economy was characterized by near hyperinflation, which was the beginning of the end for that administration.

Economic activity during the Cámpora–Lastiri–Perón–Perón period was affected – as were average Argentins – by confrontation, this time not between Peronists and anti-Peronists, but between two different groups of Peronists, the radicalized left wing and the extreme right, amid terrorist attacks and the severe state repression of the Triple A, a fiercely anticommunist, paramilitary terrorist group.[4] Having overthrown Isabel Perón, the military junta, with its corporate mentality, believed that the problem of inflation was the result of the considerable power of the Peronist trade unions, and in order to eliminate this power, political life was prohibited

---

3 See the work of Alberto Alesina and Allan Drazen, "Why Are Stabilizations delayed?" *The American Economic Review*, no. 5, 1991; and Barry Eichengreen, *Globalizing Capital*, New Jersey, Princeton University Press, 1996.

4 The Triple A is the popular name for the Argentine Anticommunist Alliance, a paramilitary ultra right-wing organization created to combat the left wing. It was later found to be led by José López Rega, Perón's own minister and personal secretary.

and unions put under control of military offices. All union activity was proscribed and wages frozen while prices were liberalized. This attempt to curb inflation also failed because despite the forced union inactivity, the price agreements to control inflation were not honored either; as the economy recovered, wages increased and prices did as well. Desperate to find a solution to the economic woes afflicting the country, the government considered any economic framework as long as it would not cause a recession and would maintain employment levels.

Amid terrorist attacks and very severe repression that infringe every limit of legality, reaching its apex in 1978, a number of economic plans were attempted and all failed. These attempts also further complicated the economy with problems such as foreign debt that were even more difficult to resolve. The military government could not find a political solution to the seemingly uncontrollable economic problems that had again emerged. Having lost the *Malvinas* (Falkland) Islands War, there were dissident voices within the military that ended up being the preface to its hurried demission.

Constitutionally elected President Raul Alfonsín, bolstered by overwhelming support for democracy, believed that inflation could be controlled by means of gradual measures and agreements between economic sectors. Central to his idea was that democracy in Argentina was fragile and only recently regained, such that drastic measures that would cause civil strife were ruled out. Despite the pro-democratic support, the president was constantly hounded for the economic circumstances that were largely beyond his control; he had inherited enormous difficulties and considerable foreign debt, which only caused the problems to intensify. After trying several different measures, all of which were partial attempts, he suffered a resounding failure: the hyperinflationary period of 1989. Conflicting interests of different corporate sectors long in a war of attrition had reached a culminating moment. The hyperinflation of 1989 would be the culmination of a long cycle in the economic life of Argentina.

Peronist Trienium: 1973–1976

After eighteen years of the proscription of his party, Perón returned to power, marking a new period, and promising to fulfill a number of expectations, among them that with his return, the violent confrontations would end. This upheaval had begun in 1946 with Perón's victory, as the candidate of the military government of 1943–1946, and were renewed in 1955 with his fall and the proscription of his party. The climate of violence was startling proof that the difficult period had not come to an end, and foretold something still worse. Interestingly, the violence this time was not between Peronists and anti-Peronists, but rather among Peronists themselves.

Peronism was a political movement that was created at the seat of power and accustomed to its favors; its followers had endured the fall of Perón, prohibition of the party, and often prison. When it was out of power, the party had become more combative and did not hesitate to use any and all means at its disposal – often violent means – to destabilize the governments in office. It was a relentless movement that faced particularly harsh retaliation. This "resistance" Peronism was associated with a new type of follower, markedly different and more left leaning than the earlier generation of Peronists. Amid the effervescent climate in Latin America, some believed that the Cuban revolutionary experience was a cautionary tale against the reformist tendencies of the democratic left, of which they had become disillusioned. Ignoring the Fascist cultural aspects of Peronism, they joined the movement arguing that they had to support those who represented the working classes, attempting to give the movement new meaning. Others, encouraged by the process of Catholic Church reform, sought objectives that went beyond those of the Second Vatican Counsel. Despising their education and culture, while he was out of power, Perón supported the activities of groups he disliked, in an attempt to destabilize the military that had overthrown him. Inspired by his popularity, these groups looked beyond simply the return of the old leader to the revolution they hoped would lead to a socialist fatherland (*patria socialista*). Of course, once in power, Perón had no intention of following that course and quickly demonstrated this by firing Cámpora from the government, scolding the Peronist youth representatives in front of TV cameras, and finally, in 1974, forcing the *Montoneros* out of the *Plaza de Mayo*. General Perón's death only intensified the internal Peronist warfare, unleashing a conflict that would affect the movement and the country for decades. Thus, an end to the long conflict was again out of reach, and the conflict itself had furthermore changed markedly.

This critical political framework made it more difficult to change the economy or allow it to evolve. After the failure of the Krieger Vasena plan in 1970, the same inflationary processes reared their ugly heads. These were more intense and complex because the government was trying to extract resources from the population by evermore sophisticated means. The population, attempting to prevent this, responded in a similar fashion, being ever more sophisticated in avoiding paying. This new trend would only come to exacerbate future difficulties.

Because inflation had taught people to reduce monetary holdings, which reduced the size of the inflationary tax that the government collected, the government sought to obtain voluntary savings, creating debt instruments that would protect against inflation. This allowed for the emergence of a financial and capital market but increased future liabilities. While nominal debt was liquidated with inflation, loans that had monetary correction clauses were not. Henceforth, the government would have to find other means of confiscating savings.

Although the Perón administrations ran deficits and issued enormous amounts of currency, which would ultimately lead to the 1975 crisis, it must be added in fairness that many of the fundamental problems, which they albeit managed very poorly, dated from previous administrations. For the new administration, the plans that in the past were meant to eradicate inflation were misguided because they had not taken into account that behind the causes of inflation had been the struggle for income distribution that incited the fiscal deficit and the monetary expansion. They understood that only an agreement between entrepreneurs and workers about equitable income distribution could put an end to this struggle and stave off inflation. For this task an arbiter was necessary, and who better, went the conventional wisdom, than Perón himself? He also had the support of two important organizations, the CGT (Trade Union Confederation, *Confederación General del Trabajo*) and the CGE (General Entrepreneurs Confederation, *Confederación General Económica*). Later the UIA (Argentine Industrial Union, *Unión Industrial Argentina*) would be included, joining with the Industrial Confederation of *CINA*. In this way social organizations and entrepreneurs were brought to the table and were finally able to reach agreements regarding prices and wages. These entities subscribed in May 1973 to the final agreement: "The Declaration of National Commitment to Reconstruction, National Liberation and Social Justice" (*Acta de Compromiso Nacional para la Reconstrucción, Liberación Nacional y Justicia Social*).

Henceforth, the Commission on Prices, Income, and Standard of Living would make recommendations to the executive regarding prices and wages. Increases would be authorized only if they could be justified by proving that costs had increased. When these affected purchasing power, wages would be increased. This reflected Perón's own corporatist beliefs. The policies were intended to prevent inflation of costs and expectations but ignored fiscal and monetary aspects of the problem. In fact, through agreements the government sought to establish a relative price structure, which, it was thought, should be reasonably equitable and long lasting. This was based on the strength of the government's political pressure. Following the adjustments, prices and wages would remain frozen for a period of two years. One thing is that the general level of prices remains stable; another entirely is that the changing conditions of supply and demand not be reflected in changes in relative prices. It was therefore not surprising that readjustments occurred, resulting from changing market conditions and availability of resources.

It was an insurmountable obstacle in a system of controlled prices, not discerning to what extent the increases were the result of changes in supply or demand (changes in relative prices) or of inflationary pressure and expectations on the general level of prices. In a world consisting of thousands of prices, how was it possible to prevent increases authorized to some from being granted to everyone, thus spurring inflation? Furthermore, when the price structure was frozen in May 1973, some had managed to beat the date, earning substantial profits, while others did not, and complained about their losses. Although unions had greater expectations, in 1973 they had reluctantly accepted a moderate wage increase. Entrepreneurs, for their part, concerned about an outbreak of the inflation experienced in 1972, and fearing the extreme alternatives that would follow left-wing Peronist, believed that the Gelbard option was reasonably acceptable because behind him was Perón, the only one who could enforce discipline on forces that Perón himself had unleashed.

What became known as the three-year plan (*el plan trienal*) was devised in an increasingly conflictive political context. At war were two radical wings of the Perón party, the extreme left, committing violence as in the case of the *Montoneros*, and the extreme right, with the no less violent Triple A (Argentine Anticommunist Alliance). Once certain adjustments were made, prices and wages were frozen for a period of two years. But the freeze itself had to be administered with greater flexibility within ten months, in March 1974. Sensing the imminent Perón's victory, business owners had raised prices beforehand, for which wages were readjusted, showing in 1974 an average increase of 38.5% in real terms compared to 1969.[5] In May 1975 the collective bargaining system (discontinued in 1966) was reimplemented. The program was initially successful because it served to scale back expectations (based on the considerable power Perón wielded not only over the indomitable unions but also over business owners). While for the first time some prices dropped in the first month, they increased only later, reaching a monthly average rate of 1.9% between July and December 1973, compared to the extremely high annual rate of 64% the previous year. The peso, quoted at 12.5 per dollar, in May dropped to 10 per dollar and remained there the rest of the year. In 1973 there were important factors that changed the terms of trade: an increase in the price of commodities, coupled with excellent crop yields. Thus, in 1973 there was a 68% increase in exports with respect to the previous year.

The agreement had established a reduction in the nominal interest rate, implementing a policy of cheap credit. Paradoxically, the decrease in the inflation rate (like during 1967–1969) intensified the trend of negative real rates, which went from −30.9% in 1972 to −18.6% in 1973. Later, in 1974, the trend reversed and the number became positive:

5 Roberto Domenech, "Estadísticas de la Evolución Económica de Argentina 1913–1984", *Estudios*, no. 39, July–September 1986.

0.9%.[6] GDP grew in 1973 by 3.7% and by 5.4% in 1974. Nevertheless, the government appeared indifferent to fiscal deficit and unconcerned by significant monetary expansion.[7] The deficit burgeoned, going from 4.6% of GDP in 1972 to 6.9% in 1973. Financing government operations had been the main factor in money supply, which was also used to finance the private sector (partly to absorb wage increases). During the first five months of 1973 the treasury deficit equaled one-half of spending, while the money supply (M_1)[8] grew in April at an annual rate of 119%.[9] It is clear that economic stability was growing more precarious by the day; government expenditures as a proportion of GDP increased more than revenue, increasing the deficit.

Entrepreneurs and unions clamored for increases toward the end of the year, complicating the favorable initial situation. External forces, the increase in the cost of imports in 1974, made wage and price freezes more difficult. The price of imports grew sharply in 1974, due to international inflation following an increase in the price of oil. Entrepreneurs who used imported parts threatened to halt production if they would not be permitted to increase prices. The government responded by subsidizing the import exchange rate, and the Central Bank absorbed the losses incurred when foreign currency was sold more cheaply than the price at which it was purchased from exporters. Soon there were shortages of some goods, which fetched higher prices than the official ones. Slowly, increases were permitted. Thus, in March 1974, when the CGT requested a wage increase, it was granted.

During the following months, the economy heated up. Inflation increased in the second semester of 1974, though somewhat contained by price controls, which triggered shortages. Import prices increased by 57% from 1973 to 1974.[10] The fiscal deficit also increased, and the inflation rate, which was 5.5% in the last trimester of 1973, grew to 14.3% during the same period in 1974. Thus, the real interest rate turned negative again, dropping to −52.8% in 1975. Because of the growth in the public sector, spending for this sector was greater than 25% of GDP and the fiscal deficit reached 14.5% of GDP in 1975. Fiscal contributions from 1975 and 1976 were extraordinarily low. Public sector real wages reached their height in 1974 and 1975 and were 30% higher than those in the private sector in

6 Adrián Guissarri, *La Argentina Informal: Realidad de la Vida Económica*, Buenos Aires, Emecé Editores, 1989, p. 308.

7 On this subject, see Guido Di Tella y Rudiger Dornbusch, *The Political Economy of Argentina, 1946–1983*, Oxford, St. Anthony's/Macmillan.

8 M_1 is currency in pubic hands + deposits in the current account.

9 BCRA Statistical Bulletin, 1974.

10 CEPAL, *Estadísticas Económicas de Corto Plazo de la Argentina: Sector Externo y Condiciones Económicas Internacionales*, vol. 1, Buenos Aires, May 1986.

Table 6.1. *Relative Real Wages:*
Government/Private Nonagricultural
Sector

Year	Relative Real Wage
1970	112.9
1971	110.9
1972	112.7
1973	132
1974	121.9
1975	119.1

Source: Roberto Domenech, "Estadísticas de la Evolución Económica de Argentina, 1913–1984", *Estudios*, no. 39, 1986.

1973.[11] Government spending increased in 1973 by 20% with respect to 1972, while income did so by only 6%. This increased the primary deficit by 69% compared with 1972 (see Table 6.1 and Figure 6.1).

The increase was due to the effect of wages on the government, on decentralized agencies and state enterprises, and on transferences as well. Aggregate salaries of the National Administration grew by 38% in real terms between 1972 and 1973 and by 10% between 1973 and 1974. The fiscal deficit also came from the deficit of state enterprises that had long plagued the country. This was due, among other reasons, to lags in tariffs utilities, a policy implemented in 1971 to subsidize the cost of living. The tariff utilities were partially corrected in 1973 before the change in administration and not implemented until April 1974, at which point there was a significant adjustment that remained unchanged until May 1975. The government financed the imbalances with significant money creation that was also used to finance the private sector through rediscounts and, among other things, to finance wage increases (see Figure 6.2).

Subsidies to the private sector for wage increases and the official sector were the principal sources of creation of the monetary base. The enormous monetary expansion had less effect on prices due to government controls that obscured significant repressed inflation. Thus it seemed that, with limitless financing through the Central Bank, the economy could certainly become one "for the people" just as the government slogan declared, with equitable income distribution. But this impression was short lived.

In July 1974 General Perón was dead and Vice President María Estela (Isabel) Martínez would succeed him. Gelbard, an entrepreneur with the

---

11 The calculation excludes public employee salaries.

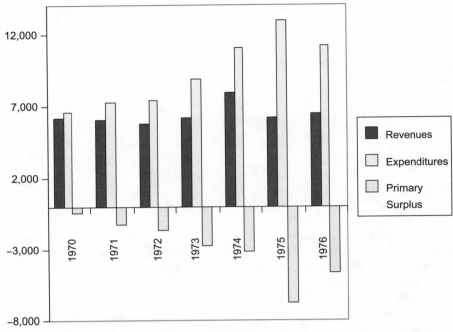

Figure 6.1. Public Nonfinancial Sector: Revenues and Expenditures, 1970–1976 (in australs, at constant 1974 prices). *Source*: Ministerio de Economía, *Sector Público Argentino no Financiero: Cuenta Ahorro-Inversión-Financiamiento*, Secretaría de Hacienda de la República Argentina, Buenos Aires, December 2004.

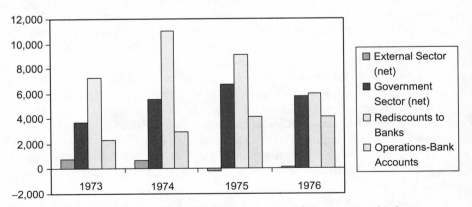

Figure 6.2. Evolution of BCRA Liabilities, 1973–1976 (in 1974 australs). *Source*: BCRA Yearbooks, 1973–1976, and BCRA Statistical Bulletins, 1975 and 1979.

Table 6.2. *Value of Dollar on Official (Financial) Market and on Parallel Market (Pesos Ley per Dollar – Annual Averages)*

Year	Official (Financial) Market	Parallel Market
1970	3.79	3.86
1971	5.42	6.14
1972	9.05	11.52
1973	9.80	11.29
1974	9.98	16.25
1975	32.03	71.41
1976	140.00	257.75

Source: *Boletín Informativo Techint*, no. 205, Buenos Aires, November–December 1987.

CGE, who had started with Cámpora and Perón, remained in the Martinez de Perón cabinet until September of that year amid an evermore difficult situation in which shortages, the black market, and violations of the initial act of the agreement between CGT, CGE, and the government (*Acta de compromiso*) were widespread. In September, Gómez Morales, a well-known and prestigious professional who led the economy during the difficult 1951–1952 recession, became minister of economy. Given these circumstances, the administration had no other choice but to loosen the control on prices.

In February 1975 the peso devalued by 50%; the financial exchange went from 10 to 15 pesos per dollar, and the commercial exchange from 5 to 10 pesos per dollar. In March new wage increases were authorized. In May, collective agreements were to be renegotiated and unions had begun to exert pressure. In the middle of this process a political upheaval occurred. The president, guided by the social welfare minister, López Rega, designated Celestino Rodrigo as minister of economy, who was sworn in on June 2 and who tried to implement a severe adjustment plan to combat inflation. The peso was devalued by 100%, as it went from 15 to 30 per dollar on the financial market, while on the commercial market it went from 10 to 26 per dollar. Again, this was the second devaluation of the year that had started with 10 pesos per dollar (see Table 6.2).

In order to reduce the deficit, rates for public services and fuel were increased by nearly 189%, although they later dropped in real terms by 6.5%.[12] By now wage negotiations had already begun with an opening of a 40% increase. Unions balked, given the increase in rates for public

12 Adjusted for inflation using CPI. Horacio Núñez Miñana and Alberto Porto, "Inflación y Tarifas Públicas: Argentina, 1945–1980", *Desarrollo Económico*, no. 84, 1982.

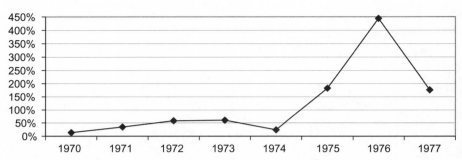

Figure 6.3. Consumer Price Index Rate of Change (annual average compared with
the average from the previous year). *Source*: INDEC, www.indec.gov.ar.

services. They confronted the president and, allied with the opposition and
with the military, managed to unseat the de facto prime minister, López
Rega, whose coattails also ensnared Rodrigo, causing his political demise.
So the brief and traumatic anti-inflationary experiment had ended, like at
other times, with the opposite result than the one desired; only this time
the price increases were exorbitant.

The agreements were signed between a 60/80% to a 200% increase
(making an average increase of 170%).[13] Prices increased in July by 35%,
and Argentina entered a new and more difficult period. Inflation from then
on had jumped to three digits annually and would not drop from there
during the following years – except for exceptional and brief periods. A
decade and a half of decline in GDP had begun, which would constitute
the long decline of the years 1974–1989 (see Figure 6.3).

The Military Government: 1976–1983

Argentina suffered profound and extremely negative consequences when the
three commanders of the armed forces deposed the democratically elected
president in March 1976, illegitimately seizing power and taking over the
government in a corporate decision The economic results were as bleak
as the sociopolitical ones. The efforts to fix the financial mess created by
successive failures on the part of the military government of 1966–1973
and the extravagances of the three-year Perón period were fruitless; the
attempts to stabilize the currency, finances, and the export sector in order
to lead the country to economic growth had all failed and left the country
in dire straits.

13 Roberto Domenech, "Estadísticas de la Evolución Económica de Argentina 1913–1984", *Estudios*,
no. 39, 1986.

At the Edge of Hyperinflation

The military government began under extreme circumstances, namely rampant inflation toward the end of 1975: 335% on retail prices.[14] Inflation during 1976 registered at 9% in January, 19% in February, 38% in March, and 34% in April. The first and only time that the country had experienced three-digit inflation rivaling this one was in 1959, as a result of the huge devaluation in December 1958, and the corresponding adjustments in public services prices and consumers and producer prices.

As has been shown, in 1973 revenues covered only 47% of basic expenditures, while the rest had to be financed, as did the interest payments on public debt. The Central Bank issued money to cover government and private sector needs, causing prices to increase and extraordinary capital flights, which left it without foreign reserves to tend to the most pressing needs abroad. The country was at the edge of hyperinflation.

After the series of failures of anti-inflation programs such as the Krieger Vasena's one and the Perón-Gelbard program for zero inflation, the military leaders thought that by simply taking over the government they could rid the country of inflation. As they saw it, their mere presence would be the necessary condition to end the recession that had begun in the last trimester of 1974 and start on the road to sustained growth.

Employment was a serious concern of this government. The military junta thought that if anti-inflation measures caused unemployment, this would lead to more upheaval and workers would join those involved in political violence. Thus, the government sought economic measures that would reduce inflation without eliminating jobs, in a period of violence and attacks carried out by armed groups from the extreme left and right and the bloody and illegal repression with which the military government responded.

Inflation was understood to be caused by an increase in costs due to substantial increases in wages that were a result of the conflict over income distribution that had broken out during the Perón government and of expectations of inflation. Moreover, the recession was produced by the erosion of business profitability and the paucity of incentives for the agricultural sector, whose income was reduced by a notoriously outdated exchange rate.

To combat these problems, Minister of Economy José A. Martínez de Hoz announced on April 2, 1976, a restructuring, stabilization, and growth program that included among other measures a devaluation, which led the financial market exchange rate of 76.9 pesos per dollar, and a financial

---

14 Data from December 1975/December 1974. Calculation based on INDEC data.

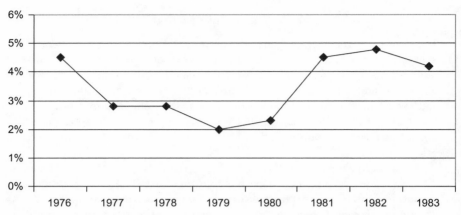

Figure 6.4. Evolution of the Unemployment Rate. *Source*: B. R. Mitchell, *International Historical Statistics: The Americas, 1750–1993*, New York, Stockton Press, 1998, p. 115.

market special rate of 109.37 pesos per dollar to a single (financial) rate of 140.33 pesos per dollar.[15] Unification of the exchange rate to a single one, replacing the multiple rate system and elimination of price controls left from the Perón administration, was carried out along with the freezing nominal salaries. Finally a policy of obtaining minimal leeway in international reserves was proposed. It was decided that if adjustments had to be made, it would not be to employment levels, but rather to real wages. This was managed until 1980 because the military government began its administration with an unemployment rate of 4.5%, which had dropped to 2% by 1979, although in 1982 it reached a maximum of 4.8% (see Figure 6.4).

It was expected that price liberalization, which would apparently produce a wage decrease in real terms, in fact would not affect them because actually their purchasing power was already reduced and it was apparently greater because it had been measured in relation to controlled prices. But effective purchasing power was not affected by the new rise in free prices because to obtain the goods on the market before, consumers should pay higher effective prices, so the government did not expect a strong opposition from the workers. Besides, the CGT was intervened and political activity prohibited. The devaluation had a positive impact on the agricultural sector, which during that year increased production, which meant improved exports from this sector, which in 1976 increased by 32% and in 1977 by 44% (see Table 6.3).

15 BCRA Yearbook, 1976.

Table 6.3. *Grain Exports (in thousands of dollars)*

	First Trimester of 1975	First Trimester of 1976	First Trimester of 1977
Total grains	253,198	278,308	437,686
Wheat	119,568	197,449	273,958
Corn	104,332	40,496	59,609
Sorghum	2,581	15,983	28,447
Bran and ground bran	8,747	11,988	24,403
Others	17,970	12,392	51,269

Source: CEPAL, *Estadísticas Económicas de Corto Plazo de la Argentina: Sector Externo y Condiciones Económicas Internacionales*, vol. 2, Buenos Aires, May 1986.

Improvement in exports from the agricultural sector allowed better results in the trade account and consequently in the balance of payments. Rates for public services, which had remained remarkably outdated in 1976, were increased because the need to finance this sector was a primary factor in the fiscal deficit. Increases in tariffs utilities and the drop in the administration's real salaries produced better fiscal accounts. As early as 1977, income covered 83% of primary expenditure and 75% of total expenditures. Total remuneration paid in the national administration in constant terms (australs, at 1975 prices) dropped from 5,308 in 1976 to 5,004.5 in 1977, or nearly 6%. Furthermore, to eliminate expectations of price increases, agreements were made with a powerful group of large enterprises to not change their prices.

In 1976 an agreement with the IMF was signed in which the government committed to the gradual implementation of a single and floating exchange rate. The government also guaranteed that export taxes would not increase. It promised to reduce import duties and free them from obstacles so as to allow international competition and to eliminate other restrictions on payments and transfers originated in current and capital transactions. (Minimum requirements for financing imported capital goods, minimal cap of 180 days financing for imports and the obligation to purchase investment bonds for foreign trade for the financed portion of private sector imports).

The new conditions caused a reversion in the flow of capitals, as a significant amount entered from abroad, including many of Argentines' savings. This considerably improved foreign reserves at the Central Bank, which increased from $618 million in 1975 to $1,772 million in 1976 and $3,862 million in 1977. This also had a positive effect on investment levels (see Table 6.4).

Toward the end of the year, it was clear that the government had managed to prevent hyperinflation, which, given the conditions under which it assumed power, was no small feat. Also, promising signs were the increase

Table 6.4. *Gross Domestic Investment: Construction and Durable Goods (as a percentage of GDP)*

Year	Construction[a]	Production Durable Goods
1973	11.3	8.3
1974	11.5	7.8
1975	12.1	7.3
1976	13.8	7.7
1977	14.2	10.2
1978	14.0	8.1
1979	13.0	9.0
1980	12.9	9.9

[a] Includes private and public construction.

Note: Estimate made on data at 1970 prices.

Source: CEPAL: *Estadísticas Económicas de Corto Plazo de la Argentina: Cuentas Nacionales, Industria Manufacturera y Sector Agropecuario Pampeano*, vol. 1, Buenos Aires, July 1988.

in reserves at the Central Bank, growing investment levels, and the agricultural sector had shown great capacity for recovery. While inflation had been reduced considerably, and the 1978–1976 recession seemed to dissipate, after the first and drastic fall in GDP toward the end of the year, the country appeared to reach a new low from which it would be difficult to fall any further (see Figure 6.5 and Tables 6.5 and 6.6).

If what was at issue was inflation of costs and expectations and real wages had dropped and expectations had reversed course (also the outflow

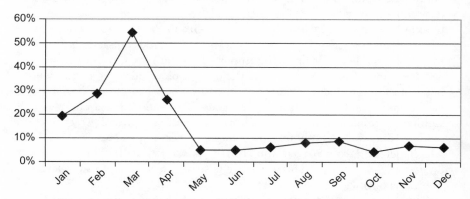

Figure 6.5. Change in Wholesale Prices Compared with the Previous Month, General Level, 1976. *Source:* "Serie Histórica del Sistema de Índice de Precios Mayoristas (IPM)," INDEC, www.indec.gov.ar (accessed May 2005).

Table 6.5. *Gold and Foreign Exchange Reserves at the Central Bank, Balance at the End of Each Year (in millions of dollars)*

Year	Reserves
1975	617.7
1976	1,771.9
1977	3,862.4
1978	5,828.9
1979	10,137.6

Source: BCRA Yearbook, 1979 and 1981.

of capital and the speculation against the peso), then the government said – to what was this stubborn resistance due to? Insisting that at the root of inflation were expectations, the government managed to come to a price freeze or "truce" with business owners. For a period of 120 days, entrepreneurs agreed not to increase prices, assuming that once the inertial effects of periodic adjustments were over, prices would ultimately stabilize. The prices of goods produced by a group of 700 leading businesses were set at February 22, 1977, levels and the previous intervention of the commerce secretary was stipulated for the authorization of changes to the same. The truce would be valid for 120 days starting March 9.

But again it was impossible to put the brakes on escalating prices. The military government handily enforced the price truce during the period in question, but when it ended, everyone was ready to begin the game anew, and when the opportunity arrived – keeping in mind that in the inflationary game he who hesitates is lost – everyone tried to keep ahead of the change. Thus, the size of the increase easily outstripped the stability from the period of the price freeze.

Because this instrument also failed in May 1977, the government tried to curb inflation by orthodox monetary methods. Recognizing that there

Table 6.6. *Gross Domestic Product at Factor Cost, Several Sectors (in australs at 1970 prices)*

	1975	1976	1977
General Total	8,951.0	8,949.9	9,521.4
Agriculture, hunting, wildlife, and fishing	1,171.9	1,226.8	1,257.0
Manufacturing industries	2,485.3	2,409.9	2,598.2
Construction	527.3	605.9	679.8

Note: Because the partial data do not cover all items, sector totals differ from the general total.
Source: CEPAL, *Estadísticas de Corto Plazo de la Argentina: Cuentas Nacionales, Industria Manufacturera y Sector Agropecuario Pampeano*, vol. 1, Buenos Aires, July 1988.

was excess supply of money, they tried to control the expansive factors: the monetary base, containing the increase in domestic and foreign assets (these last ones mainly due to swaps and exchange insurances), and issues of banking money, with required minimum cash reserves. According to the BCRA Yearbook for 1977, the measures of the economic program tended to curb monetary expansion, government credits and debits, proposing the following quantitative objectives: the increase in the Central Bank's foreign net assets to no less than $249 million during the first five months of the year, $258 million during the first semester, and $534 million for the year; a reduction in the exchange rate guarantees on short-term foreign loans valued at more than $230 million granted by the Central Bank by the end of May and those valued at $140 million by the end of June to its complete elimination by the year end. The final item was to limit net domestic credit expansion to 750 billion pesos by the end of May, to 793 billion by the end of June, and to 1,219 billion by the end of December. Restrict the treasury deficit to no more than 340 billion pesos by the end of May, to 420 billion by the end of June, and to 736 billion for the year.

Restrictions on money issues and credit expansion made the rate of inflation decrease more than the nominal interest rate, which caused a situation that had rarely been seen in the second half of the twentieth century, an increase in real interest rates. This increase made entrepreneurs angry. The sectors that had access to the restricted official credit market at rates that had been lower than inflation had gotten used to going into debt because during a series of inflationary processes their debt also ended up being liquidated. Accumulating debt in real terms was something new and in fact dangerous. These measures began to break the alliance established since the end of 1975 between business sectors and the military government. This debt would also have another important consequence: enterprises began to liquidate inventory, limiting stock, for which they limited production. The increase in real interest rates caused a drop in GDP in 1978. See Figure 6.6 and the table of nominal and real interest rates in the Appendix, Table A.C.6.8.

Moreover, an exchange rate that would gradually adjust to the inflation rate – a crawling peg – was established to maintain competitiveness. Other measures whose objective was to reduce inflation, part of the 1977 reforms, were the reduction in customs tariffs. The government maintained that the resistance to price reductions was because the industrial sectors were not competitive, and that the only way to become so was to open the economy.

At the beginning of 1976 it was clear that the Argentine tariff level was greater than most other countries. Furthermore, the extremely differentiated tariff structure caused unwanted distortions by overprotecting some industries to the detriment of the agricultural as well as industrial export sectors. Thus, one of the economic authorities' concerns was to eliminate the distortions caused by the tariff structure. With this in mind, in November

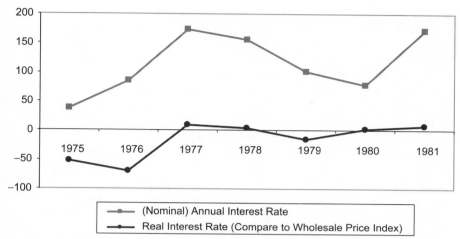

Figure 6.6. Nominal and Real Interest Rates, 1975–1981. *Source*: Adrián Guissarri,
La Argentina Informal: Realidad de la Vida Económica, Buenos Aires, Emecé, 1989,
p. 308.

1976 a global tariff reduction was established for all of the import items.
This policy was pursued in 1977, when, in addition to reducing tariffs,
the prohibition on the importation of certain goods was lifted. The tariff
adjustments signified a reduction of around 40 points (from 90% to around
40%), which was associated with a reduction of export taxes on agricultural
products, which went from 10–50% down to 5–25% and previous deposits
for imports were eliminated.[16]

Central Bank Reforms: Guarantee of Deposits

*The Monetary Regulation Account (Cuenta de Regulacion Monetaria). The Finan-
cial Intermediaries Law.* In order to eliminate the system of nationalization
of deposits, the Central Bank's charter was changed. The 1957 system by
which each commercial bank would have the deposits of its customers at
its own disposal was again implemented. Concession of rediscounts was
limited to temporary illiquidity situations, as the Central Bank resumed
its role as lender of last resort. Regulation of the money supply would be
related to banks' credit capacity, with the system of required minimum
reserves, while the Central Bank's financing of the government would be
considerably reduced. Interest rates, which had been controlled ever since
World War II, were, with few exceptions, fixed at a rate that was permanently lower than that of inflation. This increase had favored debtors to

16 *Política Económica y Procesos de Desarrollo: La Experiencia Argentina entre 1976 y 1981*, Estudios e
Informes de la CEPAL, Santiago de Chile, 1983, p. 17.

the financial system, among them the government, but was an obstacle to the formation of a debt market for public bonds (the reason for which was, for a long time, they had been placed in the pension fund in the state social security system). The new system included a National Government guarantee of deposits in financial institutions, something that dated back to World War II. Lastly, the Monetary Regulation Account was created. It was thought that such an instrument was necessary for a chronically inflationary economy. This instrument required the Central Bank to charge a fee for sight deposits (with lending capacity) and remunerated reserves (that accrued no interest) in banks and other financial institutions. A plan that seemed equitable, and offered seigniorage to checking accounts, faced the only problem that there was an inflationary mentality, and with liberalized rates, fewer people put their money in these accounts and transferred them instead to time deposits, where they earned interest at a rate that was greater than inflation. The monetary regulation account became a source of quasi-fiscal deficit and of money creation on the part of the Central Bank.[17]

The 1978 Recession

A 3.2% fall in GDP was caused mainly by a 10.5% reduction in industrial product, which had been affected by monetary policy that resulted in positive real interest rates[18] and a relative opening in trade. Positive real interest rates led entrepreneurs to reduce their stocks, an adjustment that was initially achieved through a reduction in production. Table 6.7 shows that the most significant reduction in 1978 was in the manufacturing sector. With regard to fiscal accounts, the substantial decrease in expenditure and the increase in revenue from 1975 to 1976 allowed a reduction in the primary deficit and in the overall deficit (see Tables 6.7 and A.28, and Figures 6.7 and 6.8).

December 1978: The Monetary Approach to the Balance of Payments

The monetary policies (quantitative control of monetary expansion) had not reduced the annual inflation rate that in 1978 remained near 175.5%.[19] Moreover, the increase in real interest rates led to the 1978 recession that

---

17 The fiscal deficit is the difference between income and expenditures in the nonfinancial public sector. The Central Bank quasi-fiscal deficit is the difference between income and expenditures that have not been considered in the fiscal deficit. It is the "difference between Central Bank income from domestic and net international assets and net expenditures for interest and/ or adjustments of instruments it uses to control the expansion of monetary aggregates." Piekarz, Julio, "El Déficit Cuasifiscal del Banco Central", Buenos Aires, Banco Central de la República Argentina, 1987, p. 2.

18 On average 4.2%, according to A. Guissarri, *La Argentina Informal: Realidad de la Vida Económica*, Buenos Aires, Emecé Editores, 1989.

19 Average variation of the CPI between 1977 and 1978. *Source*: INDEC.

Table 6.7. *Gross Domestic Product at Factor Cost*

Year	1977	1978	1979
General total	9,521.4	9,214.6	9,861.2
Agriculture, hunting, wildlife, and fishing	1,257.0	1,292.4	1,328.9
Manufacturing industries	2,598.2	2,324.8	2,556.3
Construction	679.8	647.4	644.4
Mine and quarry exploitation	214.8	218.9	232.8
Electricity, gas, and water	285.0	294.5	326.1
Wholesale and retail businesses, restaurants, and hotels	1,401.1	1,314.0	1,490.8
Transportation, storage, and communications	1,003.8	981.8	1,054.2
Financial institutions, insurance, and real estate	691.5	738.1	796.9
Community, social, and personal services	1,390.4	1,402.7	1,430.9

Source: CEPAL, *Estadísticas de Corto Plazo de la Argentina: Cuentas Nacionales, Industria Manufacturera y Sector Agropecuario Pampeano*, vol. 1, Buenos Aires, July 1988.

broke the recovery begun the previous year. Toward the end of 1978, conscious of the recent Chilean experience, another way to curb inflation was explored. The December 1978 program was intended to make domestic and international prices converge. To this end, the government sought to eliminate the uncertainty regarding the change in the exchange rate by announcing a decreasing rate of devaluation for a prolonged period of time, which was initially eight months. It was thought that the decline in the exchange rate would affect local inflation, which would also tend to decrease. This was based on the assumption that if all goods had to

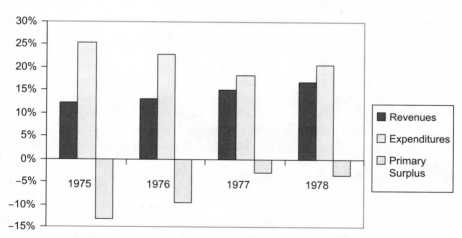

Figure 6.7. Fiscal Revenues and Expenditures as a Percentage of GDP. *Source*: Ministerio de Economía, *Sector Público Argentino no Financiero: Cuenta Ahorro-Inversión-Financiamiento*, Secretaría de Hacienda de la República Argentina, Buenos Aires, December 2004.

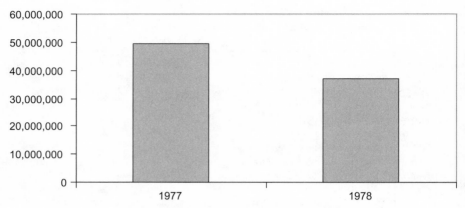

Figure 6.8. Real Monetary Base, 1977–1978 (in millions of pesos Ley at 1980 prices). *Source*: BCRA Statistical Bulletins, 1975 and 1979, and BCRA Yearbooks, 1975 and 1979.

compete internationally, domestic prices would converge with international ones, multiplied by the exchange rate. If the uncertainty over the change in the exchange rate was eliminated, followed by a decreasing way until parity was reached, prices would end up converging with international ones.

It was clear that this would not happen immediately with goods that did not compete with foreign products, the nontradable ones. However, in this case, it was assumed that more expensive nontradable domestic goods would be substituted for cheaper ones. An excess in supply of nontradable goods would end up pushing prices down.

Because reaching equilibrium between the two markets meant a recession in the domestic goods sector, the government tried to avoid this by previously regulating a sliding scale of the devaluation rate, announcing it so that people could adapt their expectations and thus allow a rapid adjustment that would render unnecessary an excess supply and a recession to achieve domestic and foreign price convergence. Although inflation began to decrease, it was belated with respect to the devaluation, which led many people to note that the local currency was being overvalued (see Figure 6.9).

A heated debate erupted over whether or not the peso was overvalued; Rodríguez and Sjaastad maintained that in 1978 it was not but they accepted that in 1979 it was. To a large extent, the program's failure was due to the way in which the government financed the deficit. Local debt at rates that should have been competitive was issued in a market with a floating interest rate. Individuals acquired debt abroad, and with this money, they bought financial assets in pesos. If the local interest rate,

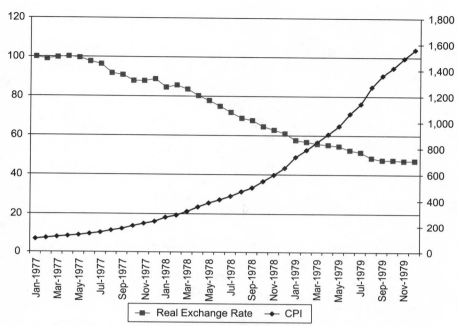

Figure 6.9. Change in the Real Exchange Rate (Index numbers: January 1977 = 100). *Source*: INDEC, Federal Reserve of St. Louis (Web), and CEPAL, *Estadísticas Económicas de Corto Plazo de la Argentina: Cuentas Nacionales, Industria Manufacturera y Sector Agropecuario Pampeano*, vol. 1, Buenos Aires, July 1988.

minus the devaluation rate, was greater than what was paid to obtain loans abroad, the operation was profitable. The risk of devaluation was always there, but this was rather improbable in the beginning and became ever greater (which was reflected in increasing interest rates) as the end of the sliding-scale devaluation period, called the *tablita*, approached. Initially, this contributed to an increase in reserves, but it also contributed to the increase in foreign debt, which gave little credence to sliding-scale exchange rate (*tablita*); total foreign debt, both public and private, increased from 20.7% of GDP in 1977 to 21.8% in 1979 (see Figure 6.10 and Table 6.8). The government had encouraged state enterprises to assume foreign debt. The inflow of foreign loans, by increasing reserves, was a factor in monetary expansion and had the same characteristics as Central Bank money financing.

Private foreign debt had to do with loans that Argentines obtained abroad, which were backed by their own assets in foreign financial institutions. These funds were deposited locally at much higher interest rates. But while in order to pay the debt they had to make remittances abroad,

Table 6.8. *Evolution of Public External Debt*[a]
(in millions of dollars)

Year	Stock	Percentage of GDP
1977	8,126.7	14.3
1978	8,357.0	14.4
1979	9,960.3	14.4
1980	14,459.0	18.8
1981	20,024.0	25.5

[a] Only capital. Values recorded at year's end.
Source: BCRA Yearbooks, 1977, 1979, and 1981, and World Bank, *World Bank Tables 1995*, Baltimore, MD, The Johns Hopkins University Press, May 1995.

the same was not true with interest from savings deposited abroad, which did not return to the country.

An inconsistent fiscal policy and money issues based in part on the inflow of foreign exchange, acquiring debt abroad (and in the case of private debt, utilized to purchase domestic debt from the government), inspired very little confidence and were a negative factor in achieving domestic and foreign price convergence (see Table 6.8).

Public expenditure that had been greater than 20% of GDP in 1974–1976 dropped to 18% in 1977, and later increased to 22% in 1980–1981. At the beginning of the 1980s, the fiscal deficit was greater than 10%

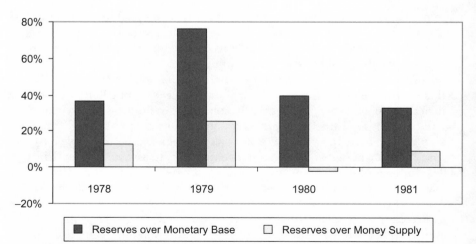

Figure 6.10. Ratio Reserves to Monetary Base and to Money Supply, 1978–1981.
Source: BCRA Yearbooks, 1979–1981, and BCRA Statistical Bulletin, 1978.

Table 6.9. *Percent Change in*
Wholesale Prices (general level,
average annual change)

Year	Change (%)
1976	499.0
1977	149.4
1978	146.0
1979	149.3
1980	75.4

Source: INDEC, www.indec.gov.ar.

of GDP.[20] The other problem had to do with the very highly restricted trade opportunities that disallowed an easy flux between the domestic and foreign markets.

The fiscal deficit and the fact that there was no external trade opening parallel to the financial market were the main factors in the failure of the program. Also worthy of note were the political circumstances in which there was a change of president and ministers and a prolonged silence about the will to continue with the economic program's objectives. Around the end of 1980 the annual increase in wholesale prices, which in 1976 had been 499% and in 1978 146%, had dropped to 75.4% (see Table 6.9).

Interest Rates and the 1980 and 1981 Banking Crisis

Interest rate liberalization led to increasing indebtedness of entrepreneurs who in the past had been accustomed to negative rates; because with inflation their liabilities were liquidated, they were free from solvency problems. This led many enterprises to default on their debts to banks and let the interest accumulate on the unpaid loans, hoping for a government bail out. In order for the banks to, in turn, continue paying depositors, they tried to attract more savings by increasing the interest rate, which pushed interest up and made the situation evermore precarious. But the public made deposits in dubious banks because these were guaranteed by the National Government. The Central Bank would pay in the event that the banks could not, which in effect happened in 1980 in some highly publicized cases (*Banco de Intercambio Regional*/Regional Commerce Bank). A banking crisis ensued and the Central Bank responded by rediscounting assets that were largely unrecoverable. Thus several of these banks were liquidated. Paying depositors of liquidated entities caused an enormous

20 8%, 13%, 15%, and 16% in 1980, 1981, 1982, and 1983, respectively.

Table 6.10. *Ratio Rediscounts[a] to Money Supply (M₃)*

Year	1978	1979	1980	1981
Ratio (%)	1.9	1.3	14.1	24.4

[a] Includes rediscounts, advances, resources from bank debt, and other financial sector liabilities.
Source: BCRA Yearbooks, 1979–1981, and BCRA Statistical Bulletin, 1978.

increase in monetary issues and put an end to the stabilizing program. Table 6.10 shows how the ratio between rediscounts and monetary supply increased between 1980 and 1981.

Before the General Videla presidency had ended, Minister Martínez de Hoz decided to abandon the preannounced exchange rate path and ordered a 10% devaluation, with which the exchange gap was expected to be closed. By the time the transfer of government occurred and General Viola, along with his minister of economy, Lorenzo Sigaut, had assumed office, expectations had changed. No one thought that the devaluation would be enough and a new run on the dollar ensued.

The failure of the 1981 adjustments caused a series of devaluations that, in order to keep ahead of prices, were ever greater. It was a whirlwind of new increases in the exchange rate and prices. Inflation was 105% in 1981, 165% in 1982, and 344% in 1983,[21] and the devaluation was 118% in 1981.[22] By the time the huge mess was over, real devaluation had been achieved (see Figure 6.11).

The devaluation, because it caused a drop in real income, had a negative effect on economic activity. The reduction in GDP was 5.4% in 1981 and 3.2% in 1982; a recovery (4.1% growth) followed in 1983 (see Table A.9). Each of the frustrated stabilization attempts not only left higher inflation in its wake, but caused even more serious economic imbalances. Hastened by the crisis, the government took measures that compromised the economic future of the country. During the sliding-scale devaluation period (*tablita*) public and private debt had increased. Public debt consisted of foreign loans that were used to finance the government and public enterprises. Private debt was obtained by a number of mechanisms, which intensified the flight of capital that begun in 1975. This required a complex process of remittances of savings to foreign countries, in an effort to prevent loss due to depreciation. Carlos Rodríguez[23] pointed out that while individuals who had assets abroad (which were the guarantee of the debt they had

21 Consumer Price Index. *Source*: INDEC.
22 On average, compared with 1980.
23 Carlos Rodríguez, "La Deuda Externa Argentina", *Serie Seminarios*, Seminary 2/87, Centro de Investigaciones Económicas, Torcuato Di Tella Institute, 1987.

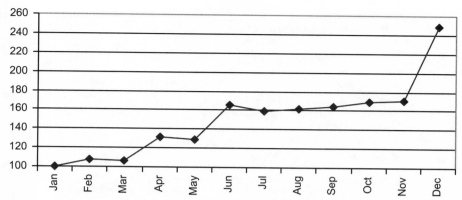

Figure 6.11. Evolution of the Real Exchange Rate in 1981 (Index numbers: January 1981 = 100). *Note*: Until May, the nominal exchange rate is free; from June on, it is a commercial rate. The single exchange rate was used for December, as it became valid from December 23. Real exchange rate = Nominal exchange rate × CPI (USA)/CPI (Argentina). *Source*: INDEC, Federal Reserve of St. Louis (Web), and CEPAL, *Estadísticas Económicas de Corto Plazo de la Argentina: Cuentas Nacionales, Industria Manufacturera y Sector Agropecuario Pampeano*, vol. 1, Buenos Aires, July 1988.

assumed) maintained abroad the interest gained for those assets, they had instead to remit the interest due for the foreign liability. Thus, while in the current account payments for interest for the loans abroad were filed, there was no inflows for the earnings of assets held abroad, creating the explosive problem of foreign debt (which was largely owned by Argentines) (see Table 6.11).

Table 6.11. *Gross Domestic Product at Market Prices, Several Sectors*

Year	1980	1981	1982	1983
General total	10,301.4	9,742.9	9,435.2	9,823.2
Agriculture, hunting, wildlife, and fishing	717.0	738.6	781.1	793.6
Manufacturing industries	2,890.4	2,544.1	2,475.8	2,658.3
Construction	841.3	738.4	667.3	657.3
Mine and quarry exploitation	231.4	228.4	221.8	227.1
Electricity, gas, and water	151.1	152.8	160.3	171.4
Wholesale and retail businesses, restaurants, and hotels	1,844.6	1,682.2	1,546.4	1,619.2
Transportation, storage, and communications	418.1	393.8	402.2	416.3
Financial institutions, insurance, and real estate	1,451.1	1,541.9	1,499.0	1,497.0
Community, social, and personal services	1,761.4	1,769.9	1,782.3	1,824.0

Source: CEPAL, *Estadísticas Económicas de Corto Plazo de la Argentina: Cuentas Nacionales, Industria Manufacturera y Sector Agropecuario Pampeano*, vol. 1, Buenos Aires, July 1988.

Table 6.12. *Buenos Aires Stock Market, Total Operations (in millions of australs)*

	Constant Values 1983 Prices		
	1981	1982	1983
Total	34,932.1	60,382.7	45,920.2
Public securities	28,236.0	54,300.7	38,063.8
Adjustable public securities	11,874.1	11,253.0	–
Variable national bonds	382.7	–	–
Foreign bonds	15,979.2	41,558.1	38,063.8
Argentine mortgage loans	–	1,489.6	–
Private securities	6,696.1	6,082.0	7,856.4

Note: 1981–1982 values are adjusted using the Wholesale Price Index, general level.
Source: BCRA Yearbook, 1983.

Lastly, because of the devaluation shock of 1981, the state assumed a large share of foreign private debt, replacing it with debt bonds in pesos, which, adjusted at a rate lower than inflation and much more to devaluation, ended up being a subsidy to debtors. Because these loans had been assumed abroad, backed by assets abroad, the value of liabilities in pesos was reduced compared with that of assets in dollars, which meant an enormous transfer of taxpayer income to those debtors abroad. All of this created a climate of distrust and resentment, wherein the very legitimacy of the system was questioned (widespread tax evasion) as was the political regime itself.

With positive real rates for a prolonged period (from the hope of a devaluation bailout) enormous public and private debt had accumulated. Thus, in July and August of 1982, indexed public debt (VAVIS – Adjusted National Bonds) was purchased issuing money – as were mortgage loans with a monetary correction clause, which were adjusted with a two-month lag, by money issues. This purchase caused a substantial inflationary surge, reducing the real weight of foreign debt. Debtors quickly took advantage

Table 6.13. *Prices of Public Enterprises, at Constant Values (yearly averages, index: 1960 = 100)*

Year	General Level
1978	120.9
1979	97.7
1980	103.3
1981	117.6
1982	91.6
1983	100.4

Source: BCRA Yearbooks, 1982 and 1983.

Table 6.14. *United States of America Interest Rate: Federal Reserve Bank Rediscount Rate*[a]

Year	Interest Rate (%)
1978	7.52
1979	10.41
1980	11.74
1981	13.33
1982	10.83
1983	8.50

[a] Rate average for each year.

Source: CEPAL, *Estadísticas Económicas de Corto Plazo de la Argentina: Cuentas Nacionales, Industria Manufacturera y Sector Agropecuario Pampeano*, vol. 1, Buenos Aires, July 1988.

of this, paying off debt with a regulated rate that was lower than inflation, and liquidated their liabilities. At the end of the military period, wages were adjusted upward and the public service prices gap was at least partly rectified (see Tables 6.12 and 6.13, and Figure 6.12).

For the new constitutional government, its legacy was extremely serious: the CPI variation rate in the second trimester of 1982 compared with the same period in 1981 was 130%, while the rate in this period in 1983 compared with 1982 was 314%. Fiscal circumstances were indeed grave and the considerable foreign debt represented an even greater liabilities because of the increase in international interest rates (see Tables 6.14 and A.C.6.8, and Figure 6.13). The evolution of GDP

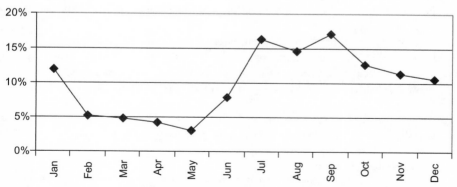

Figure 6.12. 1982 Consumer Price Index (percent change compared with the previous month). *Source*: INDEC, www.indec.gov.ar.

had been frustrating: up in 1977, down in 1978, up in 1979 and 1980, and later slid ever lower in 1981 and 1982. The 1983 GDP was only 2% greater than that of 1976.[24] Yet another failure, and the decline continued.

The *'Radical'*[25] Government Years

No supe, no quise, no pude.
(I didn't know, I didn't want to, I couldn't.)
President Alfonsín

The new constitutional government assumed office during particularly difficult circumstances, which deteriorated only because of its insistence on ignoring them. Not only were urgent problems put off for a later date, but those problems that were resolved were also done so timidly or even inappropriately that it demonstrated scant conviction about expected results. When things became unbearable and the country was at the precipice, the government finally reacted with measures that afforded only fleeting relief. But because problems were not attacked at their root level, and solutions were implemented half-heartedly, they ended up aggravating only already tenuous circumstances. Each failure led to a new attempt at recovery, but because this was insufficient, it contributed to the downward spiral of the economy.

In the wake of the military government's chaotic withdrawal, after having lost the war in *Malvinas* (Falkland) Islands and having failed economically, was burgeoning inflation and an enormous fiscal deficit. Of equal significance was government foreign debt (and the part of private debt that had been assumed by the state), which had reached new heights ($31 billion by the end of 1983). The difference between this constitutional government and the others that preceded it was that it enjoyed broad public support. For the first time since 1930, the opposition viewed the government as legitimate.

President Alfonsín and his minister of economic, Grispun (who had been in the Illia administration), believed that they could confront the problems with the same measures that had led to the years of economic growth between 1963 and 1966. At that time, as previously indicated, following the 1962–1963 recession, with idle capacity, measures that tended to increase aggregate demand (with the payment of arrears of the state to suppliers and to salaried employees, as well as wage increases and monetary

24 Calculated at 1970 prices.
25 *Radical* refers to the government of Raúl Alfonsín, who came from the UCR (*Unión Cívica Radical*), a center-left moderate political party.

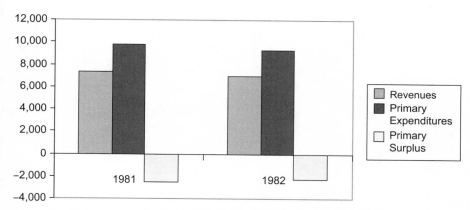

Figure 6.13. Treasury Revenues and Expenditures, 1981–1982 (values in constant australs, at 1974 prices). *Source*: Ministerio de Economía, *Sector Público Argentino no Financiero: Cuenta Ahorro-Inversión-Financiamiento*, Secretaría de Hacienda de la República Argentina, Buenos Aires, December 2004.

expansion) contributed to growth in GDP with little inflationary impact. But by 1983, things had completely changed. Beginning in 1975 three-digit inflation had been the norm. Attempts at reducing it had failed, with serious consequences, and had left precipitously high levels of inflation. People understood that the government intended to pay for its expenses by confiscating their savings; thus, those who were informed and had greater income took their money out of reach of the government, while wage earners, with less access to more sophisticated financial markets, suffered the full effect of inflation. The government thus received fewer benefits from the inflationary tax, losing a resource with which it and other governments had grown accustomed.

Capital flights intensified. In order to protect their savings from being eroded by inflation, individuals deposited them abroad. Reduction of the use of domestic money had a perverse consequence. If the inflationary tax is collected from the sum total of primary money, the supply of which diminishes, its proportional value (aliquot) should increase, which resulted in an upward trend in inflation.

But the government understood that inflation was related to the lack of elasticity of supply and cost pressure. The first of these would be solved only if the economy grew, so that, instead of contracting demand – as was the customary IMF recommendation – demand should expand. Cost pressure would be controlled by gradual, staged increases in wages and tariffs utilities, beginning with an anticipatory wage hike, because this was considered long overdue, considering the price increases.

Table 6.15. *Debt Service (as a percentage of GDP)*

Year	Debt Services
1980	3.3
1981	7.1
1982	10.2
1983	5.8
1984	4.9

Source: Ministerio de Economía, *Sector Público Argentino no Financiero: Cuenta Ahorro-Inversión-Financiamiento*, Secretaría de Hacienda de la República Argentina, Buenos Aires, December 2004.

After declaring a wage raise to improve income distribution, Minister Grispun established stages of gradual increase in prices, wages, and tariffs utilities. With this, inflation was expected to moderate. By 1983 it had reached a staggering 343.8%. Moreover, the primary fiscal deficit reached 10% of GDP (see Table 6.15). The government was also faced with the daunting task of making payments on ballooning foreign debt (largely private loans that the government assumed in 1981).

While in 1980 debt interest payments represented 3.3% of GDP, in 1982 they reached 10.2%. Regarding these payments, there were also necessary negotiations with the IMF for a program than had not been renewed toward the end of the military government of General Bignone (the last military president). For Minister Grispun, the nostalgia for the university *reformist* years led him to show that the *radicals* were in effect anti-imperialist and during much of 1984 delayed an agreement with the IMF, going as far as to send a letter of unilateral intention, to which no response was given. President Alfonsin trusted that European countries with friendly governments would help him pressure banks to refinance loans, and the IMF to reach an agreement with less stringent commitments than desired. But he was disappointed to find that all of these governments responded the same way: "You must negotiate [this] with the IMF." Finally, in December 1984 a fifteen-month agreement was reached, giving Special Drawing Rights (SDR) for 1,419 million.[26] This payment was subject to a series of commitments referred to as "nominal trimestral" limits on net domestic assets and on the regulated liabilities interest rate level, stipulating that it should not be negative by more than one-half point in real terms; nominal trimestral limits on the combined deficit of the nonfinancial public sector and for unpaid

26 BCRA Yearbook, 1984.

treasury drafts; and trimestral limits on Central Bank reserves. With respect to external debts, caps were established on payment of arrears of international payments not subject to refinancing, and a maximal period was established to complete refinancing debt with the private banking system. Limits on total foreign debt and on short-term public sector debt were declared. And finally, in relation to the exchange rate were established maximum time periods for lifting restrictions on the concession of foreign currency at the official exchange rate for tourism, financial debt interest payments, royalties and dividends, and the obligation of not imposing or intensifying restrictions on payments and international transfers and on exports.

In December 1984, after not having fulfilled the fiscal and monetary objectives to which the government had committed, the IMF denied authorization for the February payment. From that point on, Argentina would embark on a tortuous path from which minimal relief was provided only during the first months of the *Austral Plan*. Nevertheless, following the severe recession of 1981–1982, the economy had grown by 4.1% in 1983 and 2.0% in 1984. Inflation however, which in 1983 had been 343.8%, rose to 626.7% in 1984, while the primary deficit dropped from 9.9% to 5.7% of GDP.

A significant fiscal surplus was required to make payments on the public debt that had reached $7,037 million in 1984. The large devaluations since 1982 had caused a great scarcity of imports, leaving as a result, a considerable trade surplus that provided sorely needed foreign currency. The trade surplus went from –$287 million in 1981 to 2,287 million in 1982 and 3,331 million in 1983. But the problem was not only a current account one but also one of having the fiscal surplus necessary to buy it from exporters. In 1933 – as has been demonstrated herein – this was done with the margin of exchange. During the 1955 provisional government and that of Frondizi taxes were again levied on exports in order to improve fiscal income. Export taxes on agricultural products, which had been reduced in 1976, were increased.[27]

The high cost of foreign exchange import purchases having decreased, a significant positive commercial balance, which translated into significant monetary expansion when the Central Bank bought foreign exchange from exporters, because, with the peso devalued, foreign exchange was more expensive and demand from importers diminished. The government bought foreign exchange but not with pesos (as importers did) nor with a fiscal surplus (in either case, this would have had a contractive effect); rather, it bought it with Central Bank loans through money issues. The expansive effect of these loans was compensated, however, with a monetary contraction caused by paying the debt with foreign reserves. Instead, money creation to

27 See also in this chapter "Monetary and Fiscal Policies of the Alfonsin Administration."

pay the net interest balance on interest-earning deposits, minus the interest received for rediscounts (quasi-fiscal deficit), was a main factor in monetary expansion and burgeoning inflation.[28]

People kept an ever-smaller proportion of their assets in checking accounts and financial instruments.[29] Thus the capacity of the government to capture funds from the financial system diminished in real terms. The difference between interest payments that the Central Bank made on reserves and frozen deposits (*depósitos indisponibles*) and those that it received from rediscounts to the public sector or to the financial system was the so-called quasi-fiscal deficit.

All of these circumstances led to ever-higher inflation. Following the year-end acceleration, in February 1985 President Alfonsin decided to abandon his old friend Grispun, making a strategic move by appointing Juan Sourrouile as minister of economy in his place and putting Grispun in Sourrouile's place as secretary of the National Counsel on Development. At the Central Bank another famous character remained from university days as president: Alfredo Concepción.

Rejecting the failed program of gradual increases in tariffs and wages (*pautas*) and concerned by its effect on relative prices, and consequently on incentives for economic activity, the new team chose a new approach. They decided to increase public prices (rates for services) to reduce their effect on the deficit of these enterprises and improve the fiscal situation. Moreover, the government sought to stimulate exports, so it devalued the peso by 230% (between February and July 1985) continuing with a system of small adjustments so that the devaluation would follow inflation and prevent loss of competitiveness. The government did not renounce an income redistribution policy favoring labor, though harming labor was not intended either, a wage adjustment of only 90% with respect to the change in prices was stipulated.[30] In truth, the adjustment came to set the stage for what would be – albeit briefly – the greatest success of the *radical* administration.

The Austral Plan

The first months of 1985 saw accelerated inflation. Because of the destabilizing factors themselves, the asymmetrical effect of inflation on revenue

---

28 Ibid.

29 See Table A.44 of monetary indicators in the Appendix.

30 The 1985 BCRA Yearbook: "To make up for the loss of purchasing power that occurred with wages since the last adjustment before the freeze (which was greater than 1% daily) the criterion of regulated wage adjustments valid to that point (90% of inflation in consumer prices from the previous month) was respected. In this way, June wages increased by 22.6%, while retirement payments incorporated 100% of the change in said index, increasing 25.1%."

and expenditures was intensified by the deliberate increase in public prices (tariffs of public utilities) and other prices considered to be outdated or more sensitive. The government tried to pursue a new adjustment of relative prices that would improve public sector ones and provide a fiscal cushion once an eventual freeze (which did occur) were put in place.

The plan, which authors called heterodox, attempted to affect costs, freezing prices and wages (before their readjustment), and exchange rates. In order to palliate the inertial effect of inflation, a new element was added, *desagio* of contracts (deflating the inflation premium that was usually added to the contracts), the face value of which, presumably having future inflation incorporated into it, was divided using a trace index of past inflation. The drastic decrease in prices had been conceived as a way of preventing the maintenance of these clauses from causing substantial lack of equity, which would make the contract's premium greater than actual inflation. The new thirty-day interest rates on deposits and loans were at 3.5% and 5.0% per month respectively, in nominal terms, which were less by 11 and 12 percentage points than those in effect previous to the reform. In addition to these measures, there was a devaluation and renewed control over the flows of capital.

To the extent that the government demonstrated an eclectic recognition of the causes of inflation, it sought to reduce the fiscal deficit and committed to not resorting to the Central Bank to finance government operations with money issues. The budget would be balanced thanks to an increase in income, to a large degree because of an increase in the VAT and an improvement in export taxes. It was also expected that a decrease in inflation would prevent significant erosion of the tax base. Table A.C.6.6 shows how current income dropped from 1983 to 1984 and how after the austral conversion, particularly export taxes and the VAT increased.

There were taxes, such as those on income, which because of the time lapsed in their collection were more affected by inflation, so that other taxes to be collected immediately were created, like on fuel, which were practically charged at the pump[31] and which increased a great deal between 1983 and 1984. To mark the start of a new period, a monetary reform established a new monetary unit, the austral, and to erase all memory of the devalued peso, it was fixed so that 80 cents of one austral equaled $1 (see Figure 6.14).

Lastly, to prevent future loss of competitiveness a system of small and gradual adjustments to prices (crawling peg) was established and to renew

---

31 The 1983 BCRA Yearbook states, "During the 1983 fiscal year there was a change in the tax collection structure that resulted in a predominance of taxes on specific goods (like fuel) and export goods, over those on transactions and wealth, such as the value added tax, income tax, and business capital gains tax."

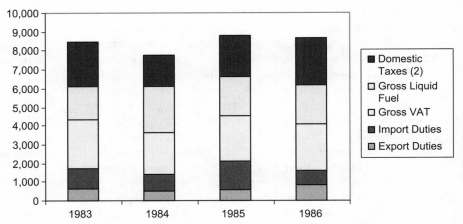

Figure 6.14. National Government Tax Revenues (in millions of australs, at 1986 prices). *Notes:* (1) Provincial revenues are not included. (2) Figure includes unified domestic taxes, income taxes, and capital gains taxes. *Source: Dirección Nacional de Investigaciones y Análisis Fiscal*, with data from AFIP, ANSeS, *Dirección Nacional de Coordinación Fiscal con las Provincias, Oficina Nacional de Presupuesto*, and other entities.

confidence in the new period, a standby agreement with the IMF was reached. The Central Bank agreed that its net international reserves would be negative by no more than $1.65 billion, "which meant in stock terms, a net liabilities situation that would not be greater than $9,913 million." It was agreed that public sector debt should not exceed an "$39.7 billion for the duration of the contract, while net short-term payments of bonds contracted as of 9/30/84 can not be greater than $2.5 billion." They promised a gradual reduction in arrears to $1.1 billion by the end of the year. The Central Bank agreed to control the exchange rate and eliminate the majority of restrictions on payments and transfers for current international transactions, a reduction in export and import taxes and to no adjustment of the average payment for exports over their 9/25/84 level.[32]

Back to Life: The Brief Recovery

People reacted favorably to the drama of the circumstances, the novelty of the instruments, especially, *disagio*, a negative premium, and the promise that the Central Bank would not issue money. The program produced an increase in tax collection; probably the most remarkable aspect of this was that it caused an increase in demand for money.[33] The economy became

32 BCRA Yearbook, 1985, p. 150.
33 BCRA Yearbook, 1985: "The evolution of monetary assets, measured as a proportion of GDP, showed a slight recovery in the first trimester of the year. In the second trimester, however, the

Table 6.16. *Currency and Bank Deposits, 1983–1988 (in millions of australs, at 1986 prices)*

Year	1983	1984	1985	1986	1987	1988
Total currency	7,055	6,910	5,681	5,246	5,161	5,582
Total bank deposits	20,777	18,933	17,027	17,531	19,362	23,941

Source: BCRA Yearbooks, 1983–1988, and BCRA Statistical Bulletin, 1988.

Table 6.17. *Evolution of Real M_1 (first trimester 1985 = 100)*

Period	Trimester	M_1
1985	1	100.0
	2	94.2
	3	126.8
	4	154.4
1986	1	166.9
	2	168.5
	3	157.9
	4	158.9
1987	1	157.4
	2	157.0
	3	129.4
	4	129.0

Source: BCRA Statistical Bulletins, 1986–1988, and INDEC, www.indec.gov.ar.

monetized once again, as seen in Table 6.16, where an increase in deposits in constant money since 1985 is shown. Bank deposits in real terms increased from 17,027 million australs in 1985 to 19,362 million in 1987 (by 14%). Demand for money (quantity of real money) increased during the third and fourth trimesters of 1985 until the second trimester of 1986 (see Table 6.17).

In 1985 the Central Bank increased its reserves by 67%[34] and inflation dropped from 28.4% in the second trimester to 3.8% in the third and 2.5% in the fourth,[35] a decrease that was difficult to surpass. GDP, which had grown very slightly in 1984 (by 2%) following a decrease of 7% in 1985, increased by 7.1% in 1986. It was generally agreed that the country had

lowest liquidity coefficients in the last few years were registered. After implementation of the Austral Plan, a sharp increase in demand for money is apparent, and this provoked significant increases in liquidity coefficients starting in the third trimester of the year."

34 Measured in current dollars.
35 Simple averages per trimester.

avoided the worst, that it had reached the edge of hyperinflation and finally retreated.

But everything was not alright. Toward the end of the last trimester, inflationary pressure was again felt. With regard to prices, a differentiated approach was adopted that included an absolute freeze price on goods from the secondary sector and control of trade margins (without a freeze) for products with prices that were more sensitive to changes in supply and demand (legumes and fruit, among others).

Although the treasury deficit had diminished, the same was not true for the quasi-fiscal deficit. Moreover, the Central Bank was directed by Alfredo Concepcion, who did not share the vision of the economic team (which would have been admirable had it not been for his belief that maintaining monetary stability was not his priority as president of the Central Bank). He embarked on a very expansive rediscount policy. Aid to official banks, the Mortgage Bank (*Hipotecario*), and provincial banks played no small part in the increase in rediscounts.[36]

In April 1986 a policy of price administration was implemented in order to prevent a situation similar to that of 1975 in which the rigidity of the freeze ended with a price explosion (see Figure 6.15).

Downhill Slide

Minister Sourrouille announced the new guidelines system, with price agreements.[37] Meanwhile, the Central Bank continued with a passive monetary policy that appeared to follow prices,[38] a policy that changed

---

36 According to José Luis Machinea, "the increase in rediscounts was very important in the first nine months of the Austral Plan. A preliminary estimation indicates that the increase of net rediscounts was equivalent to around 3% of the GDP during that period. One important question is if these rediscounts were or not fiscal expenditures. The answer depends on the characteristics of these rediscounts, but unfortunately there is not enough information. We only know that around 20% of them (0.6% of GDP) were applied to refund the deposits of financial entities intervened or liquidated by the Central Bank." In *Stabilization under Alfonsin's Government: A Frustrated Attempt*, Buenos Aires, CEDES, 1990, p. 37.

37 The 1986 BCRA Yearbook states, "During April the end of the price and wage freeze dating from June 1985 was stipulated, and was replaced with managed prices. . . . This instrument consisted of providing norms and managing prices and wages so as to decelerate the struggle over income distribution, while on the other hand postponed relative price adjustments were paced over time."

38 The BCRA Yearbook further states, "The reasons for the accelerated inflation of the second trimester are found in the change in the exchange rate, tariffs and wages, made thanks to the policy of flexibility begun in April and *confirmed with a passive monetary policy*. The monetary policy did not put a limit on this inflationary acceleration. The expansion of the monetary base was mainly a result of the *increase in rediscounts awarded* and to the manipulation of required minimum reserves and of the proportion of the incorporation of financial assets that the entities should keep in relation to deposits. *Rediscounts and their counterpart, increases in interest and non-interest earning reserves, acted as a means of income transfer between sectors and were established because of the increase of the quasi fiscal deficit. . . . The return of inflation*

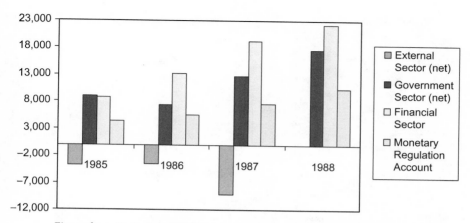

Figure 6.15. Evolution of BCRA Assets, 1985–1988 (in millions of australs at 1986 prices). *Source*: BCRA Statistical Bulletins and BRCA Yearbooks, 1985–1988.

when in September 1986, President Concepción was ousted and José Luis Machinea assumed the presidency as second in charge of economic matters. Inflation surged anyway and 1986 ended with 90.1%. Demonetization increased, the economy increasingly relied on the dollar. The dollar not only was used as store of value, as in previous decades; with very high inflation, the dollar began to be used also in everyday transactions. The process of substitution of currencies began to intensify.

The attempts to administer prices failed. These only increased in 1987 by 131.3%. The deficit of the nonfinancial public sector in 1987 was 7.2% of GDP, while the quasi-fiscal deficit was 0.59% (see Figure 6.16). The quasi-fiscal deficit was not registered in the treasury accounts that appear in Table A.28 (see also Table A.C.6.7). After implementation of the Austral Plan, revenue increased in 1985 in constant money but by 1986, it began to drop. Expenditures increase, although by a lower rate. In addition to this deficit was the quasi-fiscal one, the total of which would reach heights shown in Figure 6.17.

The growth rate of GDP decelerated in 1987, at 2.5%, following the 7.1% growth of 1986, and began to decline in 1988 (see Figure 6.18).

In October 1987 the economic team, reacting to events, announced the implementation of a program, with a new price freeze and rate adjustment, the so-called *Australito*. A wage freeze was also stipulated, together with steps to reduce the fiscal deficit, the establishment of long-term rules that would allow permanent reduction of the deficit, and measures to achieve

in the third trimester determined a new inflexion point in the design of monetary policy; the Central Bank adopted measures to gain better control over the monetary base and decelerate the growth of monetary supply of domestic origin."

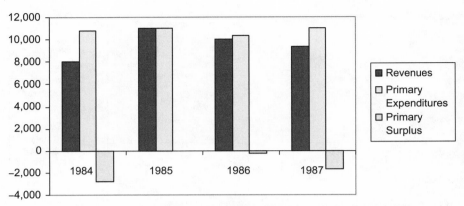

Figure 6.16. Nonfinancial Public Sector, 1984–1987 (in australs in constant 1974 prices). *Source:* Ministerio de Economía, *Sector Público Argentino no Financiero: Cuenta Ahorro-Inversión-Financiamiento*, Secretaría de Hacienda de la República Argentina, Buenos Aires, December 2004.

greater control of the monetary supply and fortify and deregulate financial markets. In order to reduce the deficit, the government sent Congress a program of tax laws along with increase in public service rates and greater control over tax evasion. Included were changes to the income tax law and

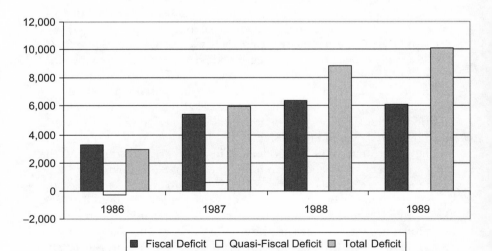

Figure 6.17. Fiscal and Quasi-Fiscal Deficit, 1986–1989 (millions of 1986 australs). *Source:* FIEL, *El Gasto Público en la Argentina, 1960–1988*, Buenos Aires, FIEL, 1987, and Ministerio de Economía, *Sector Público Argentino no Financiero: Cuenta Ahorro-Inversión-Financiamiento*, Secretaría de Hacienda de la República Argentina, Buenos Aires, December 2004.

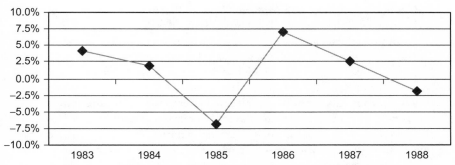

Figure 6.18. Gross Domestic Product (percent annual change). *Source*: Dirección Nacional de Cuentas Nacionales, *Cuentas Nacionales: Oferta y Demanda Globales 1980–1995*, Buenos Aires, 1996.

the personal net worth laws.[39] Measures that would tend to restrict the expansion of Central Bank loans were adopted.

The collection of new taxes did not manage to compensate the loss of the inflationary tax. The primary deficit was 3.6% of GDP and the total reached 7.2%. This imbalance was greater than the two previous years but was considerably lower than that recorded before the Austral Plan. The 1987 deficit was greater than that of 1986 because of an increase in expenditures and a drop in revenues. By the end of 1987, economic perspectives were bleak. The government lost the partial elections for the Congress of that year.

The evolution of the main economic indicators of 1988 shows that the situation deteriorated. The economic approach of the government appeared to react late and timidly, and with little conviction, amid an unfavorable climate and with a governing party unwilling to support changes. Toward the second semester, the approaching presidential elections of 1989 prompted a final, and again frustrated, attempt at stabilization. It too failed.

The Freefall, February 1989: Failure of the Primavera Plan

Having lost the elections, so began the *radical* government's decline. In August 1988 a new economic program, the Primavera Plan based on a price and wage agreement and an increase in public service prices was attempted, also in pursuit of public confidence. Some structural reforms that the government had promised and never delivered were implemented.

The exchange measures comprised the main aspects of the program. This consisted of the establishment of a regime of differential parities according to which agricultural exports were liquidated at a commercial exchange rate

39 In January of 1988 a tax on debits in checking accounts and one on fuel were levied, in addition to postponing obligatory savings. See Law 23549.

and industrial exports at an intermediary dollar between the commercial and free rate, while imports would be made at a floating rate. A correction in the commercial exchange rate was included, and public service rates were increased. The Primavera Plan was based on an agreement on prices. A commercial exchange rate by which exports were liquidated and managed by the Central Bank was established at 12 australs per dollar, and a financial rate at 14.4 australs per dollar for all other operations, including imports, in a *dirty* float market, with Central Bank intervention. The difference between the two meant an implicit tax of 20% on exports, for which it awoke the rejection of the agricultural sector whose displeasure was evident at that year's inauguration of the Rural Society Exposition. Because at the end of 1987 Congress had voted on a law that reestablished free wage negotiations, there were no measures related to this, nor was there a price freeze. Instead, the government negotiated an agreement with representative entities of the business community regarding rules for price corrections. It was expected that wage contracts in the private sector would be negotiated in line with the rules for price adjustments.

It was also thought that the exchange differential would be a resource, from the real increase in tax collection because of declining inflation (the Olivera–Tanzi effect) and the decrease in the deficit of public enterprises whose real prices increased between January and May of 1988 by 10% and from that point on, they decreased in real terms. Although inflation diminished, it did not do so at the pace of the established rules for the exchange rate and public utilities prices. Consumer prices rose 27.6% per month (wholesale 31.9%), dropped to 11.7%, then to 9%, then to 5.7% from September to November and began to increase in December.

The nonfinancial public sector deficit increased in 1988 to more than 8% of GDP (the primary deficit was 5.1%), increasing by 18.7% compared to 1987 in constant terms (although the figure was less than that of other years that decade). A process of demonetization occurred (drop in the real quantity of money) because the public, having lost confidence, intensified the substitution of *australs* for dollars (flight of domestic money). Real means of payment dropped considerably, representing only 4.9% of GDP in 1988 (see Figure 6.19).

The deficit persisted. Public rates began to deteriorate in real terms when the general level of prices rose more than the established guidelines for increases. Between January and February 1989, people lost confidence in the ability of the government to maintain the changes and a speculative attack grew against the austral toward the purchase of dollars. To curb this movement, the Central Bank increased minimum reserve requirements, the interest rate, and sold dollars. But at the end of January, fearing insufficient foreign reserves, the government abandoned the intervention

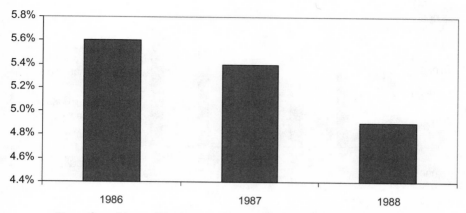

Figure 6.19. Means of Payment as a Proportion of GDP. *Note:* Currency in the hands of the public plus deposits in current accounts. *Source*: BCRA Statistical Bulletins, 1986–1988.

in the free sector of the exchange market. At the same time, in order to prevent its effects on prices, a third market of regulated exchange rates for imports was established. The estimates that assumed that with a 20% depreciation rate the flight of domestic money would stop were mistaken. In just one month the austral depreciated by 49%, in March by 140% with respect to January, and by 282% in April with respect to January,[40] punishing those who, trusting the word of the Central Bank president, had kept their assets in *australs*. Following this, the entities that had signed the price agreement broke ties with the government. Prices increased by 33.4% in April (wholesale prices by 58%) with which the hyperinflationary period officially began, further complicating the forthcoming presidential elections.

Near fiscal collapse and the ever more dramatic flight of domestic money characterized the last months of the *radical* administration. After the elections in which the Peronist candidate won, the processed ended with the July hyperinflation with prices that increased by nearly 200% during the month. During the very same month of July President Alfonsín stepped down, anticipating by several months his expected December exit.

Monetary and Fiscal Policies of the Alfonsín Administration

Monetary policy was conditioned by the need to finance the government, including the need to make rediscounts to the official banking system (national and provincial) and provide loans to the financial sector. That

40 Estimated with free market values.

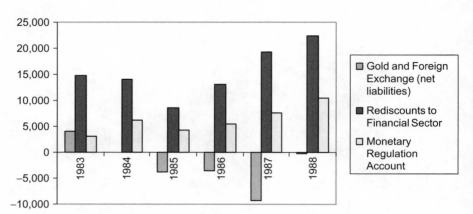

Figure 6.20. Evolution of BCRA Assets, 1983–1988 (in millions of australs at 1986 prices). *Note*: Includes resources earned from loans to the financial system. *Source*: BCRA Statistical Bulletins, 1983–1985.

produced an enormous monetary expansion and very high inflation, which when accompanied by drop in demand for money culminated in hyperinflation. Fiscal policy was itself conditioned by the need to pay the foreign debt. It was also conditioned by the effect that inflation had on fiscal revenues and that of the drop in demand for money on the possibility of gaining seigniorage.

In this tortuous and nearly impossible mission, the Central Bank faced contradictory objectives. On the one hand – as we have seen – it had to generate financing for the government, and on the other, it had to counter the effect of those loans and rediscounts on money supply, for which it increased minimum reserve requirements by rewarding them, by issuing bonds (among them *Bonin, Bonor, Denor*, etc.). When the interest it had to pay was greater than what was perceived from rediscounts, an expansion in the Monetary Regulation Account (*Cuenta de Regulación Monetaria*) occurred, creating money. This was a quasi-fiscal activity of the Central Bank and for this reason, its effect is part of what is called the quasi-fiscal deficit that reached enormous heights.

The concept of the traditional monetary base, which included monetary liabilities that did not pay interest (currency and bank deposits in the Central Bank), was broadened to include interest-earning deposits (broad monetary base). The main categories of assets and liabilities at the Central Bank, financial sector liabilities, and monetary aggregates evolved between 1983 and 1988, as Tables A.44 and A.45 in the Appendix demonstrates (see also Figure 6.20).

The government was forced to implement policies in a climate of severe restrictions caused by the constraint of the preexisting debt (to a large degree resulting from the state having assumed private debt) and in foreign exchange, which increased during that administration because interests were partially refinanced at an increasing and extremely high international interest rate due to the U.S. Federal Reserve's restrictive policies to curb inflation.

Public foreign debt rose from $14.5 billion in 1980 to $31.7 billion in 1983, reaching $53.5 billion in 1988.[41] Foreign debt was in a unit of account that could not be controlled by the government and whose cost was higher because of the devaluation. The government made a new discovery, the devaluation was not sufficient, as it had been in the past, to liquidate debts. All of this led to a crisis of large proportions. The government needed foreign exchange to pay for the debt. Devaluations had been a device used for a number of purposes, among others, to obtain foreign exchange through a positive balance of trade. The trade surplus was $3.3 billion in 1983, $3.5 billion in 1984, and $4.6 billion in 1985,[42] as a result of import restrictions due to large devaluations occurring since 1981.

While exchange policies created a foreign exchange surplus, the government had to resolve how it would buy this foreign exchange. Because the current primary fiscal surplus was not enough and because the government did not believe that it could obtain financing by placing bonds on the market, it did so by resorting to the Central Bank that increased the minimum reserve requirements of the commercial banks, transferring their deposit to the government. However, because these funds were used to pay debt abroad, the external sector had a contractionary effect on money supply.[43] But the Monetary Regulation Account was nevertheless a very significant source of money expansion. Its proportion of the Broad Monetary Base was 14.5% in 1983, increasing to 39.4% in 1984, 32.2% in 1985, 45.9% in 1986, 63.7% in 1987, and 62.3% in 1988.

The repeat inflationary cycles had diminished non-interest-bearing monetary assets, notes, and checking accounts, so that very few seigniorage resources were available. It order to seize savings, these had to earn interest

---

41 BCRA Yearbook, 1982 and 1988.

42 FIEL, *El Control de Cambios en la Argentina: Liberación Cambiaria y Crecimiento*, Buenos Aires, Manantial, 1987.

43 The 1983 BCRA Yearbook explained, "Starting January 1, 1983 the Central Bank began to utilize minimum reserves as an additional instrument of monetary regulation. The reduction in legal minimum reserves, applied to deposits and bonds subject to maximum interest rates regulated by the Central Bank, was more relevant during the first trimester, during which time a 9 point drop was recorded, such that reserves were 91% in March. After that point, the reductions were less significant. During the second trimester of the year, the minimum reserves rate remained at 89%, with successive reductions of one point during the months of July, August, November, ending the year with legal minimum reserves of 86%."

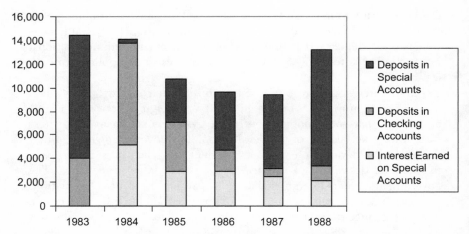

Figure 6.21. BCRA Liabilities with the Private Financial Sector, 1983–1988 (in millions of 1986 constant australs). *Source*: BCRA Balance Sheets, 1983–1988.

at nominal rates that were greater than inflation – or have monetary correction clauses – which snowballed and became an explosive situation. Because they earned interest but they were not paid the accumulated interest, this made the debt much greater than what was originally assumed. The second period of hyperinflation exploded in February 1990 (see Figure 6.21).

The increases in minimum reserves requirements in commercial banks had begun in 1982; while in December 1981 the sole rate of required minimum cash reserves was 15.5%, starting in July 1982 it was 100%.[44] The government sought refinancing from foreign banks to pay a portion of the debt it had with them, and it partially succeeded after 1985, when the trade surplus diminished and the economy endured strong inflationary pressure from the Monetary Regulation Account. Rediscounts were a significant factor in monetary expansion. This was especially the case in 1987, when important rediscounts were given to help the official banking system of the provinces, and particularly the National Mortgage Bank (*Banco Hipotecario Nacional*) (see Table 6.18).

While real demand for non-interest-bearing monetary liabilities decreased, interest-earning liabilities increased, and therefore so did the cost of government financing. The drop in inflationary tax as a result of this situation was no compensated by the creation of new taxes. The nonfinancial public sector deficit had reached 15.6% of GDP in 1983, dropping in 1984, 1985, and 1986, only to increase to 8.3% in 1988 and 7.8% in 1989 (see Figure 6.22).

---

44 See Footnote 42 and the Table A.C.6.3 in the Appendix.

Table 6.18. *Net Foreign Financing of the Central
Government (in millions of australs, at 1986 prices)*

Year	Net Foreign Financing
1983	396.6
1984	−704.7
1985	704.5
1986	767.9
1987	2,363.7
1988	1,673.8

Source: Ministerio de Economía, *Sector Público Argentino no
Financiero: Cuenta Ahorro-Inversión-Financiamiento,* Secretaría de
Hacienda de la República Argentina, Buenos Aires, December
2004.

To a certain degree, the deficit between 1985 and 1989 is underestimated, especially because of the social security high debt and from public
enterprise or companies, with suppliers, recognized in 1991–1992 as *Provisional BOCON* public bonds and *BOCON* to pay government suppliers.
As Table 6.19 shows, while there is disagreement over proper imputation
to suppliers (if it should be complete or partial), there is no doubt with
respect to which belongs to the social security component.

As has been highlighted previously, it is not enough to know the Treasury
deficit, but also the quasi-fiscal one that, as shown in Table 6.20, reached
3.2 of GDP in 1988 and 5% in 1989, which together gave a total deficit
of 11.6% of GDP in 1988 and 12.8% in 1989.

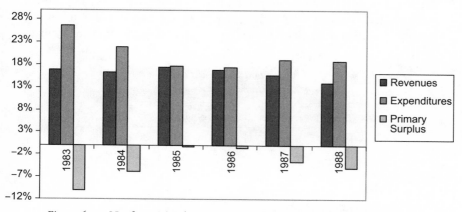

Figure 6.22. Nonfinancial Public Sector, 1983–1988 (as a percentage of GDP).
Source: Ministerio de Economía, *Sector Público Argentino no Financiero: Cuenta
Ahorro-Inversión-Financiamiento,* Secretaría de Hacienda de la República Argentina,
Buenos Aires, December 2004.

Table 6.19. *Imputed Expenditures due to the Debt*
(as a percentage of GDP)

Year	Social Security	Providers	Total
1985	0.69	0.8	1.5
1986	0.67	0.78	1.45
1987	0.99	0.99	1.97
1988	1.24	1.15	2.4
1989	3.19	2.28	5.47

Source: DNPGS, *Caracterización y Evolución del Gasto Público Social: Período 1980–1997*, Dirección Nacional de Programación del Gasto Social, 1999.

From Inflation to Hyperinflation

While inflation was an outcome of the need to issue money to finance the government, hyperinflation was related to the drop in the demand for money. There was a sharp demonetization of the economy, with diminished possibilities of collecting an inflationary tax. The government tried to substitute this tax with explicit taxes, but was never fully able to replace the lost revenue. The accumulation of interest earned from rediscounts to the financial system and not paid in the assets of the Central Bank and the interest earned on reserves and unavailable deposits not paid, which the Central Bank in turn owed in its liabilities, led to the conviction that the deposits and money would experience some kind of confiscation.

The drastic drop in the demand for money was due to a money substitution phenomenon and prices increased precipitously. In 1985 annual inflation had reached 672%. It dropped to 90.1% in 1986 following the Austral Plan and then increased in 1988 to 343% and in 1989 to

Table 6.20. *Fiscal and Quasi-Fiscal Deficits,*
1986–1989 (as a percentage, millions of 1986 australs)

Year	Fiscal	Quasi-Fiscal	Total
1986	4.4	–0.4	4.0
1987	7.2	0.8	8.0
1988	8.3	3.2	11.6
1989	7.8	5.0	12.8

Source: FIEL, *El Gasto Público en la Argentina, 1960–1988*, Buenos Aires, FIEL, 1987, and Ministerio de Economía, *Sector Público Argentino no Financiero: Cuenta Ahorro-Inversión-Financiamiento*, Secretaría de Hacienda de la República Argentina, Buenos Aires, December 2004.

3,080%.[45] Hyperinflation was now a fact, and with it, a fifteen-year cycle of declining growth, numerous conflicts, and imbalances, came to a close. President Alfonsín would hand over the government to his elected successor at an anticipated date. But the problem would not end there. Hyperinflation return in February of the following year and only then, with the conversion of deposits in a long-term dollar bond (*Bonex*), did stability return. It would be the beginning of what later became a convertibility system that reigned for ten years and the start of new and complex scenarios whose description is beyond the scope of the present book.

45 INDEC, www.indec.gov.ar.

Epilogue

There is an undeniable feeling of frustration in reaching the end of this story. It includes periods of economic boom and others of crisis and recovery. But even with the latter, there was never sustained growth during the second half of the twentieth century. There were relapses, new breaks, and finally a long decline. The country grew very little and lagged behind other more developed countries.

Nevertheless, the moments of growth impetus were repeated. Although among the policies implemented there were countless errors and follies, during nearly all of the growth periods, it seemed that the country had overcome the difficulties, whether external or inherited, and the expansion promised to continue. But frustration was invariably the result.

There was no transformation as ambitious as what Perón tried, benefiting from a growth trend that had begun in the mid-thirties and the considerable impetus that exports received in the immediate postwar period. But his abuse of the instrument of appropriation of savings of the public, and of discretionality, was also unequaled. His legacy was one of grave imbalances and inflation. To this was added a complex regulatory system, an insular mentality, and income distribution conflicts. After the fall of Perón several subsequent administrations tried to reverse the greatest imbalances that his administration had left behind, seeking to somewhat deregulate the economy (with a less pronounced role for the state), but the efforts had little success. The assault on the state had become the mechanism by which privatization of public goods was pursued. The problem was political. When imbalances due to overspending led to intolerable inflation – or during the last few decades, to the accumulation of debt – efforts to reverse these trends clashed with vested interests. Every attempt at stabilization had more enemies than proponents, which explains the repeated failures.

The growth during the 1960s – the only prolonged period of economic expansion in the last half-century – was largely the result of changes and painful adjustments carried out during previous years. The changes had unleashed severe social and political upheaval, instability, and among other things, the political crisis of 1962. Without going to the question of why growth occurred, which is beyond the scope of this book and because others have tried to do so,[1] we cannot ignore the temporal association of certain phenomena and how these in turn affected in some way the growth trends. It is the task of future researchers[2] to determine to what extent there is a relationship between growth trends and some of the factors mentioned here.

What is evident at first glance is the coincidence between the period of greatest growth and that of greatest investment. The period of greatest growth, 1900–1914, was also one of a very high rate of investment (on growth periods, see Figure I.1 in the Introduction; and on investment, Figure E.1).[3]

Although, as indicated in Chapter 2, investment levels were not expected to return to the same levels as in the first decade of the twentieth century, during the 1920s investment, in various forms, recovered. Foreign investment participation diminished following World War I but especially after 1930. The exchange control regime was an obstacle to foreign investment, which intensified during the postwar period because of nationalist rhetoric against foreign capital promoted initially by Perón, despite the fact that later Perón himself appeared to seek this capital.

Foreign investment would never again assume the role it had until 1914, offsetting reduced domestic savings. Domestic savings after 1918, for their part, appear to have played a less significant role in Argentina than in Canada or Australia,[4] although, as indicated in Chapter 2, there are no indications that there had been a change in trend or that savings had diminished or that this was due to a greater demographic dependency rate. The 1930 financial crisis had a negative effect on investment, but during

---

1 Authors cited the following throughout this book: Carlos Díaz Alejandro, Juan José Llach, Víctor Elías, Gerardo della Paollera y Allan Taylor, Pablo Gerchunoff, and Lucas Llach.

2 As has been done recently, Leandro Prados de la Escosura and Isabel Sanz-Villarroya, "Growth in Argentina: A Long Run View," Working Paper 04-67, Universidad Carlos III de Madrid, Getafe, España, 2004; Alan Taylor, "Argentina and the World Capital Market: Saving, Investment, and International Capital Mobility in the Twentieth Century," NBER Working Paper W6302, 1997. Also: Juan Carlos de Pablo, *La Economía Argentina en la segunda mitad del siglo XX*, Buenos Aires, La Ley, 2005.

3 As indicated in Chapter 4, the most well-known estimates at 1950 prices count capital goods at higher prices than the international ones. Díaz Alejandro and Davis and Gallman came up with new investment estimates at 1937 and 1914 prices, and they give lower results. Because for our intents and purposes, the level of investment is not the issue but rather the variations in its rates of growth, we use them with due reservations as indicators of overall trends.

4 Alan Taylor, "Argentina and the World Capital Market: Saving, Investment, and International Capital Mobility in the Twentieth Century," NBER Working Paper W6302, 1997; Robert Gallman and Lance Davis, *Evolving Financial Markets and International Capital Flows: Britain, the Americas, and Australia*, Cambridge, Cambridge University Press, 2001.

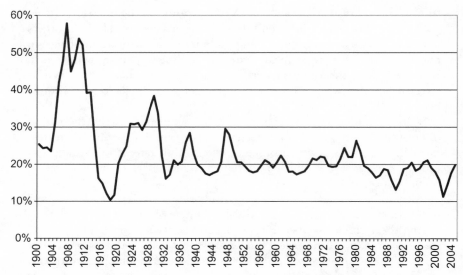

Figure E.1. Gross Domestic Investment as a Percentage of GDP, 1900–2004.
Sources: 1900–1949: BCRA, *Cuentas Nacionales de la República Argentina, Series
Históricas,* V.3, 1976; Naciones Unidas-CEPAL, "El desarrollo económico de la
Argentina," E/CN 12/429, Santiago de Chile, 1958. 1950–1959: Conade-CEPAL,
Cuentas Nacionales de la República Argentina, Buenos Aires, 1964. 1960–1979:
CEPAL, *Estadísticas Económicas de Corto Plazo de Argentina,* V.1, Buenos Aires, 1988.
1980–1992: Ministerio de Economía, Cuentas Nacionales, *Oferta y Demanda
Globales, 1980–1995,* Buenos Aires, 1996. 1993–2004: Ministry of Economy,
online database.

the decade there was a slight recovery, whereas during the war years there
had been a noticeable decline.

The war caused decapitalization of the infrastructure, transportation,
energy, and industrial sectors because of an interruption in imports of
machinery and equipment that should have been offset by a significant
inflow of imports at the end of the war (Chapter 2). It is true that until 1949
imports increased considerably (despite world's difficulties in rebuilding
supply), but during the following decade they were severely restricted
for domestic reasons: the balance-of-payments crisis due to the drop in
agricultural prices, export stagnancy and the reduction in reserves that
were consumed by the repatriation of foreign debt, the purchase of British
railroads, and the political exigencies of maintaining consumption and
employment.

From then on and because of measures that made capital goods more
expensive, more difficult, if not impossible to obtain, and profit remittances
less predictable, investment dropped to much lower levels during the second
half of the twentieth century, with rare exceptions (see Figure E.1). The
high cost of capital goods, as noted by Díaz Alejandro and more recently

pointed out by Taylor, Hopenhayn, and Neumeyer, was rooted in distortions caused by multiple exchange rates, tariffs, and quantitative restrictions that prioritized imputs imports before capital goods. Díaz Alejandro argued that in the period 1935–1961, "real capital formation in the form of new producers durable equipment...was determined mainly by supply conditions," and these in turn were mainly influenced by foreign trade policies in the postwar period. He maintained that "the extraordinary increases in capital goods' relative prices resulted first from the war and afterwards from those government policies that also led to low rates of capital formation and technological change." These postwar high relative prices for capital goods, he claimed, were the result of bad public policies and were not the result of a "meager capital market."

Their high levels may be taken as an index of the deterioration in the capacity to transform of the Argentine economy, because they imply a situation where a given amount of current savings bought less real investment. The saving effort of an economy should be defined in terms of how many units of consumption goods must be given up to obtain one unit of investment goods. So, while the real level of capital formation is best measured using constant international relative prices, the saving effort should be measured using current Argentina relative prices.[5]

"In 1962 relative prices for new machinery and equipment were between 2.5 and 3.3 times higher in Buenos Aires than in two major United States cities."[6]

Taylor maintained the same thing, pointing out that policies which he called "inward looking" had accumulation and growth impacts that "distorted the domestic cost of capital goods." He argued that "such price distortions diminished the incentives for accumulation, and, thus, the motivation for foreign capital inflows."[7]

The establishment of the exchange control in 1931 and the regime that divided seller and buyer rates created a margin of exchange in 1933. This regime became complicated by multiple exchange rates during the Perón years (Chapter 3) that allowed the state to appropriate part of individuals' earnings in foreign money, paying a price for it that was below those they would have gotten on foreign markets. Furthermore, after 1946 (in a framework in which there was no capital market) the government used as a means of financing expenditures Central Bank rediscounts,[8] causing an

5 Carlos Díaz Alejandro, *Essays on the Economic History of the Argentine Republic*, New Haven and London, Yale University Press, 1970, pp. 310–311.

6 Ibid., p. 318.

7 Alan Taylor, "Argentina and the World Capital Market".

8 On using rediscounts in Latin America in this way, see Adolfo Diz, *Oferta Monetaria y sus instrumentos*, México, Centro de Estudios Monetarios Latinoamericanos, 1997, p. 157: "In several Latin American countries rediscount operations underwent a drastic change. They became instruments through which policies of 'selective' subsidized credit at negative interest rates in real terms."

1900 –1945

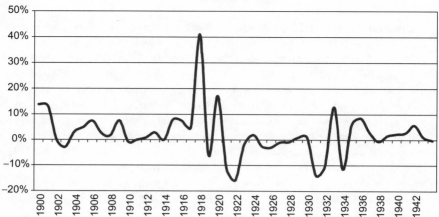

1945–1975

1975: 335%

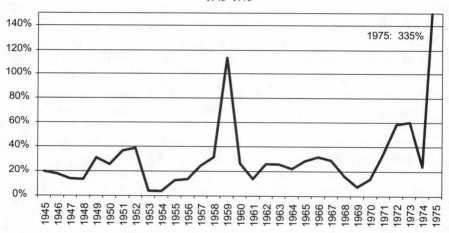

1975–2004

1989: 4,924%
1990: 1,344%

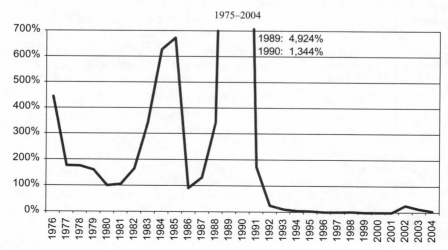

inflationary phenomenon that would last for the next half of the century (see Figure E.2).

The fears of savings confiscations were an obstacle to the development of financial institutions and a capitals market and led the public to reduce its real monetary holdings, which was a significant disincentive. Fomenting savings requires the development of institutions that bring together those who have excess savings with those who need it, but especially a framework of confidence to place savings in long-term instruments.

The demonetization of the economy reflected a climate of great lack of confidence. When inflation became accelerated the public reduced its liquid holdings in real terms. If this occurred with the most liquid of assets, it was hardly expected that excess earnings would be channeled into financial instruments, much less in long-term ones. This is shown in the decline in M_3, an indicator of financial deepening that explains the persistent absence of a financial and capital market (see Figure E.3).

There were other attempts at alternative plans, such as Pinedo's, which propose to convert short-term deposits into loans backed by the Central Bank, which would rediscount the loans in the event of lags between the time when loans mature (long term) and when deposits are exigible (short term). After 1946, this practice was generalized, giving the Central Bank rediscount a new function and causing an enormous monetary issue that resulted in elevated and persistent inflation, yet another disincentive for savings.

As for other factors, whereas trends in investment, economic monetization, and financial deepening show coincidences, the evolution of the terms of trade is much more volatile; it spikes during short periods followed by sharp drops. Nevertheless, in general, an increase coincides with an improvement in terms of trade, as in 1934, 1946, 1963, 1973, and so on, though the economic expansion is never sustained (see Figure E.4).

The years of rising investment were also years of monetary stability (e.g., 1920s, 1960s). This stability allowed the assumed debt in foreign currency, and when the value of the peso rose in foreign currency the price of imports diminished. Moreover, the period of greatest growth was also the period of greatest economic openness; this receptiveness to the outside world favored imports of machinery and equipment and facilitated the incorporation of more advanced technologies that came with more modern equipment, all of which spurred improvements in productivity (see Figure E.5).

Figure E.2. Annual Inflation Rate: Change CPI Annual Average, 1900–1945, 1945–1975, 1975–2004. *Sources: Anuario Geográfico Argentino*, Comité Nacional de Geografía, Buenos Aires, 1941.; DNEC, *Costo del Nivel de Vida en la Capital Federal*, Survey of living conditions of working families carried out in 1960, Buenos Aires, 1968; INDEC, www.indec.gov.ar.

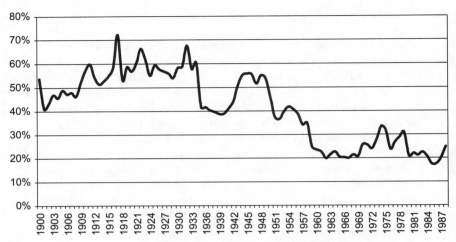

Figure E.3. Monetary Supply (M₃) as Percentage of GDP, 1900–1988. *Sources:*
Monetary Statistics: Treasury Yearbooks, BCRA Yearbooks, and BCRA Statistical
Bulletins. GDP: 1900–1934: Roberto Cortés Conde with the collaboration of
Marcela Harriague, "Estimaciones del Producto Bruto Interno de Argentina,
1875–1935," Documento de Trabajo, Departamento de Economía, Universidad de
San Andrés, Buenos Aires, 1994 (Updated series). 1935–1949: BCRA, Cuentas
Nacionales de la República Argentina, Series Históricas, V.3, 1976. *Original source:*
United Nations–CEPAL, "El Desarrollo Económico de la Argentina," E/CN
12/429, Santiago de Chile, 1958. 1950–1959: Conade-CEPAL, Cuentas Nacionales
de la República Argentina, Buenos Aires, 1964. 1960–1979: CEPAL, Estadísticas
Económicas de Corto Plazo de Argentina, V.1, Buenos Aires, 1988. 1980–1988:
Ministry of Economy, *Cuentas Nacionales, Oferta y Demanda Globales, 1980–1995,*
Buenos Aires, 1996.

Katz analyzed two periods in the industrialization process and concluded
that between 1945 and 1955 industrial growth was a result of the domestic
accumulation of capital, but it did not incorporate significant new technologies. Instead, technological improvement came with the inflow of foreign
capital between 1955 and 1961.[9]

9 According to Jorge Katz (1969), "Clearly, between 1955 and 1961 the technological process was not
independent of the process of capital accumulation. During those years the industries that reached
the greatest capital formation also achieved greater rates of technological change. At the same time
lower rates of capital formation tended to be associated also with lower rates of technological change.
During the postwar period and until the 1950's [sic] the manufacturing sector received very little
foreign capital and technology. Thus, the manufacturing sector operated as a closed economy. With
respect to the accumulation rate as such, isolation from foreign influences did not turn out to be a
terrible disadvantage, but with respect to technological inflows it was a great disadvantage." Katz
points out, "The diminished cost of using capital services allowed for a significant number of new
investments with more capital intensive techniques, which brought superior technology.... Fixed
capital in use during 1946–55 did not receive significant modifications to existing technology, but
it did between 1955 and 1961." Jorge Katz, "Una interpretación de largo plazo del crecimiento
industrial argentino," *Desarrollo Económico,* vol. 8, no. 32, 1969.

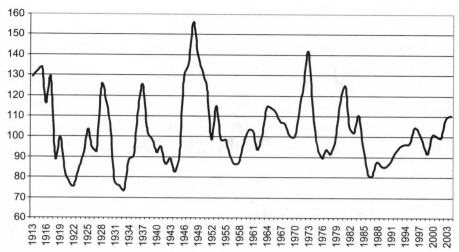

Figure E.4. Evolution of the Terms of Trade Index: 1970 = 100, Period
1900–2004. *Sources:* 1913–1950: M. Balboa, "La Evolución del Balance de Pagos de
la República Argentina, 1913–1950," *Desarrollo Económico*, no. 45, April–June
1972. 1951–1984: CEPAL, *Estadísticas Económicas de Corto Plazo de la Argentina:
Sector Externo y Condiciones Económicas Internacionales*, Buenos Aires, 1986.
1985–1986: P. Gerchunoff and L. Lach, *El Ciclo de la Ilusión al Desencanto*, Buenos
Aires, Ariel, 2003. 1987–2004: Ministry of Economy, online database.

The period of greatest decline in GDP, from 1975 to 1989, as Hopenhayn and Neumeyer maintain, coincided with a fall in productivity. This
was due to shift in the labor force from sectors of greater productivity
(manufacturing, etc.) to backward service sectors characterized by low productivity. Whereas this labor shift from manufacturing to service is a fact
among all of the most developed countries, in Argentina the difference is
that the shift was toward less productive service sectors, such as domestic
workers and community services.[10] The labor shift to the service sector was
also most likely the result of distortive policies that raised the prices of
capital goods and discouraged investment.

10 Hopenhayn and Neumeyer point out, "In addition to the direct distortionary effect of tariffs, we
argue that uncertainty about future protection had a detrimental force on investment. To make this
point, we present a model where uncertainty about future protection drives up the cost of capital
in a multisector economy with irreversible investment. The two sectors in the model are a sector
where capital/labor substitution is low (tradable goods) and another one where it is high (nontraded
goods). An increase in the cost of capital that reduces investment also induces labor to flow from
the tradable goods sector (with low capital/labor substitution) to the non-traded sector (with high
capital/labor substitution). The reallocation of labor induced by the fall in the capital stock reduces
income per worker, labor productivity and wages, as observed in the data." Hugo A. Hopenhayn and
Pablo Neumeyer, "The Argentine Great Depression, 1975–1990," Internal Seminary, Department
of Economy, Universidad de San Andrés, Buenos Aires, 2004, p. 3.

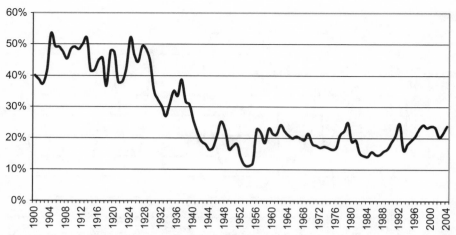

Figure E.5. Index of Economic Openness: Imports plus Exports as Percentage of
GDP, 1900–2004. *Sources:* 1900–1949: BCRA, *Cuentas Nacionales de la República
Argentina*, Series Históricas, 3, 1976. *Original source:* UN-CEPAL, *El Desarrollo
Económico de la Argentina*, E/CN 12/429, Santiago de Chile, 1958; *Anuario Geográfico
Argentino*, Comité Nacional de Geografía, Buenos Aires, 1941; Banco de Análisis y
Computación, *Relevamiento Estadístico de la Economía Argentina, 1900–1980*, Buenos
Aires, 1982. 1950–1959: Conade-CEPAL, *Cuentas Nacionales de la República
Argentina*, Buenos Aires, 1964. 1960–1979: CEPAL, *Estadísticas Económicas de Corto
Plazo de Argentina*, V.1, Buenos Aires, 1988. 1980–1992: Ministry of Economy,
National Accounts, *Oferta y Demanda Globales 1980–1995,* Buenos Aires, 1996.
1993–2004: Ministry of Economy, online database.

Lastly, to the degree that governments throughout the second half of
the twentieth century sought financing with devices that required the
appropriation of financial and monetary assets, individuals sought refuge
that would protect them (capital flight), which was not lack of savings but
rather lack of savings within the country because they save abroad.

The institutional frameworks created in response to the 1930 crisis
were the foundation of the tendency to appeal to the state to prevent the
damage of collapsing markets. At first, the state's role was to spread losses.
Thus, a constellation of interests emerged, promoting a new institutional
framework based on state intervention in pricing mechanisms that lasted
even longer than the circumstances to which they had been a response.

But in Argentina it was not only a matter of corporate conflicts that
emerged following the 1930s depression. The period following World War
II was characterized by social change that had been insinuated since the end
of World War I. Greater political participation, migratory influence, rural
to urban population shift, growth of manufacturing, and enormous urban
development produced strong political demands that resulted in important

economic and social changes during the Perón period. If the resources those changes required would have been obtained from a tax reform approved by Congress, they would have had greater legitimacy and duration. But as we have seen in Chapter 3, these were obtained through bureaucratic decisions such as exchange control or by the inflationary tax.

The goals of keeping real wages high and maintaining full employment required protection of domestic industry and intervention in the pricing of goods and services, which in the long run were negative for investment and growth. Full employment and protection of domestic industry was assured with tariff measures and quantitative restrictions on imports, and high real wages were achieved by overvaluing the peso to provide inexpensive food and keeping tariff utilities provided by public enterprises low. Capital formation was also subsidized with loans at a negative real interest rate.

Keeping real wages high conflicted with a system based on protection and subsidies to the industrial sector, because these subsidies indicated that they had a productivity rate lower than that of their international competitors. These policies, as I showed in Chapters 3 and 5, led to intractable problems and accentuated income distribution conflicts.

In the most developed countries the multiplicity of interests, within pluralistic and stable political systems, put limits on the excessive demands from each sector and allowed the state to maintain relative autonomy. What was peculiar to Argentina was not state protection of industry or privileges, but the extent of these. In effect, the state was too weak to keep a distance between vested interests and the government. Unsure of how long the favor would last and understanding their lack of legitimacy, those who benefited form them sought the maximum advantage in the shortest period of time. The lack of consensus regarding property rights of economic rents was a source of constant insecurity and was very detrimental for investment.

In this game in which everyone wanted to be a winner, but in which the profit gained by one was a loss for others, ended with an enormous mass of losers. Those who were most informed and most capable of managing demand and more from markets to prevent losses were the winners. Because information is a costly good, especially in an increasingly chaotic and confusing system, the wealthy were winners and the poor were losers.

In a society without great social distances, information, though costly, could not be permanently hidden. Thus, nearly everyone tried to follow the behavior of the most successful. Demands multiplied, making competition more costly and reducing income. All of this caused great instability and a latent war of attrition. Moreover, the public discovered several defense mechanisms, such as responding to the inflationary tax by refusing to use domestic money. The economy became demonetized, subtracting resources from the government; inflation rose and, later on, so did public debt. The income distribution conflicts were increasingly difficult and perverse because no one wanted to change the system; rather everyone preferred to try and benefit from it.

All of this led to a climate of instability and illegitimacy, which made life in Argentina much more difficult, discouraged investment, and created a culture that was hostile to hard work, effort, and cooperation factors – among others that contributed to the decline of Argentina in the second half of the twentieth century.

Statistical Appendix

1. Population and Migration

Table A.1. *Argentine Population, According to National Census, 1869–2001 (annual rate of growth)*

Year	Population Total	t^a	Average Yearly Growth Rate[b]
1869	1,737,076		
1895	4,044,911		
1914	7,903,662	19.080	36.0
1947	15,893,827	33.000	21.0
1960	20,013,793	13.390	18.0
1970	23,364,431	10.000	16.0
1980	27,949,480	10.000	18.0
1991	32,615,528	10.564	15.0
2001	36,260,130	10.507	10.1

[a] Time interval in years.

[b] The average annual growth rate expresses a particular population's pace of growth. That is, it tells how much it increases or decreases on average for every 1,000 people, during a specified period of time – in this case, a year.

Note: Rate values are found at the beginning of each period.
Source: INDEC, *Censos Nacionales de Población.*

Table A.2. *Population by Region, 1800–1914*

Regions	Percentage of Total Population			
	1800	1869	1895	1914
Pampas and Litoral	29	41.3	58.2	64.3
Northeast	6	7.4	7.3	5.9
Central and Northwest	52	40.9	26.8	21.9
Cuyo	11	10.4	7.0	6.5
Patagonia	0	0.0	0.7	1.4

Source: Ernesto Maeder, "Población e Inmigración en la Argentina entre 1880 y 1910," in *La Argentina del Ochenta al Centenario*, ed. G. Ferrari and E. Gallo, Buenos Aires, Editorial Sudamericana, 1980, p. 559.

Table A.3. *Migratory Balances, 1870–1910*

Year	Entering	Leaving	Balance
1870	40.0	0.0	40.0
1871	20.9	10.7	10.2
1872	37.0	9.1	27.9
1873	76.3	18.2	58.1
1874	68.3	21.3	47.0
1875	42.0	25.6	16.4
1876	31.0	13.5	17.5
1877	36.3	18.3	18.0
1878	43.0	14.9	28.1
1879	55.1	23.7	31.4
1880	41.6	20.4	21.2
1881	47.5	22.4	25.1
1882	51.5	8.3	43.2
1883	63.2	9.5	53.7
1884	77.8	14.4	63.4
1885	108.7	14.6	94.1
1886	93.1	13.9	79.2
1887	120.8	13.6	107.2
1888	155.6	16.8	138.8
1889	261.0	40.6	220.4
1890	110.6	80.2	30.4
1891	52.1	81.9	−29.8
1892	73.3	43.8	29.5
1893	84.4	48.8	35.6
1894	80.7	41.4	39.3
1895	81.0	36.8	44.2
1896	135.2	45.9	89.3
1897	105.1	57.5	47.6
1898	95.2	53.5	41.7
1899	111.1	62.2	48.9
1900	105.9	55.4	50.5
1901	126.0	80.2	45.8
1902	96.1	79.4	16.7
1903	112.7	74.8	37.9
1904	161.1	66.6	94.5
1905	221.6	82.8	138.8
1906	302.2	103.8	198.4
1907	257.9	138.1	119.8
1908	303.1	127.0	176.1
1909	278.1	137.5	140.6
1910	345.3	135.4	209.9

Source: Roberto Cortés Conde, *El Progreso Argentino, 1880–1914*, Sudamericana, Buenos Aires, 1979.

Table A.4. *Net Balance of Nonnative Migrants in the Economically Active Population at the End of Each Period between Censuses, by Age and Sex*

	1869–1895		1895–1914		1914–1947		1947–1960	
Age	Men	Women	Men	Women	Men	Women	Men	Women
15–65 years	64%	36%	64%	36%	56.7%	43.3%	52%	48%
Total of both genders	759,157		1,502,491		1,167,476		548,836	

Source: Z. Lattes and A. Lattes, *Migraciones en la Argentina. Estudio de las Migraciones Internas e Internacionales Basado en Datos Censales, 1869–1960*, Instituto Di Tella, Buenos Aires, 1969, pp. 34–40 and 123.

Table A.5. *Sex of Immigrants (in percentages)*

	Male	Female
1857–1860	80.5	19.5
1861–1870	76.4	23.5
1871–1880	70.4	29.6
1881–1890	69.6	30.4
1891–1900	70.7	29.3
1901–1910	72.6	27.3
1911–1920	69.9	30.1
1921–1924	70.4	29.6
1857–1924	71.1	28.9

Source: Roberto Cortés Conde, *El Progreso Argentino, 1880–1914*, Buenos Aires, Sudamericana, 1979, p. 77.

Table A.6. *Illiteracy Rate in Argentina*

Year	Rate
1870	77
1890	56
1910	36
1930	22
1940	15
1950	13
1960	10
1980	6.1
1990	4

Source: Roberto Cortés Conde, *Tendencias de la Educación en la Argentina*, Mimeograph, 1998.

2. GDP and Investment

Table A.7. *GDP per Cápita, 1875–1935, at 1900 Prices (index numbers: 1900 = 100)*

Year	1900 = 100	Year	1900 = 100	Year	1900 = 100
1875	55.91	1896	123.25	1917	111.70
1876	55.37	1897	97.07	1918	144.62
1877	59.23	1898	102.20	1919	133.53
1878	54.63	1899	116.73	1920	133.58
1879	55.35	1900	100.00	1921	132.98
1880	52.58	1901	105.84	1922	144.46
1881	51.80	1902	106.09	1923	160.11
1882	63.35	1903	123.16	1924	174.66
1883	68.80	1904	139.74	1925	159.65
1884	71.52	1905	159.00	1926	159.57
1885	81.33	1906	150.42	1927	169.90
1886	79.19	1907	140.49	1928	165.09
1887	82.06	1908	157.89	1929	163.73
1888	92.37	1909	162.42	1930	145.76
1889	98.23	1910	161.45	1931	140.47
1890	87.45	1911	160.38	1932	131.27
1891	80.24	1912	178.71	1933	131.17
1892	92.95	1913	173.57	1934	141.66
1893	95.58	1914	134.62	1935	153.57
1894	106.81	1915	136.91		
1895	114.91	1916	134.89		

Source: Roberto Cortés Conde with the collaboration of Marcela Harriague, "Estimaciones del Producto Bruto Interno de Argentina, 1875–1935," Universidad de San Andrés, 1994.

Table A.8. *GDP per Capita Growth, 1936–2000, at 1970 Prices (index numbers: 1900 = 100)*

Year	GDP per Capita	Year	GDP per Capita	Year	GDP per Capita
1936	174.94	1958	278.96	1980	383.87
1937	190.74	1959	257.13	1981	351.77
1938	176.42	1960	272.31	1982	328.32
1939	207.40	1961	288.68	1983	331.95
1940	191.69	1962	279.94	1984	334.08
1941	195.80	1963	269.24	1985	313.79
1942	207.56	1964	290.58	1986	325.88
1943	210.15	1965	304.75	1987	327.91
1944	228.53	1966	302.49	1988	314.46
1945	212.24	1967	306.27	1989	296.10
1946	238.00	1968	315.15	1990	296.40
1947	281.61	1969	337.39	1991	322.78
1948	279.27	1970	350.74	1992	400.24
1949	247.38	1971	359.10	1993	412.25
1950	238.15	1972	361.75	1994	441.11
1951	242.84	1973	370.28	1995	436.70
1952	226.84	1974	385.16	1996	454.17
1953	235.40	1975	377.90	1997	481.42
1954	241.36	1976	372.85	1998	486.23
1955	254.37	1977	391.49	1999	457.06
1956	257.65	1978	374.14	2000	452.49
1957	266.78	1979	395.30		

Source: FIEL, BCRA, and Ministry of Economy and Industry.

Statistical Appendix

Table A.9. *Gross Domestic Product, Total and by Sectors, 1875–1935 (total in millions of 1914 pesos; index numbers: 1900 = 100)*

Year	Total	Industry	Agriculture	Cattle	Trans	Trade	Government	Construction
1875	17.45	14.46	4.70	54.34	7.80	19.41	0.00	0.00
1876	17.48	13.13	5.44	58.02	7.81	18.44	0.00	0.00
1877	19.71	15.96	6.30	62.12	7.61	20.98	0.00	0.00
1878	18.89	14.83	7.30	58.31	7.93	19.87	0.00	0.00
1879	20.33	15.95	8.46	61.48	8.76	21.31	0.00	0.00
1880	21.78	14.57	7.98	61.39	8.41	20.87	0.00	44.63
1881	21.86	15.84	8.95	63.75	10.33	21.69	0.00	32.56
1882	29.58	18.38	11.28	76.55	13.07	25.24	52.89	65.13
1883	33.75	20.67	14.83	80.95	16.79	28.09	42.92	86.84
1884	37.23	19.85	18.45	82.47	20.60	29.11	51.46	109.75
1885	44.70	22.40	20.03	89.28	24.99	34.22	59.04	157.62
1886	43.00	25.50	20.46	94.14	26.02	35.82	57.93	116.86
1887	46.27	31.76	30.49	90.70	32.67	41.86	48.55	99.62
1888	55.12	31.75	33.42	98.55	39.32	43.99	56.97	170.32
1889	64.41	30.00	32.92	81.63	52.46	44.27	74.89	287.56
1890	58.59	31.62	46.30	71.95	45.94	48.82	56.53	199.69
1891	51.00	35.62	53.58	77.70	43.09	48.62	63.44	71.01
1892	63.66	40.61	62.97	81.61	52.33	56.43	73.11	143.38
1893	68.08	39.85	72.12	76.67	59.99	57.82	77.81	169.35
1894	80.00	58.10	94.03	86.23	66.72	76.56	75.68	134.38
1895	82.69	60.37	108.62	100.74	75.94	79.63	79.87	86.85
1896	86.63	73.39	96.99	104.78	86.59	87.15	101.52	78.70
1897	79.14	70.27	70.86	106.22	76.51	78.61	87.16	98.32
1898	84.97	81.42	68.27	111.15	79.72	86.76	104.74	99.70
1899	109.77	104.83	96.80	130.91	94.97	108.75	123.80	139.44
1900	100.00	100.00	100.00	100.00	100.00	100.00	100.00	100.00
1901	115.33	108.92	109.84	130.23	108.87	117.10	91.24	99.84
1902	112.81	109.05	89.62	131.49	109.69	110.85	110.56	134.70
1903	134.10	130.12	153.62	132.50	128.46	134.21	102.43	125.63
1904	150.50	149.97	184.37	129.03	149.41	154.47	108.73	197.11
1905	164.38	169.56	178.61	141.64	167.39	166.62	108.39	346.65
1906	166.51	185.40	181.93	131.53	201.80	170.70	125.37	274.68
1907	163.63	179.12	159.28	135.36	218.30	166.34	145.97	288.66
1908	185.07	182.08	219.19	151.30	250.37	187.72	144.25	268.44
1909	192.64	207.93	209.77	146.06	250.51	193.35	153.10	408.52
1910	197.58	217.85	181.72	156.48	277.11	197.25	175.68	477.36
1911	193.59	231.79	141.57	157.54	291.85	194.91	176.72	491.17
1912	230.25	247.18	248.85	175.95	334.17	235.87	194.08	384.79
1913	231.28	266.19	255.63	154.84	354.57	239.93	199.67	379.46
1914	201.19	223.99	223.78	152.84	298.84	200.63	185.19	254.75
1915	216.47	230.15	279.62	167.39	298.42	215.02	163.73	187.42
1916	204.55	240.27	218.53	176.53	304.71	207.05	142.87	115.80

Year	Total	Industry	Agriculture	Cattle	Trans	Trade	Government	Construction
1917	176.49	235.93	99.25	192.53	269.07	178.37	141.74	67.06
1918	223.49	245.44	248.50	212.52	317.96	232.36	107.32	69.78
1919	226.71	266.77	249.60	196.03	346.53	239.30	116.58	75.10
1920	231.93	251.85	294.59	175.10	366.56	247.96	113.28	165.37
1921	239.98	273.38	266.99	196.37	327.86	257.16	147.97	195.33
1922	265.80	293.24	240.07	249.29	353.85	287.49	192.79	264.76
1923	292.54	314.33	263.23	268.70	402.48	321.62	202.13	363.10
1924	318.45	310.11	343.87	283.83	464.40	343.70	210.59	346.02
1925	305.06	342.57	277.37	271.03	453.51	327.01	230.10	327.29
1926	324.85	339.25	364.17	269.08	479.81	343.80	247.72	288.57
1927	350.68	360.98	381.16	270.09	527.76	376.83	351.98	368.58
1928	352.69	367.51	406.57	260.51	536.19	372.83	311.32	428.73
1929	356.19	359.82	422.62	254.42	545.56	372.68	331.66	494.57
1930	327.16	347.74	311.17	262.95	498.69	338.82	362.64	469.07
1931	335.75	334.33	422.00	236.93	504.81	354.27	350.58	286.57
1932	323.86	335.55	383.88	247.07	469.30	332.92	372.37	192.97
1933	331.48	372.19	369.04	255.48	449.40	348.21	341.98	215.01
1934	359.18	410.04	401.36	262.01	464.89	369.78	409.29	325.58
1935	403.97	490.80	470.82	278.12	482.30	425.22	405.49	315.56

Source: Roberto Cortés Conde with the collaboration of Marcela Harriague, "Estimaciones del Producto Bruto Interno de Argentina, 1875–1935", Buenos Aires, Universidad de San Andrés, 1994.

Table A.10. *Gross Domestic Product at Factor Costs (millions of pesos at 1950 prices)*

Year	Agriculture	Cattle	Industry	Construction	Trade	Other	Total
1936	5,021	3,793	7,247	1,806	6,348	11,335	35,550
1937	5,205	3,905	7,699	2,317	7,139	11,880	38,145
1938	4,360	3,929	8,001	2,581	7,199	12,219	38,289
1939	5,197	4,050	8,316	2,365	7,189	12,629	39,746
1940	5,705	4,186	8,330	2,092	7,129	12,957	40,399
1941	6,523	4,523	8,658	2,187	7,149	13,428	42,468
1942	6,243	4,668	8,782	2,183	7,159	13,930	42,965
1943	4,676	4,878	9,179	2,256	7,099	14,557	42,645
1944	6,479	5,028	10,412	2,755	7,469	15,325	47,468
1945	4,277	4,953	10,481	2,685	7,439	16,115	45,950
1946	4,693	4,958	11,823	2,863	8,530	17,168	50,035
1947	5,442	4,948	13,632	2,884	10,052	18,642	55,600
1948	5,573	4,836	13,796	3,733	10,673	20,068	58,679
1949	4,803	4,799	13,303	4,171	9,962	20,850	57,888
1950	4,378	4,677	13,700	4,330	10,012	21,502	58,599
1951	5,166	4,453	14,043	4,253	10,112	22,396	60,423
1952	3,923	4,574	13,015	3,621	8,750	22,528	56,411
1953	6,125	4,799	12,741	3,439	9,011	23,384	59,499
1954	5,875	4,775	13,837	3,875	9,732	23,978	62,072
1955	6,068	4,981	15,152	3,862	10,132	24,466	64,661

Source: CEPAL, *El Desarrollo Económico de la Argentina*, Santiago de Chile, CEPAL, 1958.

Table A.11. *Gross Domestic Product at Factor Cost (millions of 1960 pesos)*

Year	Primary Prod	Industry	Trade	Construction	Other	Total GDP
1950	1,242.8	1,923.7	1,339.8	331.2	2,062.9	6,900.4
1951	1,327.5	1,974.1	1,391.7	339.2	2,135.7	7,168.2
1952	1,138.4	1,936.8	1,294.0	311.8	2,122.5	6,803.5
1953	1,488.4	1,926.0	1,272.4	310.4	2,175.1	7,172.3
1954	1,479.9	2,078.6	1,351.0	297.1	2,258.0	7,464.6
1955	1,540.9	2,332.9	1,484.0	304.6	2,333.0	7,995.4
1956	1,470.5	2,494.6	1,550.3	295.5	2,406.8	8,217.7
1957	1,463.3	2,691.6	1,652.0	346.9	2,485.4	8,639.2
1958	1,527.0	2,916.5	1,743.4	411.7	2,569.0	9,167.6
1959	1,511.5	2,615.0	1,549.6	309.6	2,591.2	8,576.9
1960	1,536.6	2,878.0	1,749.4	369.9	2,715.5	9,249.4
1961	1,526.6	3,166.3	1,945.3	391.4	2,878.7	9,908.3
1962	1,588.4	2,991.6	1,868.5	359.1	2,940.2	9,747.8
1963	1,619.2	2,870.1	1,718.6	338.0	2,968.4	9,514.3
1964	1,732.2	3,411.2	1,876.7	352.4	3,126.0	10,498.5
1965	1,834.9	3,882.1	2,069.6	365.9	3,305.3	11,457.8
1966	1,766.3	3,907.7	2,058.4	388.5	3,408.7	11,529.6
1967	1,842.1	3,966.9	2,079.4	438.5	3,513.8	11,840.7
1968	1,742.1	4,224.7	2,189.7	517.9	3,670.7	12,345.1
1969	1,837.6	4,682.4	2,416.7	616.9	3,850.1	13,403.7
1970	1,940.6	4,977.9	2,516.7	674.8	4,011.3	14,121.3
1971	1,842.8	5,458.5	2,681.4	651.9	4,165.7	14,800.3
1972	1,697.8	5,783.9	2,765.9	683.6	4,331.0	15,262.2
1973	1,983.6	6,151.6	2,843.3	649.0	4,568.6	16,196.1

Source: BCRA, *Sistema de Cuentas del Producto e Ingreso de la Argentina*, Vol I y II, Buenos Aires, BCRA, 1975.

Table A.12. *Gross Domestic Product (millions of 1993 pesos)*

Year	Primary Production	Industry	Construction	Trade	Other	GDP
1980	9,660	38,588	16,149	29,446	83,817	200,922
1981	9,998	33,930	14,229	26,343	83,983	190,494
1982	10,745	32,975	12,898	24,643	85,946	189,093
1983	10,963	35,223	12,712	25,655	90,514	197,317
1984	11,002	36,095	11,342	26,741	92,583	200,416
1985	10,816	32,684	9,703	24,194	90,959	190,017
1986	10,835	35,969	11,586	26,279	94,347	201,709
1987	10,540	36,357	13,222	26,480	97,979	207,165
1988	11,369	34,577	12,846	25,219	98,882	204,907
1989	10,434	31,988	9,783	22,678	94,952	190,242
1990	11,319	30,259	7,831	23,264	93,432	185,548
1991	11,783	33,398	10,168	27,300	99,552	202,495
1992	11,805	36,801	11,956	30,559	104,545	218,567
1993	12,091	38,101	13,255	31,701	113,028	236,505
1994	12,995	39,814	14,018	33,744	119,579	250,308
1995	13,726	36,958	12,315	30,955	120,619	243,186
1996	13,568	39,350	13,351	33,286	125,921	256,626
1997	13,630	42,950	15,565	36,812	133,576	277,441
1998	14,820	43,733	16,919	37,869	138,411	288,123
1999	15,186	40,275	15,591	35,072	138,567	278,369
2000	14,920	38,732	14,138	34,063	141,191	276,173
2001	15,077	35,867	12,500	31,375	138,861	263,997
2002	14,733	31,955	8,322	25,581	131,648	235,236
2003	15,745	37,058	11,180	29,151	136,899	256,023
2004	15,505	41,492	14,470	33,225	144,824	279,141
2005	17,358	44,613	17,459	36,739	155,229	304,764

Source: INDEC and Argentine Ministry of Economy.

Table A.13. *Gross Fixed Investment by Sector (five-year averages in millions of 1950 pesos)*

Year	Total	Agricultural	Industry	Transportation, Communications, and Energy	Trade, Finance, Personal Services, and Housing	State	Railroads Investment	As a Percentage of Total
1901–1905	3,514.8	420.8	581.8	590.6	1,380.2	541.4	529.2	15.1
1906–1910	8,498.2	833.4	1,067.2	1,776.0	3,562.8	1,078.8	1,753.6	20.6
1911–1915	6,977.0	847.0	1,131.2	1,318.2	2,761.0	919.6	958.0	13.7
1916–1920	2,777.8	791.6	433.8	293.6	1,044.4	214.4	45.0	1.6
1921–1925	7,649.6	1,269.6	1,178.6	1,286.8	3,367.8	546.8	501.0	6.5
1926–1930	11,591.8	1,774.0	1,838.2	2,470.2	3,997.0	1,512.4	789.0	6.8

Note: Railroads are included in the Transportation, Communications, and Energy sector.
Source: CEPAL, *El Desarrollo Económico de la Argentina*, Appendix, Santiago de Chile, CEPAL, 1958.

Table A.14. *Consumption and Investment (in millions of pesos at 1950 prices)*

Year	Total Consumption	Change	Private Consumption	Change	Public Consumption	Change	Gross Domestic Investment	Change
1941	33,805	–	29,698	–	4,107	–	9,291	–
1942	35,380	4.66	31,058	4.58	4,322	5.23	8,050	−13.36
1943	34,042	−3.78	29,310	−5.63	4,732	9.49	7,508	−6.73
1944	38,746	13.82	32,861	12.12	5,885	24.37	8,010	6.69
1945	37,939	−2.08	31,253	−4.89	6,686	13.61	7,230	−9.74
1946	38,946	2.65	32,426	3.75	6,520	−2.48	11,577	60.12
1947	42,346	8.73	35,410	9.20	6,936	6.38	18,726	61.75
1948	46,311	9.36	38,056	7.47	8,255	19.02	19,160	2.32
1949	49,670	7.25	42,080	10.57	7,590	−8.06	13,872	−27.60
1950	48,282	−2.79	40,566	−3.60	7,716	1.66	13,548	−2.34
1951	49,776	3.09	41,876	3.23	7,900	2.38	15,963	17.83
1952	46,919	−5.74	38,875	−7.17	8,044	1.82	14,479	−9.30
1953	50,348	7.31	42,090	8.27	8,258	2.66	11,607	−19.84
1954	50,764	0.83	42,060	−0.07	8,704	5.40	13,918	19.91
1955	54,600	7.56	45,942	9.23	8,658	−0.53	14,818	6.47

Source: BCRA, *Cuentas Nacionales de la República Argentina*, vol. 3, Buenos Aires, BCRA, Gerencia de Investigaciones Económicas, 1976.

Table A.15. *Capital Stock at Current Prices, Year Base 1993* (*in millions of pesos*)

	1990	1991	1992	1993	1994	1995	1996	1997	1998	1999	2000
Aggregate capital stock	197,218	405,545	470,450	543,164	579,635	596,532	603,806	625,960	674,282	666,872	641,717
Durable goods	62,830	115,747	124,294	129,502	133,956	139,051	144,602	150,462	155,627	153,460	150,037
Machinery and equipment	51,634	94,270	100,715	103,648	106,199	108,802	112,422	115,604	118,707	118,158	115,784
National	36,361	77,488	80,485	80,375	77,807	76,140	76,060	74,224	72,665	69,206	64,498
Imported	15,272	16,782	20,229	23,273	28,393	32,662	36,363	41,381	46,042	48,952	51,286
Transportation goods	11,196	21,476	23,579	25,854	27,757	30,249	32,179	34,858	36,920	35,301	34,253
National	7,503	16,034	17,198	18,234	18,905	20,418	21,559	22,835	23,335	21,105	20,712
Imported	3,693	5,442	6,381	7,621	8,853	9,831	10,640	12,023	13,585	14,196	13,542
Construction	125,423	270,555	325,743	395,881	428,377	438,488	440,051	453,839	495,239	489,989	469,518
Residential	59,104	128,514	157,020	189,210	206,356	209,504	212,795	220,563	244,703	238,584	226,303
Nonresidential	66,319	142,040	168,723	206,671	222,021	228,985	227,256	233,276	250,536	251,405	243,216
Private	25,282	55,845	70,320	90,158	101,131	104,340	107,619	113,896	129,681	128,929	122,744
Public	41,038	86,196	98,403	116,514	120,890	124,645	119,637	119,381	120,855	122,476	120,472
Farming assets	8,965	19,243	20,413	17,780	17,302	18,993	19,153	21,658	23,416	23,423	22,161
Cattle	4,221	10,819	10,673	8,087	7,375	7,785	7,553	9,228	10,995	9,974	9,436
Agricultural constructions	4,462	8,136	9,444	9,393	9,624	10,912	11,349	12,186	12,150	13,162	12,456
Other	282	289	296	301	302	296	251	244	271	287	270

Source: Dirección Nacional de Cuentas Nacionales (Center for National Accounts) – INDEC. IDB-UNPRE Project Estudio 1.EE.88: "La Riqueza Nacional en Argentina." National Director: Fernando Cerro. Coordinator: Ariel Coremberg.

3. Prices and Wages

Table A.16. *Monthly Wages of Unskilled Workers*

Year	Nominal[a]	Real Wages[b]	Real Wages[c]
1882	24	38	36
1883	27	45	43
1884	27	42	
1885	27	50	
1886	29.5	55	45
1887	30	39	37
1888	30	39	
1889	30	39	36
1890	30	30	32
1891	47.5	42	
1892	47.5	48	
1893	47.5	52	
1894	47.5	44	
1895	47.5	40	
1896	47.5	36	41
1897	47.5	41	
1898	55	57	
1899	55	69	63
1900	55	60	58
1901	55	53	54
1902	55	53	54
1903	55	55	55
1904	60	58	54
1905	60	56	54
1906	60	52	53
1907	60	50	49
1908	60	50	
1909	60	46	
1910	65	50	51
1911	65	50	
1912	80	62	60

[a] In pesos.
[b] Adjusted for the price of food.
[c] Adjusted for the cost of living.
Source: Roberto Cortés Conde, *El Progreso Argentino, 1880–1914*, Buenos Aires, Sudamericana, 1979.

Table A.17. *Wages in Argentina and Italy (in 1882 pesos)*

Year	Argentina	Italy	Difference (%)
1882	19.85	11.30	76
1883	23.14	11.22	106
1884	20.10	12.21	65
1885	23.37	10.44	114
1886	27.20	10.49	159
1887	19.49	14.90	31
1888	22.09	15.13	46
1889	21.63	15.25	12
1890	18.10	18.97	−5
1891	17.97	21.47	−16
1892	20.94	19.04	10
1893	20.57	17.66	16
1894	19.32	21.55	−10
1895	17.55	23.62	−26
1896	19.00	23.64	−20
1897	26.27	23.90	10
1898	36.07	19.55	85
1899	42.82	16.41	161
1900	37.38	18.34	104
1901	37.54	20.79	81
1902	38.45	20.82	85
1903	41.09	19.98	106

Source: Roberto Cortés Conde, *El Progreso Argentino, 1880–1914*, Buenos Aires, Sudamericana, 1979.

Table A.18. *Real Wage Index, 1929–1955*

Year	Index: 1929 = 100	Year	Index: 1929 = 100
1929	100	1943	101
1930	91	1944	114
1931	98	1945	108
1932	104	1946	104
1933	96	1947	128
1934	99	1948	157
1935	101	1949	162
1936	95	1950	157
1937	96	1951	147
1938	96	1952	133
1939	97	1953	141
1940	99	1954	156
1941	97	1955	154
1942	97		

Source: Anuario Geográfico Argentino, Comité Nacional de Geografía 1941, and Juan Llach, "Los Determinantes del Salario en Argentina. Un Diagnóstico de Largo Plazo y Propuestas de Políticas," in *Revista Estudios*, Instituto de Estudios Económicos sobre la Realidad Argentina y Latinoamericana (IEERAL), Córdoba, year VII, no. 29, 1984.

Table A.19. *Series of the Consumer Price Index (CPI) in Gran Buenos Aires (linkage of the series bases 1943, 1960, 1974, and 1988 with a base of 1999 = 100)*

Year	CPI General Level	Percent Change Compared with the Same Month in the Previous Year
1943	0.00000000000201451	
1944	0.00000000000200818	−0.3
1945	0.00000000000240488	19.8
1946	0.00000000000282900	17.6
1947	0.0000000000032135	13.6
1948	0.0000000000036342	13.1
1949	0.0000000000047630	31.1
1950	0.0000000000059803	25.6
1951	0.0000000000081736	36.7
1952	0.0000000000113387	38.7
1953	0.0000000000117889	4.0
1954	0.0000000000122363	3.8
1955	0.0000000000137439	12.3
1956	0.0000000000155873	13.4
1957	0.0000000000194388	24.7
1958	0.0000000000255791	31.6
1959	0.0000000000546606	113.7
1960	0.0000000000692148	26.6
1961	0.0000000000787138	13.7
1962	0.0000000000992788	26.1
1963	0.0000000001250665	26.0
1964	0.0000000001527617	22.1
1965	0.0000000001964440	28.6
1966	0.000000000259038	31.9
1967	0.000000000334730	29.2
1968	0.00000000038905	16.2
1969	0.00000000041853	7.6
1970	0.00000000047536	13.6
1971	0.00000000064042	34.7
1972	0.00000000101478	58.5
1973	0.00000000162672	60.3
1974	0.00000000202065	24.2
1975	0.00000000571430	182.8
1976	0.0000000310863	444.0
1977	0.0000000858081	176.0
1978	0.0000002364090	175.5
1979	0.000000613507	159.5
1980	0.000001231702	100.8

(continued)

Table A.19 *(continued)*

Year	CPI General Level	Percent Change Compared with the Same Month in the Previous Year
1981	0.000002518500	104.5
1982	0.0000066686	164.8
1983	0.0000295952	343.8
1984	0.0002150780	626.7
1985	0.001660790	672.2
1986	0.00315700	90.1
1987	0.00730320	131.3
1988	0.0323500	343.0
1989	1.028554	3079.5
1990	24.828900	2314.0
1991	67.4531	171.7
1992	84.2489	24.9
1993	93.1890	10.6
1994	97.0818	4.2
1995	100.3594	3.4
1996	100.5156	0.2
1997	101.0469	0.5
1998	101.9813	0.9
1999	100.7915	−1.2
2000	99.8449	−0.9

Source: INDEC, (Dirección de Índices de precios de consumo).

4. Foreign Trade

Table A.20. *Argentine Trade Balance, 1880–1910 (in thousands of gold pesos)*

Year	Imports	Exports	Trade Balance
1880	45,535	58,38	12,845
1881	55,705	57,938	2,233
1882	61,246	60,388	−0,858
1883	80,435	60,207	−20,228
1884	94,056	68,029	−26,027
1885	92,221	83,879	−8,342
1886	95,408	69,834	−25,574
1887	117,352	84,421	−32,931
1888	128,412	100,111	−28,301
1889	164,569	90,145	−74,424
1890	142,24	100,818	−41,422
1891	67,207	103,219	36,012
1892	91,481	113,37	21,889
1893	96,223	94,09	−2,133
1894	92,788	101,687	8,899
1895	95,096	120,067	24,971
1896	112,163	116,802	4,639
1897	98,288	101,169	2,881
1898	107,428	133,829	26,401
1899	116,85	184,917	68,067
1900	113,485	154,6	41,115
1901	113,959	167,716	53,757
1902	103,039	179,486	76,447
1903	131,206	220,984	89,778
1904	187,305	264,157	76,852
1905	205,154	322,843	117,689
1906	269,97	292,253	22,283
1907	285,86	296,204	10,344
1908	272,972	366,005	93,033
1909	302,756	397,35	94,594
1910	351,77	372,626	20,856

Source: Dirección General de Estadística de la Nación, *Extracto Estadístico de la República Argentina Correspondiente al año 1915*, Compañía Sudamericana de Billetes de Banco, Buenos Aires, 1916.

Table A.21. *Argentine Trade Balance, 1910–2000 (in thousands of current dollars)*

Year	Exports	Imports	Balance
1910	373,122	363,797	9,325
1911	328,270	388,397	−60,127
1912	481,097	428,523	52,574
1913	497,848	475,865	21,983
1914	388,220	310,593	77,627
1915	553,598	290,502	263,096
1916	551,822	352,585	199,237
1917	548,421	379,123	169,298
1918	813,170	507,902	305,268
1919	1,018,739	648,000	370,739
1920	934,213	836,575	97,638
1921	485,764	542,516	−56,752
1922	554,657	565,848	−11,191
1923	604,517	680,586	−76,069
1924	787,192	645,000	142,192
1925	792,209	800,321	−8,112
1926	728,907	756,802	−27,895
1927	971,992	825,127	146,864
1928	1,015,508	805,763	209,746
1929	906,946	819,707	87,238
1930	509,380	613,139	−103,759
1931	420,751	339,249	81,503
1932	331,054	214,987	116,067
1933	346,997	277,740	69,257
1934	467,013	318,023	148,990
1935	498,190	332,861	165,329
1936	537,565	323,681	213,884
1937	755,229	479,292	275,936
1938	437,505	427,160	10,345
1939	464,063	346,001	118,062
1940	408,948	377,901	31,047
1941	412,337	322,225	90,112
1942	491,202	319,309	171,893
1943	601,114	239,281	361,834
1944	658,234	256,745	401,488
1945	723,782	294,910	428,872
1946	1,159,338	588,073	571,265
1947	1,611,985	1,340,484	271,501
1948	1,628,975	1,561,490	67,484
1949	1,043,469	1,179,597	−136,128
1950	1,177,535	964,214	213,322
1951	1,169,441	1,480,220	−310,779
1952	687,813	1,179,335	−491,522
1953	1,125,147	795,138	330,009
1954	1,026,638	979,001	47,637

(*continued*)

Table A.21 *(continued)*

Year	Exports	Imports	Balance
1955	928,595	1,172,590	−243,995
1956	943,753	1,127,579	−183,826
1957	974,821	1,310,443	−335,622
1958	993,919	1,232,633	−238,714
1959	1,008,952	993,019	15,933
1960	1,079,155	1,249,273	−170,118
1961	964,116	1,460,379	−496,263
1962	1,216,028	1,356,502	−140,474
1963	1,365,086	980,677	384,409
1964	1,410,350	1,077,164	333,186
1965	1,493,409	1,198,551	294,858
1966	1,593,242	1,124,306	468,936
1967	1,464,529	1,095,542	368,987
1968	1,367,865	1,169,189	198,676
1969	1,612,079	1,576,091	35,988
1970	1,773,167	1,694,042	79,125
1971	1,740,348	1,868,067	−127,719
1972	1,941,098	1,904,682	36,416
1973	3,266,003	2,235,331	1,030,672
1974	3,930,702	3,634,918	295,784
1975	2,961,264	3,946,501	−985,237
1976	3,916,058	3,033,004	883,054
1977	5,651,842	4,161,539	1,490,303
1978	6,399,540	3,833,655	2,565,885
1979	7,809,924	6,700,055	1,109,869
1980	8,021,418	10,540,603	−2,519,185
1981	9,143,044	9,430,226	−287,182
1982	7,624,936	5,336,914	2,288,022
1983	7,836,063	4,504,156	3,331,907
1984	8,107,405	4,584,672	3,522,733
1985	8,396,017	3,814,148	4,581,869
1986	6,852,213	4,724,053	2,128,160
1987	6,360,160	5,817,818	542,342
1988	9,134,812	5,321,565	3,813,247
1989	9,579,271	4,203,194	5,376,077
1990	12,352,532	4,076,665	8,275,867
1991	11,977,785	8,275,271	3,702,514
1992	12,234,949	14,871,754	−2,636,805
1993	13,117,758	16,783,513	−3,665,755
1994	15,839,213	21,590,255	−5,751,042
1995	20,963,108	20,121,682	841,426
1996	23,810,717	23,761,809	48,908
1997	26,430,855	30,450,184	−4,019,329
1998	26,433,698	31,377,360	−4,943,662
1999	23,308,635	25,508,157	−2,199,522
2000	26,341,029	25,280,485	1,060,544

Source: INDEC.

Table A.22. *Imports, Exports, and Trade Opening as a Percentage of GDP*

Year	Imports (%)	Exports (%)	Trade Opening (%)
1900	25.0	15.0	40.1
1901	24.0	14.8	38.7
1902	21.1	16.2	37.3
1903	24.0	17.6	41.6
1904	34.4	19.0	53.4
1905	28.8	20.6	49.4
1906	31.5	17.7	49.2
1907	30.0	17.6	47.6
1908	25.3	20.1	45.3
1909	27.9	20.5	48.4
1910	30.0	17.8	47.8
1911	31.9	15.0	46.9
1912	28.7	21.1	49.8
1913	31.2	20.9	52.1
1914	21.5	18.4	39.9
1915	16.3	29.3	45.5
1916	20.1	29.3	49.5
1917	19.1	32.3	51.4
1918	14.7	39.8	54.5
1919	17.6	49.4	67.0
1920	22.1	46.6	68.7
1921	20.4	29.2	49.6
1922	19.1	27.2	46.4
1923	22.5	28.0	50.5
1924	21.6	34.1	55.6
1925	25.1	29.3	54.5
1926	25.0	25.6	50.6
1927	26.5	30.4	57.0
1928	24.7	29.9	54.6
1929	24.1	25.9	49.9
1930	20.9	17.4	38.2
1931	14.6	19.5	34.1
1932	11.7	17.8	29.6
1933	13.2	14.8	28.0
1934	12.8	17.6	30.5
1935	14.2	21.0	35.2
1936	14.5	19.0	33.6
1937	18.3	20.4	38.7
1938	17.4	14.4	31.8
1939	13.7	17.0	30.8
1940	11.8	13.7	25.5
1941	8.6	13.2	21.8

(*continued*)

Table A.22 *(continued)*

Year	Imports (%)	Exports (%)	Trade Opening (%)
1942	7.1	12.0	19.1
1943	4.9	13.3	18.1
1944	4.5	11.8	16.3
1945	4.7	12.2	16.9
1946	8.0	13.0	21.0
1947	14.3	11.0	25.3
1948	13.8	8.8	22.6
1949	9.9	6.6	16.5
1950	8.2	9.2	17.4
1951	10.0	8.2	18.2
1952	8.3	5.4	13.7
1953	4.7	6.6	11.3
1954	5.3	5.7	11.1
1955	6.6	5.5	12.1
1956	11.9	10.8	22.7
1957	12.1	9.6	21.7
1958	10.1	8.4	18.5
1959	11.3	11.8	23.1
1960	11.3	10.1	21.4
1961	12.5	8.7	21.2
1962	12.2	12.0	24.2
1963	9.7	12.5	22.3
1964	10.2	10.6	20.9
1965	9.3	10.7	20.0
1966	8.9	11.7	20.6
1967	8.7	11.2	19.9
1968	8.9	10.6	19.5
1969	10.1	11.4	21.4
1970	9.0	9.2	18.2
1971	9.7	8.0	17.7
1972	9.0	8.0	17.0
1973	8.6	8.8	17.4
1974	8.6	8.4	17.0
1975	8.8	7.6	16.4
1976	7.0	10.0	17.0
1977	9.0	12.0	21.0
1978	8.8	13.5	22.3
1979	12.7	12.2	24.9
1980	11.9	7.0	19.0
1981	11.6	7.8	19.4
1982	6.9	8.4	15.2
1983	6.1	8.3	14.4

(continued)

Statistical Appendix

Table A.22 *(continued)*

Year	Imports (%)	Exports (%)	Trade Opening (%)
1984	6.3	7.9	14.2
1985	5.9	9.8	15.7
1986	6.5	8.2	14.7
1987	7.0	7.7	14.8
1988	6.5	9.3	15.9
1989	5.9	10.8	16.6
1990	5.8	12.9	18.8
1991	9.5	11.3	20.8
1992	14.4	10.2	24.6
1993	9.3	6.9	16.2
1994	10.7	7.5	18.2
1995	9.9	9.5	19.4
1996	11.0	9.7	20.7
1997	12.9	10.0	23.0
1998	13.5	10.7	24.2
1999	12.4	10.9	23.3
2000	12.5	11.3	23.8
2001	11.2	12.2	23.4
2002	6.3	14.1	20.4
2003	8.0	13.7	21.7
2004	10.2	13.6	23.8
2005	11.3	14.1	25.4

Sources: 1900–1935: Argentine Statistical Study (Relevamiento Estadístico de la República Argentina).

1900–1949: Central Bank National Accounts (BCRA Cuentas Nacionales), 1976. Millions of pesos at 1950 prices.

1950–1959: Conade-CEPAL, Argentine National Accounts (Cuentas Nacionales de la República Argentina), 1964. Millions of current pesos.

1960–1979: CEPAL, Short-Term Economic Statistics of Argentina; 1960–1969, 1960 australs; 1970 to 1979, 1970 australs.

1980–1992: National Accounts: Global Supply and Demand, 1980–1995. Thousands of 1986 pesos.

1993–2004: MECON, online database. Thousands of Pesos at 1993 prices.

5. Public Finances

Table A.23. *Revenues, Expenditures, and National Debt, 1880–1900 (in millions of gold pesos)*

Year	Revenues	Expenditures	Domestic Debt	Foreign Debt	Total Debt
1880	19.59	26.92	24.83	34.13	58.96
1881	21.35	28.38	24.22	36.18	60.40
1882	26.82	58.01	43.15	96.08	139.23
1883	30.95	44.83	42.25	106.48	148.73
1884	37.72	56.44	47.73	122.60	170.33
1885	36.42	55.51	47.14	71.19	118.33
1886	42.25	54.46	43.77	73.39	117.15
1887	51.58	65.08	51.24	90.47	141.72
1888	51.64	76.36	188.65	88.81	277.46
1889	68.71	100.39	180.91	115.76	296.67
1890	75.19	98.42	227.24	128.21	355.44
1891	72.93	125.91	234.89	135.58	370.47
1892	107.24	127.27	238.25	187.34	425.60
1893	124.38	123.27	237.36	190.44	427.81
1894	122.36	143.61	202.37	190.99	393.36
1895	131.49	166.86	202.65	199.24	401.90
1896	124.34	231.51	204.65	216.76	421.41
1897	149.69	177.54	205.16	233.29	438.45
1898	136.62	311.71	201.70	316.40	518.10
1899	163.94	172.42	204.78	344.59	549.37
1900	149.82	158.42	58.40	389.06	447.46

Source: Anuario Geográfico Argentino, Comité Nacional de Geografía, Buenos Aires, 1941, p. 394.

Table A.24. *National Treasury Cash Balance Accounts (in millions of pesos)*

In Millions of Current Pesos

Year	1900	1901	1902	1903	1904	1905	1906	1907	1908	1909	1910	1911	1912	1913	1914	1915
Revenues	211	225	233	231	280	328	333	418	335	519	390	457	521	432	333	298
Expenditures	162	165	207	179	205	331	244	272	269	383	385	379	414	352	399	382
Primary surplus	49	60	26	52	76	-2	89	146	66	136	6	78	107	80	-66	-84
Public debt payment	47	54	56	70	53	53	57	51	55	52	46	45	41	86	81	82
Surplus	2	7	-30	-18	23	-55	32	95	11	84	-41	33	66	-6	-148	-166
Financing (1) + (2)	-2	-7	30	18	-23	55	-32	-95	-11	-84	41	-33	-66	6	148	166
Use of net credit (1)	30	12	-7	-36	-13	99	-17	-81	-2	-6	12	-14	6	15	144	180
Difference in inventory (2)	-32	-19	37	53	-10	-44	-14	-14	-9	-78	29	-19	-72	-9	3	-14

In Millions of Pesos at 1914 Prices

Year	1900	1901	1902	1903	1904	1905	1906	1907	1908	1909	1910	1911	1912	1913	1914	1915
Revenues	311	292	302	309	364	407	384	470	370	534	405	474	536	432	333	277
Expenditures	238	214	269	239	266	409	281	306	297	394	399	393	426	352	399	354
Primary surplus	72	78	33	69	98	-3	102	164	73	140	6	81	110	80	-66	-78
Public debt payment	69	70	73	93	69	65	66	57	60	54	48	46	42	86	81	76
Surplus	3	8	-39	-23	30	-68	37	107	13	86	-42	34	68	-6	-148	-154
Financing (1) + (2)	-3	-8	39	23	-30	68	-37	-107	-13	-86	42	-34	-68	6	148	154
Use of net credit (1)	44	16	-9	-48	-16	123	-20	-91	-3	-6	12	-15	6	15	144	167
Difference in inventory (2)	-47	-24	49	71	-13	-55	-17	-16	-10	-80	30	-20	-74	-9	3	-13

In Millions of Current Pesos

Year	1916	1917	1918	1919	1920	1921	1922	1923	1924	1925	1926	1927	1928	1929	1930
Revenues	318	414	354	441	732	556	556	639	894	1,010	947	1,238	1,010	996	908
Expenditures	333	337	332	357	428	471	571	587	646	675	731	1,015	770	726	949
Primary surplus	-16	76	22	84	303	85	-15	52	248	335	217	223	240	270	-42
Public debt payment	78	80	99	107	106	109	112	107	122	121	139	175	181	192	201
Surplus	-93	-3	-77	-23	198	-24	-126	-56	125	214	78	48	59	78	-243
Financing (1) + (2)	93	3	78	26	-198	24	126	56	-125	-214	-78	-48	-59	-78	243
Use of net credit (1)	96	86	72	11	-185	35	153	-6	-33	-248	-42	-68	-2	81	317
Difference in inventory (2)	-3	-83	5	15	-13	-11	-26	62	-92	34	-36	20	-57	-159	-74

In Millions of Pesos at 1914 Prices

Year	1916	1917	1918	1919	1920	1921	1922	1923	1924	1925	1926	1927	1928	1929	1930
Revenues	274	305	207	275	389	333	396	463	635	738	713	941	775	758	683
Expenditures	288	249	194	223	228	282	406	426	459	494	550	772	591	552	714
Primary surplus	-14	56	13	52	161	51	-11	37	176	245	163	169	184	206	-31
Public debt payment	67	59	58	67	56	65	79	78	87	89	105	133	139	146	151
Surplus	-81	-2	-45	-14	105	-14	-90	-40	89	156	59	37	45	60	-183
Financing (1) + (2)	81	2	45	16	-105	14	90	40	-89	-156	-59	-36	-45	-60	183
Use of net credit (1)	83	64	42	7	-98	21	109	-4	-24	-181	-31	-52	-1	62	239
Difference in inventory (2)	-2	-61	3	9	-7	-7	-19	45	-65	25	-27	15	-44	-121	-56

(*continued*)

Table A.24 (*continued*)

In Millions of Current Pesos

Year	1931	1932	1933	1934	1935	1936	1937	1938	1939	1940	1941	1942	1943	1944	1945
Revenues	1,077	1,286	1,302	1,338	3,618	1,954	2,479	2,043	1,865	2,382	2,421	2,226	3,819	5,400	4,228
Expenditures	733	1,030	926	1,196	2,315	1,328	1,859	1,795	1,728	1,767	1,451	2,185	2,847	4,329	4,219
Primary surplus	343	256	376	142	1,303	626	620	248	137	615	970	41	972	1,072	9
Public debt payment	228	271	274	229	192	258	1,002	247	220	256	463	314	374	734	349
Surplus	115	-15	103	-87	1,110	368	-382	2	-84	358	507	-274	598	338	-340
Financing (1) + (2)	-115	15	-103	87	-1,110	-368	382	-1	84	-358	-507	274	-597	-338	340
Use of net credit (1)	53	141	-28	-20	-871	39	41	177	67	129	352	63	497	345	255
Difference in inventory (2)	-168	-125	-75	107	-239	-407	341	-177	17	-487	-859	211	-1,094	-683	85

In Millions of Pesos at 1914 Prices

Year	1931	1932	1933	1934	1935	1936	1937	1938	1939	1940	1941	1942	1943	1944	1945
Revenues	941	1,253	1,125	1,304	3,328	1,657	2,048	1,699	1,527	1,907	1,889	1,621	2,753	3,893	2,540
Expenditures	641	1,004	800	1,165	2,129	1,126	1,535	1,492	1,415	1,415	1,132	1,592	2,052	3,120	2,534
Primary surplus	300	249	325	139	1,198	531	512	206	112	492	757	30	701	772	6
Public debt payment	200	264	237	223	177	219	828	205	180	205	361	229	270	529	210
Surplus	100	-15	89	-85	1,021	312	-315	1	-69	287	396	-199	431	244	-204
Financing (1) + (2)	-100	15	-89	85	-1,021	-312	315	-1	69	-287	-396	199	-430	-244	204
Use of net credit (1)	47	137	-24	-20	-801	33	34	147	54	103	275	46	358	248	153
Difference in inventory (2)	-147	-122	-65	104	-220	-345	282	-148	14	-390	-670	154	-788	-492	51

Source: Treasury Yearbook, several years.

Table A.25. *National Government Revenue and Expenditures, 1945–1956 (in millions of pesos, 1945 prices)*

	1945	1946	1947	1948	1949	1950	1951	1952	1953	1954	1955	1956
1. Revenues	2,386	2,587	4,083	4,904	4,997	4,884	5,204	4,440	4,865	5,290	5,298	6,629
Current revenue	2,386	2,587	4,083	4,904	4,997	4,884	5,204	4,440	4,865	5,290	5,227	6,583
Social security	474	528	915	1,305	1,342	1,333	1,284	1,089	1,312	1,554	1,538	1,683
Capital revenue	0	0	0	0	0	0	0	0	0	0	71	46
2. Expenditures	2,990	3,041	4,531	8,333	6,050	5,402	5,493	4,677	5,330	6,279	6,180	6,327
Current expenditures	2,283	2,350	3,203	4,380	4,276	3,920	4,081	3,635	4,142	5,140	5,251	5,362
Social security	292	267	303	356	545	474	445	449	586	821	1,008	1,193
Capital expenditures	706	691	1,328	3,954	1,774	1,482	1,412	1,042	1,188	1,139	929	965
3. Primary surplus	-604	-454	-448	-3,429	-1,053	-517	-289	-236	-465	-989	-882	302
4. Debt payment	305	240	214	219	154	108	110	100	70	51	51	71
5. Surplus	-909	-694	-662	-3,648	-1,207	-626	-399	-336	-535	-1,040	-933	231
6. Financing	909	694	662	3,648	1,207	626	399	336	535	1,040	933	-231

Source: OAS/IDB/CEPAL, *Programa Conjunto de Tributación: Estudio sobre Política Fiscal en la Argentina*, OAS/IDB/CEPAL, 1963.

Statistical Appendix

Table A.26. *National Government Revenues and Expenditures, 1957–1961*
(in millions of pesos, 1955 prices)

	1957	1958	1959	1960	1961
1. Revenue	28,947	30,761	26,490	31,793	34,916
Current revenue	28,849	29,663	25,742	30,820	34,916
Social security	7,729	7,283	5,634	6,465	7,494
Capital revenue	98	1,098	749	972	0
2. Expenditures	28,827	41,687	32,774	35,010	39,114
Current expenditures	24,171	31,684	26,640	27,014	30,991
Social security	6,089	7,506	6,488	6,340	8,103
Capital expenditures	4,656	10,003	6,133	7,997	8,123
3. Primary surplus	120	−10,926	−6,283	−3,218	−4,198
4. Debt payment	195	172	292	414	447
5. Surplus	−74	−11,098	−6,576	−3,632	−4,646
6. Financing	74	11,098	6,576	3,632	4,646

Note: 1957 includes only January/October. The following ones include November/October.

Source: OAS/IDB/ECLA, *Programa Conjunto de Tributación: Estudio sobre Política Fiscal en la Argentina*, OAS/IDB/CEPAL, 1963.

Table A.27. *National Government and Public Enterprises Fiscal Balance Sheet, 1962–1972 (in millions of 1961 pesos)*

	1962	1963	1964	1965	1966	1967	1968	1969	1970	1971	1972
1. Revenue	150,952	144,832	162,609	181,550	179,085	223,419	212,710	228,372	239,421	232,862	224,154
2. Expenditures	209,679	200,588	216,538	212,343	220,123	234,683	231,283	242,756	255,970	282,034	286,678
3. Primary surplus	–58,727	–55,756	–53,928	–30,793	–41,038	–11,264	–18,573	–14,384	–16,549	–49,172	–63,524
4. Public debt payment	11,536	10,611	15,505	11,576	10,274	10,690	11,445	10,634	10,598	12,602	16,129
5. Surplus	–70,263	–66,368	–69,433	–42,369	–51,311	–21,954	–30,019	–25,017	–27,146	–61,774	–78,654
6. Net financing	70,263	66,368	69,433	42,369	51,311	21,954	30,019	25,017	27,146	61,774	78,654
6.1 Use of net credit and advances	47,627	32,463	6,395	11,448	4,409	–4,277	5,182	13,363	13,373	28,465	26,918
6.2 Central Bank	7,770	14,872	6,142	11,223	3,616	13,032	9,147	10,214	49,146	37,328	28,996
6.3 Increase in net financial liabilities	4,866	19,032	56,896	19,698	43,286	12,199	15,690	1,441	–35,373	–4,018	22,739

Note: Includes public enterprises. International methodology.

Source: Ministerio de Economía, *Sector Público Argentino no Financiero. Cuenta Ahorro-Inversión-Financiamiento*, Buenos Aires, Secretaría de Hacienda de la República Argentina, 2004.

Table A.28. *Nonfinancial Public Sector Revenues and Expenditures 1967–1990 (constant values in million of australs at 1974 prices)*

	1967	1968	1969	1970	1971	1972	1973	1974
1. Revenue	5,735.4	5,460.4	5,862.5	6,146.2	5,977.8	5,754.2	6,106.1	7,892.6
2. Expenditures	6,024.5	5,937.2	6,231.8	6,571.0	7,240.1	7,359.3	8,810.7	11,028.0
3. Primary surplus	−289.2	−476.8	−369.2	−424.8	−1,262.3	−1,605.1	−2,704.6	−3,135.5
4. Public debt payment	274.4	293.8	273.0	272.0	323.5	414.1	417.1	547.1
5. Surplus	−563.6	−770.6	−642.2	−696.9	−1,585.8	−2,019.1	−3,121.7	−3,682.6
6. Net financing	563.6	770.6	642.2	696.9	1,585.8	2,019.1	3,121.7	3,682.6

	1975	1976	1977	1978	1979	1980	1981	1982
1. Revenue	6,139.3	6,509.1	7,504.0	7,576.1	7,477.6	8,198.6	7,292.7	6,995.7
2. Expenditures	12,858.6	11,182.6	8,978.6	9,173.0	9,335.5	10,250.6	9,800.2	9,243.0
3. Primary surplus	−6,719.3	−4,673.5	−1,474.6	−1,597.0	−1,858.0	−2,052.0	−2,507.5	−2,247.3
4. Public debt payment	622.0	981.2	983.9	1,357.1	1,439.2	1,547.7	3,134.6	4,571.8
5. Surplus	−7,341.3	−5,654.7	−2,458.5	−2,954.0	−3,297.2	−3,599.7	−5,642.2	−6,819.1
6. Net financing	7,341.3	5,654.7	2,458.5	2,954.0	3,126.9	3,599.7	5,642.2	6,819.1

	1983	1984	1985	1986	1987	1988	1989	1990
1. Revenue	7,817.3	8,025.9	8,438.0	7,978.1	7,479.8	6,789.4	6,286.8	5,613.3
2. Expenditures	12,414.9	10,838.2	8,483.7	8,258.4	9,216.8	9,268.8	7,977.3	6,403.5
3. Primary surplus	−4,597.7	−2,812.3	−45.7	−280.2	−1,737.0	−2,479.4	−1,690.5	−790.1
4. Public debt payment	2,695.1	2,451.8	2,601.5	1,805.7	1,706.8	1,609.5	2,220.1	779.7
5. Surplus	−7,292.8	−5,264.1	−2,647.3	−2,085.9	−3,443.8	−4,088.9	−3,910.6	−1,569.8
6. Net Financing	7,292.8	5,264.1	2,647.3	2,085.9	3,443.8	4,088.9	3,910.6	1,569.8

Note: In this and the remaining tables that contain tax information, revenue, and contributions to the Federal Government from the provinces have not been included. The austral was the currency in effect starting June 1985. However, federal entities publish data from previous years in this currency in order to establish comparisons to other periods, as long as the monetary unit is constant.

Source: Ministerio de Economía, *Sector Público Argentino no Financiero. Cuenta Ahorro-Inversión-Financiamiento*, Buenos Aires, Secretaría de Hacienda de la República Argentina, 2004.

Table A.29. *National Government Revenues and Expenditures, 1990–2000 (in millions of current pesos)*

	1990	1991	1992	1993	1994	1995	1996	1997	1998	1999	2000
I. Total revenue	7,159	20,192	27,833	38,539	39,006	37,815	35,882	40,944	41,216	40,388	43,189
1. Current revenue	7,159	20,192	27,833	35,669	38,264	36,188	35,482	40,205	40,905	40,170	42,768
Operating revenue				391	397	324	146	153	204	201	188
Social security contributions	3,121	8,970	13,169	13,255	14,015	12,533	10,630	10,901	10,566	9,655	9,438
Net tax revenue	3,335	9,060	12,574	19,012	20,992	20,849	22,239	25,846	26,867	25,733	27,348
Transfers				6	53	68	76	90	202	262	1,341
Other revenues	703	2,163	2,090	2,130	1,871	1,408	1,303	1,796	2,032	3,320	3,455
2. Capital revenue				2,870	742	1,627	400	739	311	219	421
II. Total expenditures	7,454	20,196	26,565	37,683	41,220	42,677	43,617	45,155	46,463	48,874	49,238
1. Current expenditures	6,945	20,122	26,446	34,131	37,903	39,174	39,725	41,238	42,520	45,028	46,250
Consmption expenditures	2,213	6,711	7,102	7,869	9,105	9,655	9,444	9,423	9,334	9,470	9,241
Personnel	1,711	5,121	5,358	5,700	6,557	7,156	7,206	6,968	6,777	7,145	7,202
Goods and services	502	1,589	1,743	2,169	2,548	2,499	2,239	2,454	2,556	2,325	2,039
Social security benefits				14,174	16,572	15,934	17,023	17,306	17,344	17,355	17,498
Interest on public debt	616	2,240	2,622	2,570	3,194	4,228	4,160	5,655	6,631	8,176	9,647
Transfers	4,116	11,171	16,723	9,505	9,026	9,341	9,039	8,831	9,205	9,732	9,545
Other		0	0	12	6	15	58	22	7	294	320
2. Capital expenditures	509	74	119	3,552	3,317	3,503	3,892	3,917	3,942	3,847	2,988
Real investment	166	378	526	935	1,033	634	634	743	855	666	424
Financial investment	171	-452	-707	725	263	159	260	185	122	818	36
Capital transfers	171	149	300	1,892	2,021	2,710	2,998	2,990	2,965	2,362	2,529
Current account balance (I.1–II.1)	214	70	1,386	1,538	361	-2,986	-4,243	-1,033	-1,615	-4,858	-3,482
Primary balance	322	2,236	3,890	3,426	980	-634	-3,574	1,444	1,384	-309	3,598
Global balance (I–II)	-245	37	1,307	855	-2,214	-4,862	-7,735	-4,212	-5,247	-8,486	-6,049

Note: Savings – Investment account – adjusted base.
Source: Ministry of Economy.

Table A.30. *Evolution of Debt (in millions of pesos)*

Year	Domestic Debt	External Debt	Total Debt
1900	135	900	1,035
1901	131	898	1,029
1902	126	901	1,027
1903	115	855	970
1904	127	843	970
1905	126	748	874
1906	126	737	863
1907	224	727	951
1908	191	716	907
1909	314	709	1,023
1910	332	697	1,029
1911	505	690	1,196
1912	531	676	1,208
1913	536	701	1,237
1914	531	714	1,246
1915	525	714	1,239
1916	557	683	1,240
1917	670	649	1,319
1918	649	611	1,260
1919	649	611	1,260
1920	706	647	1,353
1921	866	761	1,627
1922	843	630	1,474
1923	886	664	1,550
1924	944	849	1,793
1925	927	878	1,806
1926	976	927	1,903
1927	1,062	1,132	2,195
1928	1,155	1,110	2,265
1929	1,224	1,071	2,295
1930	1,230	1,037	2,267
1931	1,406	996	2,403
1932	1,912	946	2,858
1933	1,823	1,218	3,041
1934	1,812	1,237	3,049
1935	2,242	1,162	3,404
1936	2,260	1,224	3,484
1937	2,843	934	3,777
1938	3,041	1,003	4,044
1939	3,292	1,141	4,433
1940	3,446	1,114	4,560
1941	3,948	1,063	5,011

Year	Domestic Debt	External Debt	Total Debt
1942	4,219	1,013	5,232
1943	4,690	929	5,619
1944	5,758	567	6,325
1945	6,535	520	7,055
1946	8,580	114	8,694
1947	9,623	102	9,725
1948	11,563	67	11,630
1949	13,440	54	13,494
1950	16,458	41	16,499
1951	20,291	27	20,318
1952	24,622	13	24,634
1953	32,797	0	32,797
1954	40,360	0	40,360

Source: Treasury Yearbook, several years.

Table A.31. *Debt, 1913–1931 (in millions of gold pesos; changes are absolute)*

Year	Consolidated Debt	Floating Debt	Total Debt
1913	544.7	41.4	586.1
1914	545.0	112.8	657.8
1915	537.6	185.9	723.5
1916	546.7	227.0	773.7
1917	595.4	276.1	871.5
1918	578.2	313.0	891.2
1919	565.5	323.2	888.7
1920	553.3	300.2	853.5
1921	562.2	327.9	890.1
1922	569.7	392.8	962.5
1923	578.9	384.8	963.7
1924	670.4	328.6	999.0
1925	768.1	213.5	981.6
1926	812.2	288.4[a]	1,100.6[a]
1927	948.4	220.1[a]	1,168.5[a]
1928	998.0	253.3	1,251.3
1929	1,010.2	380.9	1,391.1
1930	995.6	522.1	1,517.7
1931	1,055.9	543.1	1,599.0

[a] Estimates.

Source: Harold Peters, *The Foreign Debt of the Argentina Republic*, Baltimore, MD, The Johns Hopkins University Press, 1934.

Table A.32. *Consolidated and Floating Public Debt, 1928–1940 (in millions of pesos)*

Year	Consolidated Debt						Floating Debt	Total Public Debt in Circulation
	Domestic	External	Issued by December 31	To the Exchange Board	Treasury Bonds	In Circulation on December 31	Floating Debt	Total Public Debt in Circulation
1928	1,156.4	1,111.8	2,268.2	–	16.4	2,251.8	623.7	2,875.5
1929	1,224.5	1,071.4	2,295.9	–	87.8	2,208.1	827.8	3,035.9
1930	1,227.9	1,034.9	2,262.8	–	48.8	2,214.0	1,181.4	3,395.4
1931	1,259.8	1,138.3	2,398.1	–	167.4	2,230.7	1,341.8	3,572.5
1932	1,500.3	1,057.4	2,557.7	166.5	167.1	2,557.1	1,009.2	3,566.3
1933	1,534.5	1,325.9	2,860.4	153.4	265.1	2,748.7	888.4	3,637.1
1934	1,574.9	1,300.3	2,875.2	145.3	185.4	2,835.1	872.4	3,707.5
1935	2,242.7	1,248.9	3,491.6	–	142.0	3,349.6	110.7	3,460.3
1936	2,656.0	1,224.0	3,880.0	–	272.7	3,607.3	77.2	3,684.5
1937	2,816.6	932.5	3,749.1	–	6.2	3,742.9	172.2	3,915.1
1938	2,990.2	993.7	3,983.9	–	132.9	3,851.0	427.5	4,278.5
1939	3,292.1	1,153.3	4,445.4	–	46.8	4,398.6	391.5	4,790.1
1940	3,445.7	114.2	4,559.9	–	49.5	4,510.4	687.2	5,197.6

Source: Anuario Geográfico Argentino, Comité Nacional de Geografía, Buenos Aires 1941, p. 409.

Table A.33. *National Government Financial Balance Sheet (in millions of pesos)*

Year	To Cover by Cash Resources			To Cover by Bonds			Total Difference
	Expenditures	Resources	Difference	Expendit	Resources	Difference	Total Difference
1928	738.6	738.6	0	180.3	177.6	−2.7	−2.7
1929	795	747.6	−47.4	193.2	25.7	−167.5	−214.9
1930	905.6	663.3	−242.3	186.2	71.5	−114.7	−357
1931	813.9	685.7	−128.2	94.6	91.4	−3.2	−131.4
1932	783.8	742.4	−41.4	66.1	66.1	0	−41.4
1933	777.3	753.7	−23.6	103.1	103.1	0	−23.6
1934	773.9	764.4	−9.5	160.3	160.3	0	−9.5
1935	821.9	846.8	24.9	159	159	0	24.9
1936	872.2	872.8	0.6	179.6	179.6	0	0.6
1937	977.8	991.3	13.5	243.3	243.3	0	13.5
1938	1,007.8	991.4	−16.4	270.4	90.7	−179.7	−196.1
1939	1,075.5	1,015	−60.5	384.9	384.9	0	−60.5
1940	1,133.9	963.8	−170.1	182.7	182.7	0	−170.1

Source: Anuario Geográfico Argentino, Comité Nacional de Geografía, Buenos Aires, 1941, p. 406.

6. Money and Banking

Table A.34. *Monetary Indicators, 1880–1900 (in millions of pesos)*

Year	Money Supply	Total Deposits	Currency (in hands of the public)
1880	74.23	31.06	43.17
1881	82.70	48.77	33.93
1882	86.46	53.82	32.64
1883	125.97	75.71	50.26
1884	153.71	95.51	58.20
1885	187.60	116.91	70.69
1886	210.30	130.00	80.30
1887	280.00	144.90	135.10
1888	403.07	231.07	172.00
1889	576.55	312.55	264.00
1890	570.09	304.09	266.00
1891	519.66	258.66	261.00
1892	409.88	127.88	282.00
1893	429.94	122.94	307.00
1894	421.18	123.18	298.00
1895	452.47	156.47	296.00
1896	440.95	145.95	295.00
1897	432.48	139.48	293.00
1898	446.46	154.46	292.00
1899	463.93	172.93	291.00

Source: Roberto Cortés Conde, *Estadísticas Monetarias y Fiscales Argentinas: 1810–1914*, Mimeograph, 1995.

Table A.35. *Currency Board Primary Items and Other Monetary Indicators, 1900–1914 (in millions of pesos)*

	1900	1901	1902	1903	1904	1905	1906	1907	1908	1909	1910	1911	1912	1913	1914
Gold inventory		0.6	0.6	87.4	114.8	205.2	233.8	239.2	288.2	392.2	422.8	429.7	506.5	529.9	510.0
Currency	295.2	295.2	296.0	380.2	407.7	498.2	526.7	532.2	581.3	685.4	716.0	722.9	799.8	823.3	803.3
Previous issues	295.2	295.2	296.0	293.3	293.3	293.3	293.3	293.3	293.3	293.3	293.3	293.3	293.3	293.3	293.3
Conversion															
Law 3871	–	–	–	86.9	114.4	204.9	233.5	238.9	288.0	392.1	422.7	429.7	506.5	530.0	503.9
Law 9480	–	–	–	–	–	–	–	–	–	–	–	–	–	–	6.1
Total deposits	392.6	391.6	407.3	504.0	585.0	720.0	755.0	778.5	875.8	1,157.0	1,331.0	1,374.0	1,480.0	1,411.0	1,189.0
Ratio reserves/															
currency				0.23	0.28	0.41	0.44	0.45	0.50	0.57	0.59	0.59	0.63	0.64	0.63
Monetary															
aggregate (M_3)	688	687	703	884	993	1,218	1,282	1,311	1,457	1,842	2,048	2,098	2,281	2,234	1,993

Source: Pedro J. Baiocco, "La Economía Bancaria Argentina a través de sus Índices más Representativos en el Período 1901–1935," Universidad de Buenos Aires, 1937.

Table A.36. *Central Bank Assets and Liabilities (in millions of current pesos)*

Assets

Year	1935	1936	1937	1938	1939	1940	1941	1942	1943	1944	1945	1946
Gold and foreign exchange	1,354	1,528	1,417	1,296	1,396	1,329	1,542	2,096	3,200	3,828	4,673	5,807
Public bonds	354	537	558	595	560	592	571	619	988	964	950	1,311
Rediscounts	–	–	–	–	–	–	–	–	–	–	–	3,719
Other	22	22	332	405	544	939	28	56	55	72	70	5,820
TOTAL	1,730	2,087	2,307	2,295	2,500	2,860	2,141	2,771	4,243	4,864	5,694	16,658

Year	1947	1948	1949	1950	1951	1952	1953	1954	1955	1956	1957	1958
Gold and foreign exchange	3,686	2,795	2,539	3,347	2,992	2,612	3,855	3,968	3,409	4,318	5,996	3,225
Public bonds	1,301	1,786	1,770	2,028	2,077	2,127	3,907	4,177	5,145	5,379	3,823	5,527
Rediscounts	8,639	13,896	17,774	20,573	26,474	31,513	36,817	44,341	51,512	94,019	4,406	1,434
Other	6,840	7,695	10,287	12,457	15,839	17,560	21,028	25,192	33,655	10,971	129,449	180,170
TOTAL	20,466	26,172	32,370	38,405	47,382	53,812	65,607	77,678	93,722	114,686	143,674	190,356

Liabilities

Year	1935	1936	1937	1938	1939	1940	1941	1942	1943	1944	1945	1946
Currency	982	1,094	1,150	1,118	1,191	1,224	1,380	1,627	1,886	2,354	2,830	4,065
Bank accounts	482	426	355	321	428	437	561	764	1,116	1,402	1,765	286
Deposits	–											11,075
Other	266	567	802	857	881	1,199	201	380	1,242	1,109	1,099	1,232
TOTAL	1,730	2,087	2,307	2,295	2,500	2,860	2,141	2,771	4,243	4,864	5,694	16,658

Year	1947	1948	1949	1950	1951	1952	1953	1954	1955	1956	1957	1958
Currency	5,346	6,686	8,939	11,874	15,371	18,217	22,103	26,838	31,859	36,165	50,449	71,352
Bank accounts	427	1,008	1,188	1,410	2,333	3,053	4,393	4,751	5,607	6,657	13,206	14,512
Deposits	12,850	16,334	19,604	22,133	25,232	27,276	34,304	40,260	46,714	61,528	53,932	65,719
Other	1,843	2,145	2,638	2,988	4,447	5,266	4,808	5,830	9,541	10,356	26,087	38,773
TOTAL	20,466	26,172	32,370	38,405	47,382	53,812	65,607	77,678	93,722	114,686	143,674	190,356

Source: BCRA Yearbooks and Balance Sheets, several years.

Statistical Appendix

Table A.37. *Central Bank Assets (in millions of pesos)*

Year	Gold and Foreign Exchange	Government Bonds	Rediscounts and Other Private Sector Loans
1946	5,807	1,311	3,720
1947	3,686	1,301	8,639
1948	2,795	1,786	13,896
1949	2,539	1,770	17,774
1950	3,347	2,028	20,573
1951	2,992	2,077	26,474
1952	2,612	2,127	31,513
1953	3,855	3,907	36,817
1954	3,968	4,177	44,341
1955	3,409	5,145	51,512

Note: Under rediscounts and other loans to banks the following are included: operations-bank accounts, collateral bank loans, bank loans with various guarantees, rediscounts and advances on current debt accounts and advances on mortgage loans.
Source: BCRA Yearbook, 1946–1955.

Table A.38. *Money Supply Determinants (in millions of pesos)*

	1945	1946	1947	1948	1949	1950	1951	1952	1953	1954	1955
Central Bank											
Gold and foreign exchange	4,673	5,807	3,686	2,795	2,539	3,347	2,992	2,612	3,855	3,968	3,409
Government	951	1,311	1,301	1,786	1,770	2,028	2,077	2,127	3,907	4,177	5,145
Rediscounts	–	9,551	15,491	21,641	28,061	33,030	42,313	49,073	57,845	69,533	85,167
Sterlization (bonds and mortgage loans)	–	384	364	314	356	441	390	366	507	746	880
Financial system											
Deposits (private)	8,386	10,404	11,623	14,140	17,330	19,898	21,926	23,774	29,705	33,781	38,783
Currency (in public hands)	2,580	3,582	4,772	6,737	9,066	11,912	15,363	18,258	22,065	26,744	31,826
Money supply	10,966	13,986	16,395	20,877	26,396	31,810	37,289	42,033	51,770	60,525	70,608

Note: Under rediscounts and other loans to banks the following are included: operations-bank accounts, collateral bank loans, bank loans with various guarantees, rediscounts and advances on current debt accounts, and advances on mortgage loans. The same is true throughout the chapter. These pertain to accounts from Central Bank Assets.
Source: BCRA Yearbooks and Statistical Bulletins, 1946–1949.

Table A.39. *Money Supply Determinants (in millions of 1945 pesos)*

	1945	1946	1947	1948	1949	1950	1951	1952	1953	1954	1955
Central Bank											
Gold and foreign exchange	4,673	4,936	2,758	1,850	1,282	1,346	880	554	786	780	597
Government	951	1,114	974	1,182	894	815	611	451	797	821	900
Rediscounts	–	8,119	11,593	14,321	14,168	13,282	12,450	10,408	11,800	13,666	14,902
Sterlization (bonds and mortgage loans)	–	326	272	208	180	177	115	78	103	147	154
Financial system											
Deposits (private)	8,386	8,844	8,698	9,357	8,750	8,002	6,451	5,042	6,060	6,639	6,786
Currency (in public hands)	2,580	3,043	3,571	4,425	4,578	4,790	4,520	3,872	4,501	5,256	5,569
Money supply	10,966	11,639	11,987	13,530	13,328	12,792	10,972	8,915	10,561	11,895	12,355

Source: BCRA Yearbooks and Statistical Bulletins, 1946–1949.

Table A.40. *Money Supply Determinants (as a percentage of the money supply)*

	1945	1946	1947	1948	1949	1950	1951	1952	1953	1954	1955
Central Bank											
Gold and foreign exchange	42.6	42.4	23.0	13.7	9.6	10.5	8.0	6.2	7.4	6.6	4.8
Government	8.7	9.6	8.1	8.7	6.7	6.4	5.6	5.1	7.5	6.9	7.3
Rediscounts	–	68.3	94.5	103.7	106.3	103.8	113.5	116.7	111.7	114.9	120.6
Sterlization (bonds and mortgage loans)	–	2.8	2.3	1.5	1.3	1.4	1.0	0.9	1.0	1.2	1.2
Financial system											
Deposits (private)	76.5	76.0	72.6	69.2	65.7	62.6	58.8	56.6	57.4	55.8	54.9
Currency (in public hands)	23.5	26.1	29.8	32.7	34.3	37.4	41.2	43.4	42.6	44.2	45.1
Money supply	100	100	100	100	100	100	100	100	100	100	100

Source: BCRA Yearbooks and Statistical Bulletins, 1946–1949.

Table A.41. *Money Supply Determinants: BCRA Balance Sheet (in millions of 1945 pesos)*

	1946	1947	1948	1949	1950	1951	1952	1953	1954	1955
Assets										
External sector (net)	4,800	2,728	1,605	1,009	1,081	549	230	629	592	240
Government sector (net)	610	−134	1,182	894	816	611	451	797	821	900
Rediscounts to banks	3,162	6,465	9,196	8,974	8,273	7,789	6,684	7,510	8,715	9,014
Other advances and loans to banks	4,958	5,128	5,125	5,194	5,009	4,660	3,724	4,290	4,951	5,859
TOTAL	14,388	15,705	17,396	16,418	15,513	13,985	11,435	13,424	15,292	16,421
Liabilities										
Notes and coins	3,502	4,040	5,125	5,183	5,357	5,214	4,514	5,407	6,210	6,557
In public hands	3,045	3,571	4,458	4,578	4,790	4,520	3,872	4,501	5,256	5,569
In banks	458	469	667	567	693	642	906	954	989	
Deposits by order and account of the BCRA	9,414	9,417	10,809	9,898	8,900	7,424	5,785	6,998	7,913	8,174
TOTAL	14,383	15,705	17,396	16,418	15,513	13,985	11,435	13,424	15,292	16,421

Note: Because partial data do not cover all items, the totals for these differ from the overall totals.
Source: BCRA Yearbooks and Statistical Bulletins, 1946–1955.

Table A.42. *Money Supply Determinants and Monetary Aggregates, 1957–1963 (values in millions of pesos at 1970 prices)*

Year	1957	1958	1959	1960	1961	1962	1963
BCRA assets							
External sector (net)	−40,342	−94,641	−48,955	46,470	−35,198	−139,191	−36,375
Government sector (net)	848,752	1,007,164	734,582	662,138	620,317	570,505	591,701
Financial sector	885,823	759,933	375,882	299,200	285,280	241,149	227,172
TOTAL	1,960,275	1,861,022	1,341,778	1,335,778	1,163,558	1,007,100	1,046,486
BCRA liabilities							
Notes and coins	1,233,699	1,326,011	867,138	876,465	842,698	732,022	747,173
In public hands	1,022,505	1,120,214	734,120	723,613	734,868	648,213	634,970
In banks	211,194	205,797	133,019	152,852	107,831	83,808	112,203
Deposits from banks in BCRA	245,070	247,226	172,888	116,582	36,450	25,165	68,507
TOTAL	1,960,275	1,861,022	1,341,743	1,335,778	1,163,558	1,007,100	1,046,486
Monetary base	1,478,775	1,573,236	1,040,027	991,909	878,318	756,554	815,679
Monetary supply	2,351,297	2,582,925	1,624,490	1,637,871	1,691,096	1,458,480	1,541,974

Table A.43. *Primary Items on the BCRA Balance Sheet 1973–1976 (from assets and liabilities)*

1974 Australs	1973	1974	1975	1976
Assets				
External sector (net)	823	671	−148	137
Government sector (net)	3,694	5,552	6,694	5,719
Rediscounts to banks	7,232	11,070	9,135	5,966
Bank accounts – operations	2,327	2,903	4,094	4,176
Other advances and loans to banks	1,887	0	0	0
TOTAL	16,738	21,763	21,546	19,555
Liabilities				
Notes and coins	4,024	5,293	5,719	3,664
In public hands	3,280	4,313	4,379	2,676
In banks	744	981	1,340	988
Deposits by order and account of BCRA	10,072	13,321	11,254	9,763
TOTAL	16,738	21,763	21,546	19,555

Note: Because partial data do not cover all items, the totals for these differ from the overall totals.

Note: For the 1974–1976 period, advances and loans to banks are included under the heading "Rediscounts to banks."

Source: BCRA Yearbooks, 1973–1976, and BCRA Statistical Bulletins, 1975 and 1979.

Table A.44. *Monetary Indicators, 1983–1988 (in millions of australs at 1986 prices)*

	1983	1984	1985	1986	1987	1988
Central Bank (BCRA) Assets						
Gold and foreign exchange (net bonds)	3,964	−64	−3,729	−3,597	−9,282	−138
Rediscounts to financial sector[a]	14,869	13,949	8,652	13,097	19,294	22,330
Monetary regulation account	3,127	6,221	4,339	5,489	7,701	10,404
BCRA Monetary Liabilities						
Total notes	7,055	6,910	5,681	5,246	5,161	5,582
Monetary base	11,133	15,537	9,797	6,943	5,844	6,831
Broad monetary base	21,542	15,782	13,462	11,956	12,083	16,701
Financial Sector Liabilities						
Total Bank deposits	20,777	18,933	17,026	17,531	19,392	23,941
Deposits in public hands	17,065	16,160	12,449	13,639	16,597	20,733
Current accounts	2,518	1,782	1,885	1,598	1,429	1,156
Savings banks	3,290	3,526	2,807	2,562	2,640	2,312
Fixed term	9,900	7,610	5,956	8,079	9,944	14,411

[a] Includes resources accrued from credits to the financial system.

Source: BCRA Statistical Bulletins, 1983–1985.

Table A.45. *BCRA Balance Sheet, 1983–1988 (in millions of constant australs at 1986 prices)*

	1983	1984	1985	1986	1987	1988
1. Assets	42,942	32,669	30,166	32,455	43,220	46,088
1.1 External sector (net)	3,964	−64	−3,729	−3,597	−9,282	−138
1.1.0 External sector (gross)	8,630	3,597	5,682	4,046	2,304	4,570
1.1.1 Gold and foreign exchange	8,630	3,597	5,682	4,046	2,304	4,570
1.2 Government (net)	9,696	11,106	13,339	12,918	20,374	17,502
1.2.0 Government (gross)	19,132	12,801	13,823	13,019	21,255	17,599
1.2.1 Consolidated public treasury bonds	13,852	3,288	2,602	1,357	581	130
1.2.2 Public bonds	0	2,431	0	0	0	1,694
1.2.3 Advances	760	353	4,146	4,571	12,070	4,188
1.2.4 Others (2)	1,356	441	2,713	1,602	902	486
1.2.5 Resources accrued on government debt	37	67	22	1	0	697
1.2.6 Monetary regulation account	3,127	6,221	4,339	5,489	7,701	10,404
1.3 Financial sector (gross)	14,869	13,949	8,652	13,097	19,294	22,330
1.3.1 Rediscounts and loans	6,661	3,356	4,076	3,603	4,318	2,588
1.3.2 Resources accrued on debt to banks	8,208	10,593	45,760	9,494	14,976	19,742
1.4 Other items	310	2,323	2,010	2,293	367	1,588
2. Liabilities	42,942	32,669	30,164	32,455	43,220	46,088
2.1 Notes	7,055	6,910	5,681	5,246	5,161	5,582
2.2 Commercial bank deposits in BCRA current account	4,078	8,627	4,116	1,697	682	1,249
2.3 Deposits by order and account of BCRA	0	0	0	0	0	227
2.4 Deposits and debt to government	9,436	1,694	484	101	881	97
2.5 BCRA debt to the financial system	10,416	5,680	6,713	8,103	8,988	12,140
2.5.1 Other deposits in current accounts	7	20	10	10	234	33
2.5.2 Debts to the financial system	0	238	116	115	58	43
2.5.3 Mortgage debt and bonds	0	0	0	0	0	82
2.5.4 Deposits in special accounts	10,409	245	3,664	5,013	6,239	9,870
2.5.5 Accrued compensation on minimum required cash reserves	0	5,177	2,922	2,965	2,457	2,112
2.6 External sector	4,666	3,662	9,411	7,643	11,586	4,708
2.6.1 IMF, IBRD, and other international organizations	1,764	2,462	2,556	2,661	2,745	2,660
2.6.2 Other debt in foreign currency	2,742	863	6,749	4,888	3,007	1,991
2.6.3 Payment agreements	160	337	107	93	296	57
2.6.4 From exchange operations	0	0	0	0	5,538	0
2.7 Other accounts under liabilities	6,508	3,410	3,471	9,222	11,891	18,668
2.8 Profit and loss	704	2,626	113	350	3,915	2,949
2.9 Capital and reserves	79	60	177	93	115	468

Note: The heading under liabilities "Public government debt," in 1983, includes funds from exchange operations.

Source: BCRA Yearbooks, 1983–1988.

Table A.46. *Central Bank Balance Sheet, 1985–1988 (in millions of australs at 1986 prices)*

Year	1985	1986	1987	1988
Assets				
External sector (net)	−3,729	−3,597	−9,282	−138
Government sector (net)	9,000	7,429	12,673	17,599
Financial sector	8,652	13,097	19,294	22,330
Monetary regulation account	4,339	5,489	7,701	10,404
TOTAL	30,166	32,455	43,220	46,088
Liabilities				
Notes and coins	5,681	5,246	5,161	5,582
In public hands	3,844	3,990	4,004	4,214
Under bank control	1,836	1,256	1,158	1,367
Bank deposits in BCRA	4,116	1,697	682	1,249
Special accounts	3,664	5,013	6,239	11,982
BCRA debts and titles	116	115	58	125
TOTAL	30,166	32,455	43,220	46,088

Note: Because not all categories of assets and liabilities are included, the amounts of those totals differ from overall totals.

Source: BCRA Yearbooks and Statistical Bulletins, 1985–1988.

Table A.47. *Monetary Indicators (in thousands of pesos, reserves in thousands of dollars)*

Year	International Reserves	Currency Circulation	Monetary Base
1990	6,170	3,037	3,617
1991	9,377	6,605	7,565
1992	12,585	9,648	11,011
1993	18,227	12,173	14,989
1994	18,813	13,317	16,070
1995	16,752	13,050	13,050
1996	17,740	14,030	14,030
1997	18,463	15,966	15,966
1998	19,656	16,370	16,370
1999	19,146	16,493	16,493
2000	18,792	15,054	15,054

Source: BCRA data.

Table A.48. *Financial Sector Indicators (in thousands of pesos)*

Year	Deposits	Loans	Real Active Rate
1990	6,064	7,213	−75.23
1991	15,785	19,757	−34.32
1992	26,430	31,062	−5.72
1993	40,683	40,395	−0.28
1994	47,180	52,275	5.65
1995	44,759	52,388	14.00
1996	54,685	57,592	10.34
1997	70,547	66,935	8.67
1998	78,787	76,406	9.67
1999	80,996	77,241	12.31
2000	85,755	76,986	12.14

Source: BCRA data.

Appendix of Tables by Chapter

Chapter 2

Table A.C.2.1. *U.S. Tariffs (examples of goods imported from Argentina)*

	1913 Law	1922 Law	1930 Law
Linseed oil	20 cent. per bu.	40 cent. per bu.	65 cent. per bu.
Meat	Free	20%	6 cent. lb. But no less than 20%
Corn	Free	15 cent per bu.	25 cent. per bu.
Fowl	Free	6 cent. lb.	10 cent. lb.

Note: lb. = libra., bu. = bushel., cent. = centavos.
Source: Vernon Lovell Phelps, *The International Economic Position of Argentina*, Philadelphia, University of Pennsylvania Press, London, H. Milford, Oxford University Press, 1938.

Table A.C.2.2. *Argentine Balance of Payments (in millions of gold pesos)*

	1900–1914		1915–1920		1921–1929		1930–1931	
	Debit	Credit	Debit	Credit	Debit	Credit	Debit	Credit
1. Current account								
a) Merchandise								
Exports		4,280		4,515		7,815		1,267
Imports	4,050		2,915		7,000		1,325	
Net balance of trade		770		1,600		815		58
b) Services								
Travel expenditures	375	50	75	15	186	63	45	22
Interests and dividends	1,650		890	16	1,488	19	344	1
Immigrant remittances	450		150		310		50	
Miscellaneous services	250	50						
Total services	2,725	100	1,084		1,902		416	
Net balance current account	−1,855	516	−1,087	−474				
2. Capital account								
Net balance of permanent capital flow (including immig. remitt)		2,212	284			1,098		195
3. Gold flows								
Net imports	295		220			45		235
Remainder/balance	62		48			56		44
Total (debit and credit columns)	7,232	7,232	4,546	4,546	9,040	9,040	1,764	1,764

Note: Until 1930, the relationship gold peso to U.S. dollar was approximately 1.03$ = U.S.$1.

Source: Walter Beveraggi Allende, *El Servicio del Capital Extranjero y el Control de Cambios: la Experiencia Argentina de 1900 a 1943*, México, FCE, 1954.

Table A.C.2.3. *Wheat Prices*

Years	Price in Pesos per 100 kg
1923/1924	12.8
1924/1925	14.31
1925/1926	12.2
1926/1927	11.31
1927/1928	10.5
1928/1929	9.68
1929/1930	8.79
1930/1931	5.56

Source: Anuario Geográfico Argentino, Comité Nacional de Geografía, Buenos Aires, 1941, p. 207.

Table A.C.2.4. *Nominal Wages, Real Wages, and Prices, 1914–1923*

	In Current Pesos			In Pesos, at 1914 Prices	
Year	Men	Women	Cost of Living (N.I. Base: 1914 = 100)	Men	Women
1914	3.81	2.38	100	3.81	2.38
1915	3.64	2.28	107	3.4	2.13
1916	3.64	2.28	115	3.17	1.98
1917	3.7	2.26	135	2.74	1.67
1918	4.02	2.17	169	2.38	1.28
1919	5.06	2.12	160	3.16	1.33
1920	6.16	3.11	186	3.31	1.67
1921	6.75	3.42	166	4.07	2.06
1922	6.5	4.03	139	4.68	2.9
1923	6.5	4.03	136	4.78	2.96

Note: The cost of living is the average of the indices of the cost of food (meat, bread, etc.), housing, clothing, and other living expenses.
Source: Revista de Economía Argentina, Year 7, 77 (Nov. 1924), pp. 343 and 345, and "Costo del Nivel de Vida en la Capital Federal." Survey carried out in 1960 on the living conditions of working-class families. Dirección Nacional de Estadísticas y Censos (Argentine Census Bureau), March 1968.

Table A.C.2.5. *Net Monthly Gold Flows Argentina (in millions of gold pesos)*

	1913			1914			1915		
Month	At the Currency Board	In Banks	In the Country	At the Currency Board	In Banks	In the Country	At the Currency Board	In Banks	In the Country
January	1,135	−2,566	−1,431	−4,027	0.133	−3,894	16,490	−11,781	4,709
February	16,570	−1,971	14,599	0.215	−1,407	−1,192	18,302	0.502	18,804
March	17,185	1,691	18,876	2,272	9,004	11,276	22,776	−2,188	20,588
April	4,249	4,038	8,387	0.196	1,393	1,589	11,918	−0.323	11,595
May	1,480	−2,760	−1,280	−11,382	0.744	−10,638	4,712	−0.887	3,825
June	3,040	−0.399	2,641	−7,481	2,815	−4,666	6,170	−1,206	4,964
July	−7,004	−9,290	−16,294	−16,851	−5,158	−22,009	0.035	−0.910	−0.875
August	−3,682	−4,311	−7,993	25,522	−29.02	−3,498	0.184	−2,768	−2,584
September	−3,523	1,194	−2,329	0.005	0.467	0.472	0.170	−0.729	−0.559
October	−10.22	−1,636	−11,856	0.003	−0.166	−0.163	0.126	−0.035	0.091
November	−2,678	−0.765	−3,443	0.007	0.386	0.393	0.134	−0.485	−0.351
December	−6,230	1,946	−4,284	2,729	12,526	15,255	0.214	−0.886	−0.672
For the year	10,322	−14,829	−4,507	−8,792	−9,056	−17,848	81,231	−21,696	59,535

Source: Pedro Baiocco, *La Economía Bancaria Argentina a través de sus Índices más Significativos en el Período 1901–1935*, Universidad de Buenos Aires, Facultad de Ciencias Económicas, Instituto de Economía Bancaria, Buenos Aires, 1937, p. 50.

Table A.C.2.6. *Interest Rates*

Year	1919	1920	1921	1922	1923	1924	1925	1926	1927	1928	1929	1930
Interest rate	7.2	7.8	7.7	7.7	6.5	6.5	7.4	6.9	6.9	6.3	6.9	6.9
Real rate	4.5	4.1	4.6	5.5	4.7	4.6	5.4	5.2	5.3	4.8	5.2	5.2
International rate	4.6	5.3	5.2	4.4	4.3	4.4	4.4	4.6	4.6	4.5	4.6	4.5

Source: Roberto Cortés Conde, "Vicissitudes of an exporting economy," in *An Economic History of Twentieth-Century Latin America*, Cárdenas, Enrique, Ocampo, José Antonio y Thorp, Rosemary, New York, Palgrave, 2000.

Table A.C.2.7. *Change in Nominal Terms of the Principal Monetary Items, 1917–1930 (in percenatges)*

Year	Currency	Money Supply	Bank Deposits
1917	0	11	18
1918	14	32	41
1919	2	5	6
1920	16	16	16
1921	0	−3	−4
1922	0	3	4
1923	0	0	1
1924	−3	−1	0
1925	0	0	0
1926	0	1	1
1927	4	5	6
1928	2	9	11
1929	−11	−4	−1
1930	1	1	1

Source: Pedro Baiocco, *La Economía Bancaria Argentina a través de sus Índices más Significativos en el Período 1901–1935*, Universidad de Buenos Aires, Facultad de Ciencias Económicas, Instituto de Economía Bancaria, Buenos Aires, 1937, p. 50.

Table A.C.2.8. *Debt Services and Total Services in the Balance of Payments (in millions of gold pesos)*

	1920	1921	1922	1923	1924
Debt services	145.5	115.6	157.5	169.3	165.3
Total services	201.5	161.1	201.5	218.3	202.3

	1925	1926	1927	1928	1929
Debt services	153.4	177.6	187.8	197.1	180.0
Total services	190.4	236.6	241.8	248.1	223.0

Note: Debt services refer to public and private debt.
Source: Vernon Lovell Phelps, The International Economic Position of Argentina, Philadelphia, University of Pennsylvania Press; London, H. Milford, Oxford University Press, 1938.

Table A.C.2.9. *Peso Quotations in Pounds and U.S. Dollars, 1910–1933*

Year	London (pesos per pound)	New York (pesos per dollar)
1910	11.46	23,673
1911	11.46	2,368
1912	11.45	23,661
1913	11.5	2,365
1914	11.51	23,632
1915	11.37	23,914
1916	11.23	23,557
1917	10.84	22,782
1918	10.66	2,24
1919	10.18	23,005
1920	9.25	25,411
1921	12.04	3,143
1922	12.29	27,745
1923	13.23	29,045
1924	12.85	29,223
1925	11.96	24,866
1926	11.99	24,682
1927	11.48	23,618
1928	11.48	23,589
1929	11.61	23,912
1930	13.31	27,384
1931	15.49	3,455
1932	13.71	38,864
1933	13.37	32,334

Source: Anuario Geográfico Argentino, Comité Nacional de Geografía, Buenos Aires, 1941, p. 431.

Table A.C.2.10. *U.S. Federal Reserve Discount Rate*

Year	Month	Rate (%)
1927	July	4
	September	3.5
1928	July	5
	September	5
1929	July	5
	September	6

Source: Milton Friedman and Ana Jacobson, *A Monetary History of the United Satates, 1867–1960*, Princeton, Princeton University Press, pp. 282 and 288.

Chapter 3

Table A.C.3.1. *Cost of Living Index*

Year	Cost of Living (index: 1929 = 100)
1929	100.0
1930	102.1
1931	88.7
1932	80.5
1933	91.9
1934	82.4
1935	88.3
1936	96.9
1937	100.5
1938	100.8
1939	103.4
1940	106.8
1941	110.6
1942	118.0

Source: "Costo del Nivel de Vida en la Capital Federal," Dirección Nacional de Estadísticas y Censos, Argentine Census Bureau, March 1968.

Table A.C.3.2. *Revenues and Expenditures Coming from the Spread of the Rates of Exchange (in millions of pesos)*

Source	1934	1935	1936	1937	1938	1939	1940	1941	1942	1943	1944	1945
I. Funds produced	116.215	118.044	88.425	64.850	73.027	113.911	200.888	114.614	90.164	42.854	84.349	106.739
Margin of exchange	116.215	118.043	88.262	64.123	71.682	112.314	199.1791	112.835	88.2223	39.9025	76.477	98.251
Advance interests wine producers	0	0.001	0.163	0.584	1.081	1.264	1.3433	1.3227	1.1459	0.459	1.261	0.442
Interests confirmed by correspondants	0	0		0.062	0.133	0.0608	0.01334	0.2809	0.6644	1.9622	5.636	6.848
Other interests	0	0		0.081	0.131	0.2722	0.3527	0.1748	0.1315	0.5299	0.975	1.199
II. Expenditures	35.231	64.302	34.438	135.282	22.502	69.184	56.852	69.900	212.968	91.457	199.007	164.651
(a) Exchange differences	24.265	58.637	32.287	122.331	19.635	21.867	20.167	18.659	18.871	18.486	42.537	17.905
Public debt	22.799	34.947	27.31	118.458	16.782	17.842	16.043	15.2463	15.3304	14.4482	38.635	10.181
Other payments abroad	1.466	23.69	4.977	3.873	2.853	4.025	4.124	3.4122	3.5405	4.038	3.902	7.724
(b) Contribution to general revenue									50	50	120,000	120,000
(c) Contribution to budget of Exchange Bureau	0.167	0.185	0.174	0.25	0.417	0.4652	0.5007	0.4862	0.5719	0.5493	0.600	0.600
(d) Administrative expenses	0.895	1.050	1.665	2.085	2.025	3.488	2.517	5.615	7.094	6.036	4.083	4.211
Agricultural Production Regulatory Commission						0.9528	0.1523	3.3514	4.7559	3.8715	2.370	2.278
National Meat Commission						0.1638						
National Dairy Commission												
National Commission of Grain Elevators						0.938	0.6916	0.6556	0.6548	0.6043		
Cotton and Special Crops Commission (1)						1.4597	1.6669	1.6032	1.6785	1.556	1.713	1934
National Dairy Commission						0.0008	0.0039	0.0044	0.0043	0.0037		
National Fuel Commission							0.002					
Commission for the Promotion of Meat Exports												
National Dairy Commission												

(e) Grain Elevator Network												
(e) Packing Port of Rosario												
(f) National Grain and Elevator Commission (func.)												
(g) Promotion expenses (2)	9.904	4.430	0.312	10.616	0.425	34.618	25.465	35.901	133.126	14.573	23.378	11.462
Agricultural Production Regulatory Commission (3)												
Losses liquidated in crop trade									32.5318	12.9476		
Interests and commissions						18.9782	0.0104	7.8785	2.3621			
National Meat Commission										0.002		
National Dairy Commission												
Dairy Regulatory Commission												
Cotton and Special Crop Commission (1)												
Commission on Meat Export Promotion												
Difference I–II	80,984	53,742	53,987	–70,432	50,525	44,727	144,037	44,713	–122,804	–48,603	–114,658	–57,912
(1) Previously National Cotton Commission												
(2) 1939–1942 not included in the investment account												
(3) Previously Grain Regulatory Commission												

Source: Elaborated by Marcela Harriague.
Primary Source: Treasury Yearbooks, several years.

Table A.C.3.3. *Ratio Reserves/Deposits,*
1931–1942 (in percentages)

Year	Reserves/Deposits	Change
1931	15	24
1932	18	25
1933	15	−18
1934	12	−20
1935	25	104
1936	21	−15
1937	18	−16
1938	17	−6
1939	20	21
1940	19	−8
1941	19	2
1942	21	10

Source: BCRA Yearbooks and Statistical Bulletins,
several years.

Table A.C.3.4. *Annual Real Change in Reserves, Deposits, and*
Monetary Base, 1936–1940

Real Annual Growth Rate	Reserves	Monetary Base	Deposits
1936	4.0	−4.1	0.8
1937	−9.3	−3.3	3.0
1938	−8.3	−3.2	−1.7
1939	6.0	9.3	1.6
1940	−6.9	−1.1	6.4

Source: BCRA Yearbooks and Statistical Bulletins, 1936–1940.

Chapter 4

Table A.C.4.1. *Oil Imports*

Year	Volume (in thousands of tons)
1945	143
1946	911
1947	1,168
1948	1,742
1949	590
1950	2,954
1951	2,818
1952	3,013
1953	3,599
1954	3,644
1955	3,714

Source: Carmen Llorens de Azar, *Argentina Evolución Económica 1915–1976,* Fundación Banco de Boston, Buenos Aires, 1977.
Primary Source: INDEC.

Table A.C.4.2 *Consumer Prices and U.S. Dollar Quotations, 1940–1955*

Year	CPI 1940 = 100	Value of U.S. Dollar in Pesos			
		Free	Official Basic	Free/Official	Parallel
1940	100.0	4.37	4.23	1.03	n/d
1941	102.6	4.24	4.23	1.00	n/d
1942	108.5	4.23	4.23	1.00	n/d
1943	109.6	4.06	4.23	0.96	n/d
1944	109.6	4.02	4.23	0.95	n/d
1945	134.3	4.04	4.23	0.96	n/d
1946	159.5	4.09	4.23	0.97	4.15
1947	183.3	4.08	4.23	0.96	4.35
1948	217.9	4.45	4.23	1.05	6.35
1949	291.2	5.87	4.69	1.25	10.96
1950	355.6	10.72	6.58	1.63	16.09
1951	534.1	14.2	7.5	1.89	23.00
1952	636.0	14.3	7.5	1.91	22.99
1953	631.5	13.97	7.5	1.86	22.77
1954	732.6	13.97	7.5	1.86	25.26
1955	787.3	17.36	9.25	1.88	29.72

Note: CPI: Until 1942, Census Bureau (Dirección Nacional de Estadísticas y Censos): Cost of Living in the Federal Capital, March 1968. After 1943, (Institute of Statistics and Census) Instituto de Estadísticas y Censos (INDEC), Consumer Price Index (CPI) GBA, database (WEB). Consulted May 2005.
Sources: R. Olarra Jiménez, *Evolución Monetaria Argentina.* Buenos Aires, Universitaria de Buenos Aires, 1968, p. 184.

Table A.C.4.3. *Terms of Trade, Domestic and Foreign*

Period	Terms of External Trade (1935–1939 = 100)	Terms of Domestic Trade (1935–1939 = 100) Wholesale
1925–1929	102	132
1930–1934	78	87
1935–1939	100	100
1940–1944	100	62
1945–1946	107	74
1947–1949	129	80
1950–1952	114	68
1953–1955	100	68
1956–1958	86	78
1959–1961		85
1962–1964		93

Source: Carlos Díaz Alejandro, *Essays on Economic History of the Argentine Republic,* New Haven and London, Yale University Press, 1970.

Table A.C.4.4. *Exchange Spread (in percentages)*

Year	Exchange Spread
1941–1945	10
1946	11
1947	28
1948	147
1949	265
1950	275
1951	400
1952	286
1953	235
1954	345
1955	100

Source: FIEL, *El Control de Cambios en la Argentina: Liberación Cambiaria y Crecimiento*, Buenos Aires, Manantial, 1987.

Table A.C.4.5. *Inflation (in CPI Change)*
(in percenatges)

Year	CPI Change[a]
1947	14.90
1948	18.90
1949	33.70
1950	22.10
1951	50.20
1952	19.10
1953	−0.70
1954	16.00
1955	7.50

[a] Average yearly change.
Source: INDEC, www.indec.gov.ar.

Table A.C.4.6. *Annual Growth Rate in Real Terms (in percentages)*

Year	Money Supply	Total Deposits	Total Loans	Notes
1946	8.4	6.8	24.7	22.1
1947	3.2	0.8	66.1	15.8
1948	12.6	18.9	31.1	27.3
1949	–3.5	–8.6	–7.2	0.4
1950	–4.0	–9.7	–3.1	4.3
1951	–14.2	–18.0	–16.5	–2.3
1952	–18.7	–22.2	0.1	–13.4
1953	18.5	21.5	18.4	19.8
1954	12.6	14.9	3.9	14.9
1955	3.9	3.3	8.4	5.6

Note: Changes calculated with values adjusted for the CPI 1955 = 100 (Source: INDEC).
Source: BCRA Yearbook, 1946–1955, and BCRA Statistical Bulletins, 1948 and 1958.

Table A.C.4.7. *Creation of Means of Payment*

Means of Payment Created	1939	1940	1941	1942	1943	1944	1945	1946
Domestic	*Change in millions of pesos*							
Crop financing	213	–	505	242	–32	53	–75	146[a]
Total domestic	113	34	593	482	–84	493	263	2,927
Foreign	*Change in millions of pesos*							
Total frozen funds	24	51	14	114	571	650	448[b]	368[b]
Frozen pounds	11	56	53	175	559	655	–	–
Other frozen for exchange	13	–5	–39	–61	12	–5	–	–
Total foreign	148	–78	458	465	1.321	1.253	1.067	851
Total domestic and foreign	261	–44	1051	947	1,237	1,746	1,330	3,778
Domestic	*As a percentage of total*							
Crop financing	81.60	–	48.00	25.60	–2.60	3.00	–5.60	3.90
Foreign	*As a percentage of total*							
Total frozen funds	9.20	–115.90	1.30	12.00	46.20	37.20	33.70	9.70
Frozen pounds	4.20	–127.30	5.00	18.50	45.20	37.50	–	–
Other frozen foreign exchange	5.00	11.40	–3.70	–6.40	1.00	–0.30	–	–

[a] Shown in "Purchase of IAPI, Purchase of grains."
[b] "Compensatory Foreign Exchange."
Note: Because the partial data does not cover all items, the totals for these differ from the total values shown.
Source: BCRA Yearbook, 1942, 1944, 1945, and 1946.

Table A.C.4.8. *Lending Real Interest Rate*

Year	Lending Nominal Interest Rate (approximately average)	Implicit Price (percenatge yearly change)	Lending Real Interest Rate (%)
1946	5.5	20.4	−14.9
1947	5.5	9.8	−4.3
1948	6.5	15.6	−9.1
1949	6.5	27.4	−20.9
1950	6.5	22.4	−15.9
1951	6.5	40.8	−34.3
1952	6.5	34.5	−28.0
1953	6.5	9.9	−3.4
1954	6.5	2	4.5
1955	6.5	10.7	−4.2

Source: Aldo Arnaudo, *Cincuenta Años de Política Financiera Argentina (1934–1983)*, Buenos Aires, El Ateneo, 1987.

Table A.C.4.9. *Net Money Creation (in millions of current pesos)*

Year	Rediscounts	Deposits	Ratio Reserves/Deposits (%)
1946	9,551.40	11,173.10	85.49
1947	15,491.40	12,791.40	121.11
1948	21,641.10	17,204.20	125.79
1949	28,060.67	20,615.20	136.12
1950	33,029.88	23,378.30	141.28
1951	42,313.15	26,209.50	161.44
1952	49,072.68	28,291.00	173.46
1953	57,844.61	35,740.40	161.85
1954	69,532.90	42,610.10	163.18
1955	85,167.48	49,458.10	172.20

Source: BCRA Yearbooks and Statistical Bulletins, 1946–1955.

Chapter 5

Table A.C.5.1 *Exchange Reform, New Import Surcharges, and Resultant Prices (in pesos per dollar)*

Item	Before March 1967			Since March 1967			
	Cost of U.S. Dollar	Surcharge	Total Pesos	Cost of U.S. Dollar	Surcharge	Total Pesos	Change (%)
Cigarettes	255	175	701	350	110	735	5
Iron (mineral)	255	1	258	350	10	385	49
Natural rubber	255	1	258	350	60	560	91
Crude oil	255	25	319	350	30	455	43
Charcoal	255	70	434	350	70	595	37
Newspaper	255	0	255	350	0	350	37
Book paper	255	20	306	350	20	420	37
Silk thread	255	75	446	350	70	595	33
Natural rubber	255	195	752	350	60	560	−26
Natural manufacture	255	220	816	350	120	770	−6
Fish	255	195	752	350	70	595	−21
Shellfish	255	225	829	350	50	525	−37
Tomatoes	255	175	701	350	70	595	−15
Eggs	255	210	791	350	70	595	−25
Shredded coconut	255	210	791	350	110	735	−7
Almonds	255	200	765	350	80	630	−18
Coffee	255	220	816	350	110	735	−10
Ethyl alcohol	255	320	1071	350	130	805	−25
Whisky	255	235	854	350	140	840	−2
Tobacco leaves	255	220	816	350	70	595	−27
Cement	255	220	816	350	50	525	−36
Basic minerals	255	220	816	350	60	560	−31
Refined oil	255	220	816	350	70	595	−27
Pharmaceuticals	255	220	816	350	120	770	−6

Source: The Economist, Year XVII, no. 868, March 18, 1967.

Table A.C.5.2. *Tax Revenue*

	1965	1966	1967	1968
In millions of current pesos				
Tax collection	251,752	366,029	515,471	577,485
Import duties	58,525	63,152	76,151	72,154
Export duties	4,979	8,159	65,484	57,469
Domestic taxes	38,117	47,776	72,330	111,310
Income taxes	75,263	105,422	140,838	134,642
Sales taxes	49,703	105,064	114,136	133,987
In millions of 1960 pesos				
Tax collection	88,583	107,656	120,268	123,105
Import duties[a]	20,593	18,574	17,767	15,381
Export duties	1,752	2,400	15,279	12,251
Domestic taxes	13,412	14,052	16,876	23,729
Income taxes	26,482	31,007	32,860	28,702
Sales taxes	17,489	30,901	26,630	28,563

[a] The heading Import Duties includes customs and port taxes.
Source: Treasury Yearbooks, 1965–1968.

Table A.C.5.3. *Annual Change in Money Supply (in percentages)*

Year	Change
1954	17
1955	17
1956	20
1957	14
1958	45
1959	34
1960	28
1961	17
1962	9
1963	33
1964	41
1965	27
1966	32
1967	31

Source: BCRA Yearbooks, 1954–1967.

Chapter 6

Table A.C.6.1. *Evolution of National Government Real Payroll (in australs, at 1975 prices)*

Year	Total Spent on Personnel
1975	7,948.9
1976	5,307.9
1977	5,004.5
1978	5,615.7

Source: Ministerio de Economía, *Sector Público Argentino no Financiero. Cuenta Ahorro-Inversión-Financiamiento*, Buenos Aires, Secretaría de Hacienda de la República Argentina, 2004.

Table A.C.6.2. *Consumer Prices – CPI 1984 (percent change compared to the preceding month)*

Month	Consumer Price
August	22.84
September	27.55
October	19.32
November	14.97
December	19.68

Source: INDEC, www.indec.gov.ar .

Table A.C.6.3. *Consumer Prices – CPI 1985 (percent change compared to the preceding month)*

Month	Consumer Price
January	25.14
February	20.70
March	26.48
April	29.47
May	25.09
June	30.54

Source: INDEC, www.indec.gov.ar.

Table A.C.6.4. *Consumer Prices – IPC 1979–1984*
(percent change compared to the preceding year)

Month	Consumer Price
1979	159.51
1980	100.76
1981	104.48
1982	164.78
1983	343.80
1984	626.73
1985	672.18

Source: INDEC, www.indec.gov.ar.

Table A.C.6.5. *Price Index of Foreign Trade and Terms of Trade*
(Base: 1993 = 100, 1986–2000)

Year	Export Price Index	Import Price Index	Terms of Trade Index
1986	79.4	93.0	85.4
1987	81.8	96.4	84.9
1988	95.3	103.2	92.3
1989	97.0	108.0	89.8
1990	97.6	108.7	89.8
1991	96.1	103.9	92.5
1992	99.8	102.7	97.2
1993	100.0	100.0	100.0
1994	102.9	101.4	101.5
1995	108.8	106.9	101.8
1996	115.9	105.6	109.8
1997	111.9	103.2	108.4
1998	100.3	97.9	102.5
1999	89.1	92.4	96.4
2000	98.0	92.4	106.1

Source: INDEC, www.indec.gov.ar.

Table A.C.6.6. *National Government Tax Revenues (in millions of australs, at 1986 prices)*

Year	1983	1984	1985	1986
Total net tax collection	11,471	11,778	14,933	14,978
Import duties	607	485	585	831
Export duties	1,081	905	1,502	777
Import and export processing fees	0	61	118	121
Domestic taxes	977	834	1,007	1,139
Gross VAT	2,666	2,237	2,420	2,460
Income taxes	735	398	720	890
Tax on net wealth	11	14	17	109
Gross liquid fuel	1,729	2,464	2,089	2,102
Capital gains tax	653	420	471	457
Seals (stamps)	166	119	144	198
Interactions with foreign exchange	103	77	105	90

Note: Provincial contributions are not included.
Source: Dirección Nacional de Investigaciones y Análisis Fiscal, based on data from AFIP, ANSeS, Dirección Nacional de Coordinación Fiscal con las Provincias (National Directorate of Provincial Tax Coordination), Oficina Nacional de Presupuesto (National Budget Office), and other entities.

Table A.C.6.7. *Fiscal and Quasi Fiscal Deficits, 1986–1989 (in millions of 1986 australs)*

Year	Fiscal Deficit	Quasi-Fiscal Déficit	Total Deficit
1986	3,259	−314	2,945
1987	5,381	591	5,971
1988	6,388	2.475	8,863
1989	6,110	3.955	10,064

Source: FIEL, *El gasto Público en la Argentina 1960–1985*, Buenos Aires, FIEL, 1987, and Ministerio de Economía, *Sector Público Argentino no Financiero. Cuenta Ahorro-Inversión-Financiamiento*, Buenos Aires, Secretaría de Hacienda de la República Argentina, 2004.

Table A.C.6.8. *Nominal and Real Interest Rates, 1975–1981*

Year	Annual Interest Rate (nominal)	WPI Growth Rate	Real Interest Rate (adjusted for WPI)
1975	38.1	192.5	−52.8
1976	84.6	499	−69.2
1977	173.5	149.4	9.6
1978	156.3	146	4.2
1979	101.5	149.3	−15
1980	77.9	75.4	1.7
1981	171	109.6	8.4

Source: Adrián Guissarri: *La Argentina Informal. Realidad de la Vida Económica*, Buenos Aires, Emecé, 1989, p. 308.

Table A.C.6.9. *U.S. Dollar quotations on Exchange Market in 1981*
(in australs per dollar)

Month	Open Market	Commercial Market	Financial Market
January	201.7		
February	224.8		
March	233.8		
April	309.7		
May	323		
June	435.1	448.6	622.1
July		470.7	649.1
August		511.9	746.6
September		557.7	745.5
October		603.7	819.1
November		650.7	1,068.3
December		701.7	1,082.5

Source: CEPAL, *Estadísticas económicas de corto plazo de la Argentina: Sector externo y condiciones económicas internacionales*, vol. I, Buenos Aires, May 1986.

Table A.C.6.10. *Monetary Base and Money Supply (M_1 and M_3)*
(in millions of australs at 1986 prices)

Year	1985	1986	1987	1988
Monetary base	9,797	6,943	5,844	6,831
Monetary base (broad)	13,461	11,956	12,083	18,813
M_1	5,730	5,588	5,433	5,371
M_3	16,293	17,629	20,600	24,947

Note: Broad monetary base is calculated based on the traditional monetary base plus deposits in commercial bank special accounts.
Source: BCRA Yearbooks and Statistical Bulletins, 1985–1988.

Table A.C.6.11. *BCRA Assets and Liabilities to the Private Financial Sector, 1983–1988*
(in millions 1986 constant australs)

	1983	1984	1985	1986	1987	1988
Debts from financial institutions (1)	6,661	3,356	4,076	3,603	4,318	2,588
Resources yielded from bank debt	8,208	10,593	4,576	9,494	14,976	19,742
Subtotal (assets)	14,869	13,949	8,652	13,097	19,294	22,330
Deposits in current account	4,078	8,627	4,116	1,697	682	1,249
Deposits in special accounts	10,409	245	3,665	5,013	6,239	9,870
Debts to the financial system	0	238	116	115	58	43
Compensation yielded from special accounts	0	5,177	2,922	2,965	2,457	2,112
Subtotal (liabilities)	14,487	14,287	10,819	9,790	9,436	13,274

Source: BCRA Balance Sheets.

Table A.C.6.12. *Minimum Reserves Cash Requirements, 1985–1988 (ratio of cash reserves to deposits and liabilities subject to cash minimum)*

	Single Rate of Minimum Reserves	Rate of Reserves by Type of Deposit Current Accounts and Other Deposits and Debts through Financial Intermediation[a]
January 1985	86	–
February	86	–
March	86	–
April	–	96.5
May	–	96.5
June	–	95.5
July	–	90.5
August	–	89.5
September	–	88.5
October	–	88.5
November	–	88.5
December 1985	–	88.5
December 1986	–	88.5
December 1987	–	88.5
December 1988	–	88.5

[a] For Type I institutions. Type II institutions would receive one additional percentage point for the period between April 1985 and September 1987.
Source: BCRA Yearbooks, 1985 and 1988.

Table A.C.6.13. *Minimum Reserves Cash Requirements, 1978–1988 (required minimum rate of cash reserves in percentage)*

Year	Single Rate of Minimum Cash Requirement	Minimum Reserve Requirement by Type of Deposit	
		Current Accounts and Debts through Financial Intermediation	Savings Bank
December 1978	29.0	–	–
December 1979[a]	16.5	–	–
December 1980[a]	10.0	–	–
December 1981[a]	15.5	–	–
December 1985	–	88.5	11
December 1986	–	88.5	11
December 1987	–	88.5	25
December 1988	–	88.5	25

[a] Provsional data.

Note: For Group I institutions.

Source: BCRA Yearbooks, 1978–1988.

Methodological Appendix

A Methodological Note on Fiscal Series

1862–1899. For the years 1862–1899 we use the cash flows accounts of Treasury (*Cajas Nacionales*) taken from *Dinero, Deuda y Crisis*, for the years 1864–1899. The Treasury accounts reflected what was received and paid during each year, and not the credits and liabilities outstanding the same year. Besides we added to those accounts the data provided by the Budget Investment Account (*Cuenta de Inversión del Presupuesto*), which reflects the credits and debits outstanding each year. That data were published in the Statiscal Extract (*Extracto Estadístico 1915*) from the year 1900 to 1915 and in the Geographical Yearbook from the years.

Regarding the Treasury data, following current criteria, the treatment of *existencias* (credits or debits remaining from the previous periods) was changed; in this work the balances of *existencias* (positively or negativily) instead of being included as revenues were registered below the line considering its accumulating inventories as a financial investment and its use as an additional source of financing.

Interest payments on the debt are taken from the record of the Department of Treasury Public Debt. Where there are gaps in the record, Department of Treasury expenditures in gold are taken. These data were taken directly from the Treasury Yearbook and refer exclusively to the National Government.

Therefore we presented the fiscal accounts from different periods and sources in the following tables.

Revenues and Expenditure Treasury (Cajas Nacionales)

Year	Revenues (in pesos fuertes)	Expenditures (in pesos fuertes)
1864	8,045,328	6,814,612
1865	8,345,686	10,769,043
1866	8,387,026	14,545,041
1867	13,054,047	15,954,100
1868	12,598,842	16,832,169
1869	12,373,610	16,270,725
1870	14,896,938	21,938,261
1871	10,376,500	24,642,151
1872	20,683,245	23,992,973
1873	22,911,474	27,019,142
1874	18,472,588	26,065,922
1875	21,428,232	31,040,842
1876	13,623,914	26,333,874
1877	13,776,540	19,635,642
1878	17,517,508	21,214,277
1879	21,793,818	25,476,575
1880	19,760,479	26,926,772
1881	20,807,739	32,055,740
1882	26,867,107	52,821,639
1883	32,705,623	54,238,485
1884	36,169,793	59,018,873
1885	39,463,388	57,203,751
1886	46,631,506	62,849,121
1887	68,741,073	65,479,214
1888	67,831,522	74,883,058
1889	114,822,175	148,530,821

Source: Roberto Cortés Conde. *Dinero, Deuda y Crisis, Evolución Fiscal y Monetaria en la Argentina 1862–1890*, Buenos Aires, Sudamericana, 1989.

National Government Revenues and Expenditures 1864–1900, Statistical Extract and Geographical Yearbook

Year	Revenues National Government (in gold pesos)	Expenditures National Government (in gold pesos)
1864	7,005,328	7,119,931
1865	8,295,071	22,517,147
1866	9,568,555	13,702,590
1867	12,040,287	14,110,077
1868	12,495,126	16,693,406
1869	12,676,680	14,953,431
1870	14,883,904	19,439,967
1871	16,682,155	21,166,230
1872	18,172,380	26,462,786
1873	20,217,232	31,025,070
1874	15,974,042	29,784,096
1875	17,206,747	28,567,861
1876	13,583,633	22,153,048
1877	14,824,097	19,924,961
1878	18,415,898	20,840,918
1879	20,961,893	22,523,159
1880	19,594,306	26,919,295
1881	21,345,926	28,381,224
1882	26,822,320	58,007,158
1883	30,950,196	44,831,378
1884	37,724,374	56,440,137
1885	26,581,118	40,515,080
1886	30,395,792	39,178,658
1887	38,209,229	48,205,071
1888	34,892,162	51,596,824
1889	38,169,506	55,770,588
1890	29,143,767	38,145,542
1891	19,498,953	33,664,842
1892	32,597,078	38,685,227
1893	38,389,688	38,047,440
1894	34,178,105	40,114,452
1895	38,223,808	48,505,921
1896	42,008,415	78,212,817
1897	51,440,841	61,010,309
1898	53,158,969	121,289,634
1899	72,863,448	76,630,701
1900	64,858,210	68,580,237

Source: Dirección General de Estadística de la Nación, *Extracto Estadístico de la República Argentina Correspondiente al año 1915*, Compañía Sudamericana de Billetes de Banco, Buenos Aires, 1916, and *Anuario Geográfico Argentino*, Comité Nacional de Geografía, Buenos Aires, 1941.

1900–1940

Different criteria used in presenting fiscal accounts. Comparison between cash basis accounting and investment account. Fiscal accounts presented herein rely on sources that use a variety of criteria and thus provide varying results. The present comparison is made between data from Treasury balance sheets (reconstructed according to the criteria outlined earlier) and data from the Investment Account, shown in *Extracto Estadístico Argentino* and *Anuario Geográfico Argentino*.

On the one hand, data from Treasury balance sheets, tables with revenues and expeditures of the National Treasury, which were made according to cash basis accounting – from revenue in effect received and expenditures actually made – do not correspond to other official data recorded in known publications that summarize information from the Secretary of Treasury (*Ministerio de Hacienda*). These data also differ from the majority of studies that refer to the period. Furthermore, as mentioned previously, in the Treasury tables shown in the present book, the data have been re-elaborated in order to separate payments on public debt and obtain the primary deficit and surplus, which was not included in the original source.

As stated in the *Anuario Geográfico Argentino*, these differences are a result of the fact that the information regarding national revenue and National Government expenditures included therein is only a record of what was collected and covered with cash and not what was paid out in bonds. In addition, the debt figure combines both foreign and domestic debt and includes neither short-term loans nor floating debt. Likewise the information included in the *Extracto Estadístico Argentino* (Argentine Statistical Extract) for the years preceding 1914. That is, these sources include data from the Investment Account (*Cuenta Inversión del presupuesto*), what had accrued.

Information from Investment Accounts of the budget includes debits and credits accrued during the fiscal year even though they may have been neither deposited nor paid. These data are often difficult to place in a particular fiscal year.

Likewise, the data extracted from the *Anuario Geográfico Argentino* differ from the figures included in the primary source, which is the Investment Account published in the Treasury Yearbook. This is because in the secondary source, subsequent corrections have been included, along with other expenditures and revenue that are not recorded in the Investment Account, for several reasons, but that make accrual basis accounting more precise.

As indicated in the *Anuario Geográfico Argentino*, the data included therein have the following characteristics:

- The totals collected and spent under "special accounts" are excluded until 1927, in national revenue as well as in National Government expenditures. Since 1928 "special account" spending is included, and since 1933 budget expenditures met with the exchange differential. Under funds collected quantities equal to the previous ones are included for both sections.

- Starting in 1933, revenue collected from taxes on gasoline, travel, wine, Law 5313, Yerba Mate tea, and exchange revenue is not included.
- Starting in 1933 cash resources produced by the National Lottery and the fund resulting from the revenue on perfumes and medicines are included in the figures for national revenue. Furthermore, starting in 1910, funds called "miscellaneous" are included, and credit resources excluded.
- Between 1910 and 1917, the figures for National Government expenditures include budget, special law, and government contracts expenditures. As of 1917, all of these plus loans transferred from previous years are included.
- The figures for 1928 through 1936 are those adjusted by the Secretary of the Treasury (*Ministerio de Hacienda*) in 1937.

Thus, the graphs indicating fiscal results have differences relating to the sources. On the one hand, data from the Treasury of the Department of Treasury are kept according to cash basis accounting, whereas the *Extracto Estadístico de la República Argentina* (from 1900 to 1913) and the *Anuario Geográfico Argentino* (from 1914 to 1940) use accrual basis accounting for investment accounts. The data from the sources used are summarized in the following tables:

	Treasury Account Series			Argentine Republic Statistical Extract		
Year	Revenues	Expenditures	Deficit	National Revenue	Total Expenditures	Deficit
1900	211.0	162.0	49.0	148.4	158.2	−9.8
1901	225.0	165.0	60.0	149.1	161.1	−12.0
1902	233.0	207.0	26.0	151.0	198.7	−47.7
1903	231.0	179.0	52.0	171.4	182.9	−11.5
1904	280.0	205.0	75.0	188.7	195.0	−6.2
1905	328.0	331.0	−3.0	205.4	322.1	−116.7
1906	333.0	244.0	89.0	228.9	270.3	−41.4
1907	418.0	272.0	146.0	243.8	253.2	−9.4
1908	335.0	269.0	66.0	254.2	252.4	1.8
1909	519.0	383.0	136.0	275.2	392.3	−117.1
1910	390.0	385.0	5.0	302.6	411.2	−108.7
1911	457.0	379.0	78.0	310.5	416.6	−106.1
1912	521.0	414.0	107.0	336.4	404.2	−67.8
1913	432.0	352.0	80.0	349.3	403.4	−54.1

Source: Treasury Yearbook and Dirección General de Estadística de la Nación, *Extracto Estadístico de la República Argentina Correspondiente al año 1915*, Compañía Sudamericana de Billetes de Banco, Buenos Aires, 1916.

	Treasury Account Series						Argentine Geographical Yearbook (Accrued, Investment Account)			
Year	Revenues	Expenditure	Public Debt Payment	Total Expenditure	Primary Deficit	Deficit	National Revenue	Expenditure	Deficit	Consolidated Public Debt
1913	431.80	351.79	86.00	437.79	80.01	-5.99	370.21	403.44	-33.23	1,238.00
1914	332.81	399.11	81.20	480.31	-66.31	-147.51	273.40	419.64	-146.24	1,238.69
1915	298.04	382.06	82.03	464.09	-84.02	-166.05	251.90	390.84	-138.95	1,221.78
1916	317.66	333.31	77.67	410.99	-15.66	-93.33	254.74	374.65	-119.90	1,242.47
1917	413.53	337.07	79.57	416.64	76.46	-3.11	254.32	389.57	-135.25	1,353.21
1918	354.19	331.98	98.85	430.83	22.21	-76.64	321.84	421.05	-99.22	1,314.15
1919	441.26	357.45	106.88	464.33	83.81	-23.07	401.00	427.91	-26.91	1,285.25
1920	731.83	428.46	105.58	534.05	303.37	197.79	508.84	487.81	21.03	1,257.43
1921	555.99	471.00	108.96	579.96	84.99	-23.97	470.30	560.30	-90.01	1,277.73
1922	556.38	571.26	111.51	682.77	-14.89	-126.40	452.84	614.46	-161.62	1,294.89
1923	639.07	587.44	107.16	694.61	51.63	-55.53	542.45	632.34	-89.89	1,315.75
1924	893.69	646.01	122.43	768.44	247.68	125.25	596.80	671.20	-74.41	1,523.58
1925	1,010.36	675.34	121.32	796.66	335.02	213.70	662.52	713.46	-50.94	1,743.97
1926	947.49	730.57	139.04	869.61	216.93	77.88	640.19	745.82	-105.62	1,845.84
1927	1,237.80	1,015.06	174.67	1,189.73	222.74	48.07	681.39	1,048.77	-367.38	2,155.48
1928	1,009.98	770.39	180.88	951.27	239.59	58.70	738.63	918.98	-180.35	2,251.84
1929	996.30	725.90	192.10	918.00	270.40	78.30	747.62	988.23	-240.61	2,208.10
1930	907.55	949.07	201.21	1,150.28	-41.52	-242.73	663.31	1,091.79	-428.48	2,214.00
1931	1,076.60	733.42	228.42	961.85	343.17	114.75	685.69	908.45	-222.76	2,230.69
1932	1,285.76	1,030.21	271.04	1,301.24	255.56	-15.48	742.44	849.89	-107.45	2,557.15
1933	1,302.03	925.58	273.69	1,199.26	376.46	102.77	753.69	880.39	-126.70	2,748.70
1934	1,337.80	1,195.56	229.05	1,424.61	142.25	-86.81	764.41	934.15	-169.75	2,835.14
1935	3,618.16	2,315.36	192.32	2,507.68	1,302.80	1,110.48	846.79	980.86	-134.07	3,349.68
1936	1,954.16	1,328.13	258.23	1,586.36	626.03	367.80	872.80	1,051.85	-179.05	3,607.27
1937	2,478.94	1,858.76	1,002.08	2,866.85	620.18	-381.90	991.30	1,221.13	-229.82	3,742.96
1938	2,042.57	1,794.53	246.50	2,041.03	248.04	1.54	991.44	1,278.35	-286.91	3,850.98
1939	1,864.67	1,728.14	220.27	1,948.41	136.53	-83.74	1,014.98	1,460.34	-445.36	4,398.58
1940	2,381.78	1,767.16	256.48	2,023.64	614.62	358.14	973.00	1,320.90	-347.90	4,510.40

Source: Treasury Yearbook and *Anuario Geográfico Argentino*, Comité Nacional de Geografía, Buenos Aires, 1941.

1945–1961. For the period 1940–1961 the source used was the series published by the OAS and the IDB for the National Government. These series include payments to the social security system, contributions to provinces and municipalities, and subsidies to state enterprises. Regarding the latter, investment data are not available but rather operating results; thus, we have opted to consider only the subsidy component. The method of recording income and expenditures of the social security system is problematic because it inhibits visualizing this system as a source of financing, its function during the period. Rather, it shows a smaller fiscal deficit that is the actual one. This method also obscures understanding of the effective mechanism used to make the surplus from the retirement system a source of financing, such as placing public bonds (at a negative rate) in retirement accounts. During this period public bonds were absorbed largely by the retirement system or the Central Bank.

1961–1989. For this period the source is the series published in 2003 by the Department of Treasury (Secretaría de Hacienda), which uses accrual-based accounting, except for payments to the social security system and some interest, which is recorded with cash basis accounting procedures. Only Central Government expenditures (National Government, Public Agencies, and the social security system) have been considered, but because this publication has consolidated information with data corresponding to these governments, it was necessary to deduct the provincial government expenditures and add them to the Central Government expenditures, and besides, the transfers made to the provinces should be added to the Central Government expenditures. These transfers to provincial governments do not include resource sharing between the National Government and the provinces, because these are dealt with as the provinces own resources, except for the period 1985–1987, during which time the sharing revenues law did not exist and all transfers are recorded as representational. For these three years it was necessary to adjust the expenditure quantity added so as not to incorporate sharing fiscal resources and to maintain the homogeneity of the series. This adjustment was made from provincial information. It is important to point out that public enterprises have been included with international methodology, which considers the operation deficit plus investment under public expenditures.

Notes Concerning Monetary Units

During the twentieth century there were various monetary units whose designations and equivalencies are listed next.

From colonial times to independence the monetary unit was the silver *peso hispanoamericano*, weighing 27 grams of silver (equal to the dollar).

Later, an 1875 law declared the national monetary unit the *peso fuerte*, the "strong" peso, a convertible currency weighing 1.6666 grams of 0.916 fine gold, with contents equivalent to the silver peso or *peso plata*, but that never caught on as currency and remained as a simple accounting unit. A November 1881 law established as the monetary unit the gold and silver pesos, the first consisting of 1.6129 grams of gold and 25 grams of silver and the second of the designation of 0.916 fine gold. A unit of account *peso fuerte* from 1875 equaled 1.03 gold peso from 1881, and their symbols were $F and $oro.

When convertibility was suspended in 1885 the paper note called gold pesos came to be known as the national currency and its value fluctuated on the market. In 1899, the gold peso continued to the accounting monetary unit, which was convertible to the money in circulation, the legal tender peso at a fixed exchange rate of 0.44 gold pesos for each *peso moneda nacional*; the sign used in Spanish is m$n, but in the English translation is referred to as the peso. This was the monetary unit until 1970.

Starting in 1970 the monetary unit changed several times and is summarized in the following table. In the text we use pesos, pesos ley or pesos ar., and starting in June 1985, australs, although when the official source during the use of the austral refers to previous years it converts them to australs. Thus, in the text, in some cases this unit is used. From 1985 to 1991 the monetary unit is the austral and since then the convertible peso.

Evolution of the Argentine Monetary Unit Symbol with Respect to the Peso in Circulation in 2005

				Cited in Text As
Until December 31, 1969	Peso Moneda Nacional	M$n	10,000,000,000,000	Peso
Until May 31, 1983	Peso Ley 18,188	$ley	100,000,000,000	Peso ley
Until June 14, 1985	Peso Argentino	$a	10,000,000	Peso ar.
Until December 31, 1991	Austral	A	10,000	Austral
Since January 1, 1991	Peso	$	1	Peso

Source: Anuario Estadístico INDEC, Buenos Aires, 1997.

Bibliography

Abramovitz, M., "Catching Up, Forging Ahead and Falling Behind," in *Thinking about Growth, and Other Essays on Economic Growth and Welfare*, Cambridge, Cambridge University Press, 1989.

Agote, Pedro, *Informe del Presidente del Crédito Público Nacional, Libro II*, Buenos Aires, Imprenta La Universidad, 1884.

Alesina, Alberto, and Drazen, Allan, "Why Are Stabilizations Delayed?" *The American Economic Review*, no. 5, 1991.

Alesina, Alberto, and Enrico Spolaore, *The Size of Nations*, Cambridge, MA, The MIT Press, 2003.

Alhadeff, Peter, "Dependencia, Historiografía y Objeciones al Pacto Roca," *Desarrollo Económico*, no. 99, 1985.

Antonio, Jorge, *Y ahora qué*, Buenos Aires, Ediciones Verum et Militia, 1966.

Arnaudo, Aldo, *Cincuenta Años de Política Financiera Argentina (1934–1983)*, Buenos Aires, El Ateneo, 1987.

Ashton, Thomas S., "Some Statistics of the Industrial Revolution," in *Gold and Prices*, ed. George F. Warren and Frank A. Pearson, New York, John Wiley, 1935.

Baiocco, Pedro J., *La Economía Bancaria Argentina a través de sus Índices más Representativos en el Período 1901–1935*, Buenos Aires, Universidad de Buenos Aires, 1937.

Balboa, Manuel, "La Evolución del Balance de Pagos de la República Argentina, 1913–1950," *Desarrollo Económico*, no. 45, 1972.

Banco de la Nación Argentina, *El Banco de la Nación Argentina en su Cincuentenario*, Buenos Aires, Banco de la Nación Argentina, 1941.

Barro, Robert, and Xavier Sala i Martin, "Convergence across States and Regions," *BPEA*, no. 1, 1991, 107–158.

Beveraggi Allende, Walter, *El Servicio del Capital Extranjero y el Control de Cambios: la Experiencia Argentina de 1900 a 1943*, México, FCE, 1954.

Blanco, Eugenio, *La Política Presupuestaria, la Deuda Pública y la Economía Nacional*, Buenos Aires, Ministerio de Hacienda de la Nación, 1956.

Botana, Natalio, *El Orden Conservador. La Política Argentina entre 1880 y 1916*, Buenos Aires, Sudamericana, 1977.

Bulmer Thomas, Victor, *The Economic History of Latin America since Independence*, Cambridge, Cambridge University Press, 2003.

Bunge, Alejandro, *Análisis del Comercio Exterior Argentino en los años 1910 a 1922*, Buenos Aires, Dirección General de Estadística de La Nación, 1923.

"La Industria durante la Guerra," *Revista de Economía Argentina*, no. 150, 1930.

Canavese, Alfredo, Víctor Elías, and Luisa Montuschi, *Sistema Financiero y Política Industrial para la Argentina en la Década de 1980*, Buenos Aires, El Cronista Comercial, 1983.

Canitrot, Adolfo, "La Experiencia Populista de Redistribución de Ingresos," *Desarrollo Económico*, no. 59, 1976.
Carbonell Tur, Antonio, *La Estabilidad Monetaria y la Banca Comercial en la República Argentina*, Buenos Aires, Asociación de Bancos, 1971.
CEPAL, *Política Económica y Procesos de Desarrollo: La Experiencia Argentina entre 1976 y 1981*, Santiago de Chile, Estudios e Informes de la CEPAL, 1983.
Clague, C., P. Keefer, S. Knacl, and M. Olson, "Contract Intensive Money: Contract Enforcement, Property Rights and Economic Performance," *Journal of Economic Growth*, vol. 4, 181– 211.
Cortés Conde, Roberto, *Dinero, Deuda y Crisis: Evolución Fiscal y Monetaria en la Argentina, 1862–1890*, Buenos Aires, Sudamericana, 1989.
  El Progreso Argentino, 1880–1914, Sudamericana, Buenos Aires, 1979. *Estadísticas Monetarias y Fiscales Argentinas: 1810– 1914*, mimeo, 1995.
  "Finanzas Públicas, Moneda y Bancos (1810–1899)," *Nueva Historia de la Nación Argentina*, tomo V, Buenos Aires, Planeta, 1999.
  "Fiscal Crisis and Inflation in XIX Century Argentina," Buenos Aires, Documento de Trabajo, Departamento de Economía Universidad de San Andrés, 1998.
  Historia Económica Mundial, Buenos Aires, Ariel, 2005.
  La Economía Argentina en el Largo Plazo (Siglos XIX y XX), Buenos Aires, Sudamericana, 1994.
  "Las Finanzas Públicas y la Moneda en las Provincias del Interior," in *Nueva Historia de la Nación Argentina*, tomo V, Buenos Aires, Planeta, 2000.
  "Migración, Cambio Agrícola y Políticas de Protección. El Caso Argentino," in *Españoles hacia América. La Emigración en Masa, 1880–1930*, ed. Nicolas Sánchez-Albornoz, Madrid, Alianza, 1988.
  Progreso y Declinación de la Economía Argentina, Buenos Aires, Fondo de Cultura Económica, 1998.
  Tendencias de la Educación en la Argentina, mimeo, 1998.
  "The Vicissitudes of an Exporting Economy: Argentina 1875–1930," in *An Economic History of Twentieth-Century Latin America*, ed. Enrique Cárdenas, José Antonio Ocampo, and Rosemary Thorp, New York, Palgrave, 2000.
  "Tierras, Agricultura y Ganadería," in *La Argentina del Ochenta al Centenario*, ed. Gustavo Ferrari and Ezequiel Gallo, Buenos Aires, Sudamericana, 1980.
Cortés Conde, Roberto, and George McCandless, "Argentina: From Colony to Nation," in *Transferring Wealth and Power from the Old to the New World: Monetary and Fiscal Institutions in the 17th throughout the 19th Centuries*, ed. Michael D. Bordo and Roberto Cortés Conde, Cambridge, Cambridge University Press, 2001.
Cortés Conde, Roberto, with the collaboration of Marcela Harriague, *Estimaciones del Producto Bruto Interno de Argentina, 1875–1935*, Buenos Aires, Universidad de San Andrés, 1994.
Dagnino Pastore, José María., *Crónicas Económicas. Argentina, 1969–1988*, Buenos Aires, Crespillo, 1988.
Davies, Lance E., and Robert E. Gallman, "Argentine Savings, Investment, and Economic Growth before World War I," in *Evolving Financial Markets and International Capital Flows: Britain, The Americas, and Australia, 1865–1914*, Cambridge, Cambridge University Press, 2001.
della Paolera, Gerardo, and Allan M. Taylor, *Straining at the Anchor: The Argentine Currency Board and the Search for Macroeconomic Stability, 1880–1935*, Chicago, University of Chicago Press, 2001.
della Paolera, Gerardo, and Allan M. Taylor, *Tensando el Ancla: La Caja de Conversión Argentina y la Búsqueda de Estabilidad Macroeconómica – 1880–1935*, Buenos Aires, FCE, 2003.

De Pablo, Juan Carlos, *La Economía Argentina en la Segunda Mitad del Siglo XX*, Buenos Aires, La Ley, 2005.

Política Antiinflacionaria en la Argentina, 1967–70, Buenos Aires, Amorrortu, 1970.

"Precios Relativos, Distribución del Ingreso y Planes de Estabilización en la Argentina, 1967–76," *Desarrollo Económico*, vol. 15, no. 57, 1975.

Díaz Alejandro, Carlos, "Economía Argentina, 1880–1913," in *La Argentina del Ochenta al Centenario*, ed. Gustavo Ferrari y Ezequiel Gallo, Buenos Aires, Editorial Sudamericana, 1980.

Essays on the Economic History of the Argentine Republic, New Haven and London, Yale University Press, 1970.

Tipo de Cambio y Términos de Intercambio en la República Argentina, 1913–1976, Buenos Aires, CEMA, 1981.

Di Tella, Guido, and Rudiger Dornbusch, *The Political Economy of Argentina, 1946–1983*, Oxford, St. Anthony's/Macmillan, 1989.

Diz, Adolfo, *Oferta Monetaria y sus Instrumentos*, Centro de Estudios Monetarios Latinoamericanos, México, 1997.

Domenech, Roberto, "Estadísticas de la Evolución Económica de Argentina, 1913–1984," *Estudios*, no. 39, 1986.

Dornbusch, Rudiger, and Sebastián Edwards, "Macroeconomics Populism in Latin America," NBER Working Paper W2986.

Echagüe, Alfredo, "Expedientes de la Comisión Designada para Dictaminar sobre Cuestiones de Carácter Monetario," published in "Conferencia Económica Nacional," *Revista de Economía Argentina*, 17–18, tomo III, 1919.

Eichengreen, Barry, *Globalizing Capital*, New Jersey, Princeton University Press, 1996.

Golden Fetters: The Gold Standard and the Great Depression 1919–1939, New York, Oxford University Press, 1995.

Ekelund, Robert B., and Robert D. Tollison, *Mercantilism as a Rent-Seeking Society: Economic Regulation in Historical Perspective*, Austin, TX, Texas A&M University Press, 1981.

Elías, Víctor, *Sources of Growth*, San Francisco, California, Fundación del Tucumán and Internacional Center for Economic Growth, 1992.

Escudé, Carlos, *Gran Bretaña, Estados Unidos y la Declinación Argentina, 1942–1949*, Buenos Aires, Belgrano, 1983.

Eshag, Eprime, and Rosemary Thorp, "Las Consecuencias Económicas y Sociales de las Políticas Ortodoxas Aplicadas en la Argentina Durante los Años de Postguerra," *Desarrollo Económico*, vol. 4, no. 16, 1965.

Ferreres, Orlando, *Dos Siglos de Economía Argentina (1810–2004): Historia Argentina en Cifras*, Buenos Aires, El Ateneo y Fundación Norte y Sur, 2005.

Fodor, Jorge, and Arturo O'Connell, "La Argentina y la Economía Atlántica en la Primera Mitad del Siglo XX," *Desarrollo Económico*, no. 49, 1973.

Fornero, Jorge, and Alberto Díaz Cafferata, *Tendencias y Quiebres del Grado de Apertura Exportadora de Argentina, y el Marco Internacional, 1884–2002*, Córdoba, IEF y U.N. de Córdoba, 2004.

Friedman, Milton, and Anna Jacobson, *A Monetary History of the United States, 1867–1960*, New Jersey, Princeton University Press, 1971.

Fundación de Investigaciones Económicas Latinoamericana, *El Control de Cambios en la Argentina: Liberación Cambiaria y Crecimiento*, Buenos Aires, Manantial, 1987.

Fundación de Investigaciones Económicas Latinoamericana, *El Gasto Público en la Argentina 1960–1985*, Buenos Aires, FIEL, 1987.

Gallo, Ezequiel, *La Pampa Gringa: La Colonización Agrícola en Santa Fe (1870–1895)*, Buenos Aires, Sudamericana, 1984.

Gambini, Hugo, *Historia del Peronismo (1943–1951)*, Buenos Aires, Planeta, 1999.

García Heras, Raúl, *Transporte, Negocios y Política: La Compañía Anglo Argentina de Tranvías, 1876–1981*, Buenos Aires, Sudamericana, 1994.

García Mata, Rafael, and Emilio Llorens, *Argentina Económica 1939*, Buenos Aires, Compañía Impresora Argentina, 1939.

Gerchunoff, Pablo, "Capitalismo Industrial, Desarrollo Asociado y Distribución del Ingreso entre los Gobiernos Peronistas, 1950–1972," *Desarrollo Económico*, no. 57, 1975.

Gerchunoff, Pablo, and Horacio Aguirre, "Lo Nuevo por Nacer, lo Viejo por Morir: la Economía Argentina entre la Gran Guerra y la Gran Depresión" in *Serie Estudios y Perspectivas*, Buenos Aires, CEPAL, 2006.

Gerchunoff, Pablo, and Lucas Llach, *El Ciclo de la Ilusión y el Desencanto*, Buenos Aires, Ariel, 1998.

Gerschenkron, A., *Economic Backwardness in Historical Perspective*, Cambridge, MA, Harvard University Press, 1962.

Gravil, Roger, *The Anglo-Argentine Connection, 1900–1939*, Boulder and London, Westview Press, 1985.

Guissarri, Adrián, *La Argentina Informal: Realidad de la Vida Económica*, Buenos Aires, Emecé Editores, 1989.

Halperín Donghi, Tulio, *Guerra y Finanzas en los Orígenes del Estado Argentino (1821–1850)*, Buenos Aires, Editorial Belgrano, 1982.

Hopenhaym, Hugo A., and Pablo Neumeyer, "The Argentine Great Depression, 1975–1990," seminario interno Departamento de Economía UdeSA, Buenos Aires, 2004.

Hueyo, Alberto, *La Argentina en la Depresión Mundial, 1932–1933: Discursos y Conferencias*, Buenos Aires, El Ateneo, 1938.

Katz, Jorge, "Una Interpretación de Largo Plazo del Crecimiento Industrial Argentino," *Desarrollo Económico*, vol. 8, no. 32, 1969.

Katz, Jorge, and Bernardo Kosacoff, *El Proceso de Industrialización en la Argentina: Evolución, Retroceso y Perspectiva*, Buenos Aires, Centro Editor de América Latina, 1989.

Kindleberger, Charles, *The World in Depression, 1929–1939*, Berkley, University of California Press, 1973.

Lane, Frederik C., "Economic Consequences of Organised Violence," *Journal of Economic History*, vol. XVIII, no. 4, December 1958.

Lattes, Zulma, and Lattes, Alfredo, *Migraciones en la Argentina: Estudio de las Migraciones Internas e Internacionales Basado en Datos Censales, 1869–1960*, Buenos Aires, Instituto Di Tella, 1969.

Lewis, Arthur, "Economic Development with Unlimited Supplies of Labour," *Manchester School of Economic and Social Studies*, vol. XXIII, no. 2, May 1954.

Lewis, Colin, *British Railways in Argentina 1857–1914: A Case of Study of Foreign Investment*, Institute of Latin American Studies, University of London, 1983.

Llach, Juan, "El Plan Pinedo de 1940, su Significado Histórico y los Orígenes de la Economía Política del Peronismo," *Desarrollo Económico*, no. 92, 1984.

"Los Determinantes del Salario en Argentina. Un Diagnóstico de Largo Plazo y Propuestas de Políticas," *Estudios*, no. 29, Córdoba, IEERAL, 1984.

Reconstrucción o estancamiento, Buenos Aires, Tesis 1987.

Llorens de Azar, Carmen, with the collaboration of María Inés Danelotti, Antonio Pablo Grippo, and Dora Delia Puente, *Argentina, Evolución Económica, 1915–1976*, Buenos Aires, Fundación Banco de Boston, 1977.

Machinea, José Luis, "Stabilization under Alfonsin's Government: A Frustrated Attempt," Documento CEDES 42, Buenos Aires, 1990.

Maddison, Angus, *Dynamic Forces in Capitalist Development*, Oxford, Oxford University Press, 1991.

Maddison, Angus, *Monitoring the World Economy: 1820–1992*, OECD Development Centre Studies, Paris, 1995.

Maddison, Angus, *The World Economy: Historical Statistics*, OECD Development Centre, Paris, 2003.

Maeder, Ernesto, "Población e Inmigración en la Argentina entre 1880 y 1910," in *La Argentina del Ochenta al Centenario*, ed. Gustavo Ferrari and Ezequiel Gallo, Buenos Aires, Editorial Sudamericana, 1980.

Maynard Gilles, "Argentine Macroeconomic Policy, 1966–73," in *The Political Economy of Argentina, 1946–1986*, ed. Guido Di Tella and Rudiger Dorbusch, London, St. Anthony's/Macmillan Press, 1989.

Ministerio de Economía, *Sector Público Argentino no Financiero. Cuenta Ahorro-Inversión-Financiamiento*, Buenos Aires, Secretaría de Hacienda de la República Argentina, 2004.

Mitchell Brian R., *International Historical Statistics: The Americas, 1750–1993*, New York, Stockton Press, 1998.

Mitchell, Brian R., and Phyllis Deane, *Abstract of British Historical Statistics*, Cambridge, Cambridge University Press, 1962.

Newland, Carlos, "Los Años entre 1810 y 1870. Sector Externo y Desarrollo Regional en la Argentina," *Ciencia Hoy*, no. 38, 1997.

Newland, Carlos, and Barry Poulson, "Puramente Animal, Pastoral Production and Early Argentine Economic Growth, 1825–1865," Presentado en el Ciclo de Seminarios de la Universidad de San Andrés, Victoria, Buenos Aires, octubre 1995.

North, Douglass C., "Ocean Freight Rates and Economic Development, 1750–1913," *Journal of Economic History*, vol. 18, no. 4, 1958.

Novick, Susana, *IAPI: Auge y Decadencia*, Buenos Aires, Centro Editor de América Latina, 1986.

Nuñez Miñana, Horacio, and Alberto Porto, "Inflación y Tarifas Públicas: Argentina, 1945–1980," *Desarrollo Económico*, no. 84, 1982.

O'Connell, Arturo A., "La Argentina en la Depresión: los Problemas de una Economía Abierta," *Desarrollo Económico*, vol. 23, no. 92, 1984.

OEA/BID/CEPAL, *Programa Conjunto de Tributación: Estudio sobre Política Fiscal en la Argentina*, Buenos Aires, OEA/BID/CEPAL, 1963.

Olarra Jiménez, Rafael, *Evolución Monetaria Argentina*, Buenos Aires, Universitaria de Buenos Aires, 1968.

Peters, Harold, *The Foreign Debt of the Argentina Republic*, Baltimore, MD, The Johns Hopkins University Press, 1934.

Phelps, Vernon Lovell, *The International Economic Position of Argentina*, Philadelphia, University of Pennsylvania Press; London, H. Milford, Oxford University Press, 1938.

Piekarz, Julio, "El Déficit Cuasifiscal del Banco Central," Buenos Aires, Banco Central de la República Argentina, 1987.

Potash, Robert A., *Perón y el G.O.U*, Buenos Aires, Editorial Sudamericana, 1984.

Prados, Arrarte J., *El Control de Cambios*, Buenos Aires, Sudamericana, 1944.

Prados de la Escosura, Leandro, and Isabel Sanz-Villarroya, *Institutional Instability and Growth in Argentina: A Long Run View*, Working Paper 04-67, Universidad Carlos III de Madrid, Getafe, España, 2004.

"Property Rigths and Economic Backwardness in Argentina: A Historical Perspective," Working Paper 04–67, Universidad Carlos III de Madrid, Getafe, España, 2004.

Prebisch, Raúl, "Anotaciones Sobre Nuestro Medio Circulante," *Revista de Ciencias Económicas*, año IX, serie II, número 3, 1921.

La Crisis del Desarrollo Argentino: de la Frustración al Crecimiento Vigoroso, Buenos Aires, El Ateneo, 1986.

"La Experiencia del Banco Central Argentino en sus Primeros Ocho Años," *Cincuentenario del Banco Central de la República Argentina*, Buenos Aires, 1985.

Obras 1919–1948, Buenos Aires, Fundación Raúl Prebisch, 1991.

Reutz, Ted, "Ilusiones Fiscales, Dimensión y Método de Financiamiento del Déficit Fiscal del Gobierno 1928–1972," *Ciclos*, Buenos Aires, Ministerio de Economía, 1991.

Rippy, J. Fred, *British Investments in Latin America: 1822–1949: A Case Study in the Operations of Private Enterprise in Retarded Regions*, Minneapolis, University of Minnesota Press, 1959.

Roca, Eduardo, *Julio A. Roca (h)*, Buenos Aires, Consejo Argentino para la Relaciones Internacionales, 1995.

Rodríguez, Carlos, "La Deuda Externa Argentina," *Serie Seminarios*, seminario 2/87, Buenos Aires, Centro de Investigaciones Económicas, Instituto Torcuato Di Tella, 1987.

Rojnica, Paula, "Una Estimación del PBI para la Argentina en el Siglo XIX: el Impacto de la Independencia sobre la Economía," Trabajo de licenciatura en Economía, Universidad de San Andrés, Victoria, Buenos Aires, May 1998.

Sábato, Jorge Federico, *La Clase Dominante en la Argentina Moderna: Formación y características*, Buenos Aires, Imago Mundi, 1991.

Salera, Virgil, *Exchange Control and the Argentine Market*, New York, AMS Press, 1968.

Sánchez-Alonso, Blanca, "Labour and Immigration in Latin America," in *Cambridge Economic History of Latin America*, vol. 2, ed. Víctor Bulmer Thomas, John Catsworth, and Roberto Cortés Conde, Cambridge and New York, Cambridge University Press, 2005.

Sauvy, Alfred, *Histoire Économique de la France entre lês deux Guerres*, Paris, Economica, 1984.

Schenk, Catherine, *Britain and the Sterling Area: From Devaluation to Convertibility the 1950's*, London and New York, Routledge, 1994.

Schenone, Osvaldo, "Public Sector Behavior in Argentina," in *The Public Sector and the Latin American Crisis*, ed. Felipe Larraín and Marcelo Selowsky, San Francisco, International Center of Economic Growth, ICS Press, 1991.

Solow, Robert, "Technical Change and the Aggregate Production Function," *Review of Economics and Statistics*, August 1957.

"A Contribution to the Theory of Economic Growth," *Quarterly Journal of Economics*, no. 70, February 1956.

Sourrouille, Juan, "La Posición de Activos y Pasivos Externos de la República Argentina entre 1946 y 1948," *Serie Estudios y Perspectivas*, no. 29, Oficina de la CEPAL en Buenos Aires, December 2005.

Sturzenegger, Federico, "Descripción de una Experiencia Populista: La Argentina, 1973–1976," in *The Macroeconomics of Populism in Latin America*, ed. Rudiger Dornbusch and Sebastian Edwards, Chicago, University of Chicago Press, 1991.

Taylor, Alan, "Argentina and the World Capital Market: Saving, Investment, and International Capital Mobility in the Twentieth Century," NBER Working Paper W6302, 1997.

"Argentine Economic Growth in Comparative Perspective," Ph.D. Thesis, Harvard University, 1992.

"Latifundia as Malefactor in Economic Development? Scale, Tenancy and Agriculture on the Pampas," Presentado en el Ciclo de Seminarios de la Universidad de San Anrés, Victoria, Buenos Aires, November 1996.

The Economist, Year XVII, no. 868, 1 May 18, 1967.

The Economist, Year X, January 3, 1959.

Todeschini, Federico, "El BCRA y el IAPI en la Política Económica Peronista: 1946–1955," Documento de Trabajo N° 68 de la Universidad de San Andrés, 2004.

Ugalde, Alberto, *Las Empresas Públicas en la Argentina*, Buenos Aires, El Cronista Comercial, 1984.

Van der Wee, Herman, *Prosperity and Upheaval: The World Economy, 1945–1980*, Berkeley, Los Angeles, University of California Press, 1986.

Vázquez Presedo, Vicente, *Auge y Decadencia de la Economía Argentina desde 1776*, Buenos Aires, Academia Nacional de Ciencias Económicas, 1992.

Vénganzonès, Marie-Ange, and Carlos Winograd, *Argentina en el siglo XX: Crónica de un Crecimiento Anunciado*, Estudios del Centro de Desarrollo, OCDE, Paris, 1997.

Vives, Alberto Edwards, *La Fronda Aristocrática en Chile*, Santiago de Chile, Editorial Universitaria, 1997.

Villanueva, Javier, "El Origen de la Industrialización Argentina," *Desarrollo Económico*, no. 47, 1972.

Viner, Jacob, "The Bullionist Controversies," in *Studies in the Theory of International Trade*, New York, Harper, 1937.

Vitelli, Guillermo, *Los Dos Siglos de la Argentina: Historia Económica Comparada*, Buenos Aires, Prendergast, 1999.

Williamson, Jeffrey, and Kevin O'Rourke, *Globalization and History. The Evolution of a Nineteenth-Century Atlantic Economy*, Cambridge, MIT Press, 1999.

Zalduendo, Eduardo A., "Sistema de Transportes de la Argentina," en *La Argentina del Ochenta al Centenario*, ed. G. Ferrari and E. Gallo, Buenos Aires, Sudamericana, 1980.

Zarazaga, Carlos, "Crecimiento Económico en Argentina en el Período, 1900–1930: Evidencia a partir de Tasas de Retorno en el Mercado Bursátil," Federal Reserve Bank of Dallas, 1996.

Sources

Anales de Legislación Argentina.

Anuario Geográfico Argentino, Comité Nacional de Geografía, Buenos Aires, 1941.

BCRA, *Sistema de Cuentas del Producto e Ingreso de la Argentina*, vols I and II, Buenos Aires, BCRA, 1975.

BCRA, *Cuentas Nacionales de la República Argentina: Series Históricas*, vol. III, Buenos Aires, BCRA, Gerencia de Investigaciones Económicas, 1976.

BCRA, *Series Históricas de Cuentas Nacionales de la Argentina*, Buenos Aires, BCRA, Gerencia de Investigaciones Económicas, 1976.

BCRA, Boletines y Suplementos Estadísticos.

Bonos de Fondos Públicos Nacionales, período 1829–1848, Burgin.

CEPAL, *El Desarrollo Económico de la Argentina*, Santiago de Chile, CEPAL, 1958.

CEPAL, *Estadísticas Económicas de Corto Plazo de la Argentina: Sector Externo y Condiciones Económicas Internacionales*, vol. I, Buenos Aires, May 1986.

CEPAL, *Estadísticas Económicas de Corto Plazo de la Argentina: Cuentas Nacionales, Industria Manufacturera y Sector Agropecuario Pampeano*, vol. II, Buenos Aires, May 1986.

Dirección Nacional de Cuentas Nacionales, *Cuentas Nacionales. Oferta y Demanda Globales 1980–1995*, Buenos Aires, 1996.

Dirección Nacional deCuentas Nacionales (Center for National Accounts) – INDEC. IDB-UNPRE Project Estudio 1.EE.88: "La Riqueza Nacional en Argentina." National Director: Fernando Cerro. Coordinator: Ariel Coremberg.

DNEC (Dirección Nacional de Estadística y Censos), *Costo del Nivel de Vida en la Capital Federal*, Encuesta sobre Condiciones de Vida de las Familias Obreras Realizada en el Año 1960, Buenos Aires, 1968.

DNPGS, *Caracterización y Evolución del Gasto Público Social: Período 1980–1997*, Dirección Nacional de Programación del Gasto Social, 1999.

Dirección General de Estadística de la Nación, *Extracto Estadístico de la República Argentina Correspondiente al año 1915*, Compañía Sudamericana de Billetes de Banco, Buenos Aires, 1916.

Extractos del Mensaje Radiofónico del Presidente Dr. Arturo Frondizi, Transmitido el 29 de diciembre de 1958 por la Red Nacional de Radiodifusión.

INDEC, www.indec.gov.ar.

Memorias del Banco Central de la República Argentina, Años 1935–1989.

Memorias del Banco de la Nación Argentina, Años 1948–1957.

Balances del Banco Nacional, Años 1863–1881.

Memorias del Banco de la Provincia de Buenos Aires, Años 1948–1957.

Memorias de Hacienda, 1913–1918.

Memorias de Hacienda, 1939–1945.

Memorias del IAPI, Años 1948–1957.

Relevamiento Estadístico de la República Argentina, 1900–1980.

Revista de Economía Argentina.

Secretaría de Estado de Agricultura y Ganadería, Junta Nacional de Granos, *Estadísticas de Área Cultivada, Rendimiento, Producción y Exportación de Granos. Totales del País: 1900 a 1975*, Buenos Aires, 1975.

World Bank, *World Bank Tables, 1995*, Baltimore, MD, The Johns Hopkins University Press, May 1995.

Index